Disorders of
NARCISSISM

Disorders of
NARCISSISM

Diagnostic, Clinical,
and Empirical Implications

EDITED BY
Elsa F. Ronningstam, Ph.D.

JASON ARONSON INC.
Northvale, New Jersey
London

Note: The authors have worked to ensure that all information in this book concerning drug dosages, schedules, and routes of administration is accurate as of the time of publication and consistent with standards set by the U.S. Food and Drug Administration and the general medical community. As medical research and practice advance, however, therapeutic standards may change. For this reason and because human and mechanical errors sometimes occur, we recommend that readers follow the advice of a physician who is directly involved in their care or the care of a member of their family.

First softcover edition 2000

Library of Congress Cataloging-in-Publication Data

Disorders of narcissism : diagnostic, clinical, and empirical implications /
edited by Elsa F. Ronningstam.—1st softcover ed.
p. cm.
Originally published: Washington, DC : American Psychiatric Press, © 1998.
Includes bibliographical references.
ISBN 0-7657-0259-2 (softcover)
1. Narcissism. I. Ronningstam, Elsa
[DNLM: 1. Narcissism. WM 460.5.E3 D612 1998a]
RC553.N36 D57 2000
616.85'85 – dc21   99-059531

Printed in the United States of America on acid-free paper. For information and catalog write to Jason Aronson Inc., 230 Livingston Street, Northvale, NJ 07647-1726, or visit our website: www.aronson.com

To
My Father,
Yngve F. Karlsson

Contents

Section I
Diagnostic and Theoretical Considerations

Section III
Special Clinical Considerations

Section IV
Research

Contributors

Ralph H. Beaumont, M.D.
Faculty, San Francisco Psychoanalytic Institute, Oregon New Training Facility for Psychoanalysis, Northwest Center for Psychoanalysis, and Psychoanalytic Institute of New England–East, Boston, Massachusetts

Arnold M. Cooper, M.D.
Stephen P. Tobin and Dr. Arnold Cooper Professor Emeritus in Consultation-Liaison Psychiatry, Cornell University Medical College; and Training and Supervising Analyst, Center for Psychoanalytic Training and Research, Columbia University, New York City

Catherine Flanagan, Ph.D.
Clinical Instructor of Psychology in Psychiatry, Department of Psychiatry, Cornell University Medical College, New York City

Glen O. Gabbard, M.D.
Bessie Walker Callaway Distinguished Professor of Psychoanalysis and Education, Karl Menninger School of Psychiatry and Mental Health Sciences; Training and Supervising Analyst, Topeka Institute for Psychoanalysis; and Clinical Professor of Psychiatry, University of Kansas School of Medicine, Topeka, Kansas

Fady Hajal, M.D.
Medical Director, Stony Lodge Hospital, Briarcliff Manor, New York

Robert D. Hare, Ph.D.
Professor, Department of Psychology, University of British Columbia, Vancouver, British Columbia, Canada

Stephen D. Hart, Ph.D.
Associate Professor, Department of Psychology and Mental Health, Law, and Policy Institute, Simon Fraser University, Burnaby, British Columbia, Canada

Janice K. Jones, B.S.
Research Fellow, Department of Psychology, Harvard University, Cambridge, Massachusetts

Otto F. Kernberg, M.D.
Director, Personality Disorders Institute, The New York Hospital—Cornell Medical Center, Westchester Division, White Plains, New York; Professor of Psychiatry, Cornell University Medical College; and Training and Supervising Analyst, Columbia University Center for Psychoanalytic Training and Research, New York City

Paulina F. Kernberg, M.D.
Professor of Psychiatry, Cornell University Medical College; Attending Psychiatrist, The New York City Hospital—Cornell Medical Center, Westchester Division, White Plains, New York; and Training and Supervising Analyst (Adult and Child), Columbia University Center for Psychoanalytic Training and Research, New York City

Henry Krystal, M.D.
Professor Emeritus of Psychiatry, Michigan State University, East Lansing, Michigan; and Lecturer, Michigan Psychoanalytic Institute, Southfield, Michigan

Lucy LaFarge, M.D.
Assistant Clinical Professor of Psychiatry, Columbia University
College of Physicians & Surgeons; and Training and Supervising
Analyst, Columbia University Center for Psychoanalytic Train-
ing and Research, New York City

John T. Maltsberger, M.D.
Associate Clinical Professor of Psychiatry, Harvard Medical School;
Faculty, Boston Psychoanalytic Society and Institute; and Associate
Attending Psychiatrist, McLean Hospital, Belmont, Massachusetts

Theodore Millon, Ph.D., D.Sc.
Graduate Professor of Psychology, University of Miami, Miami,
Florida; Visiting Professor, Harvard Medical School, Department
of Psychiatry, Boston, Massachusetts; and Dean, Institute for Advanced Studies in Personality and Psychopathology, Coral Ga-
bles, Florida

Lesley C. Morey, Ph.D.
Professor of Psychology, Director of Clinical Training, Department of Psychology, Vanderbilt University, Nashville, Tennessee

John C. Nemiah, M.D.
Professor of Psychiatry, Dartmouth Medical School, Hanover,
New Hampshire; and Professor of Psychiatry Emeritus, Harvard
Medical School, Boston, Massachusetts

Lina Normandin, Ph.D.
Associate Professor of Clinical Psychology, School of Psychology,
Laval University, Quebec, Canada

Paul H. Ornstein, M.D.
Professor of Psychoanalysis Emeritus, University of Cincinnati,
Department of Psychiatry; Co-Director, International Center for
the Study of Psychoanalytic Self Psychology; and Training and
Supervising Analyst, Cincinnati Psychoanalytic Institute, Cin-
cinnati, Ohio

Elsa F. Ronningstam, Ph.D.
Assistant Clinical Professor of Psychology, Department of Psychiatry, Harvard Medical School, The Psychosocial Research Center at McLean Hospital, Belmont, Massachusetts; Associate Clinical Psychologist, McLean Hospital and Two Brattle Center, Cambridge, Massachusetts; and Candidate, The Boston Psychoanalytic Society and Institute, Boston, Massachusetts

Bennett E. Roth, Ph.D.
Training Analyst, The Institute for Psychoanalytic Training and Research; Fellow, American Group Psychotherapy Association; and Private Practice, New York City

Marion F. Solomon, Ph.D.
Professor, American Behavioral Studies Institute; Coordinator of Psychoanalytic Training Programs, Department of Humanities, Sciences and Social Sciences, UCLA Extension; and Director, The Lifespan Institute Continuing Education Seminars, Los Angeles, California

Michael H. Stone, M.D.
Professor of Clinical Psychiatry, Columbia University College of Physicians & Surgeons, New York City

Jeffrey Young, Ph.D.
Assistant Professor of Clinical Psychology in Psychiatry, Department of Psychiatry, Columbia University College of Physicians & Surgeons, New York City; and Director, Cognitive Therapy Centers of New York and Fairfield County, Wilton, Connecticut

Foreword

John C. Nemiah, M.D.

In a discussion of "The Ego and Its Emotional Manifestations" (1896/1902), the French psychologist Théodule Ribot commented:

> The English designate by the term of *self-feeling,* and the Germans by that of *Selbstgefühl,* a group of sentiments directly derived from the ego. . . . We might, for want of a better, include them under the term *amour-propre* . . . i.e., satisfaction or dissatisfaction with one's self. . . . These emotional forms are reducible to one primary fact of which they are the embodiment in consciousness—viz., the feeling (well-founded or not) of personal strength or weakness.
>
> The self-feeling has two forms, one positive, the other negative, of which pride and humility may respectively be taken as types. . . . Under its positive form, we find pride, vanity, contempt, love of glory, emulation, courage, daring, etc. . . . Under its negative form . . . it has for its basis a feeling of weakness and impotence. . . . It consists in belittling rather than aggrandizing, of lowering rather than raising. It is related on one side to sadness, and on the other to fear; in short, it is the complete antithesis to the positive form. From this source flow . . . humility, timidity, modesty, resignation . . . want of self-confidence, etc.
>
> Self-feeling, under its positive form, has its ultimate incarnation in a well-known pathological manifestation—the delusion of greatness or megalomania. . . . If self-love, in its positive form, reaches its culmination in megalomania . . . self-feeling under its negative form attains its supreme negation in suicide. (pp. 239–245)

Ribot played a dominant role in the development of scientific psychology during the latter half of the last century. Titular professor of experimental psychology at the Collège de France, founder and editor of the esteemed *Revue philosophique,* he had an encyclopedic knowledge of the contemporary psychological literature and was himself the author of many papers and monographs that amalgamated and publicized the recent advances in experimental psychology in Germany and England and highlighted the findings of clinicians investigating the psychopathology of psychiatric disorders. His remarkable synthesis of the vicissitudes of self-esteem, quoted above, constituted a short chapter of 9 pages in a treatise of 448 pages of text designed to provide a comprehensive discourse on the psychology of the emotions. It apparently went unnoticed by his clinical contemporaries. Indeed, his analysis of the polarity of the positive and negative forms of "self-feeling" remained isolated from the mainstream of psychopathological investigations for nearly two decades until Freud (1914/1962), quite independently, advanced similar notions in his discussion of the phenomena of narcissism.

The study of psychopathology meanwhile followed a different path. Pierre Janet, Ribot's most famous pupil and the successor to his post at the Collège de France, began his professional career with a specific focus on the investigation of the psychopathology of memory and sensation. In his epoch-making studies of the disturbance of those functions in hysterical patients, he not only provided empirical evidence for the existence of unconscious mental processes but also attributed hysterical symptoms to the underlying effect of dissociated memories of traumatic experiences.

According to Janet's (1889) theoretical formulation, dissociation was particularly liable to occur in persons with a constitutional deficiency of the mental energy (*la misère psychologique*) required by the ego for its essential task of binding together the individual mental functions (e.g., sensation, cognition, emotion, volition, memory) into an integrated whole under its conscious control. If such vulnerable persons were subjected to an emotional trauma resulting in the expenditure of a significant amount

of that energy, its already deficient quantity would be further reduced to a pathological level that compromised the capacity of
the ego to maintain the synthesis of the various mental functions.
Escaping from the ego's control, they now operated autonomously—they were, in other words, dissociated from consciousness. It is apparent from consideration of this theoretical
explanation that Janet adhered to an ego-deficit model of psychogenesis. Apart, however, from his conception of its passive role in
mental dissociation, the ego played a negligible role in his early
psychopathological formulations.

When Freud first turned his attention to a study of hysterical
phenomena (Breuer and Freud 1893/1955), he accepted Janet's
proposition that dissociation was the central factor in hysterical
symptom formation. However, he offered a radically different explanation of the etiology of dissociation itself. Dissociation, he
proposed, was not the result of a functional deficiency in a consti-
tutionally defective ego. On the contrary, it occurred when a powerful ego, motivated by its self-preservative instinct, effectively
repressed traumatic memories from consciousness in order to
protect itself from the psychic pain induced by their recollection.
With that formulation, Freud introduced the vital concept of psychological conflict that was thereafter the bedrock of psychoanalytical theory. Moreover, in three of his earliest psychoanalytical
papers (Breuer and Freud 1893/1955; Freud 1894/1962, 1896/1962),
which were devoted to the delineation of the fundamental ego
defenses, he underscored the importance of ego structure as a basic element in all of psychic functioning, both normal and pathological. Freud, in other words, was an "ego psychologist" from the
very beginning of his career as a psychoanalytical investigator.

Although his work initially adhered to the traumatic etiology
of hysteria, Freud ultimately revised his formulations to take into
account new and important psychological observations that
emerged in the course of his own self-analysis—observations that
led to the recognition of the existence of childhood sexuality, of its
orderly development in the early years of life, and of the etiological role of disturbances in that development in the production of
adult mental disorders. Those discoveries, the elucidation of

which occupied the better part of a decade, were equal in importance to the earlier recognition of the place of psychological conflict in mental functioning. Furthermore, they set the stage for the
final chapter of Freud's contributions to psychoanalytical theory
that opened with the publication of his paper "On Narcissism: An
Introduction" (Freud 1914/1962).

Whereas in the immediately preceding years Freud's attention had been primarily focused on the nature of unconscious
processes and on the role of the instinctual libidinal drives in
psychological conflict, he now returned to a consideration of the
structure and function of the ego. Partly in response to conceptual
differences with colleagues (notably Adler and Jung) and partly as
a result of his observations of patients with more serious psychiatric problems than the transference neuroses that had previously
been the major focus of his investigations, Freud was led to the
recognition of the central role of narcissistic phenomena in psychological functioning. His elaboration of the details of those phenomena (the self-observing ego, the ego ideal, the vicissitudes of
self-esteem, and the reciprocal relation between ego-libido and
object-libido) and his discovery of their origins in the early phases
of the development of ego structure formed the cornerstone of
Freud's final psychoanalytical formulations. The resulting "structural model" of the mind, with its triad of ego, superego, and id,
still serves as the conceptual basis of modern psychodynamic
psychiatry.

It was not until after Freud's death and the end of World War II
that further significant developments occurred in psychoanalytical observation and theory. The serial publications of Hartmann
and his colleagues (Hartmann and Kris 1945; Hartmann et al.
1947) in the early volumes of *The Psychoanalytic Study of the Child*,
which stressed the importance of the developmental and integrative aspects of the ego, aroused widespread interest. Simultaneously, the emergence of systematic investigations of infant and
early childhood behavior underscored the innate capacity of infants and very young children to relate to their human environment as well as the important effect of such relationships on the
subsequent development of that capacity. On the clinical side,

such studies were complemented by the evolving theories advanced by the adherents of object relations psychology and self psychology, who attributed many aspects of psychopathology to ego deficits rather than to psychological conflict. More recently, the revival of interest in psychological trauma not only has reinstated a recognition of its importance as a factor in the production of psychiatric disorders but also has demonstrated its often devastating effect on the development of the ego when the trauma occurs in childhood. Finally, mention should be made of the attempts of modern phenomenological psychiatry to delineate valid and reliable categorical diagnostic definitions of personality disorders—an endeavor that has fostered the careful clinical observation and description of their surface manifestations at the expense, however, of the dynamic understanding of the observed phenomena.

The modern study of the ego has provided new and important information about its psychopathological manifestations, both symptomatic and characterological. At the same time, modern investigators have raised numerous practical and theoretical questions and have generated often clashing conceptual views with polarization that is sometimes unnecessarily divisive. For example, is a given narcissistic disorder the result of psychological conflict, or is it a manifestation of deficits in the structure of the ego? Should psychotherapy of patients with narcissistic personality disorder be based on interpretations aimed at resolving unconscious psychic conflicts, or should the therapist provide a "holding environment" designed to modify pathogenic arrests in the formation of ego structure with "transmuting internalizations"? Are dissociative symptoms a reflection of unconscious memories of actual childhood traumatic events or of phase-specific early developmental fantasies? In the evaluation and treatment of narcissistic disorders, what are the relative merits of the categorical-descriptive and the dimensional-psychodynamic approaches to their definition and classification?

These and other questions of equal import and puzzlement are at the forefront of the modern study of narcissism, and they are creatively addressed by the authors of the chapters in this vol-

ume. Readers should not, of course, expect always to find defini-
tive answers, but they may be assured of a rich banquet of clinical
facts and clarifying formulations that admirably amplify and illu-
minate Ribot's telling insights of a century ago.

References

Breuer J, Freud S: On the psychical mechanism of hysterical phenom-
    ena: preliminary communication (1893), in The Standard Edition of
    the Complete Psychological Works of Sigmund Freud, Vol 2. Trans-
    lated and edited by Strachey J. London, Hogarth Press, 1955, pp 3–17
Freud S: The neuro-psychoses of defense (1894), in The Standard Edi-
    tion of the Complete Psychological Works of Sigmund Freud, Vol 3.
    Translated and edited by Strachey J. London, Hogarth Press, 1962,
    pp 41–68
Freud S: Further remarks on the neuro-psychoses of defense (1896), in
    The Standard Edition of the Complete Psychological Works of Sig-
    mund Freud, Vol 3. Translated and edited by Strachey J. London, Ho-
    garth Press, 1962, pp 157–185
Freud S: On narcissism: an introduction (1914), in The Standard Edition
    of the Complete Psychological Works of Sigmund Freud, Vol 14.
    Translated and edited by Strachey J. London, Hogarth Press, 1962,
    pp 67–102
Hartmann H, Kris E: The genetic approach in psychoanalysis. Psycho-
    anal Study Child 1:11–30, 1945
Hartmann H, Kris E, Loewenstein RM: Comments on the formation of
    psychic structure. Psychoanal Study Child 2:11–38, 1947
Janet P: l'Automatisme psychologique. Paris, Félix Alcan, 1889
Ribot T: The Psychology of Emotions (1896). London, Walter Scott Pub-
    lishing, 1902, pp 239–245

Acknowledgments

The collective efforts and contributions from several scholarly, clinically and scientifically accomplished, and competent colleagues have made this volume possible. I would like to thank all the contributing authors for their efforts and willingness to make their knowledge and experiences available through their chapters, as well as through comments and advice. They represent a distinguished group of experts in the field of narcissism and related areas who have made important theoretical, clinical, and empirical contributions to increase our understanding of narcissism and its related disorders.

Specifically, I would like to thank John Gunderson, M.D., director of the Psychosocial Center at McLean Hospital, for the scientific mentorship and research collaboration that have enabled me to become actively involved in the empirical exploration of pathological narcissism. The generous support and thoughtful advice from Arnold M. Cooper, M.D., in linking the latest conceptualization and diagnostic outline of narcissistic personality disorder with my empirical research and clinical observations, have been stimulating and valuable. Likewise, the clinical collaboration and exploratory psychoanalytical discussions on pathological narcissism with Ralph H. Beaumont, M.D., have contributed to a vital intellectual and personal growth. I would also like to acknowledge the many patients whose informative reports have provided invaluable knowledge about the nature and vicissitudes of narcissism.

In the progress of this book, Shervert Frazier provided expert advice, for which I am grateful.

I would like to give special thanks to my editorial secretaries Frances MacNeil and Carolyn MacLennan for their superb editorial advice, extensive computer experience, and persistence.

Finally, for warm support, I would like to thank my husband Philip.

Introduction

Elsa F. Ronningstam, Ph.D.

During the last two decades, several important clinical, theoretical, and empirical findings have influenced the conceptualization of narcissistic personality disorder (NPD). The development of two different theoretical stands and clinical approaches to NPD during the 1970s—the ego psychological–object relational school represented by Kernberg and the self psychology view represented by Kohut—stimulated an enormous worldwide discussion about the nature of pathological narcissism and the definition and treatment of NPD. The inclusion of NPD in DSM-III (American Psychiatric Association 1980) in 1980 gradually led to more systematic studies of NPD and characteristics of pathological narcissism. Results from these studies have both clarified a number of discriminating and differential diagnostic issues and proposed changes in the diagnostic criteria set. They have also challenged the diagnostic status of NPD and questioned its construct validity as a long-term personality disorder. A shift in the clinical and descriptive focus of NPD from mainly overt signs to covert signs of narcissistic pathology has stimulated additional dynamic formulations, and the existence of two clinical types of NPD has recently been suggested: one with overt grandiose desires, arrogance, entitlement, and exploitive behavior as represented by the official DSM-IV (American Psychiatric Association 1994) category and another that is an equally characterological disorder but that includes more sensitive, shy, inhibited, vulnerable, shame-ridden, and socially withdrawn behavior.

The development of treatment strategies for patients with narcissistic disorders within modalities other than psychoanalysis has inspired new conceptualizations beyond the psychoanalytical realm and pointed toward a higher degree of changeability and treatability than was earlier proclaimed. In addition, clinical explorations of other manifestations of psychopathology indicate a dimensional aspect of pathological narcissism—that is, its presence in and interaction with other states and disorders.

The impetus for this book results from several efforts during the past years to update and critically analyze the latest developments in the field of narcissism and NPD. Two symposia at the American Psychiatric Association annual meetings initiated by Eric Plakun in 1987 and 1990 ("New Perspectives on Narcissism" and "Narcissism in the '90s"), as well as his collaborative volume on narcissism (Plakun 1990), aimed to bridge the gap between psychoanalytical conceptualization and empirical psychiatric and psychological studies of NPD.

A special issue of *Psychiatric Clinics of North America* on NPD guest-edited by Otto F. Kernberg (1989) linked results from empirical research with the ongoing theoretical and diagnostic controversies of NPD and narcissism. In 1992, I chaired another symposium of the American Psychiatric Association annual meeting titled "The Validity of Narcissistic Personality Disorder." New diagnostic conceptualizations of NPD and the latest empirical studies on construct validity and differential diagnostics were discussed. Another parallel influence was the work of the Task Force on DSM-IV Axis II, which for the first time used results from empirical studies to guide their decisions about a useful criteria set for NPD (Gunderson et al. 1991).

It was natural to continue these endeavors and, within a historical context of a century of progress, bring together the latest empirical evidence, clinical diagnostic observations, and advances in treatment in this volume. The four parts of the book reflect an attempt to discuss relevant developmental areas of narcissism and narcissistic disorders, to point out major differences and lines of progress and influence, and to raise questions for further clinical and empirical investigation. Each part has an editorial introduction highlighting specific theoretical rationales and divergences, differences in diagnostic and technical approaches, and choices of empirical strategies to obtain relevant data, as well as the bearing of such data on the continuing clinical and theoretical discussions.

References

American Psychiatric Association: Diagnostic and Statistical Manual of Mental Disorders, 3rd Edition. Washington, DC, American Psychiatric Association, 1980

American Psychiatric Association: Diagnostic and Statistical Manual of Mental Disorders, 4th Edition. Washington, DC, American Psychiatric Association, 1994

Gunderson J, Ronningstam E, Smith L: Narcissistic personality disorder: a review of data on DSM-III-R descriptions. Journal of Personality Disorders 5:167–177, 1991

Kernberg O (ed): Narcissistic personality disorder. Psychiatr Clin North Am 12(3):505–776, 1989

Plakun E (ed): New Perspectives on Narcissism. Washington, DC, American Psychiatric Press, 1990

Section I

Diagnostic and
Theoretical
Considerations

Introduction

Elsa F. Ronningstam, Ph.D.

This first section presents the fundamental conceptualizations and understanding of narcissism and of its pathological conditions as they have developed and influenced recent clinical descriptions and empirical research.

The section begins with a chapter outlining normal narcissism, an essential constituent for most human functioning because it involves the self-preserving, self-regulating, and self-asserting activities. Michael H. Stone, M.D., in Chapter 1, discusses the ethological aspects of universal phenomena such as competitiveness, beauty, and status in the context of normal narcissism. Exceptional aspects of normal narcissistic development, such as charisma, leadership, humor, and wisdom, are also high lighted.

Three theoretical developmental lines are presented. An object relations–ego psychology view, described in Chapter 2 by Otto F. Kernberg, M.D., emphasizes the function of splitting in internalized self and object representations and the role of aggression and early envy in the formation of a pathological self-structure that contains the pathological grandiose self. This view, until recently the most predominant in the delineation of the overt features of narcissistic personality disorder, has been especially consequential for the diagnostic differentiation between antisocial and narcissistic personality disorders and for empirical studies on the interface between psychopathy and narcissism.

Another view brings together self psychological formulations

3

with specific relevance to the understanding of narcissism. In this view, presented by Arnold M. Cooper, M.D., in Chapter 3, pathological narcissism and the narcissistic character are considered to be a defense of a fragile and vulnerable self-structure; grandiosity in this perspective has a compensatory function. The role of shame in the development of the pathological grandiose self is particularly emphasized, whereas aggression is assumed to be secondary in the development of pathological narcissism. Based on this theoretical frame, a diagnostic conceptualization of the covert, shy type of narcissistic personality disorder is delineated.

The first two views are developed within a psychoanalytical frame of reference, whereas the third view, presented by Theodore Millon, Ph.D., D.Sc., in Chapter 4, represents a fundamentally different conceptual and descriptive view of narcissistic personality disorder. Observations of the libidinal aspects of narcissistic character pathology noted in the psychoanalytical literature are integrated into a systematic, theoretical, biopsychosocial learning model for personality and psychopathology. In a multidimensional comprehensive classification system for personality disorders, each disorder prototype is divided into several clinical domains and subtypes in which specific features are highlighted. Because of its structured format and systematic criteria–based conceptualization, this view has instigated extensive methodological development in the assessment of personality disorders, including narcissistic personality disorder, and is specifically influential in contemporary empirical research on DSM Axis II personality disorders.

Several theoretical views on the etiology of pathological narcissism (e.g., those emphasizing early self-development, separation-individuation, attachment) influence the present conceptualization of narcissistic personality disorder. Paulina F. Kernberg, M.D., in Chapter 5, outlines these theoretical divergences and identifies the differences between normal and pathological narcissism and self-esteem regulation. Clinical manifestations of narcissistic disturbances in children's play and interaction are described, as well as pathogenic family interactions that can lead to the development of narcissistic personality disorder.

The introduction of the concept of narcissism within theoretical references other than psychoanalysis, such as learning theory and cognitive theory (Beck et al. 1990), and the interest for narcissism within empirical psychology (Auerbach 1993) and neuroscience (Schore 1994) have added new and valuable perspectives to the definition and understanding of narcissism. Such additions are especially important for the possibilities to validate empirically the clinical observations of narcissism and its disorders.

References

Auerbach JS: The origins of narcissism and narcissistic personality disorder: a theoretical and empirical reformulation, in Psychoanalytic Perspectives on Psychopathology. Edited by Masling JM, Bornstein RF. Washington, DC, American Psychological Association, 1993, pp 43–110

Beck AT, Freeman A, and Associates: Cognitive Therapy of Personality Disorders. New York, Guilford, 1990

Schore AN: Affect Regulation and the Origin of the Self: The Neurobiology of Emotional Development. Hillsdale, NJ, Lawrence Erlbaum, 1994

Chapter 1

Normal Narcissism

An Etiological and Ethological Perspective

Michael H. Stone, M.D.

The term *narcissism* derives, as most are aware, from a figure in Greek mythology: someone who fell in love with his own image. To understand better how the term has evolved in meaning—specifically, how it has come to acquire overtones in the spheres of both normality and psychopathology—it is useful to repeat the myth in a little more detail.

The beautiful nymph Echo, whose main job was to distract Hera while her mate Zeus went off philandering, fell in love with the equally beautiful youth Narcissus. He did not return her affections. As a result, Echo gradually pined away, until nothing remained of her but her voice. As a punishment for this apparent heartlessness, Nemesis forced Narcissus to stare at his own image in a fountain. Narcissus became so enamored, obsessed really, with his reflection, that he too pined away, until he was finally transformed into the flower that to this day bears his name.

The term narcissism—both in psychoanalytical parlance and

in the DSM-IV (American Psychiatric Association 1994) definition of narcissistic personality disorder (NPD)—has acquired along the way many attributes, all offshoots of the central concept of self-centeredness, but very few of which were exhibited by the pathetic figure from Greek mythology. Narcissus's chief problem—his inability to love—does not even figure into the DSM definition. Instead, we find a catalog of much more malignant traits: exploitativeness, arrogance, envy, preoccupation with power and success—none of which was a part of Narcissus's "personality disorder."

Within the domain of psychoanalysis (and to the best of my knowledge, nowhere else) "narcissism" has also been co-opted to designate normal aspects of feelings and attitudes about one's self. This usage arose out of the recognition by Freud and the pioneer generation of psychoanalysts that, as inevitably social animals, people must relate to others in their external world (which they can do either normally or abnormally) and must simultaneously develop a set of impressions and attitudes about their own selves. This self-development can likewise proceed in a harmonious and realistic way or in a distorted way. Hence, the oxymoron "normal narcissism," which refers to the path of development concerning the self as opposed to the other developmental track: the object-relational path (Kernberg 1975).

The concept of normal narcissism itself has a number of subdivisions. Some fall under the heading of self-preservation. Children must, if they are to survive, develop a healthy self-regard and must learn to avoid dangers, especially those that would immediately threaten well-being or survival. They must, to adopt a phrase from lay language, "look out for number one." A related but not identical task is their need to develop an evermore accurate sense of both what they can do well and what lies beyond their powers. In this way, they aim to perfect themselves, ultimately, in vocations that not only are life sustaining monetarily but also lie within their grasp. Thus far, the author has focused on the *Arbeit* half of Freud's twofold division of what life is all about.

As for the *Liebe* component, normal narcissism would direct us to develop a realistic sense of how attractive we are sexually compared with those around us, as well as a sense of how desirable we are characterologically (how adequate and appropriate we are from the standpoints of ethics and morality). Our ability to form and to sustain gratifying relationships, both in the sphere of friendship and in the realm of intimacy, will depend in large measure on how pleasing we are in appearance but also in personality. It is therefore quite normal to devote considerable attention to these areas, steering a course between vanity or conceitedness on the one hand and self-denigration or self-effacingness on the other.

With respect to self-regard, one can discern a cultural component. Just where modesty ends and superciliousness begins will not always be defined in the same way by different cultures. In Greco-Roman antiquity, for example, it was permissible and ordinary to speak with candor about one's accomplishments, even about one's greatness. This quality has been called by classical scholars "ancient high-mindedness." Horace (1603) offers us an example in his famous ode (Bk. I, Ode #30), where he gives recognition to the eternal value of his own poetry. The poem begins: "Exegi monument'aere perenniis . . . I have built me a monument more lasting than bronze." And so he had. But in the Judeo-Christian culture, which soon came to dominate thought and social patterns in the West, we tend to wince a bit at so bold an assertion of one's worth, even if it happens to be unassailably true. One of the few Western writers to dare such an assertion is Pushkin, Russia's greatest poet, who composed an ode only months before his death in 1837. Modeled after Horace's, it begins: "Ya pamyatnik sebyeh vozdveeg nyeh-rukotvornii . . . I built for myself a monument not fashioned by hands" (Pushkin 1954).

In cultures in which Buddhism exerts a significant impact, modesty carries an even higher social mortgage than in the West: children are carefully taught to be the very opposite of narcissistic in the pathological sense. When Japan's "Babe Ruth," Sadaharu Oh, hit his 800th home run, he said, in a manner typical of his culture, "Thanks to the good advice of my coach and to the encouragements of my teammates and fans, I was fortunate enough." The "Babe" would not have been so humble.

Assertive and Aggressive
Aspects of Normal Narcissism

Freud and the early generation of psychoanalysts strove to understand the place of aggression within the panoply of human behavior (Stone 1991). One of the more controversial issues concerned human violence: was aggression of this sort something built into our genome to be suppressed (under ideal circumstances) by the forces of family and culture? Or was violent aggression purely a reaction to highly unfavorable environmental influences? The author believes it is useful in trying to resolve this issue to reflect on the role of aggression in other animals. In search of food, for example, animals show a variety of *assertive* behaviors, such as foraging (or "exploratory" behaviors) and orienting (as when scout bees signal via a special "dance" the location of flowers). Animals also show several types of *normal aggressive* behaviors, including *instrumental aggression* (threatening and scaring away other animals seeking the same food source), *competitive aggression* (pushing away others even of their own species), *defensive aggression* (protecting a food source), and *predatory aggression* (as when a cat kills a mouse for food). These forms of aggression also underlie similar patterns of behavior in relation to mating; one also speaks of *maternal aggression* in mother animals attacking other creatures who menace their young (Valzelli 1981, p. 69).

As for the human species, there is considerable evidence that our brains also come programmed for assertive and aggressive behaviors. These may be understood as attributes of normal narcissism to the extent that they serve an individual in his or her appropriate quests for the fulfillment of *Liebe und Arbeit* and do not transgress societal norms. Violence, in contrast, is the manifestation of abnormal aggression; specifically, the variety Valzelli (1981, p. 79) called *irritable aggression*. Under this rubric come many examples of inappropriate anger or rage such as are routinely encountered in patients with borderline personality disorder or in persons of a paranoid bent intent on carrying out hostile acts (as noted among murderers and political tyrants). Normal aggression in humans can extend as far as "justifiable homicide": killing someone who makes a murderous threat to you or a family member. Recently, the courts have often decided in favor of persons who have killed because of abuse short of murder, such as incest or spousal battering (Stone 1993). In people whose lives proceed seamlessly along the most comfortable lines (e.g., attractive persons whose inherited wealth allows them to bypass the need to compete and who easily secure the most agreeable mates), the neurophysiological underpinnings of aggression in its various forms remain a mere "potential," with buttons that need never be pushed. But of course, there are very few such people. There will be occasions in the lives of most people when the abilities to be assertive and—if survival is seriously threatened—aggressive are vital. To this extent, these abilities are important components of normal narcissism.

Self-Preservation and Related Aspects of Normal Narcissism

Closely related to the patterns of thought and behavior that subserve self-preservation are those that underlie self-regard and self-concern. Whereas some aspects of self-preservation—those related to warding off bodily harm, for example—may be "hard-wired" genetically and may need very little learning from parents, the many more subtle aspects seem to require a fair measure of learning during the early years. Self-preservation also includes the attitudinal and behavioral "programs" that help guarantee survival, well-being, and good health. Self-preservation depends, in addition, on other programs that became cemented during the developmental years and that help maintain or improve one's place in the social order. During the first 6 years of life particularly, when the habit-memory system is in the ascendancy (Mishkin et al. 1984)—speech and logic still being rudimentary—parents and other authority figures give copious instructions (reinforced sometimes with stern voice or corporal punishment) about what the child must and must not do; for example: "Don't get into a car with a stranger," "Don't cross when the light is red," "Always say 'thank you' when you get a present"—along with the thousands of other "lessons" the child is required to absorb. These instructions, in time, take on the fixed quality of innate hardwired behavior programs and inform the child's automatic survival-oriented responses.

Side by side with these instructions, parents also transmit evaluations of their children designed (under optimal circumstances) to enhance self-regard. Optimally, through loving words and gestures, parents communicate to their children that they are valued highly by the parents and are (or will soon become) valuable members of the human community. Ideally, parents praise what is "good" (pleasing to them or socially acceptable in general) and discourage what is displeasing, unfair, and generally unacceptable socially. Indiscriminate praise leads to becoming "spoiled" (and to a narcissism that is no longer normal); withholding of all praise leads to humiliation and to a diminution of self-esteem.

Normal and deserved self-esteem is healthy pride, in contrast to the "sin" of pride, which refers to arrogance and undeserved self-inflation. Children whose storehouse of memories is largely filled with recollections of having been the objects of their parents' sympathy, affection, unexploitative love, and generosity develop a healthy self-regard that is genuine: they are not simply told they are valuable and loved; they *are* valuable and loved. This genuine self-regard will later serve as a buffer against adversity: romantic disappointments, rebuffs in the workplace, and the myriad instances of unfairness with which our personal histories are interlarded. In this sense, proper self-regard enhances self-preservation.

Kohut (1971) paid considerable attention to the vicissitudes of the pathways related to normal narcissism as they become modified throughout the life course. The omnipotence and grandiosity that we ascribe to the infant are transformed, ideally, into healthy self-preservative attitudes; realistic self-evaluation; and, in the place of crass demandingness, an enlightened self-interest in which one by no means neglects one's own needs and hopes for advancement, but in which the rights and feelings of others are deeply and genuinely respected. Indeed, at the most highly developed level of normal narcissism, one realizes that it is specifically by giving the most (of one's attention, respect, goods, and money) that one reaps the greatest return in compassion, help when it is needed, and friendship from others. There is a payback to altruism. Appropriate self-regard and self-evaluation also mean that one's sense of worth is accurate, such that one aims, occupationally, neither below nor above one's capacities and, romantically, neither above nor below one's approximate ranking in the hierarchy of potential mates. Failures in these areas are of course accompanied by frustration and disappointment.

By self-concern, the author refers in part to matters such as the timeliness with which one consults doctors and dentists so as to preserve health at its maximum. Self-concern also includes the appropriateness of one's self-presentation. This is effected by a "golden mean" between shabbiness and showiness in dress and between endless primping and wanton disregard for one's appearance. Looking one's best subserves the need to be accepted in the workplace and attractive to potential sexual partners. A more subtle aspect of self-concern relates to the need, stemming from a genuine regard for others, to develop a pleasing personality, in contrast to the glib charm of the psychopathic person (Cleckley 1972) who adopts a pleasing facade in the service of his or her own selfish ends. Many additions could be made to this abnormal form of self-regard: for example, the abrasiveness of the person whose "me-first" policy shows itself as rudeness or contempt.

Making oneself attractive and pleasing to others in the social (as opposed to the romantic) sphere enhances the formation of alliances that strengthen one's position in the social hierarchy and contribute to the achievement of higher status (Buss 1991). From an evolutionary standpoint, appropriateness of self-concern and the friendships thus fostered may in turn promote self-preservative needs (by helping one to become more solidly en-

trenched in a network of friends, more affluent, etc.) as well as the
need to secure the best mate with whom to create children with
the best chance of surviving and flourishing in the subsequent
generation.

Heightened Self-Regard:
The Zone Just Beyond Normal Narcissism

In certain common life situations and various occupations, optimal performance seems to require a heightening of self-
regard—or an exaggerated sense of indestructibility—that goes
beyond the normal yet is adaptive to one's circumstances. To that
extent, this heightened self-regard is not really pathological.

Between two aspiring concert pianists, opera singers, or balle-
rinas of approximately equal virtuosity—the one self-effacing and
full of self-doubt, the other brimming with a self-confidence not
yet validated by critical acclaim—it is more likely that the one with
heightened self-confidence and not a twinge of stage fright will
capture the day. Performers not blessed with this supernormal
narcissism lead a tortured existence. Examples include Arthur
Schnabel, who, amidst the thunderous applause from the audience, used to cry in the wings at his "desecration" of Beethoven,
and Gregor Piatigorsky, who once refused to go out on stage
when Toscanini was about to lead the orchestra accompanying a
cello concerto. "I can't go out there, Arturo," Piatigorsky complained. "I'm a disgrace to the cello, I'm no good!" At his wit's end,
Toscanini finally said, "It's true, you're no good, Grisha—but all
the others are worse," which finally reassured Piatigorsky enough
to proceed with the concert.

Similarly, men with what Cloninger (1986) called "low harm
avoidance" and an exaggerated sense of invulnerability are those
more likely, in wartime, to storm the enemy's machine gun nest
and to become heroes (dead or alive), preserving, if not their own
lives, at least those of their comrades. The latter situation is analo-

gous, vis-à-vis the preservation of one's genes, to the deference shown by the men on the Titanic who allowed their wives and children to take to the lifeboats as the men themselves drowned. This is not mere gentlemanliness; this is nature's way of safe-guarding at least half of one's genes at the sacrifice, in extreme situations, of one's own self.

Charisma

Related to the quality of supernormal narcissism is that of cha-risma. *Charisma* derives, etymologically, from a Greek word signi-fying "to give pleasure" and is not related to the similar-sounding *charm*, which stems from the Latin *carmen*, a song. Yet, charismatic persons are those who "charm" us in the sense that they appeal, through the impact of powerful personality, more to the emotions than to the intellect. The charismatic person makes us feel loved or appreciated, singled out for special affection, as though an indi-vidual bond to each of us existed, even though we may be merely part of a large gathering. Positive and negative personalities may exhibit charisma: for example, Marilyn Monroe singing to the American troops, Pavarotti enchanting his audience, or Hitler mesmerizing the German masses. Usually, regardless of the va-lence (positive or negative), the charismatic person has tremen-dous self-confidence and, in the case of a political or religious leader, the unshakable conviction of being right.

Leadership

A generous supply of validated self-regard and self-confidence is an important asset—perhaps even a crucial ingredient—of effec-tive leadership. Not all leaders, not even outstanding leaders, need to have charisma. Among the United States presidents, F. D. Roosevelt and Kennedy had this elusive characteristic; Wil-son and Truman did not. But a well-deserved and high self-regard and a sense of one's worth (not material worth, but one's capacity to contribute to the tasks at hand) are of immense value to the leader. These attributes allow leaders to believe firmly in the plans they are trying to implement or in the ideas they are trying to disseminate. Lenin certainly had this kind of self-confidence from an early age, as his biographer, Volkogonov (1994), makes clear, although the rest of his personality partook much more of pathological than of normal narcissism. Certain leaders, besides their foresight, assertiveness, and self-confidence, rise to great heights also because of the way in which they came genuinely to personify their whole culture, embodying the virtues and ideals that the vast majority of their countrymen held high. Here one would certainly include Churchill and DeGaulle. Similarly, Tito managed to appeal sufficiently to the heterogeneous peoples of his country to actually unify them during his lifetime into a Yugoslavia that has, since his death, once again fragmented into its original factions.

The importance of assertiveness as a normal narcissistic element of leadership is obvious: it is not enough for the leader to have conviction about the correctness of his or her plans and to have high self-regard; the leader must also have the ability to take charge of situations, to speak his or her mind, and, ultimately, to dominate the task-oriented group (such as a corporate meeting) from which action is eventually to spring. The "narcissism" (here in quotation marks, because it is not pathological) of the ideal leader may extend to the outer edge of what we can still consider normal—in contrast to the clearly pathological narcissism of the arrogant, grandiose, or bullying leader.

Competitiveness

Related to the concept of assertiveness is that of competitiveness. With regard to normal narcissism, one can define a normal range of competitive behavior between passivity and ruthless ambition. Mentioned above is the analogy between competitiveness on the human plane and the territoriality of animals who defend (via aggression that is appropriate to their species) food supplies, living space, and their kin. Animals, and humans as well, show not only this horizontal (territorial) competition, but (and this is especially the case in social species) also vertical competition: competition for the highest possible spot in the social hierarchy. Subtle and complex rules develop for attaining and safeguarding one's social status. In vervet monkeys, for example, the offspring of the dominant female will be supported and protected by middle-status monkeys, even though the latter could easily overpower the immature offspring, because through such protective (altruistic) behavior they hope to win the allegiance of the dominant female. This can in turn help raise the status and safety of the middle-status monkeys (Harcourt 1988).

As for human competitiveness, it is well within normal bounds, for example, for the inventor to take credit for his or her invention and profit reasonably from its marketing. Pathological narcissism would be associated with the unscrupulous destruction of other people's opportunities to market a similar product. Within the realm of academia, politics, or other idea-based arenas, promulgation of a new idea (via publication or use of the electronic media) and taking credit for the idea are both reasonable activities consistent with normal narcissism. In this context, pathological narcissism spans a spectrum from failing to give others credit for their contributions to outright plagiarism or stealing of others' ideas. Normal versus pathological forms of competitiveness show themselves in innumerable areas of human activity. For example, dressing "to kill"—in order to outshine everybody else at a party, to incite envy, and so forth—represents going beyond the boundary; competitiveness has now become extreme and pathological.

Entitlement and the Golden Mean

As with any attempt to define normality, one is always invoking a kind of golden mean of a sort precious to the philosophers of ancient Greece and Rome. The excesses on either side of the mean are much easier to define than the normal range itself. Normal competitiveness, for example, implies, among other things, a normal degree of entitlement: that to which we indisputably have a right. The American Declaration of Independence embodies a similar notion: we have the right to life, liberty, and the pursuit of happiness. But, as the founding fathers made clear, our quest for liberty must not infringe on the rights of others (e.g., we are not free to spread our overcoats across three other seats in the movie theater just to have "space," which denies seats to three other moviegoers). We may likewise pursue happiness but not when our pursuit would make others miserable. Relative to many other cultures, America places the rights of the individual over the rights of society as a whole—for which reason there are endless disputes about "entitlement." (This must also help to explain why America has more lawyers per 100,000 inhabitants than any other country.) Whether what is at stake is my "right" to play my stereo at maximum wattage at 2:00 A.M. versus your right to a night's sleep or my "right" to use technical tricks to exonerate an obvious felon versus society's right to see the guilty brought to justice, the dispute centers on the territory between normal and pathological entitlement.

Normal Entitlement: The Golden Mean Between Moral Masochism and Arrogance

Freud and the early generations of psychoanalysts often dealt with patients whose sense of entitlement was deficient. Their patients were usually inhibited and, because of guilt over various childhood practices and peccadilloes, felt that they had no "right" to normal sexual gratification, to a kindly mate, or even to a decent job. These instances of self-denial relating to normal human pleasures to which they had every right fell under the heading of moral masochism. In the current generation, the pendulum seems to have swung, such that we see a surplus of excessively entitled and thus pathologically narcissistic patients (Lasch 1978). We often refer to this excess as arrogance. Similar traits include demandingness and selfishness.

Self-Respect: The Golden Mean
Between Depression and Haughtiness

Normal narcissism includes the element of self-respect. A related and important concept is that of dignity. Appropriate measures of these qualities maintain normal pride and keep us from groveling before a boss or from debasing ourselves with silly or offensive behavior in social settings. Depressive persons, especially those with a masochistic inclination, routinely have negative opinions about themselves. They are willing to accept much less from others than what they deserve; they let themselves be taken advantage of or needlessly endure unpleasant conditions in the workplace.

On the other side of the golden mean is haughtiness. In its most benign form, there is the truly accomplished person whose self-respect is high, and deservedly so, but who cannot refrain from reminding the rest of the world of his or her brilliance. Further along the spectrum of pathological narcissism is vanity in its literal meaning: the empty haughtiness of those who have accomplished nothing but who merely had the advantage of being "highborn" or of having had "connections."

Another aspect of normal self-respect is the quality of knowing and of being comfortable with one's place in the social hierarchy—provided that one's position is at least approximately fair and that one has not been cast undeservedly downward by prejudice. To be, as the French say, *bien a l'aise dans sa peau*—at ease in one's skin, neither envious of those who have more nor contemptuous of those who have less—is a part of normal narcissism.

Wisdom and Humor

Normal development throughout the life span on the track relating to the self should leave one with appropriate, reasonable, and realistic amounts of self-regard, self-respect, pride, self-acceptance, and self-awareness—the last being particularly important with respect to a sense of humor. Ideally, one should be able to poke gentle fun at oneself over one's shortcomings, mistakes, and peculiarities of habit. It is a characteristic of paranoid and pathologically narcissistic individuals, in contrast, that they are unable to sit comfortably with their foibles and flaws, much less to have a sense of humor about them.

Wisdom may be seen as a kind of end stage of the developmental track pertaining to normal narcissism. Wisdom is an attribute chiefly of old age, not only representing the distillation of experience over the preceding decades but also implying the mature acceptance of one's fate and of the human condition. Wisdom requires self-knowledge—as much as one can reasonably acquire, because no one can know himself or herself completely—that is tempered with the awareness and acceptance of one's flaws, frailty, and inescapable death. Wisdom emerges thus as the very opposite of pathological narcissism, that is, the opposite of vanity, pomposity, and grandiosity.

When combined with humor, wisdom can make for a rare kind of wit. The author heard this joke for the first time from a comedian in his 80s:

> Mr. Goldstein, a widower of 87, comes for an appointment with his internist. "Dr. Rosen, I need to have a checkup!" "But I saw you only 2 months ago, Mr. Goldstein. You were fine then . . . I mean, all things considered. What seems to have happened?" "Nothing, doctor. I'm just coming for a routine checkup. To tell the truth, it's a prenuptial exam. I want to make sure I'm OK." "A prenuptial?! Well, that's some news. . . . May I ask who's the bride?" "Certainly. A very lovely girl, Dr. Rosen, a beautiful girl, comes from a good family . . . she just turned 29." "Twenty-nine?! My goodness, Mr. Goldstein . . . I mean . . . it's true, you've been in pretty good shape, but . . . you know how it is . . . the exertions of marriage . . . it could be . . . well, I have to be honest: it could be fatal!" "Nu," Mr. Goldstein replied, "if she dies, she dies."

The contrast between normal and abnormal narcissism stands out clearly in this example. Mr. Goldstein is full of denial. The aged comedian is showing normal narcissism. In telling the joke, he makes it plain that he is aware of how little time he has left and of how risky lusty sex is in an octogenarian. He is aware of how we all like to deny these unpleasant verities, which he nonetheless is courageous enough to accept—and make a joke about. There is a special peculiarity of wisdom: if one boasts of it, one cannot be truly wise—for that would show a vanity incompatible with the state of wisdom. Wisdom must be accompanied by modesty, perhaps even humility—traits that are at quite the other end of the narcissistic spectrum.

The Quest for Beauty, Power, Status, and Wealth: An Ethological Perspective

During the past 20 years, there has been a burgeoning literature concerning ethological aspects of mating practices and (among social species) interactional patterns in members of the group. Included in this literature are the contributions of Eibl-Eibesfeldt (1989) and the neo-Darwinian biologist Dawkins, whose seminal work, *The Selfish Gene* (1976), has made more comprehensible some otherwise puzzling behaviors noted in "lower" animals and in the human species. Although environment and, in higher mammals, culture are important, much of behavior, including human behavior, is driven by a biologically built-in dictate to preserve and to reproduce one's genes. To anthropomorphize a bit, the apple, from the gene's point of view, is a clever device for spreading apple seeds (e.g., via our eating apples and tossing the seeds on the ground) so that the genes within the seeds replicate and make new apple trees. The genes are eternal; the fruit, ephemeral. People, in a like vein, may be seen from the viewpoint of human genes as so much bulky fruit programmed to mate, thereby passing on the eternal genes while the individual gene carriers live on for a time and die. Keeping in mind that normal narcissism is a part of the program for successful life, anyone reading this chapter may be seen as the descendant of a long line of people who were successful enough at the mating game and in the tasks of child rearing to produce your ancestors, your parents, and you.

As Dawkins (1976) pointed out, mammals (such as ourselves), in contrast to our distant ancestors, fish, reproduce via insemination that must take place within the (moist) interior of the female—with the important consequence that mammalian females are, not to put too fine a point on it, stuck with their offspring (p. 168). They have only the choices of rearing them or letting them die, whereas the males are free to wander off, if they wish, leaving their (momentary) mates with much, or all, of the burden of child rearing. In humans, the optimal strategy among men for replicating their genes would seem to be that of the philanderer, who inseminates as many different women as possible. Eventually, many women would refuse to go along with this plan, which would of course maximize their burden. A predominant strategy of coyness would arise among women to emphasize a man's long-term fidelity—the better to ensure her mate's protection and support. In a child-rearing couple, normal narcissism in the man would no longer be a kind of brutelike machismo, in which pride consisted simply of a long list of sexual conquests (of a sort that Leporello reads out about his master at the opening of Mozart's *Don Giovanni*); rather, it would be a more family-oriented normal narcissism, in which pride was derived mainly from the father's continuing participation in helping to raise his children and provide for his family. In this more adaptive scenario, that aspect of male pride relating to the "proof" his children provide of his masculinity and fertility would come to occupy only a secondary importance.

Although members of each sex must be sufficiently attractive to the other if their genes' "will" is to be done, there is a selectional advantage to the woman's being not only coy (thus taking the measure of the man's potential for steadfastness) but also choosy. Choosiness helps secure the immediate advantage of finding a mate with good genes (good, that is, for producing healthy and socially successful children), as well as the long-term advantage of finding a devoted and helpful mate during the years, especially when she and her children are maximally vulnerable. It is worth remembering that despite the complexity of modern society and cultures and despite the many generations interposed between us and our hunter-gatherer ancestors, our brain structure and our basic programs for survival have not materially changed in 100,000 years.

The more attractive the woman, at all events, the more potential mates will show interest and the better her chances of maintaining or even "upgrading" the quality of her offsprings' genetic stock. Given the prolonged period of infant helplessness (a quarter of our life span, as opposed to a mere 1% of a cat's life span), it is also nature's way to program a substantial proportion of men with the tendency to limerance (the falling deeply in love with one's sexual partner) coupled with the desire (in the men's case) to remain with their mates throughout life.

This brings us to the question, What is beauty? On the surface, this poses as a philosophical conundrum of the seemingly unanswerable type. But ethological research has recently shed some light on this issue. As it turns out, the characteristics we identify with feminine beauty—namely, a symmetrical and unwrinkled face, high cheekbones, a dimpling of the cheeks (a postpubertal phenomenon), wide hips, full breasts, and narrow waist—are the features of a woman during her fertile years. Wide hips indicate a pelvis large enough to bear children, and a narrow waist emphasizes the real (or apparent) width of the hips. Recent research suggests that men feel most attracted (and are genetically programmed to be so) to women whose waist-to-hip circumference ratio is 0.7 or less—even in thin women with small pelvises, when such a ratio preserves the illusion of a large pelvis (Ridley 1994).

For these reasons, the dictates of enlightened self-interest as a component of normal narcissism oblige women to maintain and enhance their attractiveness as much as possible as a way of safeguarding the future for themselves and for the children they may hope to produce. Likewise, in men, symmetrical features, a hand-

some face, and a nicely proportioned build are important elements in their being attractive to women, but these characteristics
are not as important for most women as women's outwardly attractive features are to men. A man's character, social status,
wealth, and power usually outweigh in significance physical attributes, because these elements are more meaningful indices of
his stability and of his ability to safeguard and promote the welfare of his children. There is a counterpart in the matter of attire
vis-à-vis sexual dimorphism: apart from the foppish male dress in
the courts of certain kings, men's attire tends to be, in most cultures, less variegated and colorful than women's.

It is to be expected, then, that men will strive to look at least
reasonably trim and attractive but will emphasize ambition,
monetary and social power, and affiliative ties to mentors or to
other men who can aid them in the scramble for these goods.
Women will continue to strive, even as they make gains in the
workplace, to look and dress in noticeably attractive ways; for
most, compassion will be a more important attribute than power.

Within each culture, there are norms for the degree to which
the goals of beauty, power, and wealth are legitimately and rightfully pursued. These norms help define the domain of culturally
syntonic normal narcissism. To exceed cultural limits is to enter
the territory of Criterion 2 in the DSM-IV definition of NPD—"is
preoccupied with fantasies of unlimited success, power, brilliance, beauty, or ideal love" (p. 661). The interconnections
between attractiveness, evolutionary fitness, and mating preferences among animals in general and humans in particular are discussed further in articles by Howlett (1993), Perrett et al. (1994),
Etcoff (1994), and Kirkpatrick and Ryan (1991).

Normal Narcissism, Empathy, and Affiliativeness

Although a lack of empathy is one of the defining features of NPD,
merely having a good empathic capacity is not incompatible with
that disorder. Empathy in its root meaning signifies merely the

ability to identify correctly the emotional states of others. The presence of empathy does not guarantee sympathy—that is, feelings of compassion about the distress that other people suffer. Clinically, one confronts two types of pathological narcissistic individuals in this regard: those who have some empathic capacity, technically speaking, but who do not care one whit about the pain or distress of others; and those who, besides lacking compassion, really do not even recognize the nature of other people's feelings. Many psychopathic persons are of the former type; the latter type includes the worst of psychopathic persons, certain extreme schizoid or autistic persons, or even the person with "schizoid psychopathy"—a most malignant form of personality aberration noted in about 40% of serial killers (Stone 1994).

Normal narcissism, in contrast, includes a healthy measure of empathy and compassion, because these attributes underlie the abilities to form friendships, collegial alliances, and sexual partnerships, all of which are ultimately valuable to oneself. Here again is the "selfish" side of altruism and affiliativeness: by being observant of and kind toward others, one furthers one's own aims and satisfaction in life. Merely the ability to diagnose correctly the other person's feeling state has high survival value, not just for humans but throughout the mammalian kingdom. Empathic ability, after all, allows social animals to distinguish potential allies from enemies (Byrne and Whiten 1988) and is thus a prelude to whatever adaptive behavior must follow the moment-to-moment exercise of this ability. In certain gifted individuals, high empathic ability not only subserves the normal narcissistic need of self-preservation, but also eventually becomes employed as oil to the delicate machinery of artistic creativity. An example from the life of Honoré, de Balzac is instructive. As Robb mentions in his recent biography (1994), "Mme. Balzac was a nervous mother; she prided herself . . . on being able to detect traces of misbehavior on her children's faces. Perhaps these silent interrogations are the origin of Balzac's lifelong interest in physiognomy: not an academic interest . . . but a means of survival" (p. 9).

Although the forces underlying creativity are still for the most part mysterious, the relationship between normal narcissism and creativity has been a matter of interest to several psychoanalytical theoreticians (Arieti 1979; Chasseguet-Smirgel 1985). Freud (1908/1962) understood creativity as an outgrowth of sublimation—"the capacity to exchange the original sexual aim [of the sexual instinct] for another one which is no longer sexual" (p. 187). Later, Freud (1911/1962) spoke of the artist as one who, having at first turned away from reality, then "allows his erotic and ambitious wishes full play in the life of phantasy. He finds the way back to reality from this world of phantasy by making use of special gifts to mould his phantasies into truths of a new kind which are valued by men as precious reflections of reality" (p. 224). Chasseguet-Smirgel (1985) adds, "the commencement of the sublimatory processes vouchsafe a greater role to the reality principle, and the admiration the public accords to the artist relates . . . to the feeling that . . . he has succeeded in achieving a symbolic narcissistic fulfillment" (p. 143).

To the extent that finding creative solutions to novel problems is a life function almost all people participate in, the interconnection between creativity and normal narcissism is relevant to the human situation in general, not just to a Balzac or a Beethoven. The wish to "leave one's mark" is an almost universal human desire, whether this takes the form of a graffiti artist's wall signature or a mural by Diego Rivera.

Finally, a comment about the survival value of empathy (when coupled with compassion): In most cultures throughout the world, adults in direct confrontations tend to spare the feelings of other people about whom they harbor negative opinions (children are not always so sparing!). This tendency is part of an unspoken bargain, one might say, to the effect that "I won't make you lose face if you don't make me lose face." The people of certain cultures, notably those of Japan and Thailand, go to extraordinary lengths to avoid embarrassing other people. In this way, we help one another preserve a sense of being "all right"; that is, we voluntarily buoy up one another's normal narcissism.

References

American Psychiatric Association: Diagnostic and Statistical Manual of Mental Disorders, 4th Edition. Washington, DC, American Psychiatric Association, 1994

Arieti S: The Magic Synthesis. New York, Basic Books, 1979

Buss DM: Evolutionary personality psychology. Annual Review of Psychology 42:459–491, 1991

Byrne R, Whiten A (eds): Machiavellian Intelligence: Social Expertise and the Evolution of Intellect in Monkeys, Apes, and Humans. Oxford, UK, Clarendon, 1988

Chasseguet-Smirgel J: The Ego-Ideal: A Psychoanalytic Essay on the Malady of the Ideal. Translated by Barrows P. New York, WW Norton, 1985

Cleckley H: The Mask of Sanity, 5th Edition. St. Louis, MO, Mosby, 1972

Cloninger CR: A unified biosocial theory of personality and its role in the development of anxiety states. Psychiatric Developments 3:67–226, 1986

Dawkins R: The Selfish Gene. New York, Oxford University Press, 1976

Eibl-Eibesfeldt L: Human Ethology. New York, Aldine De Gruyter, 1989

Etcoff NL: Beauty and the beholder. Nature 368:186–187, 1994

Freud S: Civilized sexual morality and modern nervous illness (1908), in The Standard Edition of the Complete Psychological Works of Sigmund Freud, Vol 9. Translated and edited by Strachey J. London, Hogarth Press, 1962, pp 177–205

Freud S: Formulations on the two principles of mental functioning (1911), in The Standard Edition of the Complete Psychological Works of Sigmund Freud, Vol 12. Translated and edited by Strachey J. London, Hogarth Press, 1962, pp 213–226

Harcourt AH: Alliances in contests and social intelligence, in Machiavellian Intelligence. Edited by Byrne R, Whiten A. Oxford, UK, Clarendon, 1988, pp 132–152

Horace: Odes, Bk. III, #30: in Quintus Horatius Flaccus: Opera Omnia. Antwerp, J Moretus, 1603

Howlett R: Sexual selection: beauty on the brain. Nature 361:398–399, 1993

Kernberg OF: Borderline Conditions and Pathological Narcissism. New York, Jason Aronson, 1975

Kirkpatrick M, Ryan MJ: The evolution of mating preferences and the paradox of the "lek." Nature 350:33–38, 1991

Kohut H: The Analysis of the Self. New York, International Universities Press, 1971

Lasch C: The Culture of Narcissism. New York, WW Norton, 1978

Mishkin M, Malamut B, Bachevalier J: Memories and habits: the neural system, in Neurobiology of Memory and Learning. Edited by Lynch G, McGaugh J, Weinberger NM. New York, Guilford, 1984, pp 65–77

Perrett DI, May KA, Yoshikawa S: Facial shape and judgments of female attractiveness. Nature 368:239–242, 1994

Pushkin AS: Sochineniya, Vol I. Gosudarstven, Izdatel, Moscow, 1954, p 382

Ridley M: The Red Queen: Sex and the Evolution of Human Nature. New York, Macmillan, 1994

Robb G: Balzac: A Biography. New York, WW Norton, 1994

Stone MH: Aggression, rage and the "destructive" instinct, reconsidered from a psychobiological point of view. J Am Acad Psychoanal 19:507–529, 1991

Stone MH: Abnormalities of Personality: Within and Beyond the Realm of Treatment. New York, WW Norton, 1993

Stone MH: Early traumatic factors in the lives of serial murderers. American Journal of Forensic Psychiatry 15:5–26, 1994

Valzelli L: Psychobiology of Aggression and Violence. New York, Raven, 1981

Volkogonov D: Lenin: A New Biography. New York, Free Press, 1994

Chapter 2

Pathological Narcissism and Narcissistic Personality Disorder

Theoretical Background and Diagnostic Classification

Otto F. Kernberg, M.D.

The clarification of the concept of *narcissism* is complicated by two parallel and complementary levels of conceptualization of this term. Within the first level, that of psychoanalytical theory or metapsychology (i.e., a consideration of structural, dynamic, economic, adaptive, and genetic principles of mental functioning), narcissism is defined as the libidinal investment of the self. In the ego-psychology theoretical frame of reference, the self is a substructure of the system ego, a substructure that reflects the integration of all the component self-images or self-representations that develop throughout the experiences of interactions with other human beings (*objects* in metapsychological language). The investment of libido in such objects and their psychic representations (*ob-*

ject representations) constitutes *object libido.* Object libido is in a dynamic relationship with *narcissistic libido* invested in the self.

The second level of the concept of narcissism is the clinical one, which has to do with the clinical syndromes that characterize patients with abnormal self-esteem regulation. Self-esteem or self-regard usually fluctuates according to whether our relationships with others are gratifying or frustrating and according to our evaluation of the distance between our goals and aspirations and our achievements. Beyond these commonsense observations, clinical experiences indicate that there are complex relations between self-esteem, on the one hand, and predominant affects or moods, the extent to which various self-representations are integrated or dissociated, and the vicissitudes of internalized object relations (the reciprocal relations between self- and object representations) on the other.

How are the metapsychological and clinical conceptualizations of narcissism related? Why the two levels of discourse? The first, more difficult, conceptualization provides us with models of unconscious psychic functioning that explain the clinical phenomena we observe.

Metapsychological analysis postulates that self-esteem regulation is dependent on, among other factors, the pressures that the superego exerts on the ego: the more demanding the superego (the more excessive the infantile morality of unconscious demands for perfections and prohibitions), the more self-esteem may be lowered. At bottom, such a lowering of self-esteem would reflect a predominance of self-directed aggression (stemming from the superego) over the libidinal investment of the self.

A lowering of self-esteem also may be caused by the lack of gratification of instinctual needs of both a libidinal and an aggressive nature (reflected in dependent, sexual, and aggressive strivings). In other words, unconscious ego defenses that repress the awareness and expression of instinctual needs would impoverish the ego (self) of gratifying experiences and thus "deplete" libidinal ego (self) investments and diminish self-esteem.

In addition, the internalization of libidinally invested objects in the form of libidinally invested object representations greatly reinforces the libidinal investment of the self—the presence in our mind of the images of those we love and by whom we feel loved strengthens our self-love. As a French song by George Brassens has it, "There are friends in the forest of my heart." In contrast, when excessive conflicts around aggression weaken our libidinal investments of others and, secondarily, their corresponding object representations, the libidinal investment of the self and self-love also suffer.

History

The term *narcissism*, first used in a psychiatric sense by Ellis (1898) and to describe a sexual perversion by Näcke (1899), entered the psychoanalytical lexicon through Sadger's (1908) work. After mentioning narcissism briefly in various papers, Freud published in 1914 one of his major contributions to psychoanalytical theory. In "On Narcissism: An Introduction," Freud (1914/1957) described narcissism 1) as a form of sexual perversion as well as a characteristic of all perversions; 2) as a stage in libidinal development; 3) as an underlying characteristic of schizophrenia (because of the withdrawal of libido from the external world), and 4) with reference to a type of object choice wherein the object is selected because it represents what the subject was, is, or would like to be.

These multiple applications of the word have facilitated significant psychoanalytical investigations but have also resulted in considerable confusion about the definition of narcissism. Gradually, however, narcissism as a concept in psychoanalytical theory became distinguished from the clinical use of the term. As mentioned before, the latter has come to refer to the normal and pathological regulation of self-esteem. Descriptions of narcissistic personality disorder (NPD) gradually evolved from this second context; the diagnostic category resulted from the observation of a particular constellation of resistances in the psychoanalytical treatment of certain patients—a constellation of resistances that corresponded to a particular type of character pathology also manifest in the daily lives of these patients.

Jones (1955/1964) wrote the first description of pathological narcissistic character traits. Abraham (1979) was the first to describe the transference resistances of patients with these traits; he pointed to the need for consistent interpretation of their tendencies to look down on the analyst and to use the analyst as an audience for their independent "analytic" work, and he drew attention to the link between narcissism and envy. Riviere (1936) observed that narcissistic resistances were an important source of negative therapeutic reactions; these patients cannot tolerate the idea of improvement because improvement would mean to acknowledge help received from somebody else. Riviere suggested that these patients cannot tolerate receiving something good from the analyst because of their intolerable guilt over their own basic aggression.

Elaborating on Klein's (1957) book *Envy and Gratitude,* Rosenfeld (1964, 1971, 1975, 1978) wrote the first detailed description of the psychostructural characteristics of narcissistic personalities and their transference developments in the course of psychoanalysis.

Important contributions to an understanding of the phenomenology and the psychopathology of narcissistic personalities were published in the United States by Reich (1953, 1960), Jacobson (1953/1971, 1964, 1971a, 1971b), van der Waals (1965), and Tartakoff (1966). On the basis of Jacobson's formulations, and in an effort to integrate the American and British contributions to the diagnosis and treatment of the narcissistic personality within an ego-psychology frame of reference, O. F. Kernberg (1970, 1974, 1975, 1976, 1980) proposed an alternative theoretical and clinical frame to that suggested by Rosenfeld. At the same time, Kohut (1968, 1971, 1972, 1977, 1979) proposed a completely different theoretical frame, clinical explanations, and therapeutic procedure for NPD.

The proliferation of contributions on narcissism in Great Britain and the United States had a parallel in the contributions of Grunberger (1979). Grunberger, whose work was first published in France in the 1950s and 1960s, focused on the wider clinical and metapsychological aspects of narcissism as observed in the psychoanalytical treatment of a broad range of psychopathology.

Pulver (1970) clarified this bewildering expansion of the concept of narcissism. More recent contributions to the study of the narcissistic personality and the psychoanalytical treatment of these patients have been written by Modell (1976), Volkan (1973, 1979), and Bach (1977a, 1977b). Akhtar and Thomson (1982) provided a broadly based analysis of NPD and its relation to the definition of this disorder in DSM-III (American Psychiatric Association 1980). A volume on NPD edited by O. F. Kernberg (1989a) includes updated descriptions of NPD by Akhtar (1989), Cooper (1989), Horowitz (1989), Ronningstam and Gunderson (1989), and P. F. Kernberg (1989) and exploration of the relationship between NPD and antisocial personality disorder by O. F. Kernberg (1989b), Stone (1989b), McGlashan and Heinssen (1989), and Bursten (1989). In the same volume, Plakun (1989), Stone (1989a, 1989b), and Rinsley (1989) reported on clinical observations and empirical research on etiology as well as a differential diagnosis and follow-up study of patients with NPD. Different psychoanalytical approaches to treatment of these patients are summarized by Chasseguet-Smirgel (1989), O. F. Kernberg (1989c), Goldberg (1989), and Steiner (1989). Further contributions to the psychopathology and treatment of pathological narcissism are presented in a book edited by Plakun (1990).

One major subject related to narcissism that, for all practical purposes, Freud (1914/1957) does not touch on is narcissism as character pathology. He refers to only one type of character pathology linked to narcissism, namely, that of the narcissistic object choice in male homosexual patients (p. 88). These patients may select another man who stands for themselves while they identify with their own mother; they then love this man as they would have wanted to be loved by her.

O. F. Kernberg (1984) proposed to classify narcissism along a dimension of severity, from normal to pathological. He described the following major categories (pp. 192–196):

■ *Normal adult narcissism* is characterized by normal self-esteem regulation. It is dependent on a normal self-structure related to normally integrated or "total" internalized object representations; an integrated, largely individualized, and abstracted superego; and the gratification of instinctual needs within the context of stable object relations and value systems.

■ *Normal infantile narcissism* is important because fixation at or regression to infantile narcissistic goals (infantile mechanisms of self-esteem regulation) is an important characteristic of all character pathology. Normal infantile narcissism consists of the regulation of self-esteem by age-appropriate gratifications that include or imply normal infantile "value system," demands, or prohibitions.

■ *Pathological narcissism* can be described in three types: 1) *regression to infantile self-esteem regulation,* reflecting the mildest type of narcissistic character pathology, involves precisely the fixation at or regression to this level of normal infantile narcissism. This type is represented by the frequent cases of personality or character disorders, in which the regulation of self-esteem seems to be overly dependent on expression of or defenses against childish gratifications that are normally abandoned in adulthood. Here, the problem is that the ego ideal is controlled by infantile aspirations, values, and prohibitions. One might say that, in fact, when Freud (1916/1957) described the neurotic lowering of self-esteem related to excessive repression of sexual drive, he was implicitly describing what later would be formulated as the structural characteristics of psychoneurosis and neurotic character pathology. This is a frequent and—in light of the present knowledge of more severe narcissistic pathology—a relatively mild disturbance that is usually resolved in the course of ordinary psychoanalytical treatment.

2) A second, more severe, but relatively infrequent type of pathological narcissism is what Freud (1914/1957) described as an illustration of *narcissistic object choice.* Here, the patient's self is identified with an object while the representation of the patient's infantile self is projected onto that object, thus creating a libidinal relation in which the functions of self and object have been interchanged. This condition, indeed, is

found among some people who love another as they wish to be loved.

3) A third and most severe type of pathological narcissism is the *narcissistic personality disorder* proper, one of the most challenging syndromes in clinical psychiatry. Because of the intense study of its psychopathology and the psychoanalytical technique optimally geared to resolve it, it has now become one of the standard indications for psychoanalytical treatment. It is also a frequent indication, in its more severe forms, for psychoanalytical psychotherapy.

Clinical Characteristics of Narcissistic Personality Disorder

The essential pathological character traits of those with NPD center on 1) pathological self-love, 2) pathological object love, and 3) pathological superego.

Pathological self-love is expressed in excessive self-reference and self-centeredness. These patients also manifest grandiosity, reflected in exhibitionistic tendencies, a sense of superiority, recklessness, and a discrepancy between their inordinate ambitions and what they can achieve. Their grandiosity is frequently expressed in infantile values—physical attractiveness, power, wealth, clothing, manners, and the like. Those who are highly intelligent may use their intelligence as the basis for intellectual pretentiousness.

Further expressions of self-love include an overdependence on admiration from others without an accompanying sense of gratitude—admiration is taken for granted rather than appreciated. These patients are emotionally shallow, especially in relation to others. Feelings of grandiosity alternate with feelings of insecurity or inferiority, conveying the impression that these patients feel either superior or totally worthless. What they fear most is being "average" or "mediocre." Of all these indicators, grandiosity is the most characteristic of pathological self-love.

Pathological object love is manifest by excessive—at times, overwhelming—envy, both conscious and unconscious (the latter reflected in conscious attempts to avoid or deny its existence). Such patients also use devaluation, consciously or unconsciously, in an effort to defend themselves against potential feelings of envy. Consciously, it manifests as an absence of interest in others and their work or activities and in varying degrees of contempt. Unconsciously, it manifests as a "spoiling" maneuver consisting of incorporating what comes from others and simultaneously devaluing what has been incorporated. Another way in which these patients defend themselves against envy is by exploitativeness. Excessive greed results in a wish to "steal" or appropriate what others have. A sense of entitlement is also often present.

Another manifestation of pathological object love is an inability to depend on others. A temporary idealization of others may quickly change to devaluation; the patients unconsciously seem to experience those around them first as idols, and then as enemies or fools. As might be expected, these patients are unable to empathize with or make substantive commitments to others.

Pathological superego is less decisive in establishing the diagnosis but very important in establishing the prognosis under psychotherapeutic treatment. These character patterns and affective disturbances include the incapacity to experience differentiated forms of depression (such as remorse, sadness, and self-exploration) or the presence of severe mood swings, often sparked by a failure to succeed in grandiose efforts or obtain admiration from others or following criticism that shatters grandiosity. Self-esteem is regulated by shame rather than by guilt. The patients show little interest in ethical, aesthetic, or intellectual values; their values are childish, aimed at protecting self-esteem and pride. Their inordinate dependency on external admiration indirectly reflects their immature superego functioning. Some narcissistic patients with particularly severe superego pathology present the syndrome that the author calls *malignant narcissism,* which is described in the section, "Differentiating Narcissistic Personality Disorder and Antisocial Personality Disorder," below.

The basic self state in NPD is typically that of a sense of emptiness or of being alone. These patients are usually incapable of learning from others, have an intense stimulus hunger, and feel that life is meaninglessness. They characteristically feel bored when their need for admiration and success is not being gratified.

Narcissistic persons function on a continuum of levels of severity of their pathology, ranging from almost "normal" personalities to a functioning that blends with borderline character pathology ("overtly borderline functioning"). For these borderline patients, a differential diagnosis with psychotic illness may have to be entertained.

Those functioning at the highest level (i.e., least severe pathology) do not have neurotic symptoms and seem to be adapting to social reality. They have little awareness of emotional illness except for a chronic sense of emptiness or boredom and an inordinate need for approval and success. They also have a remarkable incapacity for empathy and emotional investment in others. Few of them seek treatment, but they subsequently tend to develop complications secondary to their narcissistic pathology that may bring them to treatment.

The middle range of severe NPDs presents the typical symptoms already described.

At the lowest level (i.e., most severe pathology) of the continuum are patients who, despite the defensive functions provided by the pathological grandiose self in social interactions, show overt borderline characteristics—that is, lack of impulse control, lack of anxiety tolerance, severe crippling of their sublimatory capacities, and a disposition to explosive or chronic rage reactions or severe paranoid distortions.

Etiology of Narcissistic Personality Disorder

The clinical description of NPD derives mostly from the study of patients in the course of psychoanalytical and psychoanalytically oriented psychotherapeutic treatment. The theories proposed by

Rosenfeld (1964, 1971, 1975, 1978), Kohut (1971, 1972, 1977, 1979), and O. F. Kernberg (1975, 1976, 1980, 1984) coincide in pointing to the essentially psychodynamic etiology of these disorders and in focusing on the pathology of self-esteem regulation as the key pathogenic issue. All three approaches also agree in postulating the presence of an abnormal self-structure. The three approaches are in disagreement, however, regarding the origin of this pathological self-structure, and, as a consequence of their different psychodynamic formulations, they propose significantly different psychotherapeutic techniques within a psychoanalytically based frame of reference.

Rosenfeld (1964), a Kleinian psychoanalyst, proposed that narcissistic patients identify themselves with an omnipotently introjected, all-good, primitive "part object," thus denying any distinction between self and object. This identification permits the patients denial of any need for dependency on an originally good, external object. Dependency would imply the need for such a loved (and potentially also frustrating) object who is also intensely hated, with the hatred taking the form of extreme envy. Envy, Rosenfeld assumes, following Klein (1957), is a primary intrapsychic expression of the death instinct, the earliest manifestation of aggression in the realm of object relations. Narcissistic object relations permit the subject to avoid aggressive feelings caused by frustration and any awareness of envy. Rosenfeld (1971) also described the complication arising in these personality structures when their self-idealization is contaminated by the idealization of the aggressive parts of the self. The infiltration of the pathological "mad" self by primitive aggression results in a quality of violent self-destructiveness. In extreme cases, such patients feel secure and triumphant only when they have destroyed everyone else and particularly when they have frustrated the efforts of those who love them. Rosenfeld (1975) thinks this need is responsible for the severest forms of negative therapeutic reaction. The pathological grandiose self of these patients reflects a more primitive and intractable resistance to treatment than the unconscious guilt feelings stemming from a sadistic superego characteristic of milder forms of negative therapeutic reaction.

Kohut (1971, 1977) argued that there exists a group of patients whose psychopathology is intermediary between the psychoses and borderline conditions on the one hand and the psychoneuroses and milder character disorders on the other. This group of NPDs, which he considers analyzable, can be differentiated primarily by transference manifestations, not by clinical-descriptive criteria. Kohut diagnosed NPD within the psychoanalytical situation by recognizing the development of two types of transference: idealizing and mirroring.

Kohut proposed that these two broad types of transferences represent the activation in the psychoanalytical situation of an arrested stage of development—an archaic grandiose self. The fragility of that archaic self requires an empathic mother as selfobject whose love and ministrations and whose mirroring acceptance of the infant permit the development of that archaic self to more mature forms of self-esteem and self-confidence. At the same time, optimal empathic relations with the mirroring selfobject facilitate the development of idealization of the selfobject that stands for the original perfection of the grandiose self, now practically preserved in the relationship with such an idealized selfobject. This idealization culminates eventually in what Kohut calls the "transmuting internalization" of the idealized selfobject into an intrapsychic structure that will originate the ego ideal and provide the idealizing qualities to the superego, thus preserving the now-internalized regulation of self-esteem.

Narcissistic psychopathology, according to Kohut, derives from the traumatic failure of the mother's empathic function and from the failure of the undisturbed development of idealization processes. These traumatic failures bring about a developmental arrest, a fixation at the level of the archaic infantile grandiose self, and an endless search for the idealized selfobject needed to complete structure formation—all of which are reflected in the narcissistic transferences already mentioned.

In short, in Kohut's view, narcissistic psychopathology reflects the psychopathology of the stage of development that begins with the cohesion of the archaic grandiose self and ends with the transmuting internalization of the ego ideal. This stage centers on the gradual building up of what Kohut called the "bipolar self." He suggests that one pole, the bulk of nuclear grandiosity of the self, consolidates into nuclear ambitions in early childhood, whereas the other pole, the bulk of nuclear idealized goal structures of the self, is acquired somewhat later. These two polarities of the self derive, respectively, from the mother's mirroring acceptance (which confirms nuclear grandiosity) and her holding and caring (which allow merger experiences with the selfobject's idealized omnipotence). Nuclear ambitions and nuclear ideals are linked by an intermediary area of basic talents and skills. Kohut considered these component structures of the bipolar self as reflecting both the origin and the seed of narcissistic psychopathology, in contrast to the drives and conflict-derived psychopathology of the tripartite structure of the mind that characterizes the later oedipal period. For Kohut, then, the etiology of NPDs resides in an arrested stage of development of the normal self.

O. F. Kernberg (1975, 1980, 1984) proposed that the specific character features of patients with NPD reflect a pathological narcissism that differs from both ordinary adult narcissism and fixation at or regression to normal infantile narcissism. In contrast to the latter, pathological narcissism reflects libidinal investment not in a normal integrated self-structure but in a pathological self-structure. The pathological grandiose self, according to Kernberg, contains real self-representations, ideal self-representations, and ideal object representations. Devalued or aggressively determined self- and object representations are split off or dissociated, repressed, or projected. The psychoanalytical resolution of the grandiose self as part of the systematic analysis of narcissistic character resistances regularly brings to the surface—that is, activates in the transference—primitive object relations, conflicts, and defensive operations characteristic of developmental stages that predate object constancy. These transferences, however, are always condensed with oedipally derived conflicts, so that they are strikingly similar to those of patients with borderline personality organization.

The psychic development of NPD does not proceed smoothly

through the early stages of development described by Jacobson (1964) and Mahler (Mahler and Furer 1968; Mahler et al. 1975). Their description of the early stages of infantile symbiosis, separation-individuation, and object constancy underlies Kernberg's theoretical model. He believes that sometime between ages 3 and 5 years, the narcissistic personality, instead of integrating positive and negative representations of self and of objects— "on the road to object constancy" (Mahler et al. 1975)—puts together all the positive representations of both self and objects. This results in an extremely unrealistic and idealized pathological grandiose self. Fostering the development of a pathological grandiose self are parents who are cold and rejecting, yet admiring. Narcissistic individuals devalue the real objects, having incorporated those aspects of the real objects they want for themselves. They dissociate from themselves and repress or project onto others all the negative aspects of themselves and others.

The ideal self- and object representations that would normally become part of the superego are incorporated into the pathological grandiose self. This leads to a superego containing only the aggressively determined components (the early prohibiting and threatening aspects of the parental images distorted under the impact of the projection onto them of the child's own aggressive impulses). This successfully harsh superego also tends to be dissociated and projected, which leads to further development of "persecutory" external objects and to the loss of the normal functions of the superego in regulating self-esteem, such as monitoring and approval.

The devaluation of others, the emptying out of the internal world of object representations, is a major contributing cause of the narcissistic individual's lack of normal self-esteem and also determines the remarkable inability to empathize with others. The sense of an internal void can be compensated for only by endless admiration from others and by efforts to control others to avoid the envy that would otherwise be caused by the autonomous functioning, enjoyment of life, and creativity others enjoy.

Differentiating Narcissistic Personality Disorder and Antisocial Personality Disorder

The virtually total absence of the capacity for nonexploitative object relations and of any moral dimension in personality functioning is the key element in differentiating the antisocial personality proper from the less severe syndromes of malignant narcissism and NPD. The antisocial features in NPD may range from minor dishonesty to a full-fledged antisocial personality disorder, showing that the antisocial personality may be considered a narcissistic personality with particular additional superego pathology.

What follows is a classification of personality disorders in which antisocial features are prominent according to severity. In all patients with antisocial behavior, it is helpful first to rule out the diagnosis of an antisocial personality proper. For this reason, the potential presence of antisocial behavior in all patients with NPD is systematically investigated.

Antisocial Personality Disorder

Patients with antisocial personality disorder typically present with an NPD with symptoms described earlier in this chapter. Antisocial personality disorder proper involves even more serious superego pathology than NPD. These patients' antisocial behavior includes lying, stealing, forgery, swindling, and prostitution, all of which are characteristic of a predominantly "passive-parasitic" type; assault, murder, and armed robbery are characteristic of the "aggressive" type (Henderson 1939; Henderson and Gillespie 1969). In other words, one may differentiate clinically the behaviorally aggressive, sadistic, and usually paranoid orientation of some patients with antisocial personality disorder from the passive, exploitative, parasitic type of others.

The way to differentiate passive and aggressive antisocial behavior as part of an NPD from an antisocial personality disorder proper is by the absence in the latter of the capacity for feeling guilt and remorse. Thus, even after being confronted with the consequences of their antisocial behavior and in spite of their profuse protestations of regret, persons with antisocial personality disorder have no change in behavior toward those they have attacked or exploited or any spontaneous concern over this failure to change their behavior.

Although the differential diagnosis of the capacity for experiencing guilt and concern requires the inferential step of evaluating a patient's reaction to confrontation and the breakdown of omnipotence, other characteristics reflecting this incapacity for guilt and concern may become directly evident in the interviews—for example, in the inability to imagine an ethical quality in others.

The inability to invest in nonexploitative relationships with others may be reflected in transient, superficial, indifferent relationships; the inability to invest emotionally even in pets; and the absence of any internalized moral values, let alone the capacity to empathize with such values in others. The deterioration of these patients' affective experience is expressed in their intolerance of any increase in anxiety without developing additional symptoms or pathological behaviors, their incapacity for depression with reflective sorrow, and their inability to fall in love or experience any tenderness in their sexual relations.

Patients with antisocial personality disorder have no sense of the passage of time, of planning for the future, or of contrasting present experience and behavior with aspired ideal ones; they can plan only to improve present discomforts and reduce tension by achieving immediately desired goals. Their failure to learn from experience is an expression of the same incapacity to conceive of their lives beyond the immediate moment. Their manipulativeness, pathological lying, and flimsy rationalizations are well known. P. F. Kernberg (personal communication, December 1981) coined the term *hologram man* to refer to patients who create a vague, ethereal image of themselves in diagnostic sessions that seems strangely disconnected from their current reality or their actual past. This image changes from moment to moment in the light of different angles of inquiry and leaves the diagnostician with a disturbing sense of unreality.

Again, once the diagnosis of a narcissistic personality structure is obvious, the crucial diagnostic task is to evaluate the severity of any presenting antisocial features, their history and childhood origins, and the patient's remaining capacity for object relations and superego functioning.

Malignant Narcissism Syndrome

If an antisocial personality disorder proper can be ruled out, the next diagnostic category to be considered is an NPD with the syndrome of malignant narcissism.

These patients—characterized by a typical NPD, antisocial behavior, ego-syntonic sadism or characterologically anchored aggression, and a paranoid orientation, in contrast to antisocial personality disorder proper—still have the capacity for loyalty to and concern for others and for feeling guilty. They are able to conceive of other people as having moral concerns and convictions, and they may have a realistic attitude toward their own past and in planning for the future.

Their ego-syntonic sadism may be expressed in a conscious "ideology" of aggressive self-affirmation but also, quite frequently, in chronic, ego-syntonic suicidal tendencies. These suicidal tendencies emerge not as part of a depressive syndrome but rather in emotional crises or even out of the blue, with the underlying (conscious or unconscious) fantasy that to be able to take one's life reflects superiority and a triumph over the usual fear of pain and death. To commit suicide, in these patients' fantasies, is to exercise sadistic control over others or to "walk out" of a world they feel they cannot control.

The paranoid orientation of these patients (which psychodynamically reflects the projection onto others of unintegrated sadistic superego precursors) is manifest in their experience of others as idols, enemies, or fools in an exaggerated way. These patients have a propensity for regressing into paranoid micropsychotic episodes in the course of intensive psychotherapy; thus, they illustrate most dramatically the complementary functions of paranoid and antisocial interactions in the interpersonal realm (Jacobson 1971b; O. F. Kernberg 1984). Some of them may present rationalized antisocial behavior—for example, as leaders of sadistic gangs or terrorist groups. An idealized self-image and an ego-syntonic sadistic, self-starving ideology rationalize the antisocial behavior and may coexist with the capacity of loyalty to their own comrades.

Narcissistic Personality Disorders With Antisocial Behavior

Patients with NPD may present a variety of antisocial behaviors, mostly of the passive-parasitic type, and show remnants of autonomous moral behavior in some areas and ruthless exploitativeness in others. They do not evince the ego-syntonic sadism, self-directed aggression, or overt paranoid orientation typical of malignant narcissism. They have a capacity for experiencing guilt, concern, and loyalty to others. They have an appropriate perception of their past, and they may realistically conceive of and plan for the future. In some cases, what appears to be antisocial behavior is simply a manifestation of incapacity for commitment in depth to long-range relationships. Narcissistic types of sexual promiscuity, irresponsibility in work, and emotional or financial exploitation of others are prevalent here, although these patients are still able to care for others in some areas and maintain ordinary social responsibility in more distant interpersonal interactions.

Antisocial Behavior in Other Personality Disorders

The next level of pathology, with fewer negative prognostic and therapeutic implications, is antisocial behavior in personality disorders other than NPD. These are patients with borderline personality organization and nonpathological narcissism. Typical examples are the infantile, or histrionic, or hysteroid, or Zetzel type 3 and 4 personality disorders (not to be confused with hysterical personality proper) and paranoid personality disorder:

these are the two most frequent personality disorders of this group that present with antisocial behavior. In the infantile personality, pseudologia fantastica is not uncommon; the "paranoid urge to betray" (Jacobson 1971a) illustrates treacherousness in a paranoid context. In my experience, most patients with factitious disorder with psychological or physical symptoms, pathological gambling, kleptomania, pyromania, and malingering who do not have a typical NPD have one of these personality disorders with antisocial features.

Neurotic Personality Disorders With Antisocial Features

Patients with neurotic personality disorders with antisocial features, such as Freud's (1916/1957) criminals with an unconscious sense of guilt, are of great clinical interest. Their sometimes dramatic antisocial behavior occurs in the context of a neurotic personality organization and has an excellent prognosis for psychotherapeutic and psychoanalytical treatment.

Antisocial Behavior as Part of a Symptomatic Neurosis

Antisocial behavior as part of a symptomatic neurosis refers to occasional antisocial behavior as part of adolescent rebelliousness, in adjustment disorders, or in the presence (in many cases) of a facilitating social environment that fosters channeling psychic conflicts into antisocial behavior.

Dissocial Reaction

A clinically relatively rare syndrome, dissocial reaction, refers to the normal or neurotic adjustment to an abnormal social environment or subgroup. In clinical practice, most patients with this syndrome present some type of personality disorder that facilitates their uncritical adaptation to a social subgroup with antisocial behaviors.

Conclusion

Pathological narcissism constitutes a dimension within the field of personality disorders that includes—in order of progressive severity—NPD, malignant narcissism syndrome, and antisocial personality disorder. The clinical importance of this continuum resides in the prognostic implications of antisocial behavior for all psychotherapeutic approaches to these conditions: NPD without antisocial behavior has a good prognosis when no antisocial behavior is present, and that prognosis worsens with significant antisocial behavior; malignant narcissism syndrome has a reserved prognosis; and antisocial personality disorder has a grave outlook for all currently used psychotherapeutic measures.

Given the high prevalence of narcissistic pathology, the advances in clinical and psychopathological knowledge of these conditions represent an important contribution to the evolving understanding of the entire field of personality disorders.

References

Abraham K: A particular form of neurotic resistance against the psychoanalytic method, in Selected Papers on Psychoanalysis. New York, Brunner/Mazel, 1979, pp 303–311

Akhtar S: Narcissistic personality disorder: descriptive features and differential diagnosis. Psychiatr Clin North Am 12(3):505–529, 1989

Akhtar S, Thomson JA Jr: Overview: narcissistic personality disorder. Am J Psychiatry 139:12–20, 1982

American Psychiatric Association: Diagnostic and Statistical Manual of Mental Disorders, 3rd Edition. Washington, DC, American Psychiatric Association, 1980

Bach S: On the narcissistic state of consciousness. Int J Psychoanal 58:209–233, 1977a

Bach S: On narcissistic fantasies. International Review of Psychoanalysis 4:281–293, 1977b

Bursten B: The relationship between narcissistic and antisocial personalities. Psychiatr Clin North Am 12(3):571–584, 1989

Chasseguet-Smirgel J: The bright face of narcissism and its shadowy depths: a few reflections. Psychiatr Clin North Am 12(3):709–722, 1989

Cooper AM: Narcissism and masochism: the narcissistic-masochistic character. Psychiatr Clin North Am 12(3):541–552, 1989

Ellis H: Auto-eroticism: a psychological study. Alienist and Neurologist 19:260–299, 1898

Freud S: On narcissism (1914), in The Standard Edition of the Complete Psychological Works of Sigmund Freud, Vol 14. Translated and edited by Strachey J. London, Hogarth Press, 1957, pp 67–102

Freud S: Some character-types met with in psycho-analytic work (1916), in The Standard Edition of the Complete Psychological Works of Sigmund Freud, Vol 14. Translated and edited by Strachey J. London, Hogarth Press, 1957, pp 309–333

Goldberg A: Self psychology and the narcissistic personality. Psychiatr Clin North Am 12(3):731–739, 1989

Grunberger B: Narcissism: Psychoanalytic Essays. New York, International Universities Press, 1979

Henderson DK: Psychopathic States. London, Chapman & Hall, 1939

Henderson DK, Gillespie RD: Textbook of Psychiatry: for Students and Practitioners, 10th Edition, Revised. Edited by Batchelor IRC. London, Oxford University Press, 1969

Horowitz MJ: Clinical phenomenology of narcissistic pathology. Psychiatr Clin North Am 12(3):531–539, 1989

Jacobson E: On the psychoanalytic theory of affects (1953), in Depression. New York, International Universities Press, 1971, pp 3–47

Jacobson E: The Self and the Object World. New York, International Universities Press, 1964

Jacobson E: Acting out and the urge to betray in paranoid patients, in Depression. New York, International Universities Press, 1971a, pp 302–318

Jacobson E: Depression: Comparative Studies of Normal, Neurotic, and Psychotic Conditions. New York, International Universities Press, 1971b

Jones E: The God complex (1955), in Essays in Applied Psycho-Analysis, Vol 2. Edited by Jones E. New York, International Universities Press, 1964, pp 244–265

Kernberg OF: Factors in the treatment of narcissistic personalities. J Am Psychoanal Assoc 18:51–85, 1970

Kernberg OF: Further contributions to the treatment of narcissistic personalities. Int J Psychoanal 55:215–240, 1974

Kernberg OF: Borderline Conditions and Pathological Narcissism. New York, Jason Aronson, 1975

Kernberg OF: Object Relations Theory and Clinical Psychoanalysis. New York, Jason Aronson, 1976

Kernberg OF: Internal World and External Reality. New York, Jason Aronson, 1980

Kernberg OF: Severe Personality Disorders: Psychotherapeutic Strategies. New Haven, CT, Yale University Press, 1984

Kernberg OF (ed): Narcissistic Personality Disorder. Psychiatr Clin North Am 12(3), 1989a

Kernberg OF: The narcissistic personality disorder and the differential diagnosis of antisocial behavior. Psychiatr Clin North Am 12(3):553–570, 1989b

Kernberg OF: An ego psychology object relations theory of the structure and treatment of pathologic narcissism. Psychiatr Clin North Am 12(3):723–729, 1989c

Kernberg PF: Narcissistic personality disorder in childhood. Psychiatr Clin North Am 12(3):671–694, 1989

Klein M: Envy and Gratitude. New York, Basic Books, 1957

Kohut H: The psychoanalytic treatment of narcissistic personality disorders. Psychoanal Study Child 23:86–113, 1968

Kohut H: The Analysis of the Self. New York, International Universities Press, 1971

Kohut H: Thoughts on narcissism and narcissistic rage. Psychoanal Study Child 27:360–400, 1972

Kohut H: The Restoration of the Self. New York, International Universities Press, 1977

Kohut H: Two analyses of Mr. Z. Int J Psychoanal 60:3–27, 1979

Mahler M, Furer M: Human Symbiosis and the Vicissitudes of Individuation. New York, International Universities Press, 1968

Mahler M, Pine F, Bergman A: The Psychological Birth of the Human Infant. New York, Basic Books, 1975

McGlashan TH, Heinssen RK: Narcissistic, antisocial, and noncomorbid subgroups of borderline disorder: are the distinct entities by long-term clinical profile? Psychiatr Clin North Am 12(3):653–670, 1989

Modell A: The holding environment and the therapeutic action of psy-
    choanalysis. J Am Psychoanal Assoc 24:255–307, 1976
Näcke P: Die sexuellen perversitaten in der irrenanstalt. Psychiatrische
    en Neurologische Bladen 3:122–149, 1899
Plakun EM: Narcissistic personality disorder: a validity study and com-
    parison to borderline personality disorder. Psychiatr Clin North Am
    12(3):603–620, 1989
Plakun EM (ed): New Perspectives on Narcissism. Washington, DC,
    American Psychiatric Press, 1990
Pulver S: Narcissism: the term and the concept. J Am Psychoanal Assoc
    18:319–341, 1970
Reich A: Narcissistic object choice in women. J Am Psychoanal Assoc
    1:22–44, 1953
Reich A: Pathologic forms of self-esteem regulation. Psychoanal Study
    Child 15:215–232, 1960
Rinsley DB: Notes on the developmental pathogenesis of narcissistic
    personality disorder. Psychiatr Clin North Am 12(3):695–707, 1989
Riviere JA: A contribution to the analysis of the negative therapeutic re-
    action. Int J Psychoanal 17:304–320, 1936
Ronningstam E, Gunderson J: Descriptive studies on narcissistic per-
    sonality disorder. Psychiatr Clin North Am 12(3):585–601, 1989
Rosenfeld H: On the psychopathology of narcissism: a clinical ap-
    proach. Int J Psychoanal 45:332–337, 1964
Rosenfeld H: A clinical approach to the psychoanalytic theory of the life
    and death instincts: an investigation into the aggressive aspects of
    narcissism. Int J Psychoanal 52:169–178, 1971
Rosenfeld H: Negative therapeutic reaction, in Tactics and Techniques in
    Psychoanalytic Therapy, Vol II: Countertransference. Edited by Gio-
    vacchini PL. New York, Jason Aronson, 1975, pp 217–228
Rosenfeld H: Notes on the psychopathology and psychoanalytic treat-
    ment of some borderline patients. Int J Psychoanal 59:215–221, 1978
Sadger J: Fragment der psychoanalyse eines homosexuellen. Jahrbuch
    fur Sexuelle Zwischenstufen 9:339–424, 1908
Steiner R: On narcissism: the Kleinian approach. Psychiatr Clin North
    Am 12(3):741–770, 1989
Stone MH: Long-term follow-up of narcissistic/borderline patients. Psy-
    chiatr Clin North Am 12(3):621–641, 1989a
Stone MH: Murder. Psychiatr Clin North Am 12(3):643–651, 1989b

Tartakoff H: The normal personality in our culture and the Nobel Prize complex, in Psychoanalysis: A General Psychology. Edited by Loewenstein RM, Newman LM, Schur M, et al. New York, International Universities Press, 1966, pp 222–252

van der Waals HG: Problems of narcissism. Bull Menninger Clin 29:293–311, 1965

Volkan V: Transitional fantasies in the analysis of a narcissistic personality. J Am Psychoanal Assoc 21:351–376, 1973

Volkan V: The "glass bubble" of the narcissistic patient, in Advances in Psychotherapy of the Borderline Patients. Edited by Leboit J, Capponi A. New York, Jason Aronson, 1979, pp 405–431

Chapter 3

Further Developments in the Clinical Diagnosis of Narcissistic Personality Disorder

Arnold M. Cooper, M.D.

The term *narcissism* was originally used in psychoanalysis to refer to a pathological state, but that meaning has changed over time. Today, in its broadest sense, it refers to an interest in or concern with the self along a broad continuum, from healthy to pathological aspects. In general, concepts such as self-esteem, self-system, self-representation, and true or false self that are discussed in the literature all refer to aspects of narcissism. Many important contributions to the understanding of narcissism, primarily developed within clinical psychoanalysis, were made between those of Freud (1911/1957, 1913/1958, 1914a/1957, 1914b/1957, 1914c/1957) and those of contemporary psychoanalysts. In this chapter, the author reviews a few that are of particular significance.

Theoretical Contributions
About Self and Narcissism

In *Character Analysis,* Reich (1949) based his conception of character (or personality) on the development of narcissistic traits.
"Character is essentially a narcissistic protection mechanism . . .
against dangers . . . of the threatening outer world and the instinctual impulse" (p. 158). This significant formulation placed
narcissism at the center of a psychological explanation for the formation of defenses. In this view, threats to narcissistic well-being
(i.e., a threatened fall in self-esteem) propel the individual toward
finding other means for salvaging a potentially damaged internal
self-representation by utilizing the entire range of psychological
defenses. Reich described the narcissistic self-protective needs
that were the basis for both the "character armor" that every individual carries and the resistance to successful analytical work. The
analytical task was to break down the character armor so that the
patient could begin to see his or her inner self without the disguise
and begin to change. Reich's work formed the basis for modern
conceptions of character and resistance analysis and the place of
narcissistic needs in personality functioning.

Sullivan (1953) conceived a "self-dynamism" and "self-
system" that were at the core of both interpersonal interactions
and feelings about oneself. He believed the self-system was the
key to understanding interpersonal interactions and to therapeutic change. Contained within any self-system were concepts of
"good me," "bad me," and "not me," the last reflecting the most severe anxiety states (what Kohut later referred to as "annihilation
anxiety"). In Sullivan's view, these internal representations of self
reflected the childhood emotional and educational experience at
the hands of earliest caregivers and included the attitudes of the
caregivers toward the young child. He said, "the self-system
comes into being because of, and can be said to have as its goal, the
securing of necessary satisfaction without incurring much anxiety" (p. 169).

Horney (1939) made a signal contribution to the knowledge of narcissism by describing a basis for distinguishing healthy self-esteem from pathological narcissism. She suggested that the term narcissism be confined to unrealistic self-inflation: "the person loves and admires himself for values for which there is no adequate foundation . . . he expects love and admiration from others for qualities that he does not possess, or does not possess to as large an extent as he supposes. . . . it is not narcissistic for a person to value a quality in himself which he actually possesses or to like to be valued by others" (pp. 89–90). She believed that pathological self-inflation is always a consequence of disturbed early childhood, particularly the child's alienation from others because of fears and grievances. "His notions of himself become a substitute for his undermined self-esteem" (p. 93). Narcissistic self-inflation represents a desperate attempt to maintain self-esteem and to obtain admiration when love is perceived as unavailable. In an excellent clinical description of the significance of narcissistic pathology, Horney suggested three consequences of narcissistic grandiosity: 1) loss of work capacity because work is not satisfying for its own sake, 2) feelings that gratification is due one without effort, and 3) constant grievances and hostility in relationships. Narcissistic pathology creates a self-destructive vicious circle in which self-inflation leads to humiliation, which leads to evermore fantastic self-inflation. According to Horney, "self-esteem and self-inflation are mutually exclusive" (pp. 92–93). She also emphasized that narcissistic egocentricity impairs the capacity to be interested in or to love others. Horney is rarely credited for the depth and comprehensiveness of her description and understanding of narcissistic personality disorder (NPD).

Winnicott (1965) made an important distinction between a true self and a false self. Although not attempting a rigorous definition of the self, he said, "The True Self comes from the aliveness of the body tissues and the working body-functions, including the heart's actions and breathing" (p. 148).

> A True Self begins to have life through the strength given to the infant's weak ego by the mother's implementation of the

> infant's omnipotent expressions. The mother who is not-good-enough is not able to implement the infant's omnipotence, and so she repeatedly fails to meet the infant gesture; instead she substitutes her own gesture which is to be given sense by the compliance of the infant. This compliance on the part of the infant is the earliest stage of the False Self, and belongs to the mother's inability to sense her infant's needs. (p. 145)

Winnicott's work anticipated many aspects of Kohut's conception of the self, including the sources of pathology in maternal failure and the critical role of the self in therapy. He emphasized the cardinal role of the early "holding environment" in shaping the self and the need for adequate regression if there is to be an emergence of the true self in successful analysis.

More recently, the work of Kohut (1971, 1977, 1978) and Kernberg (1975) spurred an enormous resurgence of interest in the topic of narcissism in general and NPD in particular. Both authors have been hugely influential, not only among psychoanalysts but also among personality researchers and theorists interested in narcissism. Generally, Kernberg gave greater emphasis to the aggressive denigrating aspects of narcissistic pathology and saw the pathology as mainly a result of intrapsychic conflict. Kohut focused on the fragility and empathic needs of narcissistic individuals, emphasizing that the self in NPD largely has defects in its early structuralization. Regardless of their differences, their agreement on the dominant role of narcissism in understanding any psychopathology has immensely influenced psychodynamic thought (see Kernberg, Chapter 2, and Ornstein, Chapter 7, this volume).

Another trend in contemporary psychoanalysis has led to important contributions to the understanding of narcissism. As interest in early developmental processes has been increasing, interest has shifted from the role of guilt in intrapsychic functioning to the role of shame, especially in the early structuralization of the self. These ideas have been well summarized by Broucek (1982):

> Primitive shame experiences may occur in the first one and a
> half years of life before objective self-consciousness is ac-
> quired. They occur in the context of interest, joy or excite-
> ment when inefficacy experiences or unexpected events
> result in a sudden attenuation of such positive affects.
> Shame seems always to involve an element of cognitive
> shock—a discrepancy between expectation and actuality . . .
> Shame experiences disrupt the silent automatic functioning
> of self, and shame is therefore considered to be the basic
> form of unpleasure in disturbances of narcissism. The gran-
> diose self is viewed as an evolving compensatory formation
> instigated in large part by primitive shame experiences.
> (p. 376)

Monographs by M. Lewis (1992) and H. B. Lewis (1987) describe the basic infant observational research that has greatly expanded out of knowledge of shame in development and in
psychic organization. Shame is a consequence of a self-evaluation
process with a conclusion that one's self is inadequate. The feeling
is one of an intrinsic defect. In contrast, guilt is the consequence of
an appraisal process in which the person concludes that his or her
behavior has been bad, unacceptable, or not up to standard, but it
does not necessarily imply an intrinsic defect that is perceived as
both irreparable and apparent to others (H. B. Lewis 1987). Clinical observations of narcissistic pathology confirm the extraordinary sensitivity of individuals with NPD to experiences that they
perceive as causing them shame or humiliation.

No topic of psychological investigation is immune to cultural
influence, and this is surely true of narcissism. During the past
several decades, many social observers have voiced the conviction that there has been an abiding change within the culture that
has resulted in a change of character. The rampant consumerism
of Western society; the concept of the "now" generation; the ero-
sion of a larger sense of community in favor of individual advancement at whatever cost; the pervasive effect of commercial
television emphasizing sex, violence, and glamour; the instability
of the family; the lack of commitment in relationships—all have
been cited as either the cause of or the evidence for the rise of indi-

vidual narcissistic pathology. These ideas are intriguing, but without more careful studies, their validity remains to be established. However, it is probably more than mere happenstance that the burgeoning psychiatric and sociological interest in narcissism and its disorders occurred simultaneously.

Pathology of Narcissism:
Diagnostic Criteria

NPD broadly refers to 1) the compensatory and defensive modes that are adopted in the attempt to accommodate to an incapacity to sustain an adequate level of gratifying self-esteem and 2) a failure to establish a stable internal self-representation that includes a satisfying sense of one's relationships with other persons. As indicated elsewhere (Cooper and Ronningstam 1992), these efforts to adapt to failures of self-esteem and self-representation may elicit a variety of clinically observable behavioral responses.

Behaviors related to compensatory grandiosity:

- Fantasies of or demands for specialness and greatness
- Need for uncritical and continuous admiration
- Exhibitionistic tendencies (the "show-off")
- Perfectionism concerning one's possessions, including other persons
- Affectations of manners, dress, and speech

Behaviors directly related to fragile self-representation:

- Hypochondriasis—the somatic expression of a core weakness of the self-representation of the body
- Excessive shame, embarrassment, and humiliation when confronted with the recognition of unsatisfied needs or deficiencies in one's capacities; the defensive response to this state may be either overt rage and aggression or an inhibition of assertion and overt shyness

Behaviors related to interpersonal relationships:

- Impaired capacity for love and empathy with consequent shallowness of object relations
- Excessive self-preoccupation and feelings of entitlement, and proportionate inability to appreciate and respect the needs of another
- Lack of sustained commitment to others with a common pattern of early enthusiasm followed by later disappointment
- Envy and denigration of the achievements of others
- "Don Juanism" (i.e., compulsive sexual conquests without regard for the partner) with vengeful rage in response to experience of slight or injury (may be overtly expressed or hidden with resultant feelings of hurt and inhibition of assertion)

Behaviors related to work:

- A pattern of early success followed by later mediocrity, sometimes interspersed with flashes of brilliance
- Chronic or intermittent feelings of boredom and emptiness because actual achievements do not succeed in sustaining better feelings about one's self
- Inability to be interested in the work itself
- The fact that gratification comes from external praise, not from an inner sense of accomplishment

Behaviors related to mood:

- Sharp mood variations (from depression to hypomania), which reflect shifting levels of self-esteem and which, in turn, are excessively dependent on external events
- Disproportionate anger and envy when supplies of admiration are inadequate

Behaviors related to superego:

- Superego impairment as shown by an often subtle willingness to cut corners and "borrow" the intellectual and material belongings of others
- Harsh demand for perfection in matters pertaining to the self

- Self-destructive patterns of behavior
- Anxiety relating to feelings of being "fraudulent" and subject to exposure
- Assertiveness and exhibitionistic desires that may be severely inhibited by superego reproaches

Two Types of Narcissistic Personality Disorders

Clinical descriptions of persons with narcissistic pathology are in agreement on a number of key issues: damaged capacity for emotional ties to others, damaged capacity for sustained pleasure in one's own activities, damaged capacities for mourning and sadness, and inner feelings of deadness and boredom. Only in the last two decades has empirical research been done on NPD, much of it impelled by DSM-III (American Psychiatric Association 1980) and its successors. This research (Gunderson et al. 1991) revealed that DSM descriptions only loosely fit clinical usage and that there are important gaps between clinicians' recognition of the syndrome and DSM criteria. DSM-III and its successors, DSM-III-R and DSM-IV (American Psychiatric Association 1987, 1994), have emphasized the presentation of NPD in its aggressive, overt, extroverted form, largely following the depiction of the disorder as described by Kernberg (1975). However, over the years a number of researchers have stressed that there is an alternative presentation of narcissistic pathology—one that appears quite different on the surface but that shares similar dynamic constellations and similar affective and cognitive traits and impairments.

More recently, Cooper (1981), Masterson (1981), Akhtar and Thomson (1982), Gabbard (1989), Gersten (1991), Wink (1991), and Cooper and Ronningstam (1992) suggested that NPD has two distinct subtypes. The popular conception of the narcissistic person as the loud, ostentatious, self-centered braggart is the version that is the major concern of DSM-IV criteria. However, the group of shy, timid-seeming, inhibited individuals, hardly fitting the usual surface view of narcissism, also deserves to be considered as having NPD for reasons described below. DSM-IV criteria largely ignore this group. Cooper and Ronningstam (1992) stated that

> [t]hese patients, equally involved in grandiose, exhibitionistic fantasy and equally unable to maintain deep ties to another person with concern for the person that extends beyond the maintenance of one's own gratifications, present differently. These individuals carry on most of their narcissistic activity in fantasy (the Walter Mitty syndrome), too inhibited to expose their fantasies to public view. Their self-presentation is likely to be shy and unassuming and may appear deeply empathic, as others mistake their shy, preoccupied wish to be noticed as genuine interest in the other person. They are, however, incapable of maintaining enduring personal relationships, secretly denigrate and are envious of those close to them, and are unable to provide self-reward for their sometimes considerable accomplishments. They respond only to external praise, and that often only briefly as they feel themselves to be fraudulent. Patients with less severe forms of narcissistic personality disorder also may be quite capable of empathic registration of the needs of another; however, their hungry self-preoccupation may severely diminish their capacity to respond to those needs for more than a moment. For example, a patient had shown deep sympathy in conversation with a friend over the death of a parent; two days later he had "forgotten" that his friend's mother had died. These patients have inner guilt and emptiness over the sense of the shallowness of their relationships, and damage their interpersonal relationships by the eventual revelation of the lack of their concern for others. The descriptors necessary to bring this group to attention have been noted elsewhere (Akhtar 1989; Akhtar and Thomson 1982; Cooper 1981). Table 3–1 (Akhtar 1989) demonstrates one way of comparing the overt from the covert variety of narcissistic personality disorder. It is possible that structured interviews, self-reports, and single interviews may have difficulty capturing the phenomenologic range of narcissistic pathology. Several interviews, with the development

Table 3–1.   Clinical features of narcissistic personality disorder

I. Self-concept

Overt	Covert
Grandiosity; preoccupation with fantasies of outstanding success; undue sense of uniqueness; feelings of entitlement; seeming self-sufficiency	Inferiority; morose self-doubts; marked propensity toward feeling ashamed; fragility; relentless search for glory and power; marked sensitivity to criticism and realistic setbacks

II. Interpersonal relations

Overt	Covert
Numerous but shallow relationships; intense need for tribute from others; scorn for others, often masked by pseudohumility; lack of empathy; inability to genuinely participate in group activities; valuing of children over spouse in family life	Inability to genuinely depend on others and trust them; chronic envy of others' talents, possessions, and capacity for deep object relations; lack of regard for generational boundaries; disregard for others' time; refusal to answer letters

III. Social adaptation

Overt	Covert
Socially charming; often successful; consistent hard work done mainly to seek admiration ("pseudosublimation"); intense ambition; preoccupation with appearances	Nagging aimlessness; shallow vocational commitment; dilettante-like attitude; multiple but superficial interests; chronic boredom; aesthetic taste often ill-informed and imitative

IV. Ethics, standards, and ideals

Overt	Covert
Caricatured modesty; pretended contempt for money in real life; idiosyncratically and unevenly moral; apparent enthusiasm for sociopolitical affairs	Readiness to shift values to gain favor; pathological lying; materialistic lifestyle; delinquent tendencies; inordinate ethnic and moral relativism; irreverence toward authority

(continued)

Table 3 –1. Clinical features of narcissistic personality disorder *(continued)*

V. Love and sexuality

Overt	Covert
Marital instability; cold and greedy seductiveness; extramarital affairs and promiscuity; uninhibited sexual life	Inability to remain in love; impaired capacity for viewing the romantic partner as a separate individual with his or her own interests, rights, and values; inability to genuinely comprehend the incest taboo; occasional sexual perversions

VI. Cognitive style

Overt	Covert
Impressively knowledgeable; decisive and opinionated; often strikingly articulate; egocentric perception of reality; love of language; fondness for shortcuts to acquisition of knowledge	Knowledge often limited to trivia ("headline intelligence"); forgetful of details, especially names; impaired in the capacity for learning new skills; tendency to change meanings of reality when facing a threat to self-esteem; language and speaking used for regulating self-esteem

Source. Reprinted from Akhtar SJ: "Narcissistic Personality Disorder: Descriptive Features and Differential Diagnosis." *Psychiatric Clinics of North America* 12:505–530, 1989. Copyright 1989, W. B. Saunders Company. Used with permission.

within the interview structure of transference and countertransference interactions, may be needed to permit accurate diagnosis of the range of narcissistic pathology. This is an area where different experimental design could help to generate the data that would aid the construction of the nomenclature. (pp. 92–93)

In an important study using several scales, spouse report, and Minnesota Multiphasic Personality Inventory (MMPI) items

(Hathaway and McKinley 1989), Wink (1991) concluded that his findings "are consistent with the view that there are two distinct (covert and overt) forms of narcissism" (p. 596). He designated one form as vulnerability-sensitivity and the other as grandiosity-exhibitionism. He described the covert vulnerability-sensitivity form as "defensive, hypersensitive, anxious and socially reticent individuals whose personal relations, however, were marked by self-indulgence, conceit and arrogance, and an insistence on having their own way. High scores on Grandiosity-Exhibitionism, similar to overt narcissists, showed a consistent behavioral pattern of self-assuredness, exhibitionism, self-indulgence, and disrespect for the needs of others" (p. 596). Wink found that both types are

> associated with psychological problems and difficulties in effective functioning. In keeping with the distinction between covert and overt narcissism, the most clearly visible difficulties associated with Vulnerability-Sensitivity include anxiety and pessimism, lack of fulfillment, and vulnerability to life's traumas. In the case of Grandiosity-Exhibitionism, the difficulties center on overconfidence, aggressiveness at the cost of others, and an excessive need for admiration from others. (p. 596)

He continued:

> In spite of their outgoingness, self-assurance, and desire to be admired, high scores on Grandiosity-Exhibitionism did not report feeling fulfilled, integrated, and emotionally healthy. One possible explanation for this relative lack of effective functioning may be the detrimental effect that exhibitionism and aggressiveness have on interpersonal relations. After all, subjects scoring high on this narcissism factor were described by their spouses as more cruel, intolerant, immodest, and bossy than subjects scoring low. (p. 593)

He concluded:

> that narcissism in general, and covert narcissism in particular, are complex and multifaceted constructs, and many of

their characteristics are difficult to measure through self-report or observer judgment. (p. 596)

A variety of labels have been suggested to differentiate these two groups. Gabbard (1989) referred to these two types as the "oblivious" types (those who are unaware of the impact of their grandiose and exhibitionistic behavior on their relations with other persons) and the "hypervigilant" types (those who are overly concerned with the reactions of others and inhibit their assertive or exhibitionistic behavior) (see Gabbard, Chapter 6, this volume). Gersten (1991), referring to the same phenomena, suggested they be designated "NPD, type 1, overtly grandiose" and "NPD, type 2, overtly vulnerable." Rosenfeld (1987), in a discussion of negative therapeutic reactions, pointed out that among the earlier generation of psychoanalysts, Horney (1939), Abraham (1949), Reich (1949), and Klein and Riviere (1967) were all alert to the hidden narcissistic resistances that impeded certain analyses, and they emphasized the role that hidden envy and fear of humiliation may play in this process. Each of these psychoanalysts was pointing out the more subtle presentations of narcissistic pathology and objecting to Freud's pessimism regarding the negative therapeutic reaction and the analysis of narcissistic characters generally. Rosenfeld (1987), referring to the two types of narcissistic disorders, suggested they be called the "thick-skinned" and the "thin-skinned."

In a related development, Cooper, in a series of papers (1981, 1982, 1984, 1988), stressed the masochistic, self-defeating aspects of NPD. In his view, an intrinsic aspect of narcissistic pathology is the resort to masochistic defenses. The pursuit of self-defeating, painful, humiliating interpersonal interactions represents a defense mechanism in which the individual is simultaneously attempting to maintain a fantasy of grandiosity while acknowledging that he or she is weak and helpless. In effect, masochistic defenses are a method for claiming "No one has defeated me or deprived me of my greedy desires. On the contrary, I myself have decided that I will extract satisfaction from angry, self-pitying feelings of being injured. Therefore, I am still in full control." The masochistic aspect of NPD may be more readily apparent in the covert narcissistic personality, but it is also a significant aspect of overt narcissism accounting for a large portion of the interpersonal difficulties and frequent failures of ambition in these individuals. Cooper (1981, 1982, 1984, 1988) suggested that it would be phenomenologically more accurate to refer to the disorder as narcissistic-masochistic personality disorder.

DSM-IV and Covert Narcissistic Disorder

Although DSM-IV quite accurately describes the overtly grandiose narcissistic person, it largely neglects the covert, hypersensitive type. Furthermore, the DSM system, in its attempt to avoid psychodynamic propositions, neither provides adequate scope for understanding how apparently different surface presentations may represent a common underlying narcissistic pathology nor pays adequate attention to the broad continuum of pathology from mild to severe. A brief review of DSM-IV descriptions and criteria for NPD will provide an opportunity to elaborate the differences between the two types of NPD, emphasizing the depiction of the poorly described category of covert narcissistic personalities and suggesting the psychodynamics that are involved. (See Table 4–3 in Millon, Chapter 4, for DSM-IV criteria.)

The discussion of NPD under "Diagnostic Features" in DSM-IV begins, "The essential feature of Narcissistic Personality Disorder is a pervasive pattern of grandiosity, need for admiration, and lack of empathy that begins by early adulthood and is present in a variety of contexts" (p. 658). It is only later, in discussion of the need for excessive admiration (Criterion 4), that there is mention that "their self-esteem is almost invariably very fragile" (p. 658). These two statements would seem to present a surface incompatibility. It might be more enlightening to state that the essential feature of NPD is an invariable fragility of self-esteem regulation and an inability to sustain an adequate sense of self-worth. Overt grandiosity, need for admiration, and self-centeredness are then among the possible defensive responses to this painful defect; other defenses include shyness and inhibitions of assertion. Adopting a psychodynamic view of NPD can help to avoid the unnecessary rigidity and even contradictory aspects of the description.

For example, Criterion 1—"has a grandiose sense of self-importance (e.g., exaggerates achievements and talents, expects to be recognized as superior without commensurate achievements)" (p. 661)—describes individuals with NPD as follows:

> They routinely overestimate their abilities and inflate their accomplishments, often appearing boastful and pretentious. They may blithely assume that others attribute the same value to their efforts and may be surprised when the praise they expect and feel they deserve is not forthcoming. Often implicit in the inflated judgments of their own accomplishments is an underestimation (devaluation) of the contribution of others. (p. 658)

This accurate description of overt narcissism does not fit the group of covert narcissistic patients whose overt symptomatology is precisely the opposite of what is described. Covert narcissistic individuals are those whose fantasies, whether conscious or unconscious, are indeed grandiose, inflated, unrealistic, and self-centered. They may be preoccupied with fantasies of grandiose achievements, imagining themselves as world heroes, centers of attention, and acclaimed by all. However, for one of several dynamic reasons, these fantasies are not expressed in overt behavior and are regarded by the individual consciously as beyond attainment. The grandiose desires are not matched by a conviction of personal efficacy. These individuals are conflicted and guilty over their overweening exhibitionistic, competitive, and aggressive desires, and their defensiveness often leads them to suppress or repress any awareness of the existence of these qualities. Most often, a barrier is interposed by a severe inner conscience that finds these fantasies unacceptable, demanding both that they should be suppressed and that the person should feel guilty for harboring unacceptable wishes. In effect, the superego accurately detects that within these self-inflating ideas lie self-centered, aggrandizing desires to attribute all goodness and power to oneself and relegate all weakness and badness to others, an aspect of the angry envy that probably is involved in the genesis of all narcissistic pathology.

Routine initial interviewing and observation often will not reveal this complex, often paradoxical, internal fantasy life. The patients, like the public at large, may see only the final defensive inhibitory behaviors and perceive themselves as shy and unassertive, unable to obtain what rightfully they deserve. Often, the first hint of their underlying grandiosity comes when one realizes that adolescent types of daydreams of being heroic and acclaimed have persisted into adult life with unusual intensity and frequency. Furthermore, scrutiny of the nature of the inhibition will reveal that these individuals often think of themselves as "perfectionists." What they mean by this is that their fantasy of what they ought to be or produce is so inflated and grandiose that no actual product ever meets their internal standard. This discrepancy between unconscious fantasy and reality leads to further guilt and merciless attack from the conscience for not meeting self-set standards as well as to feelings of worthlessness concurrent with grandiosity. These individuals often come to the attention of psychiatrists because of the depression and sense of inner deadness that they experience, as nothing in the world matches the thrill of triumphant achievement that they imagine is due them.

As indicated in the above discussion, Criterion 2—"is preoccupied with fantasies of unlimited success, power, brilliance, beauty, or ideal love" (p. 661)—surely applies to the covert narcissistic persons, but again, more subtly and complexly. For narcissistic individuals, these pleasurable fantasies are also a source of guilt and conflict because of the discrepancy between the fantasy and their inner debased assessments of their self-worth. Because these individuals are convinced that they do not deserve the fruits of these fantasies, the grandiosity may be matched by an even greater degree of self-debasement. As a consequence, the covert narcissistic individual is ashamed of grandiose fantasies, hides them from others, and is guilty for having them. His or her interpersonal behavior, reflecting these conflicts, is likely to be characterized by an incapacity to sustain ambitions or to pursue even attainable goals with full dedication, yielding to others rewards that he or she may legitimately deserve. The final result is often significant masochistic self-damage, self-pity, feelings of hurt, and depression.

Criterion 3—"believes that he or she is 'special' and unique and can only be understood by, or should associate with, other special or high-status people (or institutions)" (p. 661)—also applies to the covert narcissistic person, but, once again, it may not be apparent on the surface. Narcissistic persons experience an enormous sense of unjustness and unfairness because they are not adequately appreciated for their specialness and understood for their unique qualities, but they are not capable of pursuing appropriate recognition. Because these patients lack adequate assertive capacities, they are often unable to choose friends or lovers who are appropriately at their level of accomplishment for fear that truly superior people would see through their pretensions. In fact, not infrequently, the chosen intimates of the covert narcissistic individual are conspicuously inferior in terms of talents or resources, and the narcissistic person secretly harbors fantasies that he or she is engaged in a heroic rescue of someone of lesser capacities.

Similar modifications apply to Criterion 4: "requires excessive admiration" (p. 661). The need for admiration, while present, is blended with the more masochistic beliefs that any admiration received is false and insincere. This is because these individuals lack the internal conviction of their good qualities. They can spend enormous amounts of time and psychological energy brooding with bittersweet feelings over how little they are appreciated for their goodness and how others are getting credit for successes that should have come to them. In addition, these individuals with pathologically harsh consciences are barraged by inner accusations along the lines of "Who are you kidding with your notions of being so admirable? You and I know that you're still a helpless baby. What's more, the things that you claim are so great are, in fact, either borrowed and plagiarized or, like you, secretly full of defects that will be revealed on close examination. Don't think you can get away with showing off your accomplishments. You'll instantly be laughed at and humiliated." Confronted with this onslaught, these individuals' overt behavior is the opposite of what is described under the DSM-IV rubric. They are frightened to show their accomplishments and often fail to get credit for good work that they have actually done. They procrastinate about accomplishing tasks that are well within their capacities but that they fear they cannot accomplish, and their overt demeanor is often excessively retiring, modest, and shy. Again, one sees the qualities that are described in the criteria, but they are not part of the individuals' overt behavior. They form part of a structure of masochistic defensive substitutions, leaving these individuals bitter, complaining, and depressed.

As already indicated, for the covert narcissistic person, Criterion 5—"has a sense of entitlement, i.e., unreasonable expectations of especially favorable treatment or automatic compliance with his or her expectations" (p. 661)—although true, may not show up in usual interpersonal interactions.

In the covert narcissistic person, the interpersonal exploitiveness of Criterion 6—"is interpersonally exploitative, i.e., takes advantage of others to achieve his or her own ends"—is secondary to masochistic defenses, in which the individual is more exploited than exploiter. Similarly, with regard to Criterion 7—"lacks empathy: is unwilling to recognize or identify with the feelings and needs of others"—the covert narcissistic individual may quite successfully disguise this actual lack of empathy by a surface appearance of unusually understanding and self-sacrificing interest in others—as the good listener, for example. This pose masks a shallowness of feelings, boredom, and secret feelings of superiority toward the person to whom he or she is being "empathic."

Criterion 8—"is often envious of others or believes that others are envious of him or her" (p. 661)—inadequately emphasizes the role of envy as part of the unconscious core of the disorder. These individuals are acutely attuned to the existence of the good qualities they detect in others, which they not only envy but also most often denigrate. In the case of the covert narcissistic individual, this denigration may be hidden beneath a facade of obsequious flattery of others.

Finally, Criterion 9—"shows arrogant, haughty behaviors or attitudes" (p. 661)—must be modified in the case of the covert narcissistic person, whose social behavior may be excessively modest, retiring, and shy, for reasons already discussed. Although treatment is not the topic of this chapter, clearly different strategies are necessary for the different types of NPD.

Conclusion

Narcissistic pathology is part of a variety of personality disorders and may be a central feature of several of them—most notably antisocial personality disorder and borderline personality disorder. NPD must be recognized in two different presentations, covert and overt. DSM-IV quite adequately describes the overt type. However, handicapped by the omission of a psychodynamic understanding of the pathology of narcissism, DSM-IV fails to give a description of covert narcissism. Individuals who have covert narcissism share the same defects in structure of the self-representation and self-esteem regulation and have similar fantasies of grandiosity. However, they have a different social self-presentation, which emphasizes inhibitions of assertion, exhibitionism, and grandiosity with apparent shyness, sensitivity, and empathic capacity. Both groups have excessive envy, a diminished capacity for empathy, and a lack of sustained enthusiasm for their activities or their relationships. Recognition of the alternative presentations of narcissistic pathology is essential for successful therapy.

References

Abraham K: Selected Papers of Karl Abraham. The International Psychoanalytic Library, No 13. Edited by Jones E. London, Hogarth Press and Institute of Psychoanalysis, 1949

Akhtar SJ: Narcissistic personality disorder: descriptive features and differential diagnosis. Psychiatr Clin North Am 12:505–530, 1989

Akhtar SJ, Thomson JA: Overview: narcissistic personality disorder. Am J Psychiatry 139:12–20, 1982

American Psychiatric Association: Diagnostic and Statistical Manual of Mental Disorders, 3rd Edition. Washington, DC, American Psychiatric Association, 1980

American Psychiatric Association: Diagnostic and Statistical Manual of Mental Disorders, 3rd Edition Revised. Washington, DC, American Psychiatric Association, 1987

American Psychiatric Association: Diagnostic and Statistical Manual of Mental Disorders, 4th Edition. Washington, DC, American Psychiatric Association, 1994, pp 658–661

Broucek FJ: Shame and its relationship to early narcissistic developments. Int J Psychoanal 63:369–378, 1982

Cooper A: Narcissism, in American Handbook of Psychiatry, Vol 4. Edited by Arieti S, Keith H, Brodie H. New York, Basic Books, 1981, pp 297–316

Cooper AM: Narcissistic disorders within psychoanalytic theory, in Psychiatry 1982: The American Psychiatric Association Annual Review. Edited by Grinspoon L. Washington, DC, American Psychiatric Press, 1982, pp 487–498

Cooper A: The unusually painful analysis: a group of narcissistic-masochistic characters, in Psychoanalysis: The Vital Issues, Vol II. New York, International Universities Press, 1984, pp 45–67

Cooper A: The narcissistic-masochistic character, in Masochism: Current Psychoanalytic Perspectives. Edited by Glick RA, Meyers DI. New York, Analytic Press, 1988, pp 117–138

Cooper AM, Ronningstam E: Narcissistic personality disorder, in American Psychiatric Press Review of Psychiatry, Vol 11. Edited by Tasman A, Riba MB. Washington, DC, American Psychiatric Press, 1992, pp 80–97

Freud S: Psycho-analytic notes on an autobiographical account of a case of paranoia (dementia paranoides) (1911), in The Standard Edition of the Complete Psychological Works of Sigmund Freud, Vol 12. Translated and edited by Strachey J. London, Hogarth Press, 1957, pp 9–82

Freud S: Totem and taboo (1913), in The Standard Edition of the Complete Psychological Works of Sigmund Freud, Vol 13. Translated and edited by Strachey J. London, Hogarth Press, 1958, pp 1–162

Freud S: On narcissism: an introduction (1914a), in The Standard Edition of the Complete Psychological Works of Sigmund Freud, Vol 14. Translated and edited by Strachey J. London, Hogarth Press, 1957, pp 67–102

Freud S: Instincts and their vicissitudes (1914b), in The Standard Edition of the Complete Psychological Works of Sigmund Freud, Vol 14. Translated and edited by Strachey J. London, Hogarth Press, 1957, pp 109–140

Freud S: Mourning and melancholia (1914c), in The Standard Edition of the Complete Psychological Works of Sigmund Freud, Vol 14. Translated and edited by Strachey J. London, Hogarth Press, 1957, pp 237–258

Gabbard G: Two subtypes of narcissistic personality disorder. Bull Menninger Clin 53:527–532, 1989

Gersten SP: Narcissistic personality disorder consists of two distinct subtypes. Psychiatric Times 8:25–26, 1991

Gunderson J, Ronningstam E, Smith L: Narcissistic personality disorder: a review of data on DSM-III-R descriptions. Journal of Personality Disorders 5:167–177, 1991

Hathaway SR, McKinley JC: Minnesota Multiphasic Personality Inventory—2. Minneapolis, MN, University of Minnesota, 1989

Horney K: New Ways in Psychoanalysis. New York, WW Norton, 1939

Kernberg O: Borderline Conditions and Pathological Narcissism. New York, Jason Aronson, 1975

Klein M, Riviere J: Love, Hate and Reparation. London, Hogarth Press and Institute of Psychoanalysis, 1967

Kohut H: The Analysis of Self: A Systematic Approach to the Psychoanalytic Treatment of Narcissistic Personality Disorders. New York, International Universities Press, 1971

Kohut H: The Restoration of Self. New York, International Universities Press, 1977

Kohut H: The Psychology of Self: A Casebook. Edited by Goldberg A, Basch MF, Gunther MS, et al. New York, International Universities Press, 1978

Lewis HB (ed): The Role of Shame in Symptom Formation. Hillsdale, NJ, Lawrence Erlbaum, 1987

Lewis M: Shame: The Exposed Self. New York, Free Press, 1992

Masterson JF: The Narcissistic and Borderline Disorders. New York, Brunner/Mazel, 1981

Reich W: Character Analysis, 3rd Edition. Translated by Wolfe TP. New York, Orgone Institute Press, 1949, p 158

Rosenfeld H: Impasse and Interpretation. London, Tavistock Publications, 1987

Sullivan HS: The Interpersonal Theory of Psychiatry. New York, WW Norton, 1953, pp 168–169

Wink P: Two faces of narcissism. J Pers Soc Psychol 61:590–597, 1991

Winnicott DW: The Maturational Processes and the Facilitating Environment: Studies in the Theory of Emotional Development. New York, International Universities Press, 1965

Chapter 4

DSM Narcissistic Personality Disorder

Historical Reflections and Future Directions

Theodore Millon, Ph.D., D.Sc.

Several theoretical contributions influenced the narcissistic personality disorder (NPD) criteria set at the time that the DSM-III Task Force began its work in 1974. One source was Freud's descriptive view concerning the narcissistic libidinal type. Freud (1900/1953) did not use the term *narcissism* to represent an observation noted in his investigation of dreams but reported the following as a likely basis for the personality traits of narcissistic individuals: "I have found that people who know that they are preferred or are favored by their mother give evidence in their lives of a peculiar self-reliance and an unshakable optimism

Abridged from Chapter 11 of Millon T, Davis R: *Disorders of Personality: DSM-IV, Axis II and Beyond*. New York, Wiley, 1995. Copyright 1995. Reprinted by permission of the publisher, John Wiley and Sons, and of the authors.

which often seem like heroic attributes and bring actual success to their possessions" (p. 398).

In his only major paper devoted exclusively to narcissism, Freud (1914/1957) described a type of parental style and motivation that he considered to be a central factor contributing to the development of narcissism: "They are impelled to describe to the child all manner of perfection which sober observation would not confirm, to gloss over and forget all his shortcomings. . . . Moreover, they are inclined to suspend in the child's favor the operation of all those cultural requirements which their own narcissism has been forced to respect, and to renew in his person the claims for privileges which were long ago given up by themselves" (p. 48). In contrast, in the same paper, Freud (1914/1957) stated that in certain cases, notable among "perverts and homosexuals," libidinal self-centeredness stems from the child's feeling that caregivers cannot be depended on to provide reliable love. These children "give up" as far as trusting and investing in others as love objects and decide instead that they can trust, and therefore love, only themselves. Freud (1931/1959) described a narcissistic libidinal individual for the first time in 1931: "The main interest is focused on self-preservation; the type is independent and not easily over awed. . . . People of this type impress others as being 'personalities'; it is on them that their fellow men are specially likely to lean; they readily assume the role of leader, give a fresh stimulus to cultural development and break down existing conditions" (p. 249). As noted, Freud identified several origins of narcissistic self-cathexis, one of which led to feelings of emptiness and low self-esteem, characteristic of the presently predominant NPD type, and another that led to the description of the narcissistic libidinal type corresponding more closely to the DSM-III (American Psychiatric Association 1980) portrayal of the narcissistic personality.

Reich's (1933/1949) conception of the phallic-narcissistic disorder was another source of inspiration in the task force's work. Individuals with this disorder express themselves in a blatantly self-confident way with flagrant display and superiority. Reich's theory, which adhered closely to the central role assigned to psychosexual development, asserted that sexuality among narcissistic males, by far the more prevalent narcissistic sex, served less as a vehicle of love than as one of aggression, especially directed toward women. Aggressive courage is among the most outstanding traits.

The notion of Horney (1939) that narcissism is essentially a form of self-inflation (i.e., the presentation of greater self-value than can be sustained by actual achievements) was an additional source for the task force, as were the keen observations in the then-recent writings of Kernberg (1967, 1970) and Kohut (1966, 1971). Also relevant were parallel formulations of Millon (1969), a member of the task force, in which the following narcissistic personality criteria were noted: elevated affectivity (buoyant, optimistic, and carefree), cognitive expansiveness (boundless in imagination, facile in rationalizations), admirable self-image (egotistic, self-assured), and interpersonal exploitation (presumptuous in expectation of special considerations and good will) (p. 263).

From DSM-III to DSM-IV

Responsible for presenting the initial draft to the DSM-III Task Force in 1975, Millon offered the following suggested characterizations and criteria:

> This pattern is typified by an inflated sense of self-worth, an air of supercilious imperturbability and a benign indifference to shared responsibilities and the welfare of others. A special status for self is taken for granted and there is little awareness that exploitive behavior is inconsiderate and presumptuous. Achievement deficits and social irresponsibilities are justified and sustained by a boastful arrogance, expansive fantasies, facile rationalizations and frank prevarications. Marked rebuffs to self-esteem may provoke serious disruptions in the characteristic unruffled composure. (Millon 1969, p. 263)

Since adolescence or early adulthood, at least three of the following criteria must have been present to a notable degree and not limited to discrete periods or stressful life events:

1. Inflated self-image (e.g., displays pretentious self-assurance and exaggerates achievements and talents; often seen by others as egotistical, haughty, and arrogant)
2. Interpersonal exploitiveness (e.g., divulges taking others for granted and using them to enhance self and indulge desires, expects special favors and status without assuming reciprocal responsibilities)
3. Cognitive expansiveness (e.g., exhibits immature fantasies and an undisciplined imagination, is minimally constrained by objective reality, takes liberties with facts, and often prevaricates to redeem self-illusion)
4. Insouciant temperament (e.g., manifests a general air of nonchalance and imperturbability; except when narcissistic confidence is shaken, appears coolly unimpressionable or buoyantly optimistic)
5. Deficient social conscience (e.g., reports flouting conventional rules of shared social living, viewing them as naive or inapplicable to self; reveals a careless disregard for personal integrity and an indifference to the rights of others)

Modified in certain details, notably in specifying symptoms manifested when confidence in self is shaken (e.g., rage, humiliation, unworthiness, and emptiness), the central features of these criteria served to guide the final version of DSM-III (see Table 4–1).

DSM-III-R (American Psychiatric Association 1987) followed the criteria for DSM-III rather closely. However, the criteria were changed from mixed polythetic/monothetic criteria to entirely polythetic criteria. The four-part interpersonal criterion group was separated into three individual criteria, deleting the criterion "alternating between extremes of over-idealization and devaluation" (Millon 1981). Similarly, DSM-III criteria encompassing both grandiosity and uniqueness were subdivided into two separate

---

Table 4–1. DSM-III diagnostic criteria for narcissistic personality disorder

---

The following are characteristic of the individual's current and long-term functioning, are not limited to episodes of illness, and cause either significant impairment in social or occupational functioning or subjective distress:

A. Grandiose sense of self-importance and uniqueness, e.g., exaggeration of achievements and talents, focus on the special nature of one's problems.

B. Preoccupation with fantasies of unlimited success, power, brilliance, beauty, or ideal love.

C. Exhibitionism: the person requires constant attention and admiration.

D. Cool indifference or marked feelings of rage, inferiority, shame, humiliation, or emptiness in response to criticism, indifference of others, or defeat.

E. At least two of the following characteristic of disturbances in interpersonal relationships:

　1. entitlement: expectation of special favors without assuming reciprocal responsibilities, e.g., surprise and anger that people will not do what is wanted

　2. interpersonal exploitativeness: taking advantage of others to indulge own desires or for self-aggrandizement; disregard for the personal integrity and rights of others

　3. relationships that characteristically alternate between the extremes of overidealization and devaluation

　4. lack of empathy: inability to recognize how others feel, e.g., unable to appreciate the distress of someone who is seriously ill.

---

criteria. Added to the list was the criterion "is preoccupied with feelings of envy" (see Table 4–2).

The DSM-IV Axis II Work Group (Gunderson et al. 1991) thoroughly reviewed the literature through 1989. Some 40-plus contributors provided advice, and 20 independent researchers contributed relevant unpublished data about diagnostic overlaps and provided efficiency statistics. To summarize these efforts, it was found that several of the DSM-III-R criteria frequently failed

---

Table 4–2.   DSM-III-R diagnostic criteria for narcissistic personality
disorder

A pervasive pattern of grandiosity (in fantasy or behavior), lack of
empathy, and hypersensitivity to the evaluation of others, beginning
by early adulthood and present in a variety of contexts, as indicated
by at least *five* of the following:

1. reacts to criticism with feelings of rage, shame, or humiliation
    (even if not expressed)
2. is interpersonally exploitative: takes advantage of others to
    achieve his or her own ends
3. has a grandiose sense of self-importance, e.g., exaggerates
    achievements and talents, expects to be noticed as "special"
    without appropriate achievement
4. believes that his or her problems are unique and can be
    understood only by other special people
5. is preoccupied with fantasies of unlimited success, power,
    brilliance, beauty, or ideal love
6. has a sense of entitlement: unreasonable expectation of
    especially favorable treatment, e.g., assumes that he or she
    does not have to wait in line when others must do so
7. requires constant attention and admiration, e.g., keeps fishing
    for compliments
8. lack of empathy: inability to recognize and experience how
    others feel, e.g., annoyance and surprise when a friend who
    is seriously ill cancels a date
9. is preoccupied with feelings of envy

---

to identify patients who were given primary narcissistic diagnoses by their clinicians. Although the results of the unpublished
empirical data were not entirely consistent, several studies indicated that the weakest criteria were poor response to criticism,
feelings of envy, and a lack of empathy. Among the best criteria
were grandiose self-importance, fantasies of unlimited success,
and requiring attention and admiration. Proposals were made to
diminish problematic overlaps, such as those found between narcissistic, antisocial, and passive-aggressive personalities. A comprehensive study employing the semistructured Diagnostic

Interview for Narcissism (DIN) (Ronningstam and Gunderson 1990) found three features of potential utility not included in DSM-III-R: 1) boastful and pretentious behavior, 2) arrogant and haughty attitudes and behavior, and 3) self-centered and self-referential behavior.

Proposed modifications reflected diagnostic efficiency statistics and evaluation of new, potentially more discriminative criteria. Replaced from the DSM-III-R original list was the criterion "reacts to criticism with rage, shame, or humiliation," which signified the downgrading of the essential feature of "hypersensitivity to evaluations by others." Added was the criterion "shows arrogant, haughty behaviors or attitudes." The sequencing of the criterion list was rearranged to present an order from the most to the least prominent or discriminable. This reorganization placed "grandiose sense of self-importance" and "preoccupied with success/power/fantasies" at the top of the list. In its final form, DSM-IV (American Psychiatric Association 1994) (see Table 4–3) basically continued the DSM tradition of diverse diagnostic criteria. The nine listed criteria fall into four broad clinical domains: interpersonal (criterion numbers 4, 5, 6, 7, 8), self-image (1, 3), cognitive (2), and behavioral (9).

Toward DSM-V: Expanding and Explicating Diagnostic Criteria

Although DSM diagnostic criteria facilitate clarity and enable comparability, a major problem is their variability in the clinical domains they encompass (e.g., from personality disorder to personality disorder). Moreover, many criteria are highly redundant, both within each personality category and with other categories (see Morey and Jones, Chapter 15, this volume). Most important, the extant criteria in DSM-IV are insufficiently comprehensive in the clinical domains they include. To summarize, current criteria

---

Table 4–3.   DSM-IV diagnostic criteria for narcissistic personality
disorder

A pervasive pattern of grandiosity (in fantasy or behavior), need for
admiration, and lack of empathy, beginning by early adulthood and
present in a variety of contexts, as indicated by five (or more) of the
following:

(1) has a grandiose sense of self-importance (e.g., exaggerates
     achievements and talents, expects to be recognized as
     superior without commensurate achievements)
(2) is preoccupied with fantasies of unlimited success, power,
     brilliance, beauty, or ideal love
(3) believes that he or she is "special" and unique and can only
     be understood by, or should associate with, other special or
     high-status people (or institutions)
(4) requires excessive admiration
(5) has a sense of entitlement, i.e., unreasonable expectations of
     especially favorable treatment or automatic compliance with
     his or her expectations
(6) is interpersonally exploitative, i.e., takes advantage of others
     to achieve his or her own ends
(7) lacks empathy: is unwilling to recognize or identify with the
     feelings and needs of others
(8) is often envious of others or believes that others are envious
     of him or her
(9) shows arrogant, haughty behaviors or attitudes

---

lack parallelism among corresponding personality categories and
remain deficient in their syndromal scope.

Following the viewpoint of Zigler and Phillips (1961)—that is,
that "the system employed should be open and expanding. . . .
Systems of classification must be treated as tools for further discovery, not bases for polemic disputation" (p. 75)—two broad suggestions will be prescribed. If added to those already instituted in
DSM-IV, they should increase the clarity and utility of DSM-V.

As stated elsewhere (Millon 1986a, 1986b), the same clinical
domains should be encompassed in specifying each personality
disorder's diagnostic criteria and be routinely addressed to en-

sure that all personality disorders can be systematically compared and differentiated in all realms of clinical significance. Attention should consistently be directed to realms relating to the more hidden forms of pathology (i.e., self-image, object relationships, morphological organization, and regulatory mechanisms).

The following range of eight clinical domains and their diagnostic criteria for NPD should enable the clinician to go beyond the level of surface phenomenological description to one that provides some measure of insight into the domains' underlying dynamics and purposes.

Expressive Behavior: Haughty

It is not uncommon for narcissistic persons to act in an arrogant, supercilious, and disdainful manner. They also tend to flout conventional rules of shared social living. Viewing reciprocal social responsibilities as being inapplicable to themselves, they act in a manner that indicates a disregard for matters of personal integrity and an indifference to the rights of others. When not faced with humiliating or stressful situations, narcissistic individuals convey a calm and self-assured quality in their social behavior. Their seemingly untroubled and self-satisfied air is viewed, by some, as a sign of confident equanimity. Others respond to it much less favorably. To them, these behaviors reflect immodesty, presumptuousness, pretentiousness, and a haughty, snobbish, cocksure, and arrogant way of relating to people. Narcissistic individuals appear to lack humility and are overly self-centered and ungenerous. Their self-conceit is viewed by most as unwarranted; it smacks of being "uppity" and superior, without the requisite substance to justify it.

Interpersonal Conduct: Exploitive

As noted above, narcissistic persons feel entitled, expecting special favors without assuming reciprocal responsibilities. Not only are they unempathic, but they also take others for granted, are shameless in the process, and use others to enhance their own personal desires. Narcissistic individuals seek accomplishments of normal life with minimal effort and reciprocity on their part. In fact, some assume that others feel "honored" in having a relationship with them and that others receive as much pleasure in providing them with favors and attention as they experience in accepting these tributes.

It should not be surprising that the sheer presumptuousness and confidence exuded by the narcissistic person often elicit admiration and obedience from others. Furthermore, narcissistic individuals typically size up those around them and quickly train those who are so disposed to honor them; for example, they frequently select a dependent mate who will be obeisant, solicitous, and subservient, without expecting anything in return except strength and assurances of fidelity. It is central to the interpersonal style of narcissistic persons that good fortune will come to them without reciprocity. Because they feel entitled to get what they wish and have been successful in convincing others to provide them with comforts they do not deserve, narcissistic people have little reason to discontinue their habitual presumptuous and exploitive behaviors.

Cognitive Style: Expansive

For the most part, narcissistic persons have an undisciplined imagination and seem preoccupied with immature and self-glorifying fantasies of success, beauty, or romance. Although narcissistic individuals are nondelusional, they are minimally constrained by reality. They also take liberties with facts, embellishing them and even lying to redeem their illusions about their self-worth. Narcissistic people are cognitively expansive, and they place few limits on either their fantasies or their rationalizations. They are inclined to exaggerate their powers, to freely transform failures into successes, and to construct lengthy and intricate rationalizations that inflate their self-worth or justify what they believe is their right, quickly depreciating those who refuse to accept or enhance their self-image.

Self-Image: Admirable

Narcissistic persons feel justified in their claim for special status, and they have little conception that their behaviors may be objectionable, even irrational. They believe that they are special—if not unique—persons who deserve great admiration from others. Quite frequently, they act in a grandiose and self-assured manner, often without commensurate achievements. Although they expect to be seen as meritorious, most narcissistic individuals are viewed by others as egotistical, inconsiderate, and arrogant. Their self-image is that they are superior persons, "extra-special" individuals who are entitled to unusual rights and privileges. This view of their self-worth is fixed so firmly in their minds that they rarely question whether it is valid. Moreover, anyone who fails to respect them is viewed with contempt and scorn.

It is not difficult to see why the behaviors of narcissistic people are so gratifying to them. By treating themselves kindly; by imagining their own prowess, beauty, and intelligence; and by reveling in their "obvious" superiorities and talents, they gain, through self-reinforcement, the rewards that most people must struggle to achieve through genuine attainments. Narcissistic individuals do not need to depend on anyone else to provide gratification; they always have themselves to "keep them warm."

Object Representations: Contrived

The internalized representations of past experiences are deeply embedded and serve as a template for evaluating new life experiences. For the narcissistic person, these object representations are composed far more than usual of illusory and changing memories. Problematic past relationships are readily refashioned so as to appear entirely consonant with the narcissistic individual's high sense of self-worth. Unacceptable impulses and deprecatory evaluations are quickly transformed so as to enable this personality to maintain a preferred and contrived image of both the self and his or her past. Most narcissistic individuals were led by their parents to believe that they were invariably lovable and perfect, regardless of what they did and what they thought. As a consequence, the narcissistic person must transform the less palatable aspects of his or her past so that they are consistent with what he or she wishes they were, rather than what they were in fact.

Regulatory Mechanisms: Rationalization/Fantasy

What happens if narcissistic persons are not successful, if they face personal failures and social humiliations? What behaviors do they show, and what mechanisms do they use to salve their wounds? Although they are still confident and self-assured, narcissistic individuals deceive themselves with great facility, devising plausible reasons to justify self-centered and socially inconsiderate behaviors. With an air of arrogance, narcissistic people are excellent at rationalizing their difficulties, offering alibis to put themselves in the best possible light, despite evident shortcomings or failures on their part. If rationalizations fail, they will likely become dejected, feel shamed, and feel a sense of emptiness. In contrast to the antisocial personality, most narcissistic persons have not learned to be ruthless or competitively assertive and aggressive when frustrated. Neither have most acquired the seductive strategies of the histrionic person to solicit rewards and protections. Failing to achieve their aims and at a loss as to what they can do next, they are likely to revert to themselves to provide comfort and consolation and let the talent for imagination take over. These facile processes enable them to create a fanciful world in which they can redeem themselves and reassert their pride and status.

What the narcissistic individual is unable to work out through fantasy is simply repressed—put out of mind and kept from awareness. Because narcissistic persons are unaccustomed to self-control and objective reality testing, their powers of imagination have free rein to weave intricate resolutions to their difficulties. Flimsily substantiated rationalizations are offered, but with a diminished air of confidence and authority. However, narcissistic individuals may never have learned to be skillful at public deception; they usually said and did what they liked without a care for what others thought. Their poorly conceived rationalizations may, therefore, fail to bring relief and, more seriously, may evoke scrutiny and deprecating comments from others. At these times, narcissistic people may be pushed to the point of using projection as a defense, as well as to begin to construct what may become rather primitive delusions.

Morphologic Organization: Spurious

Narcissistic persons have few conflicts; their past has supplied them with high expectations and encouragement. As a result, they are inclined to trust others and to feel confident that matters will work out well for them. As noted earlier, this sanguine outlook on life is founded on an unusual set of parent-child relationships that only rarely is duplicated in later life.

The structural organization of the narcissistic individual's inner world for dealing with life tends to be quite flimsy and transparent to the discerning observer. From a surface view, one would assume that their personality organization is more substantial and dynamically orchestrated than it is in fact. Because of the misleading nature of their early experiences, that is, that narcissistic individuals really did not have to do much to make the world work for them, this personality has never developed the inner skills necessary to regulate impulses adequately, to channel needs skillfully, or to acquire a strategy in which conflicts are resolved, failures are overcome, and a genuine sense of competence is regained following problematic experiences.

The routine demands of everyday life are experienced as demeaning, because they intrude on the narcissistic person's cherished illusion of self as almost godlike. Narcissistic individuals easily muster alibis to avoid "pedestrian" tasks and display considerable talent in rationalizing their social inconsiderateness. However, because these persons reflect minimally on what others think, their defensive maneuvers are transparent, a poor camouflage to a discerning eye. This failure to bother dissembling more thoroughly also contributes to their being seen as cocksure and arrogant.

Unable to disentangle themselves from lies and inconsistencies and driven by their need to maintain their illusion of superiority, narcissistic persons may begin to turn against others, accusing those others of the deceptions, selfishness, and irrationalities that in fact belong to narcissistic persons. It is at these not very typical times that the fragility and pathology of the narcissistic individual become clearly evident. "Breakdowns" in the defensive structure of this personality, however, are not too common. More typically, the exploitive behaviors and intrapsychic maneuvers of narcissistic persons prove highly adaptive and provide them with the means of thwarting serious or prolonged periods of dejection or decompensation.

Mood/Temperament: Insouciant

Roused by the facile workings of their imagination, narcissistic people experience a pervasive sense of well-being in their everyday lives, a buoyancy of mood, and an optimism of outlook—except when their sense of superiority has been punctured. Normally, however, affect—although based often on their semigrandiose distortions of reality—is generally relaxed, if not cheerful and carefree. There is a general air of nonchalance, an imperturbability, a feigned tranquility. Should the balloon be burst, however, there is a rapid turn to either an edgy irritability and annoyance with others or repeated bouts of dejection that are characterized by feeling humiliated and empty. Shaken by these circumstances, one is likely to see briefly displayed a vacillation between rage, shame, and feelings of emptiness.

Specifying and Elaborating Narcissistic Subtypes

Although each personality prototype displays a cluster of cohesive characteristics, it is also clear that these personalities evidence variations (i.e., subtypes) in the manner in which their clinical features are manifested. The widely publicized categorical versus dimensional debate may, in part, be resolved by identifying the numerous subtypes that exist among each personality disorder. It should be noted that only a small subset of the basic dimensions that may be theoretically (Cloninger 1987) or empirically (Costa and Widiger 1993) proposed are found to combine in clinically relevant ways. However, those that interrelate "realistically" are what clinicians see in their practices, and it is these clinically observed subtypes that are described in the following sections.

It may be useful to organize narcissistic subtypes in terms of their likely levels of severity. Hence, they are listed from the least to the most severe. "Normal" narcissistic personalities begin and "fanatic" narcissistic personalities conclude the severity sequence.

Normal Narcissistic Personalities

With the exception of the unusually well-to-do and those close to regal stature, the narcissistic personality style may be considered to be a pattern of behavior unique to the late twentieth century. And even during this period, as writers such as Lasch (1978) have noted, it may be more or less distinctive to the upper and upper-middle social classes of the United States. As international conferences have demonstrated, narcissistic styles are not prevalent among clinical populations in most nations; the failure of the ICD-10 (World Health Organization 1990) to include the narcissistic disorder attests to the preceding. Nevertheless, in narcissistic societies such as ours, the center or fulcrum of life's activities has increasingly been focused on the achievement of personal gratification and self-enhancement.

The following characterization of the normal narcissistic person stresses the competitive and self-assured elements of this personality style (Millon et al. 1994, p. 32):

> An interpersonal boldness, stemming from a belief in themselves and their talents, characterizes these persons. Competitive, ambitious, and self-assured, they naturally assume positions of leadership, act in a decisive and unwavering

manner, and expect others to recognize their special qualities and cater to them. Beyond being self-confident, they are
audacious, clever, and persuasive, having sufficient charm
to win others over to their own causes and purposes. Problematic in this regard may be their lack of social reciprocity
and their sense of entitlement—their assumption that what
they wish for is their due. On the other hand, their ambitions
often succeed, and they typically prove to be effective
leaders.

Given our dominant cultural orientation toward self-
enhancement, it is often difficult to determine which self-focused
traits indicate a narcissistic disorder and which are merely adaptive styles that fit societal modes. Where to draw the line between
self-confidence and healthy self-esteem compared with an artifi-
cially inflated and empty sense of self-worth is not always an easy
task. In addition to the usual characteristics of the personality
type, the normal narcissistic person should show a modicum of
social concern and interpersonal empathy, a measurable interest
in the ideas and feelings of others, and at least a partial willingness
to acknowledge one's personal role in problematic interpersonal
relationships. When the disorder is present, we see a persistent insensitivity to others, a general social exploitiveness, and lack of
reciprocity in everyday relationships.

The Unprincipled Narcissistic Personality

During the last two or three decades, the unprincipled narcissistic
person has been seen more often in drug rehabilitation programs,
centers for youth offenders, and jails and prisons. Because these
individuals often are successful in society, keeping their activities
just within the boundaries of the law, they enter into clinical treatment rather infrequently.

The behavior of these narcissistic people is characterized by
an arrogant sense of self-worth, an indifference to the welfare of
others, and a fraudulent and intimidating social manner. They
have a desire to exploit others and an expectation of special recog-

nitions and considerations without assuming reciprocal responsibilities. A deficient social conscience is evident in the tendency to flout conventions, to engage in actions that raise questions of personal integrity, and to disregard the rights of others. Achievement deficits and social irresponsibilities are justified by expansive fantasies and frank prevarications. Descriptively, we may characterize this type of narcissistic person as devoid of a superego, that is, evidencing an unscrupulous, amoral, and deceptive approach to his or her relationships with others. More than merely disloyal and exploitive, these narcissistic people may be found among society's con men or women and charlatans, many of whom are vindictive and contemptuous of their victims. The features that are clearly seen in the unprincipled narcissistic person support the conclusion that these individuals have an admixture of both narcissistic and antisocial personality characteristics.

The unprincipled narcissistic person evidences a rash willingness to risk harm and is notably fearless in the face of threats and punitive action. Malicious tendencies are projected outward, precipitating frequent personal and family difficulties as well as occasional legal entanglements. Vengeful gratification is often obtained by humiliating and dominating others. These narcissistic individuals operate as if they have no principles other than exploiting others for their personal gain. Lacking a genuine sense of guilt and possessing little social conscience, they are opportunists and charlatans who enjoy the process of swindling others, outwitting them in a game they enjoy playing in which others are held in contempt because of the ease with which they can be seduced. Relationships survive only as long as the narcissistic person has something to gain. People are dropped with no thought to the anguish they may experience as a consequence of the narcissistic person's careless and irresponsible behaviors.

The unprincipled narcissistic person displays an indifference to truth that, if brought to his or her attention, is likely to elicit an attitude of nonchalant indifference. Narcissistic individuals are skillful in the ways of social influence, capable of feigning an air of justified innocence, and adept in deceiving others with charm and glibness. Lacking any deep feelings of loyalty, they may successfully scheme beneath a veneer of politeness and civility. Their principal orientation is that of outwitting others, getting power, and exploiting them "before they do it to you." They often carry a chip-on-the-shoulder attitude and have a readiness to attack those who are distrusted or who can be used as scapegoats. A number of these narcissistic individuals attempt to present an image of cool strength, acting tough, arrogant, and fearless. To prove their courage, narcissistic individuals may invite danger and punishment. But punishment only verifies an unconscious recognition of deserved punishment and reinforces exploitive and unprincipled behaviors.

The Amorous Narcissistic Personality

The distinctive feature of the amorous narcissistic personality type is an erotic and seductive orientation, a building up of one's self-worth by engaging members of both the opposite and the same sex in the game of sexual temptation. These persons have an indifferent conscience and an aloofness to truth and social responsibility that, if brought to their attention, elicits an attitude of nonchalant innocence. Although these narcissistic individuals are totally self-oriented, they are facile in the ways of social seduction, often feign an air of dignity and confidence, and are rather skilled in deceiving others with their clever glibness. They are skillful in enticing, bewitching, and tantalizing the needy and the naive. Although indulging their hedonistic desires, as well as pursuing numerous beguiling objects at the same time, they are strongly disinclined to become involved in a genuine intimacy. Rather than investing their efforts in one appealing person, they seek to acquire a coterie of amorous objects, invariably lying and swindling as they weave from one pathological relationship to another. The qualities outlined support the observation that narcissistic personalities have characteristics that also can be found among histrionic personalities.

   Although a reasonably good capacity for sexual athletics sustains the vanity of many individuals, narcissistic or not, the need to repeatedly demonstrate one's sexual prowess is a preeminent obsession among amorous subtypes. Among these personalities are those whose endless pursuit of sexual conquests is fulfilled as effectively and frequently as their bewitching style "promises." Others, however, talk well and place their lures and baits extremely well—that is, until they reach the bedroom door. Maneuvering and seduction are done with great aplomb, but performance falls short. For the most part, the sexual exploits of the amorous narcissistic individual are brief, lasting from one afternoon to only a few weeks.

Some amorous narcissistic people are fearful of extended sexual relationships, afraid that their pretensions and ambitions will be exposed and found wanting. Their sexual banter and seductive pursuits are merely empty maneuvers to overcome deeper feelings of inadequacy. Although they seem to desire the affections of a warm and intimate relationship, they typically feel restless and unsatisfied when they find it. Having won others over, they seem to need to continue their pursuit. It is the act of exhibitionistically being seductive, and hence gaining in narcissistic stature, that compels and must be pursued again and again.

Not infrequently, amorous narcissistic individuals leave behind them a trail of outrageous acts such as swindling, sexual excesses, pathological lying, and fraud. This disregard for truth and the talent for exploitation and deception are often neither hostile nor malicious in intent. These characteristics appear to derive from an attitude of narcissistic omnipotence and self-assurance, a feeling that the implicit rules of human relationships do not apply to them and that they are above the responsibilities of shared living. As with the basic narcissistic pattern, individuals of this subtype go out of their way to entice and inveigle the unwary among the opposite sex, to remain coolly indifferent to the welfare of those whom they bewitch and whom they have used to enhance and indulge their hedonistic whims and erotic desires.

Caring little to shoulder genuine social responsibilities and unwilling to change their seductive ways, amorous narcissistic individuals refuse to "buckle down" in a serious relationship and expend effort to prove their worth. Never having learned to control their fantasies or be concerned with matters of social integrity, they will maintain their bewitching ways, if need be, by deception, fraud, and lying and by charming others through craft and wit. Rather than apply their talents toward the goal of tangible achievements or genuine relationships, they will devote their energies to construct intricate lies, to cleverly exploit others, and to slyly contrive ways to extract from others what they believe is their due. Criticism and punishment are likely to prove of no avail and are quickly dismissed as the product of jealous inferiors.

The Compensatory Narcissistic Personality

The compensatory narcissistic person deviates in a fundamental way from other narcissistic subtypes, as well as from the prototypical narcissistic person. Overtly narcissistic behaviors originate from an underlying sense of insecurity and weakness rather than from genuine feelings of self-confidence and high self-esteem. Beneath surface pseudoconfidence, this narcissistic person is driven by forces similar to those experienced by people who overtly display characteristics more akin to the negativistic and avoidant personalities.

The compensatory narcissistic personality style represents patients who are labeled "narcissistic" by those in the psychoanalytical community because they have suffered "wounds" in early life. Many have been exposed to experiences akin to the negativistic, masochistic, avoidant, and antisocial types. In essence, these personalities seek to make up or compensate for early life deprivations. They are similar to the antisocial personality, but the compensatory narcissistic person seeks to fill the sense of emptiness by creating an illusion of superiority and by building up an image of high self-worth rather than by usurping the power and control that others possess or by accumulating material possessions.

The compensatory narcissistic person needs others to fulfill his or her strivings for prestige. The motive of these individuals is to enhance their self-esteem, to obtain and to store up within themselves all forms of recognition that will "glorify" their public persona. Much to the annoyance of others, these narcissistic people "act drunk" as they recount their successes and record for others to acknowledge all forms of even minor public recognition. In effect, these narcissistic people actively worship themselves; they are their own gods. As this inflated and overvalued sense of self rises evermore highly, the narcissistic individual looks down on others and acquires a deprecatory attitude in which the achievements of others are ridiculed and degraded.

Life is a search for pseudostatus, an empty series of aspirations that serves no purpose other than self-enhancement. This search for these vacuous status goals may begin to run wild, resting from its very foundation on an unsure sense of self-value that has but little contact with tangible achievements. Instead of living their own lives, they pursue the leading role and achievements in a false and imaginary theater not related much to reality. Should these pursuits totally lose their grounding in reality, becoming increasingly an imaginary world peopled with self and others as in a dream, compensatory narcissistic persons begin to deceive themselves in a manner not unlike that shown by paranoid persons. However, whereas compensatory narcissistic persons strive for prestige in a world composed of real people, paranoid persons act out their aspirations in solitude. One comes to the stage in front of others, be it in the form of exaggeration and boasting; the other stands alone in an inner world, a "pseudocommunity," as Cameron (1963) phrased it, where imagination has substantially replaced reality.

Because of the insecure foundations on which their narcissistic displays are grounded, compensatory narcissistic persons are "hypervigilant," to use a term employed by Gabbard (1994) (see also Gabbard, Chapter 6, this volume). They are exquisitely sensitive to how others react to them, watching and listening carefully for any critical judgment and feeling slighted by every sign of disapproval. Although not delusional, as are their paranoid counterparts, these narcissistic persons are prone to feel shamed and humiliated, especially hyperanxious and vulnerable to the judgments of others. They "know" that they are frauds at some level, pretenders who seek to convey impressions of being of higher standing than they know is truly the case. Despite this awareness, they do not act shy and hesitant, but submerge and cover up their deep sense of inadequacy and deficiency by pseudoarrogance and superficial grandiosity.

The Elitist Narcissistic Personality

Reich (1933/1949) captured the essential qualities of what here is termed the *elitist narcissistic person* when he described the "phallic-narcissist" character as a self-assured, arrogant, and energetic person "often impressive in his bearing . . . and . . . ill-suited to subordinate positions among the rank and file" (p. 217). As with the compensatory narcissistic person, the elitist narcissistic person is more taken with an inflated self-image than with his or her actual self. Both narcissistic types create a facade that bears minimal resemblance to the actual person. However, the compensatory narcissistic person knows at some level that he or she is in fact a fraud, whereas the elitist narcissistic person is deeply convinced of his or her superior self-image, albeit one that is grounded on few realistic achievements. To elitist narcissistic persons, it is the appearance of things that is perceived as objective reality; an inflated self-image is their intrinsic substance. Only when these illusory elements to self-worth are seriously undermined will the individual be able to recognize, perhaps even to acknowledge, his or her deeper shortcomings.

As a consequence of their sublime self-confidence, elitist narcissistic persons feel quite secure in their apparent superiority. This is achieved in part by their ability to capture the attentions of others and to make them take note of how extraordinary the narcissistic individuals believe themselves to be. Most everything these individuals do is done to persuade others of their specialness rather than to put their efforts into acquiring genuine qualifications and attainments. They feel privileged and empowered by virtue of whatever class status and pseudoachievements they may have attained. Most are upwardly mobile, seeking to cultivate their sense of specialness and personal advantage by associating with those who may possess genuine achievements and recognition. Many elitist narcissistic individuals will create comparisons between themselves and others, turning personal relationships into public competitions and contests. Unrivaled in the pursuit of becoming "number one," the grounds for this goal are not determined by a genuine accomplishment, but by the degree to which they can convince others of its reality. Idolizing public recognition, narcissistic personalities of this type get caught in this game of one-upmanship, a game in which they strive vigorously to win, at least comparatively. Status and self-promotion and the wish to be celebrated and famous are all that matters to narcissistic elitist individuals. In whatever sphere of activity matters to them, they invest their efforts to advertise themselves and to brag about achievements, substantive or fraudulent.

By making excessive claims about themselves, these narcissistic persons expose a great divide between their actual selves and their self-presentations. In contrast to many narcissistic persons who recognize this disparity, elitist narcissistic persons are convinced and absolute in their belief in themselves. Rather than backing off, withdrawing, or feeling shame when slighted or responded to with indifference, elitist narcissistic persons speed up their efforts all the more, acting increasingly and somewhat erratically to exhibit deeds and awards worthy of high esteem. They may present grandiose illusions about their powers and future status. They may puff up their limited accomplishments and may seek competitively to outdo those who have achieved in reality.

By the persistence and social intrusiveness of their behaviors, narcissistic elitist individuals may begin to alienate themselves from others and the admiration they seek. Insulating themselves from signs of painful indifference and psychic injury, they may try to distance or screen out negativistic and judgmental responses. Some may become overtly hostile, acquiring characteristics of paranoid persons, quickly losing the remaining elements of their former charm and cleverness, and becoming increasingly contemptuous of people they feel are treating them so shabbily. Still believing in themselves as special persons, these elitist narcissistic individuals see little need to listen or follow the dictates of anyone else. They may begin to react with outright anger and irritability, convinced that they need no one. As these self-protective beliefs and actions gain in their defensive and negative tone, the elitist narcissistic person comes to be seen as an undesirable and embarrassing person, a touchy and inflated character whom others wish to shun.

The Fanatic Narcissistic Personality

The fanatic narcissistic personality is basically a structurally defective paranoid personality with prototypal narcissistic features that are deeply interwoven. Persons with this narcissistic/paranoid mix seek to retain their admirable self-image; act in a haughty and pretentious manner; are naively self-confident, ungenerous, exploitive, expansive, and presumptuous; and display an air of supercilious contempt and benign arrogance toward others.

Fanatic narcissistic persons are likely to have run hard against reality, and their illusion of omnipotence has periodically been shattered, toppling them from their grandiose and vaulted image of eminence. Accustomed to being viewed as the center of things, valued and admired at least in their own eyes, they cannot tolerate the lessened significance circumstances have now assigned to them. Their narcissism has been profoundly wounded. Fanatic narcissistic individuals must not only counter the indifference, the humiliation, and the fright of insignificance generated by reality but also reestablish their lost pride through extravagant claims and fantasies. Upset by assaults on self-esteem, they reconstruct their image of themselves and ascend once more to the status from which they fell. To do this, they endow themselves by illusory self-reinforcement with superior powers and exalted competencies. They dismiss events that conflict with their newly acquired and self-designated importance; flimsy talents and accomplishments are embellished, creating a new self-image that supplants objective reality.

Because these narcissistic/paranoid individuals may have lost their internal discipline and self-control, they allow their reparative fantasies free rein to embroider a fabric of high sheen and appeal, caring little for the fact that their claims are unwarranted. These grandiose assertions become fixed and adamant, too important to the individual's need to regain importance, and become an identity of significance and esteem. Fanatic narcissistic persons go to great lengths to convince themselves and others of the validity of their claims, insisting against obvious contradictions and the ridicule of others that they deserve and are entitled to special acknowledgment and privileges.

Unable to sustain this image before others and rebuffed and unable to gain the recognition they crave, fanatic narcissistic persons turn increasingly toward themselves for salvation. Taking liberties with objective facts and wandering further from social reality and shared meanings, they concoct an evermore elaborate fantasy world of grandiose delusions. Not uncommonly, they may begin to assume the role and attributes of some idolized person, someone whose repute cannot be questioned by others. As this identification takes root, fanatic narcissistic individuals assert their new identity: a noble and inspired leader, a saint or a god, a powerful and rich political figure, or an awesome and talented genius. Grandiose missions (e.g., solving insurmountable geographic, social, and scientific problems) are proposed and may be worked out in minute detail, often corresponding to objective needs, and are formulated with sufficient logic to draw at least momentary attention and recognition from others.

Conclusion

An advanced level of clinical sophistication has been reached in the understanding of the narcissistic personality; perhaps it should be called "the group of narcissistic personalities." In this chapter, the author has attempted to provide a basis for recognizing that there are several varieties of the narcissistic character, each of which reflects the different insightful deductions of theorists or of intuitively astute clinicians. What seems clear today is that the profession is ready to go beyond the early assumption that there is but "one kind" of narcissistic person, a singular personality whose descriptive features lend themselves to diverse etiological analysis. In its stead, the author believes that investigators are ready to recognize that many diverse narcissistic types exist, each of which stems from different pathogenic and developmental roots.

References

American Psychiatric Association: Diagnostic and Statistical Manual of
Mental Disorders, 3rd Edition. Washington, DC, American Psychiatric Association, 1980

American Psychiatric Association: Diagnostic and Statistical Manual of
Mental Disorders, 3rd Edition, Revised. Washington, DC, American
Psychiatric Association, 1987

American Psychiatric Association: Diagnostic and Statistical Manual of
Mental Disorders, 4th Edition. Washington, DC, American Psychiatric Association, 1994

Cameron N: Personality Development and Psychopathology. Boston,
MA, Houghton Mifflin, 1963

Cloninger CR: A systematic method for clinical description and classification of personality variants. Arch Gen Psychiatry 44:573–588, 1987

Costa P, Widiger T (eds): Personality Disorders and the Five-Factor
Model of Personality. Washington, DC, American Psychological Association, 1993

Freud S: The interpretations of dreams (1900), in The Standard Edition
of the Complete Psychological Works of Sigmund Freud, Vol 4–5.
Translated and edited by Strachey J. London, Hogarth Press, 1953,
pp 1–627

Freud S: On narcissism: an introduction (1914), in The Standard Edition
of the Complete Psychological Works of Sigmund Freud, Vol 14.
Translated and edited by Strachey J. London, Hogarth Press, 1957,
pp 67–102

Freud S: Libidinal types (1931), in Collected Papers, Vol 5. Edited by
Strachey J. New York, Basic Books, 1959, pp 242–251

Gabbard GO: Psychodynamic Psychiatry in Clinical Practice: The
DSM-IV Edition. Washington, DC, American Psychiatric Press, 1994

Gunderson JG, Ronningstam E, Smith L: Narcissistic personality disorder: a review of data on DSM-III-R descriptions. Journal of Personality Disorders 5:167–177, 1991

Horney K: New Ways in Psychoanalysis. New York, WW Norton, 1939

Kernberg OF: Borderline personality organization. J Am Psychoanal Assoc 15:641–685, 1967

Kernberg OF: Factors in the treatment of narcissistic personality disorder. J Am Psychoanal Assoc 18:51–85, 1970

Kohut H: Forms and transformations of narcissism. J Am Psychoanal Assoc 14:243–272, 1966

Kohut H: The Analysis of Self. New York, International Universities Press, 1971

Lasch C: The Culture of Narcissism. New York, WW Norton, 1978

Millon T: Modern Psychopathology: A Biosocial Approach to Maladaptive Learning and Functioning. Philadelphia, PA, WB Saunders, 1969

Millon T: Disorders of Personality: DSM-III Axis II. New York, Wiley Interscience, 1981

Millon T: A theoretical derivation of pathological personalities, in Contemporary Directions in Psychopathology. Edited by Millon T, Klerman G. New York, Guilford, 1986a, pp 639–670

Millon T: Personality prototypes and their diagnostic criteria, in Contemporary Directions in Psychopathology. Edited by Millon T, Klerman G. New York, Guilford, 1986b, pp 671–712

Millon T, Millon CN, Davis RD, et al: Millon Index of Personality Styles. San Antonio, TX, Psychological Corporation, 1994

Reich W: Character Analysis (1933). Translated by Carfagno VR. New York, Simon & Schuster, 1949

Ronningstam E, Gunderson J: Identifying criteria for narcissistic personality disorder. Am J Psychiatry 147:918–922, 1990

World Health Organization: International Classification of Diseases and Related Health Problems, 10th Edition. Geneva, Switzerland, World Health Organization, 1990

Zigler E, Phillips L: Psychiatric diagnoses and symptomatology. Journal of Abnormal and Social Psychology 63:69–75, 1961

Chapter 5

Developmental Aspects of Normal and Pathological Narcissism

Paulina F. Kernberg, M.D.

Our knowledge about the development of narcissism and narcissistic pathology has been influenced by theoretical contributions on narcissism and self and object relations as well as by studies of early childhood attachment and adaptation. In particular, the studies of parent-child interactions have highlighted a number of phenomena that have contributed to the understanding of early characterological formations and behavioral expressions of narcissistic disturbances. They have also shed light on the relation between normal and pathological narcissism in childhood and its pathological counterparts in later developmental stages. Before discussing the early development of narcissistic personality pathology, it is helpful to begin with a general distinction.

Normal and Pathological Narcissism

Normal narcissism refers to the positive investment in a normally integrated self (O. F. Kernberg 1975). It can be defined as the adaptive normal way of regulating self-esteem. Sources for normal self-esteem regulation involve the positive feelings from the body self, including health and appearance. Positive self-esteem is also regulated by positive experiences originating in early experiences of secure attachment as well as by positive resolution of the separation-individuation process leading to the capacity to gratify both autonomous and dependent needs in an adaptive way. An additional source is an integrated superego or conscience that monitors behavior and provides internal approval to oneself. A sense of competency, mastery, and safety provides crucial input to one's self-esteem. The gratification derived from sublimating activities—that is, activities or endeavors that transcend the individual's interest—contributes to self-esteem regulation and to sexual and sensual gratifications, especially if linked with deep relationships with others. All of these contributing factors operate efficiently if there is a realistic and integrated perception of oneself with one's actual positive and negative aspects in harmony with the wishful concept of oneself representing the ideal self (Reich 1960). A capacity to live up to one's ideals is a continuous source of self-esteem. Concomitantly, a realistic perception of others in their positive and negative qualities and in their separateness and autonomy exerts a positive influence on self-esteem as well. Mahler et al. (1975) called these achievements self and object constancy, respectively.

Pathological narcissism, in contrast, fails in practically all of these aspects. Thus, problems in the experience of the body self and a sense of vulnerability and deflation overshadow the experience of the whole self. The various sources of self-esteem outlined above are deficient, and an internal reward system, the superego, remains unintegrated. Therefore, the individual is under the influence of primitive, harsh superego precursors with unrealistic expectations against which the grandiose self is erected.

Regular sources of self-esteem that stem from interaction with others—first with parents and later with playmates and friends—are obstructed by the grandiose self. The grandiose self, an internal structure that by virtue of magical thinking allows the individual to believe he or she is already what he or she wishes to be, has to extrude negative aspects by projecting them onto others. There is no emotional growth with ideals to pursue, no acknowledgment of work necessary toward the realization of actual achievements, and no ideal objects such as parents or teachers to emulate. It is as if all the energies of the individual were spent in a show, a self-conscious performance (Reich 1960). A pseudolife lacking spontaneity is aimed at counteracting the painful sense of having been unacknowledged or confronted with traumatic experiences that exposed the person prematurely or abruptly with his or her own vulnerability.

Figures 5–1 and 5–2 show graphic expressions of the structural implications of normal and pathological narcissism. In normal narcissism (Figure 5–1), the representational world of the subject assumes the acceptance of positive and negative aspects of the actual self as perceived by oneself and others. The presence of ideals and thoughts about what the individual would like to attain for himself or herself is also necessary. A tension occurs between what one is and what one wishes to become in terms of self ideals or ideal objects represented by other persons. Aggression is integrated into the self representation, together with a realistic discriminative perception of other people in their positive and negative aspects. The subject has the capacity to internalize values from others, identify with others, and appreciate their separateness and autonomy. There is a normal superego that results from the integration of several factors: internal primitive superego precursors, the ideal self that has resulted from giving up one's infantile omnipotence, and the ideal object internalization of values and ideals from other people.

In contrast, in individuals with pathological self-esteem regulation and pathological narcissism (Figure 5–2), the positive perception of actual self is fused with an ideal self and an ideal object.

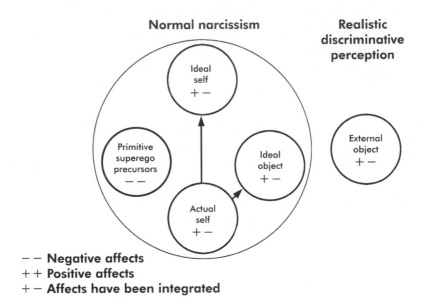

Figure 5–1.   Normal self-esteem regulation.
Source.   Reprinted from Kernberg PF: "Narcissistic Personality
Disorder in Childhood." *Psychiatric Clinics of North America*
12(3):671–694, 1989. Copyright 1989, W. B. Saunders Company. Used
with permission.

This is projected into idealized external objects that are used and
acknowledged only to confirm the individual's own grandiose
self. A splitting occurs with all other aspects of the devalued vulnerable self that are projected, resulting in a devaluation of other
objects of the external world. Primitive superego precursors (early
forms of oral and anal aggression) are also projected. Hence,
the world of others consists of devalued persecuting others and
fleeting, unstable idealized others who remain as long as they
fit into the grandiose scenario. The grandiose self structure,
consisting of the fusion of actual self, ideal object, and ideal self,
explains the sense of entitlement and self-centeredness of these
individuals.

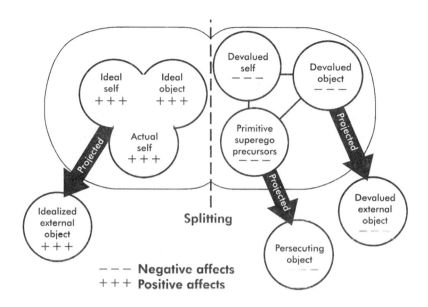

Figure 5–2. Pathological narcissism and pathological self-esteem regulation.
Source. Reprinted from Kernberg PF: "Narcissistic Personality Disorder in Childhood." *Psychiatric Clinics of North America* 12(3):671–694, 1989. Copyright 1989, W. B. Saunders Company. Used with permission.

Development of Normal and Pathological Narcissism in Children

Before a discussion of early development of narcissistic personality disorder (NPD) pathology, it is important to describe normal infantile narcissism and contrast it with child and adult pathological narcissism. In normal infantile narcissism, the child has age-appropriate fantasies, demands, and attachments. "Small children, for instance, normally have grandiose fantasies, and make angry efforts to control mother and to keep themselves at the center of attention. Fantasies of great power, wealth and beauty are common in the pre-oedipal period, but unlike in pathological narcissism, the normal child does not need to be universally admired as the sole owner of everything that is enviable and valuable" (P. F. Kernberg 1989, p. 674). In addition, in normal infantile narcissism, there is a capacity to acknowledge both dependency needs and autonomy. There are narcissistic fantasies of omnipotence, but realistic limitations tone down these narcissistic fantasies. A fluctuation between these two aspects of the self occurs that prevents the child's infantile omnipotence from interfering with further emotional development.

In contrast, in children who have pathological narcissism with the same characteristics as adults, the presence of an inability to truly depend on others and a need to maintain the illusion of a grandiosity at any cost interfere with normal emotional development. The normal narcissistic child can have grandiose fantasies but is able to accept dependence and show genuine attachment and interest in others. In contrast, pathologically narcissistic children have an inability to show such genuine attachment to others. Instead, their attachment is for immediate need gratification, leading to exploitiveness. There is no acknowledgment of gratitude and appreciation as is the case in most children. An additional important contrast is the child's pathological grandiosity, which fuels a sense of uniqueness or specialness and an attitude of entitlement. This makes the child prone to antisocial behaviors, such as lying and stealing. A sense of fulfillment, even with achievement, is not lasting, because the purpose of high performance is mainly for seeking admiration, not for internal rewards. Therefore, grandiosity is a maladaptive way of protecting self-esteem, because the grandiosity requires immature or primitive defensive maneuvers (e.g., devaluation, projective identification, denial, omnipotent control, withdrawal, and aloofness) in order to restructure an external reality to preserve this grandiosity.

Clinical Manifestations of
Pathological Narcissism in Children

All the narcissistic features found in adult patients can be observed in children (Egan and Kernberg 1984). In the case of "super Matt" (fictitious name), grandiosity and omnipotent control, serious interpersonal problems, self-centeredness, and lack of empathy had for years been characteristic of this 8-year-old boy. What follows is a description of the basic features of developmental characteristics in narcissistic personality disturbance.

Academic Performance

A consequence of a sense of grandiosity and entitlement is that in spite of superior intelligence, these children have a checkered performance at school. They can have excellent grades, have low grades, or fail altogether, depending on their wish to put forth effort or not. These children can be arrogant and haughty and devalue those around them, including their teachers. Their need to be on center stage all the time becomes a deterrent to the establishment of friendships.

Friendships

Pathological narcissism in childhood is characterized by deficient social skills and poor peer interactions in terms of level of developmental appropriateness. This is because of the inability of narcissistic children to empathize with others, their need to avoid any difference between themselves and others in order to allay their sense of vulnerability and envy, and their need to control and devalue their peers.

In adolescence, the narcissistic individual may appear charismatic. The grandiose self exerts particular attraction on peers as it resonates with the aspirations of the other members of a group.

Thus, for a while at least, the narcissistic adolescent appears to have arrived already at the ideal of perfection, beauty, and power. He or she gives an illusion of a reality that the group members seek. In turn, the group confirms the narcissistic adolescent's grandiosity so that he or she can protect himself or herself from any sense of hurt. Two noteworthy aspects of social interactions occur. One is the choice of a more popular, pretty, or handsome partner who is shown off. The other is the choice of a friend who is the least popular, ugly, or physically handicapped. In this case, the narcissistic adolescent can feel admired by the ugly partner who becomes a psychological slave and is masochistically grateful to have been chosen as an object of attention even if the quality of the attention is derision.

Gaze Aversion

Gaze aversion, which is frequently seen in narcissistic children, is the counterpart of the sense of distancing and aloofness aimed at protecting the self-inflated grandiosity (i.e., the self-inflated sense of self). It is also a way to avoid the traumatic experience of depersonification by a parent for whom the child exists only in terms of fulfilling the parent's narcissism. Last but not least, it may serve the purpose of denying dependence on the external world and other people.

Separation Anxiety

Narcissistic children frequently have separation anxiety. Paradoxically, the separation anxiety is not readily noticeable but disguised under the claim for constant attention and admiration and under the grandiosity that makes the child appear self-sufficient. However, although the child does not seem to acknowledge the presence of a parent once in the same room, the child needs to have a parent in peripheral vision. In turn, the parents report their constant apprehension on how the child will fare if he or she were to be separated from them. How does a "know-it-all," as a narcissistic child called himself, reveal such a frailty when confronted with separation? According to Rinsley (1989), the understanding of the separation-individuation process provides a clue. The parent supports the child's individuation—that is, the refinement and distinctness of his or her activities—inasmuch as the individuation rewards the parent's own needs. However, the parent does not support separation. The child exists in the service of the parent's self-esteem and does not exist as an autonomous being. Paradoxically, the power given to the child to regulate the parent's self-esteem fuels the child's grandiosity even further. In turn, the child projects his or her own unacceptable emotions and qualities onto the parent, and this permits preservation of the illusion of perfection and invulnerability. If the parent is not there, this illusion is destroyed.

Play Pathology

Narcissistic children characteristically show an inhibition of play. This appears as a boredom expressed in devaluation of the toys. Once a child begins to play, however, the fantasy play is characterized by raw aggression: dolls are dismembered or maimed, and macabre scenes of sadistic mass destruction, poisonings, and stabbings appear. The play initially lacks pleasure but later can be endowed with sadistic enjoyment. The enactment occurs of the primitive aggression that has remained "unmetabolized" and unintegrated by the grandiose self and that is now projected into the play scene.

Sibling Relations

An exaggerated sibling rivalry, which has been termed *sibling intolerance,* can be seen in narcissistic children. This can at times escalate to outright abuse. The aloofness and sadistic behavior expressed toward the siblings serve as a protection to the child's sense of narcissistic injury for not having been the only one in the family. A deep and protracted resentment continues throughout the childhood and adolescent years and beyond.

Case Vignettes

A 3½-year-old boy was seen for uncontrollable temper tantrums. Whenever his wishes were not immediately complied with, he exhibited aggressive behavior such as biting other children without remorse. He displayed sadistic behavior toward his 1-year-old sister: pulling her hair, calling her "stupid" and "dumb," pushing her down on the bed, and pushing her down the stairs.

This boy could not tolerate the awareness of his dependency or smallness. He would not have direct gaze contact with adults. If the therapist was delayed in solving a problem or fixing or finding a toy, she would be dismissed summarily by the little boy as he threatened not to return. He alienated any potential playmates with his bossiness and unresponsiveness. The other side of his split self revealed moments in which the boy would say sadly that he did not like himself and was going to kill himself; for example, "I will shoot myself with a bow and arrow." These patterns of interaction recognized at this early age prevailed for a couple of years before they could be changed in the therapeutic work with the child and family (P. F. Kernberg 1989).

A 5½-year-old boy was brought in by his parents, who complained that he had a difficult temperament. As they described it, he shied away from all physical activities such as swimming, gymnastics, and tennis. He was unwilling even to try. Similarly, he had been afraid to become toilet trained for fear that he could not do it. Indeed, he easily became frustrated with any undertaking, given the possibility of failure. For example, he was afraid to cut with scissors and would not try anything if he was not good at it, simply stating that he did not want to do it. This suggests difficulties and reluctance in following instructions from a teacher. He rarely played by himself, but he was allegedly very social and popular. Lately, however, his teacher complained about his aggressive behavior with peers when they did not carry out his will. He told another boy, for example, that he would stick nails in his eyes if he did not play with him in the way he was supposed to.

In this case, again, the mother seemed to look to her child for direction and to use him as a guide for her own behavior. The child's ongoing sense of omnipotence, as well as the deprivation he experienced, can be understood in terms of the social referencing described by Emde (1983)—that is, that the child needs to have a safe base on which to guide his behavior.

A 15-year-old boy lacked a spontaneity in his interaction with others, and his demeanor was aimed at impressing others. He was self-conscious and self-centered, as if his main purpose was to impress other people (Reich 1960). He did not have friends because of self-centeredness, and he devalued his mother to the extent of complaining to others that he was literally deprived of food at home. Her success in business made him envious, and he regarded her boyfriend as a rival whom he devalued. He felt entitled to take and steal money from his mother's purse. He felt her dissatisfaction with him was due to his resemblance to his father, her former husband. On the other hand, his mother considered him a "little boss" in her business, because she hired him to work in her firm during summers.

A 14-year-old boy had no tolerance to accept the relationship between his mother and father. Indeed, he felt that their relationship as a couple was a threat to his monopoly of his mother. His mother's undivided attention (to which he felt entitled) was an important source for his grandiosity. He experienced separation anxiety, feeling ashamed that "at my age, I cannot stand being alone." He resented deeply having his older brothers visit the parental home, because they intruded into his domain. When he was 18 months old, his mother had had two unexpected and prolonged hospitaliza-

tions for a major affective disorder. These were never discussed with the son.

Etiology

Several theories can be helpful in understanding the process of
the development of the grandiose self in narcissistic pathology.
One consideration is whether constitutional and developmental
aspects play a role. Although it is important to consider constitutional and temperamental individual differences such as hypersensitivity, frustration, tolerance, and regulation affects, it seems
that developmental experiences—more than genetically determined characteristics—are the crucial factors in the development
of dramatic personality disorder cluster (Torgersen 1994). For normal personality development, individual differences that are due
to genetics or constitutional factors are important. However, in
the development of personality disorders, environmental aspects
seem to account for the biggest share of the variance. Indeed, it is
to these aspects that some of the current theoretical understanding will be addressed, that is, theories of narcissism (Grunberger
1989), self-development (Stern 1985), separation-individuation
theory (Mahler et al. 1975), attachment theories (Patrick et al.
1994), and object relations theories (O. F. Kernberg 1975).

Grunberger (1989) proposed that the narcissistic experience
corresponds to an experience that all humans had in utero: receiving constant supplies and protection and being in a sense of om-
niscience. It is this intrauterine life that is longed for by the infant
after birth. Any circumstance that abruptly destroys this sense of
safety, security, and fulfillment might affect normal self-
development.

Stern (1985) proposed the epigenetic unfolding during the
first year of life of the emergent self, the core self, the intersubjective self, and the verbal self. This process of unfolding will depend
on the necessary parental skills that are deemed crucial for the fa-
cilitation of an integrated, cohesive continuous self with inten-

tionality and boundaries. The core self is equally dependent on the development of intersubjectivity, that is, the beginning awareness on the part of the baby that there is another with him or her who shares his or her same feelings and intentions and with whom he or she can be in contact. The verbal self or reflective self brings out the issue of language and self-observation that becomes crucial in higher levels of function. In Stern's propositions, all these stages of self coexist or become activated at different points during the life of the individual. Many aspects of the early parent-child interaction that can go awry are specifically relevant for the distortions of the sense of core self in NPD, especially because the sense of cohesion and boundary, including the experience of one's body, may be brittle (thus the hypochondriacal concerns of these patients). At the level of intersubjective self, there is no acknowledgment of the other's intentions, and reliance on one's own subjectivity infiltrates the whole world, resulting in a sense of isolation and deprivation. Problems with the verbal self are related to 1) the inability to observe oneself and to have introspection and 2) the use of words not as a means of communication but as fuel for gratification of hearing oneself talk.

There are very few prospective studies on narcissistic development in terms of attachment and separation-individuation theory. However, observations by Broussard (1983) of a boy who was "at risk for narcissistic disturbance" illustrate the insecure avoidant attachment of a child who had developed narcissistic defenses in order to deal with his mother's emotional unavailability and self-centeredness. This boy existed for his mother only inasmuch as he was her object of erotic interaction. Other needs of the child did not seem to be acknowledged. He showed gaze aversion to his mother. In adolescence, this boy had the characteristics of entitlement, aloofness, and separation anxiety, and he had not been able to enter into a true mature relationship with his parents. On the contrary, he hoped to have his mother work for him as a secretary in his chosen profession while he continued to exclude and devalue his father.

In terms of separation-individuation, the narcissistic personality may have a variety of points of fixation related to arrests in the early practicing phase, that is, when self-absorption and the illusion of self-sufficiency are such that the external object represents a minute aspect in the child's world. In terms of reactions to the rapprochement crisis, the parent does not respond enough to the toddler when confronted with his or her needs of dependence and vulnerability to support the illusion of control and to accept the child's needs of dependence.

From another vantage point, there is a pathological equilibrium between the child and his or her parents. The child can function and be supported only as long as he or she molds to the parents' expectations. Although the child's individuation is facilitated, no sense of separateness is acceptable. The child needs the parents and the parents need the child in an interlocked mutual narcissistic way, and the parents' narcissistic needs override the child's normal narcissistic needs. Consequently, the child develops a sense of unreality and pseudoexperience typical of the subjective experience of unrealistic individuals (Rinsley 1989).

Figures 5–1 and 5–2 show an application of object relations theory. The representational world of the child (Sandler and Rosenblatt 1962) includes a distinct integrated self-representation that leads to a sense of integrated identity and an internalized world of other people (i.e., object representations with integrated positive and negative aspects of others). There is, apparently, a close correspondence with the internal working models postulated by attachment theories.

According to all authors, a smooth fulfillment of basic needs as mediated by parenting functions throughout the formative years is required. Lichtenberg (1988) postulated that narcissistic needs are fulfilled by the gratification of five structure-building systems: 1) the need to fulfill physiological requirements, 2) the need for attachment and affiliation, 3) the need for assertion and exploration, 4) the need to react aversively through antagonism or withdrawal, and 5) the need for sexual and sensual pleasure. In descriptions of styles of parenting in the formation of NPDs, or in the direct observation of family interactions, one or more of these needs remain unfulfilled.

Stern (1985) addressed how different senses of self serve as organizers of the experience of others parallel to the organization of the experience of oneself. Self and other representations develop concomitantly. Not surprisingly, in the case of the grandiose self, no actual experience of others and minimal intersubjectivity causes a serious interference with a normal development of self in its continuity, cohesiveness, integration, and experience (Bach 1985).

Children at Risk for Narcissistic Personality Disorder and Their Parents

Elsewhere, P. F. Kernberg (1989) has described a variety of constellations in the family interactions. The children of narcissistic parents are at risk during their first year of life because of the parents' lack of empathy, which causes an incapability to fulfill the needs of the baby. The parents' own omnipotence leads the child to a cycle of lack of limitation, overindulgence, and inconsistency that maintains and contributes to the preservation of the grandiose self. In the mind of the parents, the child has a role, a given attribution, that contributes to his or her depersonification (Rinsley 1989). This can be seen in cases of divorced mothers with infantile personalities, who treat the child as the spouse or the sibling or as an endlessly infantile or dependent baby, an echo of mother's own sense of self.

A second group at risk for NPD is adopted children. The adopted child was in the contradictory dilemma of being chosen because he or she was "the most beautiful baby," as well as because he or she was "discarded" by the biological parents. The uncertainties of the period before the adoption are formalized and contribute additionally to the problem because they interfere with the sense of secure attachment.

A third group at risk for NPD is abused children. Here, the need to fuse with an idealized parental image to protect oneself from the external sadistic image of parent is important.

A fourth group at risk for NPD is overindulged or wealthy children. There is a fostering of prolongation of infantile narcissism, but if this is combined with narcissistic personality problems in the parents, the child can easily develop this personality style.

A fifth group at risk for NPD is children of divorced parents. These children attempt to fulfill their own infantile narcissism and combine it with the omnipotence derived from 1) fulfilling the wish to replace the other parent and 2) gratifying the custodial parent with a blurring of the normal generational roles. This leads to abnormal narcissistic development. Another variation of this occurs with the parent who aims at eradicating all traces of the child's identification with the former partner. This signifies a deep narcissistic injury of rejection for what the child cannot help but be—that is, to have acquired identification with both parents. The child then develops a grandiose self to protect himself or herself from this negative and damaging perception by the custodial parent.

Looking closer at parental contributions, the degree of adaptability of the parent to the changing needs of the child may interfere with the normal development of the self. Shapiro et al. (1979) clearly outlined that the family system serves as a repository of the internal representational world of each of its individuals. Interactions between family members can contribute and serve to maintain powerful reinforcements of the grandiose self. For example, a child is experienced as the "one who spoils our lives, our marriage." He or she is treated as a monster fitting with the perception of the omnipotent control that the child has. Parental unavailability, or parental perplexity in terms of appropriate models of interactions that are consistent and genuine toward their children, is all too frequently operative in these families. Thus, parents may submit to the child's grandiosity or abrogate their authority by withdrawing from and psychologically abandoning their child. A dramatic illustration of this point is given in Stanley Kubrick's film *A Clockwork Orange*. Here the parents of the main character replaced their son with another young man who was more responsive and appreciative.

Narcissistic rages do not contribute to an enhancement of the interaction between parents and child, and the short-term gratification of omnipotent control leaves room for only long-term dysphoria and mutual detachment.

Discussion

In summary, normal infantile narcissism is an adaptive form of self-esteem regulation that facilitates personality development. This is contrasted with pathological narcissism, which, because of the formulation of the grandiose self, reflects a pathological form of regulation of self-esteem that precludes normal development in the areas of interpersonal relations and social and moral functioning. Thus, the need to protect the grandiose self accounts for these patients' incapacity to depend on others, their envy, their ongoing need for admiration, and their exploitiveness of others. The grandiose self is a defensive formation against a variety of developmental stressors.

Although childhood NPD can be diagnosed with the same descriptive criteria of the corresponding adult personality disorder, specific descriptive features can be added, such as gaze aversion, play, separation anxiety disorder, a zigzag profile of academic performance, and severe forms of sibling rivalry. Various theories contribute to the understanding of NPD, such as constitutional aspects of hypersensitivity or low frustration tolerance; developmental aspects, such as trauma, self development, separation individuation, and attachment; and object relations theory aspects. All of these refer to the child's internal representation of his or her interactions with the environment.

References

Bach S: Narcissistic States and the Therapeutic Process. Northvale, NJ, Jason Aronson, 1985

Broussard E: Justin's Reflection (videotape). Pittsburgh, PA, University of Pittsburgh Graduate School of Public Health, Department of Health Services Administration, Infant Family Resources Program, 1983

Egan J, Kernberg PF: Pathological narcissism in childhood. J Am Psychoanal Assoc 32(1):39–62, 1984

Emde R: The representational self and its affective core. Psychoanal Study Child 38:165–192, 1983

Grunberger B: New Essays on Narcissism. London, Free Association Books, 1989, pp 15–28, 183–190

Kernberg OF: Normal and pathological narcissism, in Borderline Conditions and Pathological Narcissism. Northvale, NJ, Jason Aronson, 1975, pp 315–343

Kernberg PF: Narcissistic personality disorder in childhood. Psychiatr Clin North Am 12(3):671–694, 1989

Lichtenberg JD: A theory of motivational functional systems as psychic structures. J Am Psychoanal Assoc 36 (suppl):57–72, 1988

Mahler M, Pine F, Bergman A: The Psychological Birth of the Infant: Symbiosis and Individuation. New York, Basic Books, 1975

Patrick M, Hobson PR, Castle D, et al: Personality disorder and the mental representation of early social experience. Development and Psychopathology 6:375–388, 1994

Reich A: Pathological forms of self-esteem regulation. Psychoanal Study Child 15:205–232, 1960

Rinsley DB: Notes on the developmental pathogenesis of narcissistic personality disorder. Psychiatr Clin North Am 12(3):695–708, 1989

Sandler J, Rosenblatt B: The concept of the representational world. Psychoanal Study Child 17:128–145, 1962

Shapiro R, Zimmer J, Shapiro E: Concurrent family treatment of narcissistic personality disorders in adolescents, in Advances in Family Psychiatry. Edited by Howles J. New York, International Universities Press, 1979, pp 129–146

Stern DN: The Interpersonal World of the Infant. New York, Basic Books, 1985

Torgersen S: Genetics in borderline conditions. Acta Psychiatr Scand Suppl 379:19–25, 1994

Section II

Treatment
Implications

Introduction

Elsa F. Ronningstam, Ph.D.

The second part of this book focuses on the treatment of narcissistic personality disorder (NPD). The radical reformulations of transference and the understanding of countertransference phenomena that emanated from the works of Kernberg and Kohut paved the way for substantial advances in the psychoanalysis and dynamic psychotherapy with narcissistic patients. The new meanings of transference and countertransference and their consequences for the conceptualization of narcissistic pathology in a continuum ranging from oblivious (or overt) to hypervigilant (or covert) narcissistic patients are discussed by Glen O. Gabbard, M.D., in Chapter 6.

Two major psychoanalytical strategies to treat NPD have been developed. In Chapter 7, Paul H. Ornstein, M.D., outlines one that is based on Kohut's model of self psychology, which considers empathic and mirroring interventions to be most helpful. Another strategy, derived from the object relations theory that emphasizes an exploratory and actively interpretive approach to the pathological grandiose self, is presented by Lucy LaFarge, M.D., in Chapter 8. Each author presents the theoretical foundation and the strategy for each form of psychoanalysis of narcissistic disorders, and through illustrative case vignettes they identify the significance of the different phases in the analytical process. Whereas the self psychological approach highlights the vulnerability of the self-structure and the development of the selfobject transference in psychoanalysis as an effort to maintain the patient's self-cohesion, the object relations school focuses on the systematic interpretation of the negative transference and the pathological grandiose self. This is understood as a consequence of pathological constellations of internal representations and underlying early developmental feelings of rage and envy.

Increased interest in the treatment of severe personality disorders and the identification of narcissistic patients within other treatment modalities have inspired the development of new conceptualizations and treatment strategies for NPD. Based on defining narcissistic pathology in terms of object choice, Ralph H. Beaumont, M.D., in Chapter 9, explains how the intensive psychiatric milieu and its interventions can lead to corrective experiences that diminish narcissistic pathology. The specific problem of affect management when treating narcissistic patients in group therapy is discussed and illustrated by Bennett E. Roth, Ph.D., in Chapter 10.

Extensive advances in the realm of cognitive therapy paved the way for developing a model for treating narcissistic patients—that is, schema-focused therapy. The conceptual background and strategic techniques for changing the cognitive and behavioral patterns of pathological narcissism are presented by Jeffrey Young, Ph.D., and Catherine Flanagan, Ph.D., in Chapter 11. In the dyadic interaction of a couple relation, manifestations of narcissistic disorders are especially magnified. Marion F. Solomon, Ph.D., in Chapter 12, outlines a strategy for couples therapy built on the identification of overt symptomatic conflicts and the understanding of their relation to underlying narcissistic disturbances.

Chapter 6

Transference and Countertransference in the Treatment of Narcissistic Patients

Glen O. Gabbard, M.D.

Based on an economic model of the mind that emphasized the importance of mental energies and drive cathexis, Freud (1914/ 1963) concluded that patients with narcissistic neuroses (a term used broadly to include psychoses) were not amenable to psychoanalytical treatment because they were not psychologically capable of developing the classic features of a transference neurosis. Viewed retrospectively, Freud's conclusions can be regarded as an understandable countertransference reaction to the peculiar forms of relatedness seen in narcissistic character pathology and their dramatic differences from the more classic transferences of neurotic patients. Indeed, many narcissistic patients appear unengaged with the analyst or therapist for long periods, and it has been only relatively recently that clinicians have discerned that the apparent absence of the transference *is* the transference with such patients (Brenner 1982). From a historical perspective, the contributions of Kohut and Kernberg were instrumental in elaborating the precise nature of the narcissistic transferences.

Transference From Kohut's and
Kernberg's Perspectives—A Comparison

In his radical rethinking of Freud's notion of narcissism, Kohut suggested that patients with narcissistic personality disorder (NPD) did, in fact, develop transferences in the analytical setting (for a more detailed discussion, see Ornstein, Chapter 7, this volume). However, he stressed that the classical interpretive approaches might hinder the development of such transferences. He emphasized that the analyst needs to strive for an empathic immersion in the patient's inner world. This empathic bridge to the patient leads to the orderly unfolding of specific narcissistic transferences.

Kohut (1971) believed that NPD was a psychoanalytical diagnosis corroborated by the development of one of two related transferences reflecting the patient's effort to maintain self-cohesion. The first he called the *mirror transference,* which refers to the patient's efforts to capture the gleam of admiration or validation in the mother's eye, displaced in the present to the analyst. The other narcissistic transference he postulated was the *idealizing transference,* which involves an attribution of exaggerated, near-perfect qualities to the analyst.

Part of the theoretical revision in Kohut's psychology revolved around the privileging of the self's needs for self-esteem and self-cohesion over the drives of sexuality and aggression. The mirror and idealizing transferences were regarded as reflecting two poles of the bipolar self (Kohut 1977), respectively, the grandiose self and the idealized parent imago. Self psychology is a deficit-based model, so the transferences are conceptualized as efforts to complete the self by treating the analyst or therapist as an extension of the self.

In Kohut's posthumously published and final book (1984), he suggested that a third transference must be considered alongside the other two. He called this one the *twinship transference* and described it as a situation in which the patient regards the analyst as being like a twin. He also came to view all three transferences under the umbrella of *selfobject transferences,* reflecting the notion that the analyst in these transferences performs functions for the self of the patient.

Following Kohut's death, his colleague and collaborator Wolf (1988) identified two other selfobject transferences. The *adversarial selfobject transference* is one in which the patient experiences the analyst as a benignly opposing individual who nevertheless maintains some degree of supportiveness. The analyst is also perceived as encouraging a measure of autonomy for the patient's self by accepting the patient's need to be adversarial. The second selfobject transference observed by Wolf is related to the mirror transference but, because of its relationship to an intrinsic motivation to achieve mastery, is sufficiently different to deserve status as a distinct transference. Known as the *efficacy selfobject transference,* it involves a perception by the patient that the analyst is allowing the patient to effectively produce necessary selfobject behavior in the analyst.

Kernberg's (1970, 1974) understanding of transferences in narcissistic patients is based on a mixed model of ego psychology and object relations theory rather than on self psychology (see Kernberg, Chapter 2, this volume). Although Kernberg acknowledged transferences that have the phenomenological features of mirroring and idealization, he understood these as defensive structures behind which envy, rage, and contempt are concealed. When the pathological grandiose self is projected in the analytical setting, the analyst becomes idealized, and the patient manifests an idealizing transference. When it is reintrojected, it operates along the lines of Kohut's mirror transference.

The disengagement or distance so often seen in patients with NPD is viewed by Kernberg as related to an underlying process of devaluation and denigration of the analyst. At the core of the patient's transference is intense envy of the analyst's ability to be helpful and offer insights of which the patient is unaware. To defend against this envy, the patient devalues and spoils the analyst's interpretive work and refuses to become dependent on the analyst's help in any way.

Systematic interpretation of the negative transference is the cornerstone of Kernberg's approach to narcissistic patients (see LaFarge, Chapter 8, this volume). Whereas Kohut would argue that idealization should be accepted at face value rather than interpreted, Kernberg emphasized the importance of interpreting the underlying envy and contempt to the patient. However, Kernberg (1974) also stressed the need to acknowledge positive affects in the transference so that patients do not view the analyst's interpretations as condemning them as "all bad." Kernberg, then, would also interpret and clarify the positive aspects of the narcissistic defenses.

In Kohut's formulation, the selfobject transferences eventually give way to more classical transferences related to oedipal concerns dealing with competitiveness, rivalry, and retaliation. In Kernberg's understanding of narcissism, however, he noted a different development that follows from the systematic interpretation of pathological narcissistic defenses. Frequently, the interpretive work results in paranoid transferences as well as feelings of guilt and severe depression. Narcissistic patients begin to recognize the destructive effect they have had on others, and they may either project their sadism onto the analyst and become paranoid or acknowledge that sadism and become depressed. Ultimately, when these feelings have been worked through, Kernberg shares Kohut's view that the treatment takes on the form of a classical transference neurosis (Kernberg 1970).

The Narcissistic Continuum

The variations in the phenomenology and psychoanalytical understanding of narcissistic transferences also reflect the diversity in usage of NPD as a diagnostic term. Patients are categorized as "narcissistic" who have significantly different interpersonal characteristics. These differences can be heuristically conceptualized as residing on a continuum of narcissistic vulnerability, ranging from oblivious individuals impervious to slights on the one end to hypervigilant patients on the other end who are continually experiencing devastating narcissistic injuries (Gabbard 1989, 1994a; Gabbard and Twemlow 1994) (see also Cooper, Chapter 3, this volume).

Patients with *oblivious narcissistic personality disorders* appear to be narcissistically invulnerable because the reactions of others are screened out of their conscious awareness. Much like DSM-IV descriptors, and more similar to Kernberg's patients than Kohut's, these individuals are boastful, arrogant, and self-absorbed and use others as an audience for their "performance." Their character armor is impenetrable and serves to protect them from feeling inferior, vulnerable, or hurt. Rosenfeld (1987) described such narcissistic persons as "thick-skinned," whereas Broucek (1982) characterized patients of this type as egotistical. The transference emerging in analysis or therapy with such patients reflects this character style. They may spend the hour in boastful self-aggrandizement in an effort to impress the therapist with their superior status while not really listening to the therapist's comments.

> Mr. O typically came to his psychotherapy hours several minutes late and always greeted the therapist by saying, "How's it going?" Before the therapist could ever answer, Mr. O launched into a lengthy discourse about events in his external life. He looked over the therapist's head much of the time so that the therapist felt like something of a nonentity. Mr. O's voice was louder than necessary for small offices. This raised volume conveyed the impression that he might be talking to a large audience, or anyone in earshot, rather than engaged in a one-to-one relationship. He seemed relatively unconcerned with the therapist's response to his comments, and when the therapist attempted to make an observation, Mr. O usually said, "Please let me

finish." When he did stop long enough to listen to his therapist's words, Mr. O seemed impatient, as though he were
waiting for his therapist to finish speaking so he could pick
up where he left off. At one point, the therapist confronted
him with this tendency to pay little attention to what other
people said. Mr. O responded by saying, "I'd much rather
hear myself say something three times than someone else
say something for the first time."

At the opposite end of the continuum, patients with *hypervigilant narcissistic personality disorder* are exquisitely sensitive to the
reactions of others and therefore eschew the limelight because the
potential for narcissistic injury is magnified in such settings. Their
grandiosity is quieter and takes the form of a conviction that they
are entitled to be treated in a highly special way by others. When
others fail to note their exceptional status and fail to treat them
with the kind of exclusivity and specialness they desire, these patients feel terribly slighted. They approach the analyst or therapist
in a clinical setting with the expectation that at any moment they
will be humiliated or rejected. Rosenfeld (1987) called these patients "thin-skinned" narcissistic personalities, and their proneness to fragmentation is reminiscent of some patients described
by Kohut. Broucek (1982) referred to this subtype of narcissistic
patient as dissociative, but in his formulation these patients project their grandiosity onto others, whereas the hypervigilant patients described here retain their grandiosity within, and others
are seen as persecutors.

> Ms. H sat through each psychotherapy session with her eyes
> glued to her therapist. She carefully scrutinized his facial ex-
> pressions and his bodily movements to see if she could dis-
> cern his reaction to what she was saying. The therapist often
> felt exhausted at the end of the session because he felt that
> he was required to listen with intense concentration for the
> full 50 minutes so that he did not miss a detail. He once re-
> ferred to Ms. H as being one of four sisters, and she reacted
> indignantly, "How can you say that? I've told you that there
> are five of us, not four! Aren't you listening to anything

I say?" On another occasion, he looked out the window at lightning during a thunderstorm, and the patient was deeply hurt. She said to him that it was obvious to her that the storm was much more important than anything she was saying. With tears in her eyes, she asked, "Would you rather I leave so you can enjoy the lightning show without being bothered by me?"

Although this distinction is not reflected in DSM-IV criteria (American Psychiatric Association 1994), which fail to capture the hypervigilant subtype, empirical studies (Hibbard 1992; Wink 1991) support the validity of these two subtypes, which are often labeled as *overt* and *covert*. Although certain patients cluster around one end of the continuum or the other, many others reside along the midpoint of the continuum, with some characteristics of both subtypes. Kernberg (1974), for example, described narcissistic patients who are characterized by arrogance and aggressiveness alternating with shyness and sensitivity to slights.

These two dimensions are connected with shame propensity. The hypervigilant type is more overtly prone to feelings of shame when the desired response is not forthcoming from others. Oblivious types are constantly defending against shame by seeking acclaim and admiration. As Kinston (1983) noted, striving for this acclaim may be a way of denying a negative valuation of the self associated with shame.

Countertransference

The concept of countertransference has evolved considerably since Freud (1910/1957) first used it to refer to the analyst's transference to the patient. In the Freudian perspective, often referred to as the "narrow" view, countertransference is an obstacle or impediment to the clinical work. The patient is unconsciously viewed as someone from the analyst's or therapist's past, thus impeding the analyst's ability to hear the patient with an open mind.

The more contemporary conceptualization of countertransference, often referred to as the "broad" view (Gabbard 1994a), derives from the work of Heiman (1950) and Winnicott (1949). These authors regarded countertransference as an important communication from the patient that tells the analyst about meaningful aspects of the patient's inner world. The broad form of countertransference has less to do with the analyst's own conflicts and past internal object relationships and more to do with what the patient induces in others, including the analyst. For example, Winnicott (1949) used the term *objective hate* to describe a particular form of countertransference that virtually everyone felt in relationship to certain patients who evoke hate in others.

This shift in conceptualization has led to an outpouring of interest in the notion of projective identification (Boyer 1987, 1990; Gabbard 1994a; Goldstein 1991; Grotstein 1981; Kernberg 1975, 1987; Ogden 1979, 1982; Porder 1987; Sandler 1987; Scharff 1992; Searles 1986; Tansey and Burke 1989). Although the original concept as used by Klein (1946/1975) involved an intrapsychic fantasy rather than an interpersonal coercion, the modern use has focused to a great extent on changes in the recipient of the patient's projective identification. Racker (1968) divided these changes in the therapist into concordant and complementary countertransferences. Concordant countertransferences are those involving an empathic link between therapist and patient (i.e., the therapist identifies with the patient's subjective affective state or self-representations). Complementary countertransferences involve identifications with an internal object representation of the patient that has been projectively disavowed and attributed to the therapist. Racker viewed this complementary reaction as an instance in which the analyst's own conflicts were activated by the patient's projections.

Ogden (1979, 1982) developed a useful definition of projective identification that captures this objective or broad form of countertransference in an object relations framework. In his formulation, patients unconsciously disavow and project an internal self- or object representation onto the analyst and then through interpersonal pressure coerce the analyst to identify with what has been projected. In this manner, projective identification can be seen as a primitive forerunner of empathy that helps the analyst to understand what is going on inside the patient. In the Ogden formulation, the analyst contains and modifies what has been projected so that ultimately a new form of object relatedness is reinternalized by the patient.

Projective identification, a concept originating in the thinking of Klein (1946/1975), Bion (1984), and members of the British school of object relations (Winnicott 1949), has begun to influence classical American analysts, who now speak of transference-countertransference enactments in a manner highly reminiscent of projective identification. Enactments may be viewed as re-creations of internal object relationships initiated by either analyst or patient in which both play a role (Chused 1991; Jacobs 1986; McLaughlin 1991; Roughton 1993). As Abend (1989) noted, it is now accepted in all quarters that the analyst's countertransference reaction provides important information about the patient.

In most cases, the countertransference experience of the analyst or therapist will be determined partly by the clinician's past relationships and conflicts and partly by what is evoked in the analyst by the patient's behavior. In this regard, countertransference is generally a joint creation (Gabbard 1993, 1994b, 1994c; Gabbard and Wilkinson 1994). Indeed, one of the therapist's principal tasks is to monitor constantly the extent to which the countertransference is narrow versus broad.

With this conceptualization of countertransference as joint creation, we can approach the therapist's countertransference with NPDs as reflecting transference-countertransference enactments that provide useful information about the patient as well as about the therapist's own conflicts. As Groopman and Cooper (1995) pointed out, because the narcissistic patient tends to treat the analyst as a self-extension, the patient is likely to evoke certain states in the analyst that reflect the patient's own internal struggles. Obviously, by dint of personal characteristics, some therapists will be more likely to respond to particular aspects of the patient's internal world than others.

Boredom

One countertransference issue that confronts most therapists at some point in the treatment of narcissistic patients is the feelings of being bored and of being distanced by the patient, what Kernberg (1970) referred to as a "satellite existence." Most mental health professionals have a need to be needed (Gabbard 1994a), and patients with NPD deprive the therapist of fulfilling that need. Many narcissistic patients, especially those near the oblivious end of the continuum, drone on as though anyone in earshot is welcome to hear. They may only rarely make eye contact and speak "at" the therapist instead of "to" the therapist. A common countertransference feeling is to have a sense that one is being used as a sounding board and that one's separate existence as an individual with an independent center of autonomy is not being acknowledged.

To some extent, this transference-countertransference development reflects the narcissistic patient's inability to depend on others for help and defense against the intense underlying envy. Projective identification may be involved in that the therapist may be distanced and excluded by the patient in the same way that the patient was once distanced or excluded as a child (Adler 1986; Finnell 1985; Gabbard 1994a). In other words, via projective identification, a self-representation within the patient is projected onto the therapist, and the therapist is pressured into identifying with what has been projected. The narcissistic patient may actively master passively experienced childhood trauma in this manner.

If this role reversal is relatively clear from the clinical material, the therapist can make constructive us ? of the countertransference by interpreting the process to the patient. For example, a comment such as the following might be useful: "I wonder if to some extent you're attempting to keep me at a distance in the

same way that you were kept at a distance by your parents."
Therapists must be aware of their own narcissistic issues when
making a comment like this, however, because the countertransference boredom may grow out of the therapist's own need to be
important to the patient.

Many individuals enter careers in psychotherapy or psychoanalysis because of a wish to be idealized, needed, and loved (Finnell 1985). Treating narcissistic patients may result in feelings of
quite an opposite valence. The therapist may feel ineffectual, incompetent, invisible, and impotent. As the therapist's narcissistic
injury and narcissistic rage mount, such feelings may be dealt
with projectively by seeing narcissistic issues as residing only in
the patient and not in the therapist.

Even when the analyst is idealized by the patient, feelings of
guilt and shame at the enjoyment of basking in the idealization
may interfere with the analyst's ability to tolerate such transferences. Kohut (1984) noted that many analysts find it acutely uncomfortable to be idealized for prolonged periods and may
prematurely interpret the idealization to deal with their anxiety.
On the other hand, analysts who have difficulties handling their
own aggression as well as the patient's may fend off all hostility
and aggression in the dyad by fostering idealization and encouraging it. One therapist allowed a narcissistic patient to call him at
any time of day or night so that the patient would have the experience of a "good father" who was available around the clock. In supervision, it was pointed out to this therapist that such behavior
made it virtually impossible for the patient to express aggression
to the therapist while making it more likely that the patient's envy
would mount.

Control

A particular transference-countertransference enactment is likely
to unfold with the hypervigilant narcissistic patient (Gabbard
1994a). As the patient monitors the therapist's every movement
for signs of rejection, lack of interest, or distraction of attention,

the therapist begins to feel controlled. Therapists may worry that they cannot clear their throat, glance at the clock, shift their weight in the chair, or take their eyes off the patient without devastating the patient's self-esteem. In the same manner, therapists may feel that the hypervigilant patient is trying to control how they think and what they say. Symington (1990) noted that projective identification can be construed as an attempt by the patient to control the therapist's freedom of thought. Therapists may feel confined to a very narrow range of thoughts and words. They may feel bullied or badgered by the patient into speaking only certain thoughts and leaving out others. Lewin and Schulz (1992) referred to this form of transference-countertransference enactment in borderline patients as a situation in which the patient is like a ventriloquist and the therapist is the ventriloquist's dummy.

When therapists feel controlled in this manner, they can begin to empathize with the deep-seated terror in narcissistic patients about the potential for others to hurt them. If they do not control every move, every word, and every thought of significant others, they are convinced they will be abandoned or rejected. Therapists can make constructive use of their countertransference by pointing out the patient's anxiety about allowing the therapist to have freedom of thought and action. This fear can often be traced back to difficulties with self-esteem and an inability to believe that anyone would want to be in a relationship with the patient unless forced to do so.

Contempt

Another highly disconcerting countertransference phenomenon regularly encountered in the treatment of narcissistic patients involves being the target of the patient's contempt. Certain patients may need to remind the therapist repeatedly that nothing the therapist says is new or useful. They may have to assert that any information provided by the therapist was already known to the patient so as not to feel ashamed, humiliated, and envious. They

may also treat the therapist with contempt because of the therapist's insistence on a professional role vis-à-vis the patient, as in
the following example:

> *Mr. C:*   I need to get treatment from somebody more expe-
> rienced than you. I don't think you can handle me.
>
> *Therapist:*   Sometimes I get the feeling that you're talking
> down to me, and I wonder if you do that to other
> people.
>
> *Mr. C:*   Of course I talk down to you because you act like
> an asshole. You maintain a professional aloofness in-
> stead of acknowledging that you're a real person like
> me who has problems of his own. You haven't helped
> me a bit in the entire time I've seen you.
>
> *Therapist:*   Would you like to see someone else?
>
> *Mr. C:*   There you go again! Instead of trying to figure out
> what you need to do to change so you can be more
> helpful, you just want to get rid of me. None of your
> insights has helped me. I already knew all of them.
> I need you to be a real person who will interact with
> me spontaneously and tell me what to do and what
> not to do.
>
> *Therapist:*   I doubt it if you'd appreciate it if I started tell-
> ing you what to do.
>
> *Mr. C:*   At least then we could have an argument instead
> of you just listening to what I say and commenting
> from your perspective on what you think is going on
> inside of me. I don't know why I come here. I guess
> because I have nothing better to do. I doubt if there
> are any shrinks who are much better than you. You
> all learn from the same textbooks.

Such interactions tend to erode the therapist's confidence
and feelings of effectiveness. Countertransference tendencies
to retaliate sarcastically to the patient or to refer the patient
elsewhere (as the therapist in the above example offered to do)
may emerge as countertransference enactments that repeat interactions from the patient's past that have been internalized in
childhood. In other words, the patient may bring about rejec-

tion and abandonment by coercing such responses from the therapist through contemptuous and devaluing remarks. Being a durable object that can contain the aggression may be the most therapeutic path for the therapist in such moments.

Admiration

Certain aspects of psychotherapeutic technique can also be appropriated by the therapist's unconscious in the service of countertransference enactments. For example, some of the more charming narcissistic patients may elicit a mirroring response in the therapist that coincides with the fantasized internal object who is admiring, affirming, and unconditionally loving. The therapist consciously may be attempting to empathize with the patient's need for mirroring but unconsciously may be colluding with a transference-countertransference enactment that excludes all aggression and other negative affects from the dyad. If the patient is sufficiently entertaining and engaging, the therapist may be "conned" into abdicating a therapeutic role with the patient and simply enjoying "the show."

Similarly, adhering to Kohut's dictum that one should accept the idealization rather than interpret it can lead to a mutual admiration society between therapist and patient that excludes the rest of the world—a world in which the patient's interactions with others are problematic. A frequent development in the treatment of narcissistic patients is that while the transference idealization flourishes, the rest of the patient's life deteriorates. For example, the therapist may be empathizing with the patient's experience as a victim while the patient is abusing those around him or her and making others into victims. One difficulty created by providing unconditional acceptance of the patient is that narcissistic patients may develop the idea that they are entitled to such acceptance and are simply not getting it from other people. They may experience the fact that the therapist provides such acceptance as a sign that they do not need to change their internal world but simply find "Mr. (or Ms.) Right" in the environment who will fulfill all their needs.

Integrative Technical Strategies

The techniques and psychodynamic formulations espoused by Kohut and Kernberg are significantly different from one another in their approach to the patient's transferences. Most psychoanalysts and psychoanalytical therapists, however, probably do not work with a technical strategy that rigidly adheres to one model or the other (Gabbard 1994a; Mitchell 1988). There is increasing support in the psychoanalytical literature for the flexible use of multiple models in practice (Jacobson 1994; Pine 1988, 1990; Pulver 1993; Sandler 1990). The greater problem clinicians face is trying to force patients to accommodate to their favorite theory or technical strategy when the patient is clearly a square peg being forced into a round hole.

No current controlled studies suggest clear superiority of one technical strategy over another. Glassman (1988) attempted to test the models of Kernberg and Kohut and concluded that the Kernberg model has some advantage. However, generalization from his data must be limited because of the modest design of the study. In the absence of hard data, many clinicians believe that both models have considerable value and that elements of both can be used to benefit the same patient (Bromberg 1983; Gabbard 1994a; Groopman and Cooper 1995; Mitchell 1988). There appears to be some convergence within the literature that beginning with a self psychological approach involving empathic immersion in the patient's point of view may serve to forge a therapeutic alliance. In addition to the therapist's empathy with the patient's experience, another aspect of this integrated technical strategy is to help the patient to develop the ability to reflect and think about the process of the treatment in a useful way (Bromberg 1983). Transference interpretations are used sparingly until the alliance is strengthened. The little interpretive work that is done in the early stages primarily deals with extratransference themes.

As the therapy or analysis progresses, a point of diminishing returns is reached at which accepting the patient's grandiosity or idealization in an empathic framework is limiting. As Mitchell (1988) stressed, such empathy is in tune only with the most superficial level of the patient's defenses, whereas the underlying issues are kept out of the dyad's awareness. Mitchell argued that both Kernberg and Kohut are empathic but that Kernberg empathizes with a different dimension of the patient, namely, the greedy, selfish, and desperately envious aspect.

At the point at which one can shift from a self psychological approach to more of a Kernberg model, the therapist must begin suggesting that the patient is contributing to the difficulties encountered with others. Tentative formulations of this may be useful as follows: "If most interpersonal conflicts are a two-way street, which they probably are, can you think of anything that you might be contributing to the difficulties with your friend that we could work on here?" Posed as a question, such ideas may be more readily entertained by the patient. Ultimately, in the context of a solidified therapeutic alliance, the narcissistic patient can more openly deal with the transference themes of devaluation, envy, and feelings of inadequacy.

This integrated formulation may apply to many patients with NPD, but others require more specific tailoring of the technical strategy. For example, certain patients who are prone to shame and humiliation may hear any transference interpretation of unconscious conflict as an attack or criticism. The only way they can remain engaged in a psychoanalytical or psychotherapeutic process is to feel that they are empathized with and understood. On the other hand, certain highly contemptuous and aggressive patients may experience empathy as insincere and dishonest and virtually coerce the therapist into a more confrontational and interpretive approach.

In summary, the emerging transference and countertransference paradigms in psychoanalysis and psychoanalytical psychotherapy with narcissistic patients serve as guideposts that help the clinician chart the therapeutic strategy with each patient. Careful monitoring of transference-countertransference developments reveals important information about the patient's internal object relationships and his or her current difficulties in interpersonal relationships. Fundamentally, however, a good deal of trial and error is necessary to find a "good fit" between the therapist's interventions and the patient's capacity to use such interventions. We now know from empirical research from the Menninger Foundation Psychotherapy Research Project (Wallerstein 1986) that both supportive and expressive approaches may lead to durable and long-lasting structural change in disturbed patients. Analysts and therapists must be wary of bias toward highly interpretive approaches that are designed to meet the therapist's needs more than the patient's needs.

Especially with narcissistic patients, interpretations themselves may be countertransference enactments, in which the insight is used as a cudgel to make the patient stop whatever he or she is doing. When such efforts appear to fall on deaf ears, therapists may escalate their interpretive attacks in an all-out assault on the patient's character armor. The patient will simply circle the wagons against the assault and become more defensive and less amenable to expressive work. Therapists working with narcissistic patients must always remember that an insecure and poorly developed self is at the core of the psychopathology. A climate of affirmation and acceptance must be created before the introduction of meaningful interpretive work.

References

Abend SM: Countertransference and technique. Psychoanal Q 48:374–395, 1989

Adler G: Psychotherapy of the narcissistic personality disorder patient: two contrasting approaches. Am J Psychiatry 143:430–436, 1986

American Psychiatric Association: Diagnostic and Statistical Manual of Mental Disorders, 4th Edition. Washington, DC, American Psychiatric Association, 1994

Bion WR: Second Thoughts: Selected Papers on Psychoanalysis. New York, Jason Aronson, 1984

Boyer LB: Regression and countertransference in the treatment of a borderline patient, in The Borderline Patient: Emerging Concepts in Diagnosis, Psychodynamics, and Treatment, Vol 2. Edited by Grotstein JS, Solomon FM, Lang JA. Hillsdale, NJ, Analytic Press, 1987, pp 41–47

Boyer LB: Countertransference and technique, in Master Clinicians on Treating the Regressed Patient. Edited by Boyer LB, Giovacchini PL. Northvale, NJ, Jason Aronson, 1990, pp 303–324

Brenner C: The Mind in Conflict. New York, International Universities Press, 1982

Bromberg PM: The mirror and the mask: on narcissism and psychoanalytic growth. Contemporary Psychoanalysis 19:359–387, 1983

Broucek FJ: Shame and its relationship to early narcissistic development. Int J Psychoanal 63:369–377, 1982

Chused JF: The evocative power of enactments. J Am Psychoanal Assoc 39:615–639, 1991

Finnell JS: Narcissistic problems in analysts. Int J Psychoanal 66:433–445, 1985

Freud S: The future prospects for psycho-analytic therapy (1910), in The Standard Edition of the Complete Psychological Works of Sigmund Freud, Vol 11. Translated and edited by Strachey J. London, Hogarth Press, 1957, pp 139–151

Freud S: On narcissism: an introduction (1914), in The Standard Edition of the Complete Psychological Works of Sigmund Freud, Vol 7. Translated and edited by Strachey J. London, Hogarth Press, 1963, pp 67–102

Gabbard GO: Two subtypes of narcissistic personality disorder. Bull Menninger Clin 53:527–532, 1989

Gabbard GO: An overview of countertransference with borderline patients. Journal of Psychotherapy Research and Practice 2:7–18, 1993

Gabbard GO: Psychodynamic Psychiatry in Clinical Practice: The DSM-IV Edition. Washington, DC, American Psychiatric Press, 1994a

Gabbard GO: On love and lust in erotic transference. J Am Psychoanal Assoc 42:513–531, 1994b

Gabbard GO: Sexual excitement and countertransference love in the analyst. J Am Psychoanal Assoc 42:1083–1106, 1994c

Gabbard GO, Twemlow SW: The role of mother-son incest in the pathogenesis of narcissistic personality disorder. J Am Psychoanal Assoc 42:171–189, 1994

Gabbard GO, Wilkinson SM: Management of Countertransference With Borderline Patients. Washington, DC, American Psychiatric Press, 1994

Glassman M: Kernberg and Kohut: a test of competing psychoanalytic models of narcissism. J Am Psychoanal Assoc 36:597–625, 1988

Goldstein WN: Clarification of projective identification. Am J Psychiatry 148:153–161, 1991

Groopman LC, Cooper AM: Narcissistic personality disorder, in Treatments of Psychiatric Disorders, 2nd Edition, Vol 2. Gabbard GO, editor-in-chief. Washington, DC, American Psychiatric Press, 1995, pp 2327–2343

Grotstein JS: Splitting and Projective Identification. New York, Jason Aronson, 1981

Heiman P: On counter-transference. Int J Psychoanal 31:81–84, 1950

Hibbard S: Narcissism, shame, masochism, and object relations: an exploratory correlational study. Psychoanalytic Psychology 9:489–508, 1992

Jacobs TJ: On countertransference enactments. J Am Psychoanal Assoc 34:289–307, 1986

Jacobson JG: Signal affects and our psychoanalytic confusion of tongues. J Am Psychoanal Assoc 42:15–42, 1994

Kernberg OF: Factors in the psychoanalytic treatment of narcissistic personalities. J Am Psychoanal Assoc 18:51–85, 1970

Kernberg OF: Further contributions to the treatment of narcissistic personalities. Int J Psychoanal 55:215–240, 1974

Kernberg OF: Borderline Conditions and Pathological Narcissism. New York, Jason Aronson, 1975

Kernberg OF: Projection and projective identification: developmental and clinical aspects, in Projection, Identification, Projective Identification. Edited by Sandler J. Madison, CT, International Universities Press, 1987, pp 93–115

Kinston W: A theoretical context for shame. Int J Psychoanal 64:213–226, 1983

Klein M: Notes on some schizoid mechanisms (1946), in Envy and Gratitude and Other Works, 1946–1963. New York, Delacorte, 1975, pp 1–24

Kohut H: The Analysis of the Self. New York, International Universities Press, 1971

Kohut H: The Restoration of the Self. New York, International Universities Press, 1977

Kohut H: How Does Analysis Cure? Edited by Goldberg A, Stepansky P. Chicago, IL, University of Chicago Press, 1984

Lewin RA, Schulz CG: Losing and Fusing: Borderline and Transitional Object and Self Relations. Northvale, NJ, Jason Aronson, 1992

McLaughlin JT: Clinical and theoretical aspects of enactment. J Am Psychoanal Assoc 39:595–614, 1991

Mitchell SA: Relational Concepts in Psychoanalysis: An Integration. Cambridge, MA, Harvard University Press, 1988

Ogden TH: On projective identification. Int J Psychoanal 60:357–373, 1979

Ogden TH: Projective Identification and Psychotherapeutic Technique. New York, Jason Aronson, 1982

Pine F: The four psychologies of psychoanalysis and their place in clinical work. J Am Psychoanal Assoc 36:571–598, 1988

Pine F: Drive, Ego, Object, and Self: A Synthesis of Clinical Work. New York, Basic Books, 1990

Porder MS: Projective identification: an alternative hypothesis. Psychoanal Q 56:431–451, 1987

Pulver SE: The eclectic analyst, or the many roads to insight and change. J Am Psychoanal Assoc 41:339–358, 1993

Racker H: Transference and Countertransference. New York, International Universities Press, 1968

Rosenfeld H: Impasse and Interpretation: Therapeutic and Anti-Therapeutic Factors in the Psychoanalytic Treatment of Psychotic, Borderline, and Neurotic Patients. London, Tavistock, 1987

Roughton RE: Useful aspects of acting out: repetition, enactment, and actualization. J Am Psychoanal Assoc 41:443–472, 1993

Sandler J (ed): Projection, Identification, Projective Identification. Madison, CT, International Universities Press, 1987

Sandler J: On internal object relations. J Am Psychoanal Assoc 38:859–880, 1990

Scharff JS: Projective and Introjective Identification and the Use of the Therapist's Self. Northvale, NJ, Jason Aronson, 1992

Searles HF: My Work With Borderline Patients. Northvale, NJ, Jason Aronson, 1986

Symington N: The possibility of human freedom and its transmission (with particular reference to the thought of Bion). Int J Psychoanal 71:95–106, 1990

Tansey MJ, Burke WF: Understanding Countertransference: From Projective Identification to Empathy. Hillsdale, NJ, Analytic Press, 1989

Wallerstein RS: Forty-Two Lives in Treatment: A Study of Psychoanalysis and Psychotherapy. New York, Guilford, 1986

Wink P: Two faces of narcissism. J Pers Soc Psychol 61:590–597, 1991

Winnicott DW: Hate in the counter-transference. Int J Psychoanal 30:69–74, 1949

Wolf E: Treating the Self: Elements of Clinical Self Psychology. New York, Guilford, 1988

Chapter 7

Psychoanalysis of Patients With Primary Self-Disorder

A Self Psychological Perspective

Paul H. Ornstein, M.D.

Thirty years ago, Kohut presented his paper "Forms and Transformations of Narcissism" (Kohut 1966) and shortly thereafter a second paper, "The Psychoanalytic Treatment of Narcissistic Personality Disorders" (Kohut 1968). The first paper had broad implications, but the second paper, which suggested a new psychoanalytical treatment approach—as well as his ensuing monograph, which detailed and exemplified it (Kohut 1971)—brought the whole issue of narcissism into the center of clinical and theoretical concerns (P. H. Ornstein 1991a). Kohut emphasized the healthy aspects of narcissism and suggested that, contrary to prevailing opinion, patients with narcissistic personality and behavior disorders were analyzable without parameters. Thus, it seemed that he simply expanded the realm of analyzable clinical conditions and thereby enlarged the domain of clinical psychoanalysis. Few suspected, including Kohut himself, that this was a move toward introducing a new psychoanalytical paradigm.

This chapter includes a brief overview of the development of Kohut's ideas on narcissism and their further evolution into self psychology. In addition, the conduct and process of the psychoanalytical treatment of primary self-disorder are explicated with the aid of illustrative clinical vignettes.

From Narcissism to Self Psychology

At the outset, Kohut defined his own work as the direct continuation of Freud's study of narcissism. Freud (1914/1957) stated:

> The disturbances to which a child's original narcissism is exposed, the reactions with which he seeks to protect himself from them and the paths into which he is forced in doing so—these are the themes which I propose to leave on one side, as an important field of work which still awaits exploration. (p. 92)

Kohut undertook the detailed clinical and theoretical exploration of the fate of the "child's original narcissism" in health and illness in his two papers (1966, 1968) and mainly in his monograph *The Analysis of the Self* (1971). He completed his basic clinical and theoretical contributions of this first phase of his work on narcissism with the landmark essay "Thoughts on Narcissism and Narcissistic Rage" (1972) (see P. H. Ornstein 1974, 1978, 1979a, 1982; P. H. Ornstein and Kay 1990).

Kohut initially described the development of the infant's "original [primary] narcissism" in the language of libido theory and classic metapsychology. He assumed that primary narcissism was inevitably disturbed by the shortcomings of maternal care. The infant was "forced" (to use Freud's expression) to attempt to save the original experience of perfection in two different ways, developing along two separate lines: by assigning this perfection to the "grandiose self" on the one hand and to the "idealized parent imago" on the other—the two healthy nuclei of what later became the two poles of the bipolar self.[1]

It is important to note, however, that Kohut did not start with reformulating the theory of narcissism or its developmental vicissitudes; he began with his observations in the clinical situation. His major innovative ideas concerned the core of psychoanalysis: the identification of new transference configurations.[2]

The Selfobject Transferences

In analyzing patients with narcissistic personality disorders (NPDs), Kohut found that the patients' expectations, needs, demands, and fantasies clustered around three major themes, coalescing into three major cohesive transference constellations.[3]

In the first cluster, the *mirror transference,* patients express their

---

[1]Primary narcissism is a construction and not an observable fact. Balint (1937/1949) long ago replaced it with the concept of primary love, which is close to the selfobject concept of self psychology. Kohut initially used Freud's construct of primary narcissism for deriving the developmental origin of the archaic (narcissistic) configurations of the "grandiose-exhibitionistic self" and the "idealized parent imago." Later on, however, after he left the concept of narcissism behind and replaced it with the concept of self, Kohut postulated that these constellations reflected innate (hard-wired?) capacities to elicit the developmentally needed responses from the caregivers—a revision with validity that has been affirmed by contemporary observers of mother-infant pairs.

[2]The schematic description of the three selfobject transferences is a composite of many previous renderings of this aspect of the development of self psychology from the author's previous publications on this subject, used here liberally (A. Ornstein and P. H. Ornstein 1995; P. H. Ornstein 1979a, 1979b, 1982, 1991a, 1991b; P. H. Ornstein and Kay 1990; P. H. Ornstein and A. Ornstein 1995).

[3]Originally, Kohut described two such clusters, subsuming twinship needs under needs for mirroring. Further clinical experience convinced him of the necessity to separate twinship needs into a developmental line of its own (Kohut 1977).

needs for the analyst to serve as an echo—an affirming, approving, validating, and admiring presence—thereby bolstering patients' fragile self-esteem. Kohut noted that in these instances the analyst mattered only to the extent that he or she could or could not be experienced by the patient as available to perform these needed functions. These needs and the patient's efforts to have them met coalesce into a sustained, cohesive, mirror transference. The establishment of such a transference leads to a notable improvement in the patient's functioning, as if the analyst served as the necessary "psychic glue" that held the patient's self together. From here on, whenever the patient is disappointed in his or her expectations, which is inevitable, the disruptions in the transference are reflected either in the return of disturbed functioning or in outright fragmentation. Therefore, the analytical effort has to be focused on the immediate precipitating cause for the disruption, commonly related to some form of (even if inadvertent) "unempathic" response by the analyst. Thus, the reconstruction of the intraanalytical precipitants (often including the genetic precursors for the patient's vulnerability and proneness to fragmentation) would temporarily restore the cohesiveness of the transference and the cohesiveness of the self.

In the second cluster, the *idealizing transference,* patients express their need to attach themselves to the analyst—whom they put on a pedestal and experience as an all-knowing, all-powerful, and perfect presence—so they might partake of, or "borrow," that greatness and perfection. When the patient experiences these expectations and needs as having been met, this, too, lends the patient a modicum of cohesiveness, vitality, and inner calm. However, disappointments are inevitable. They are experienced as renewed traumata, and the vulnerable, fragmentation-prone patient responds with narcissistic rage or any of the other well-known consequences of a disrupted idealizing transference (i.e., sexual promiscuity, sadomasochistic and other perverse behaviors, addictions, and delinquencies). The analyst's response has to be given in the form of reconstructive interpretations.

In the third cluster, the *twinship* or *alter ego transference,* patients express their needs for an echo of affirmation, and they search for their own likeness. They feel the need for the analyst to think as they do, so that in relation to him or her the unfolding of hitherto thwarted skills and talents may belatedly occur. They feel the need for kinship and expect that with their alikeness, the analyst will confirm their belonging to the human community from which they have remained alienated or never felt quite at one with. Here, too, inevitable disruptions create opportunities for reconstructive interpretations that reestablish the cohesiveness of the transference.

From these transference manifestations and their working through, Kohut reconstructed both the necessary ingredients for the development of a healthy self and the variety of infantile and childhood traumata that left the psyche insufficiently "structuralized." Under optimum developmental conditions, the availability of the emotional nutrients in infancy and childhood—the selfobject responses of the original caregivers—leads to the acquisition of specific psychic structures in each line of development (i.e., the grandiose self and the idealized parent imago).

The Development of the Bipolar Self

The *grandiose self* will become transformed into *self-assertive ambitions* that constitute one pole of the bipolar self. This transformation will entail the capacity for regulating self-esteem, for being goal directed and ambitious, and for being able to enjoy physical (body—e.g., physical dexterity) and mental (mind—e.g., ways of thinking, creativity) activities. Deficient development in this area will lead to low self-esteem and disturbances in its regulation, in the inability to pursue goals and ambitions (to feel "unmotivated"), and in the inability to enjoy either physical or mental activities (to feel general malaise, boredom, and laziness). These are the frequently observed "deficits" in the group of self-disorders with psychopathology that are rooted in fixations on the archaic grandiose self.

The *idealized parent imago* will become transformed into internalized values and ideals that constitute the other pole of the bipolar self. Successful internalization will lead to the capacity to live up to values and ideals and to maintain mature enthusiasm in keeping with them. These values and ideals will serve as the regulators of manifold tension states, as if they were an invisible but effective stimulus barrier in the psyche. They function as self-soothing, self-calming, affect-containing structures, maintaining and restoring internal balance. Deficient development in this area will lead to the many forms of tension regulatory problems, such as addictions, perversions, and certain forms of criminality as well as lack of enthusiasm, empty depression, and chronic despair. These are frequently observed "deficits" in the group of self-disorders that are rooted in fixations on archaic idealizations.

The *twinship or alter ego needs* (Kohut gave no special designation to their archaic constellation), when successfully met, will safeguard the unfolding of innate skills and talents and make the child feel like a member of the human family. The availability of twinship or alter ego experiences will impart to the growing child a feeling of belonging, which will also bolster self-esteem and contribute an "I can do" feeling, a sense of effectiveness. Deficiencies in this area will lead to many forms of inhibition in the application of skills and talents and will engender feelings of alienation, never fitting in, not belonging, being outside of the human community, or being a freak or some other kind of misfit. These are some of the frequently observed "deficits" in the group of disorders that are rooted in the unavailability or unreliable availability of twinship experiences.

Psychic structures and structural deficits.   The concept of *deficit* needs further clarification because it has brought about controversies regarding self psychology (P. H. Ornstein 1991b). Developmentally, deficit simply refers to the unavailability or inadequate or erratic availability of needed selfobject functions, without which the basic capacities of the self (psychic structures) will not develop or will develop only deficiently. Structurally, deficit refers to those missing psychic functions described above as the felicitous healthy outcome of optimal developmental experiences. Dynamically, deficit refers to the fact that in response to it, secondary conflicts arise and codetermine the nature of the patients' psychopathology. Most important, it is these deficits (the underlying thwarted developmental needs) that motivate the remobilization of the selfobject transferences.

When Kohut spoke of "missing psychic structures," critics conjured up the idea of a "hole" in the psyche, which, rightfully, they could not accept as valid. However, Kohut spoke of "primary structures" that develop in relation to the responsiveness and ministrations of the original caregivers, of "defensive structures" that fill the deficit and create the manifest psychopathology, and of "compensatory structures" that develop when the infant or child can turn to a substitute caregiver/selfobject and make up for earlier unavailable selfobject experiences for structure building. It is the considerable defensive overlay to fill the void or the breakdown of the insufficiently consolidated compensatory structures that characterizes the specific narcissistic disturbances. If healthy, phase-appropriate narcissism (Hartmann's [1964] "libidinal investment of the self") is the "glue" that holds the self together, then patients with these disturbances could no longer be described as exhibiting "too much narcissism," but, in Kohut's view, too little. In other words, narcissism per se is the normal "fuel" for structure building. Pathology in this context is not a pathology of narcissism but a pathology of the structures of the self (deficiencies, defects, or defensive structures) that is due to inadequate "narcissistic cathexis" and not to excessive amounts of pathological forms of narcissism. Thus, Kohut drastically reformulated the nature of psychopathology in narcissistic personality and behavior disorders and later extended this formulation throughout the entire spectrum of psychopathology.

Developmental lines of narcissism and object love.   It is immediately evident, even from this schematic portrayal, that Kohut replaced Freud's psychosexual schema of development with his own schema of the need for selfobject experiences as the impetus for development. His clinical observations led to a heuristic claim that narcissism and object love have two separate lines of development. In one line, archaic narcissism becomes transformed into higher forms; in the other line, archaic object love develops into mature object love. The clinical implications of this small but significant correction of Freud's developmental schema—from autoerotism to narcissism to object love—were far-reaching. Narcissism could no longer be seen in this context only as a defense against or as a regressive evasion of the oedipal passions. It had to be accepted and analyzed on its own terms as a revival of hitherto thwarted but genuine infantile or childhood developmental needs that were never adequately met rather than only as a defense (resistance) in the transference.

The defensive structures enter powerfully into the analytical process and often require a lengthy analytical effort before the patient is able to make use of the analyst's empathic interventions (A. Ornstein 1974, 1991). Kohut recognized that resistances against the remobilization of archaic needs and wishes are mainly caused by the patient's desperate efforts at warding off feared retraumatization. The analyst is enjoined by Kohut to watch for signs of the patient's hopes for a different outcome and to focus interpretively on these in order to facilitate as full a remobilization of the patient's archaic needs and wishes as possible and necessary. This is a precondition for a successful psychoanalytical "cure."

Narcissistic rage.   The essential features of Kohut's contribution to the psychoanalytical treatment process were already in place in 1971 and were significantly expanded with his essay on narcissistic rage (Kohut 1972). The most significant of its elements is that narcissistic rage is reactive. Its most severe forms are a consequence of attacks on archaic grandiosity or massive disillusionment in the archaic idealized imago—the two "absolutarian constellations" of the developing psyche. Another significance is that analytical focus is not on the rage itself but on the circumstances that triggered its eruption. The focus is on the "narcissistic matrix"—the patient's specific vulnerabilities— from which the rage arose. This approach is often mistaken by the external observer as sidestepping or minimizing a direct confrontation with the rage, as an avoidance of its analysis—that is, avoidance of tracing it to its roots in the aggressive drive as is followed in some other approaches (P. H. Ornstein 1993; P. H. Ornstein and A. Ornstein 1993).

Self Psychology

In *The Analysis of the Self,* Kohut (1971) had already found his own voice but not yet his own language. By the time *The Restoration of the Self* was published (1977), he had found both his authentic voice and his authentic language. Having left drive theory (not the drives!) behind, as well as the language of classic metapsychology with all of its no-longer-tenable implications, he was well on the way to offering us more explicitly than before a new psychoanalytical paradigm.

Kohut did have a self psychology from the outset (later he called it a "self psychology in the narrower sense"), which was still embedded in a drive psychology–based ego psychology. Once he included neuroses in his clinical studies, his findings compelled him to extend his theory throughout the entire spectrum of health and illness. This is what gave birth to "self psychology in the broader sense" as he then described it to differentiate it from his earlier conceptualization.

The centerpiece of this new psychology of the self (Kohut 1977)—which led to the inclusion of neuroses—was the reformulation of the Oedipus complex. Kohut viewed oedipal wishes and fantasies as normal developmental vicissitudes and spoke of an oedipal stage or phase as universal and not the Oedipus complex. The Oedipus complex was viewed as a pathological manifestation based on a prior self-disorder or as the result of punitive or seductive responses of the oedipal selfobjects to the child's budding sexuality and assertiveness.[4]

The distinguishing features of self psychology in the broader sense, that is, in its basic concepts and their wider implications, can be summarized only in the present context.

---

[4]It is in this connection that the terms *primary* and *secondary self-disorder* were introduced. The former is independent of (and before) the oedipal-phase issues; the latter is a consequence of unempathic (punitive or seductive) responses to oedipal strivings. But the main point of the reformulation had to do with Kohut's claim that whether oedipal wishes and fantasies led to the development of a normal oedipal phase or to a pathological Oedipus complex depended on parental (or caregiver) responses.

Leaving drive theory and the tripartite model of the mind behind, Kohut placed the bipolar self into a central supraordinate position in the psychological universe. Thus, the development of the self—its cohesiveness, vitality or enfeeblement, and proneness to fragmentation—became the analyst's prime concern. The key concepts of this new psychoanalytical paradigm—*the selfobject transferences*—were derived from careful clinical observations and experience-near theorizing, amply illustrated throughout Kohut's writings. These concepts gave rise to the selfobject as a developmental concept, a theoretical concept, and a bridging concept, bringing the "outside" into the "inside" via transmuting internalization as the specific form of structure building.

The selfobject transferences represent the revival of infantile and childhood developmental needs that were never adequately responded to. This inadequate response led to structural deficits or defects in the self. When these needs are revived in the clinical situation, they manifest themselves in intensified, dramatized, and often variously distorted forms—the normal developmental needs are not seen in pure form in the transference. Yet the unextinguished hopes and needs behind the manifest psychopathology have to be actively searched for to offer the patient a chance for belated structure building.

The *selfobject as a developmental concept* was also introduced in the context of Kohut's reconstruction of normal development in the working through of the selfobject transferences. The identity of the selfobject as a clinical and as a developmental concept buttresses the notion that psychoanalysis is—and always was—at its base a developmental theory. Its curative processes also have to be viewed in developmental terms.

The *selfobject as a theoretical concept* defines the other as the "self's object." The concept of selfobject includes the experiencing of the "other"—the intrapsychic experience of the other—so it reflects that experience. It also reflects that the other serves specific functions in the process of the structuralization of the bipolar self, that is, the attainment and maintenance of its cohesion and vitality as well as the unfolding of its various capacities. This other is then experienced either as a part of the self or as someone to whom the self is attached. Kohut spoke of archaic and mature self-objects and maintained that selfobjects were needed from birth to death—both archaic selfobjects in order to become who we are and mature selfobjects in order to maintain cohesiveness and vitality as well as creativeness.

The *selfobject as a bridging concept* brings the external other into a person's inner world. It refers to how we experience "inside" of us what exists on the "outside." It is a felicitous way of dealing with an otherwise complex and often insoluble problem of how the outside is "represented" (as if it were possible to represent it concretely, like taking a photograph of the outside with a camera inside of us) by focusing on a person's subjective experience of an other. This permits a psychoanalytical (i.e., intrapsychic) view of external reality.

Transmuting internalization refers to the ongoing process in infancy and childhood (or later in the treatment process) whereby the so-called archaic narcissistic structures (the grandiose self, the idealized parent imago) are transformed and become laid down as permanent psychic structures in Kohut's view. It is significant here that the caregivers' (and later the analyst's) selfobject responsiveness catalyzes the maturation and transformation of these archaic structures. It is not identification or introjection of the caregivers' (or the analyst's) characteristics that is conceived of as the process whereby permanent psychic structures are built. It is the phase-appropriate responsiveness to the infant's and child's own innate propensities that leads to the bit-by-bit acquisition of psychic structures (see Figures 7–1 and 7–2).

In addition to these specific concepts, a new view of the human condition emerges from Kohut's self psychology, which permeates his theorizing as well as the psychoanalytical treatment process, and which the remainder of this chapter is focused on.

The Psychoanalytical Treatment Process

The various propositions of self psychology (its theoretical innovations, its reformulation of the nature of psychopathology and of the psychoanalytical treatment process) can be understood and

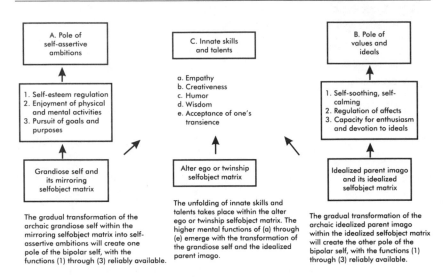

Figure 7–1. Structure and functions of the supraordinate bipolar self (normal development).
Source. Reprinted from Ornstein PH, Kay J: "Development of Psychoanalytic Self Psychology: A Historical-Conceptual Overview," in *American Psychiatric Press Review of Psychiatry*, Vol. 9. Edited by Tasman A, Goldfinger SM, Kaufmann CA. Washington, DC, American Psychiatric Press, 1990, pp. 303–322. Used with permission.

fully appreciated only if we recognize that Kohut placed empathy (i.e., vicarious introspection) as a mode of observation into a central position in psychoanalysis (Kohut 1959; P. H. Ornstein 1979b). To take up the empathic vantage point of observation means that the analyst as consistently as possible tries to grasp the patient's subjective experience from the patient's perspective, which includes the way the patient feels about the analyst. All other observational modalities that are inevitably also present remain subordinated to the effort the analyst has to make to grasp the patient's subjectivity.[5]

---

[5]By defining empathy as vicarious introspection, Kohut extricated this observational method conceptually from its murky past. In addition, however, he considered empathy as the definer of the field of psychoanalysis. The encompassing or potential encompassing (to include what is disavowed or repressed) of subjective inner experience via empathy constitutes psychoanalysis. Empathy is thus first and foremost a method of data gathering, whatever other meanings we may attach to it.

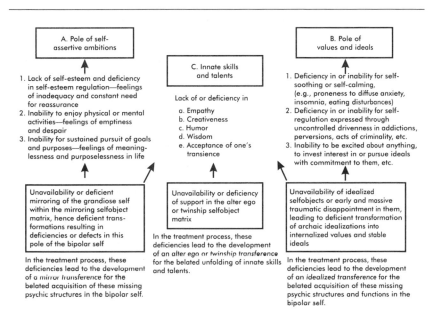

Figure 7–2. Structure and functions of the supraordinate bipolar self (deficient or derailed development).
Source. Reprinted from Ornstein PH, Kay J: "Development of Psychoanalytic Self Psychology: A Historical-Conceptual Overview," in *American Psychiatric Press Review of Psychiatry,* Vol. 9. Edited by Tasman A, Goldfinger SM, Kaufmann CA. Washington, DC, American Psychiatric Press, 1990, pp. 303–322. Used with permission.

One of the most important consequences of this shift in observational method is that the primary analytical focus is not on highlighting the discrepancy between the patient's inner experience and current reality but on capturing (i.e., understanding and explaining) the archaic logic of that inner experience without judging it from the perspective of the analyst's own current reality. Thus, whatever the specific features of the patient's psychopathology, or whatever its dominant features (such as grandiosity and omnipotence, sadomasochism, or narcissistic rage), it is the matrix of the archaic constellation of the self into which these are embedded and from which they arise that commands our analytical attention.

To put it more pointedly, it is the sustained, cohesive selfobject transference, within which aspects of the patient's psychopathology become activated, that will determine the nature of the analyst's interpretive participation in the treatment process. In contrast to the classical transference, which focuses on repetition and distortion, the selfobject transferences also contain the patient's strivings for a new beginning. Repetition is always present. It is considered here to be in the service of finding a better solution to derailed or thwarted development. The patient revives the interrupted process of structure building and strives to complete this in the analysis (Kohut 1970/1978). It is this analytical focus on the patient's unextinguished hope and push for belated acquisition of missing psychic structures that is a prominent feature of the working through of selfobject transferences. Nonjudgmental acceptance of archaic needs and longings and their understanding and explanation are the analytical vehicles that bring about structure building.

Clinical Vignettes

Three clinical vignettes are presented to illustrate various facets of the psychoanalytical treatment process.[6]

Archaic Grandiosity in the Idealizing Transference

Mr. I was in his mid-20s and single when he came for analysis. He had a variety of diffuse complaints: not being able to perform adequately on his new job, being too preoccupied with his unhappiness with himself, and having a lack of direction in his life. He was tall, handsome, carefully dressed, and soft-spoken. He was extremely anxious and spoke rapidly and in a somewhat rambling fashion during our initial contact.

Mr. I began his analysis by wishing to give a detailed,

---

[6]The three clinical vignettes were culled from a lengthier report about the analysis of Mr. I (Goldberg 1978).

chronological history of his life experiences, which he thought might take several months to accomplish. He carefully planned and controlled what he would say, and at what pace, in order not to be overwhelmed. However, he was soon derailed because of the intensity of his day-to-day analytical experience. The early phase was dominated by his detailed focus on his continuous, compulsive, sado-masochistic sexual exploits. As was later understood, these exploitive behaviors were in the service of either calming himself, exciting himself, or regaining lost self-esteem in his daily encounters at work. His self-regulatory capacities were profoundly disturbed.

He later mentioned that he told the analyst whom he consulted for a referral, "I need somebody who is an all-around he-man because he will give me credit for this," —meaning his sexual exploits—"someone who will think it is wild and great and who will really appreciate it." He thus introduced his need to be admired by someone whom he could put on the pedestal. Both the mirror transference and the idealizing transference were thus quickly foreshadowed, which determined the functions he unconsciously assigned to his analyst.

During the initial phase of his analysis, Mr. I became aware of how much he needed center stage. It was no longer unconscious, and that was the embarrassing aspect of it. He wanted to be the best analysand there ever was. He hated to admit that he needed somebody else to do the job; he thought he could do his analysis himself and become famous. "Maybe I am on the verge of it now, and you are going to get the credit for it. My case has to be the greatest!"

Mr. I slowly retreated from these grandiose, omnipotent fantasies, and his helplessness, powerlessness, and feelings of insignificance moved into the center of his analytical experience, establishing a more sustained idealizing transference. This became quite clear when he once asked thoughtfully, with some despair in his voice: "Why do I have to have you acknowledge that I feel good before I know I feel good?" His own further reflections were of considerable significance. He felt that he was "a splat on the wall—when you throw hot rubber against the wall, it hardens and is like an octopus with suckers on it, clinging to the wall. Then nothing matters, only the clinging like the splat. It can't tolerate the rumbling of the wall. Any disconnection is a threat to the survival of the splat. That's how I am with T [his girlfriend] and with you. I want you to be the wall—shut up and listen! If I would no longer have to be a splat on the wall, it would be a major accomplishment."

At this point, he could feel strong, powerful, and important only in his attachment to the idealized analyst. Whatever disrupted this attachment—weekend separations, vacations, or even slight unempathic rebuffs—all felt like the "rumbling of the wall" endangering the splat. As long as he felt this oneness with the analyst, that is, as long as the idealizing transference was not disrupted, Mr. I's sadomasochistic sexual exploits decreased considerably and finally abated, only to return as emergency measures related to specific disruptions in the idealizing transference. It was important to discover the intraanalytical precipitants for these disruptions and to understand their meaning and origin in order to reestablish the analytical bond. Mr. I reinfused these with borrowed strength and power until much later, when, bit by bit, he could establish his own bonds.

A sample intervention will be introduced here that is representative of what the analyst had done to facilitate the repair of the frequent inevitable disruptions during this phase of the analysis. Mr. I spoke with some urgency in his voice about wanting to marry his girlfriend. The analyst mistakenly rushed in to prevent a "rash acting-out"—a premature marriage—by focusing on the urgency, without any real indication that Mr. I contemplated immediate action. In a dream that followed, Mr. I was nasty and derogatory to an old man. His father criticized him for it and reminded him that his grandfather knew this man. Mr. I felt overwhelmed with kindly warm feelings and wanted to go up and hug the old man. He couldn't hug him, and then he just wanted to be able to talk to him.

Mr. I's associations and the broader context in which this dream occurred revealed his intense longing for the idealized analyst-father. The analyst acknowledged that it pained him whenever his admiring and loving feelings were not accepted but seen only (mistakenly) as "the other side of the ambivalence." Mr. I was tearful in response and, for the first time, said with emotion: "I am really ready to love the old man, but he couldn't take it, he'd brush it off!" The analyst was then able to clarify that earlier focusing on the "urgency" in connection with his marriage plans, rather than on the urgency with which he presented it, must have contributed "to the rift in here along with my not accepting your admiring and loving feelings. This must have added to your anguished retreat and made you turn to T for consolation." Invariably, such interventions quickly reestablished the disrupted transference and regularly brought forth some relevant, hitherto unavailable memories. Whenever the analyst could appropriately introduce these interventions, even if somewhat belatedly, it was always done with concrete and specific references to the events within the analytical experience.

The working through of the idealizing transference led to a decisive improvement in Mr. I's life outside of the analysis at work and in his relationships, but his vulnerability in the analytical situation increased as a prelude to the remobilization of his archaic grandiose self.

Archaic Grandiosity
From a Transitional Stage

An example from this transitional stage[7] will illustrate the analyst's contention that there is no need for confronting the patient with what he or she is not yet able to introduce into the analytical dialogue. An acceptance and understanding of the meaning of what he or she does bring into the sessions will open up otherwise unavailable parts of himself or herself.

---

[7]Mr. I's oscillations between his idealization of the analyst and his need for mirroring affirmation of his greatness and uniqueness provide an opportunity to witness his object-bound as well as subject-bound grandiosity and omnipotence. These vignettes also show his subtle and not-so-subtle efforts at controlling the analyst and the analytical situation to forestall being retraumatized by the analyst's responses.

An abrupt cancellation of his session on Washington's birthday infuriated Mr. I, and he warned the analyst to give him considerable notice before termination when the time came. He then announced in a celebratory tone that this was his 400th session. "A special occasion, yet it gives me an empty feeling." The analyst referred to the abrupt cancellation and said that it must again have felt arbitrary to Mr. I; he must have felt at the analyst's mercy because the analyst could cut him off any time. "I don't want to be at your mercy," he responded angrily. "I associate it with being a damned fool. I take it [meaning his analytic experience] seriously and somebody else [meaning his analyst] doesn't."

Not taking him seriously was the most painful treatment anyone could accord him. He recognized that in response he felt "depressed, lonely, empty, and dead inside" on Washington's birthday. He needed "some exciting sensations, some kicks, to get me out of it." The hot shower was not enough, and then he fell asleep, exhausted. After a brief silence, he added, "If I perceive you as uninterested, I lose my complete sense of wholeness—then I need more stimulation to make up for it."

For the next few days, Mr. I's feeling of emptiness continued, further intensified by the fact that the analyst did not celebrate the 400th session with him. As Mr. I berated the analyst for this, he felt dizzy on the couch. The analyst responded by saying, "It must have seemed to you a very insensitive rejection that I did not share your mood to celebrate, or at least recognize your mood; you acknowledged the anniversary, I didn't, so it was all the more painful." Mr. I replied, "I almost cried when you recalled all the feelings for me. If I felt rejected here last Wednesday, I must have felt it lots of times elsewhere. How much I must demand someone's 100% constant attention."

In a reflective mood he described himself as a globe with a defect on it like the Grand Canyon: "In analysis, you try to work on it, excavate the surface of it so it can heal in. It's comforting that somebody, your analyst, knows how sick you are and he is not alarmed, not scared, not discouraged, but optimistic of what can be done about it." Then he became more anxious: "What if I suspect that even deeper defects are there and my analyst does not know they are there? I can't tell him because even he might get discouraged. But I don't want to conceal that."

Archaic Grandiosity in
the Mirror Transference

During the arduous working-through process of Mr. I's mirror transference, he again watched Fellini's movie 8½, about which he had spoken during the first week of his analysis. At that time, he strongly identified with the provocative, arrogant director of the movie who (these are his words) collected all past important figures around himself and controlled and manipulated them—he was in complete charge. Now, as he saw the movie, he recognized the flashing back and forth between reality and fantasy, present and past. He still identified with the movie director, and he said "I could not understand it some years ago. Now I see it as the eventual death of infantile sexuality in a man—omnipotence, grandiosity, thousands of girls with no real relationship to them, narcissistically having the center stage, conducting. It's all neurotic, infantile, oedipal, Catholic church versus the whores. Shooting himself is giving up all that stuff—that is what analysis has been for me. It's difficult to give up all these infantile things."

He was wondering how it all happened in the analysis that he could give up so much. "One reason, I tell you, one reason, you are a good analyst; you have always consistently maintained your confidence in the potential of my health. Whatever I said—even when I argued with you about the twenty dollars extra charge when I missed a session—even when I said I was psychotic, you reacted as if I were capable of responding in a healthy way. Having gone through this time with you, it was a real therapeutic experience for me. If you had ever given me back the twenty dollars, deciding you were wrong, I would have resented it for the rest of my life; it was so solid, you would have destroyed it by undoing."

Near termination of therapy, Mr. I repeatedly reflected

on what he had accomplished. He said at one point that what he achieved "isn't mostly insight, but [he gained] ego-capacities, and different functioning. Every minute of the day I am different from what I used to be. The underlying force was the stability of this relationship. Once it got me stabilized, then I was able to develop a stable relationship with others—with myself too. Now I can leave with more stability and transfer my ties to others."

Conclusion

The author has presented three "psychological biopsies" from different phases of the analysis of a young man, in whom tension regulation, affect containment, grandiosity, and omnipotence (including omnipotent control) played a central role in his psychology and psychopathology. Working within the selfobject transferences entailed a focus on the function the patient unconsciously assigned to his analyst-selfobject. Thus, it was the vicissitudes of the state of his self and its enfeeblement, depletion, frequent entanglement in conflicts, fragmentation, and other identifiable states (such as rage and revengefulness) that claimed interpretive attention. The function the patient assigned to his analyst demanded a focus on the here and now of the transference, which replicated his lifelong thwarted needs as well as his habitual ways of attempting to satisfy them. The transference also offered numerous hints regarding the earliest psychogenetic precursors of the patient's psychopathology and reflected his efforts to acquire the missing psychic structures that gave rise to these transferences.

The focus of the interpretive process was not on this or that specific content (e.g., omnipotence) but on the matrix (the vulnerable self) from which the contents arose. It was only with the therapeutic reactivation of the original need for the selfobject's responses that the actual lessening of grandiosity, omnipotence, and omnipotent sadistic control and a return to healthy assertiveness and reliable self-esteem regulation could be achieved.

Therefore, the analytical aim with regard to these archaic fantasies, emotions, and behaviors is always the gradual transformation of the archaic matrix from which they arise and are later integrated into the adult self. It is this transformation and integration that makes their use ultimately unnecessary.

A focus on the defensive aspects of the patient's behavior—whenever that is necessary—entails explaining what function or purpose such defensive behavior has in maintaining the cohesiveness of a fragile, vulnerable, fragmentation-prone self. An exclusive or all-too-aggressive focus on the patient's defensiveness often engenders an adaptation but drives the archaic needs underground. A preferred focus on the patient's efforts at a belated acquisition of psychic structures decreases the patient's vulnerability and with it the need for constantly available narcissistic supplies from archaically experienced selfobjects. The essence of cure, then, lies in the acquisition of psychic structures that make the finding of an appropriate selfobject milieu after analysis possible.

References

Balint M: Early developmental states of the ego: primary object love (1937). Int J Psychoanal 30:265–273, 1949

Freud S: On narcissism: an introduction (1914), in The Standard Edition of the Complete Psychological Works of Sigmund Freud, Vol 14. Translated and edited by Strachey J. London, Hogarth Press, 1957, pp 67–102

Goldberg A (ed): The Psychology of the Self: A Case Book. New York, International Universities Press, 1978, pp 1–106

Hartmann H: Comments on the psychoanalytic theory of the ego, in Essays on Ego Psychology. New York, International Universities Press, 1964, pp 113–141

Kohut H: Introspection, empathy and psychoanalysis. J Am Psychoanal Assoc 7:459–483, 1959

Kohut H: Forms and transformations of narcissism. J Am Psychoanal Assoc 14:243–272, 1966

Kohut H: The psychoanalytic treatment of narcissistic personality disorders—outline of a systematic approach. Psychoanal Study Child 23:86–113, 1968

Kohut H: The Analysis of the Self. New York, International Universities Press, 1971

Kohut H: Thoughts on narcissism and narcissistic rage. Psychoanal Study Child 27:360–400, 1972

Kohut H: The Restoration of the Self. New York, International Universities Press, 1977

Kohut H: Narcissism as a resistance and as a driving force in psychoanalysis (1970), in The Search for the Self, Vol 2. Edited by Ornstein PH. New York, International Universities Press, 1978, pp 547–561

Ornstein A: The dread to repeat and the new beginning: a contribution to the analysis of narcissistic personality disorders. Annual of Psychoanalysis 2:231–248, 1974

Ornstein A: The dread to repeat: comments on the working through process in psychoanalysis. J Am Psychoanal Assoc 39:377–398, 1991

Ornstein A, Ornstein PH: Marginal comments on the evaluation of self psychology. Psychoanalytic Dialogues 5:421–425, 1995

Ornstein PH: On narcissism: beyond the introduction. Highlights of Heinz Kohut's contributions to the psychoanalytic treatment of narcissistic personality disorders. Annual of Psychoanalysis 2:127–149, 1974

Ornstein PH: The resolution of a mirror transference: clinical emphasis upon the termination phase, in Psychology of the Self—A Case Book. Edited by Goldberg A. New York, International Universities Press, 1978, pp 1–106

Ornstein PH: Self-pathology in the psychoanalytic treatment process, in Integrating Ego Psychology and Object Relations. Edited by Saretzky L, Goldman GD, Milman DS. Dubuque, IA, Kendall/Hunt Publishing Company, 1979a, pp 180–195

Ornstein PH: Remarks on the central position of empathy in psychoanalysis. Bulletin: The Association for Psychoanalytic Medicine 18:95–109, 1979b

Ornstein PH: On the psychoanalytic psychotherapy of primary self-pathology, in Annual Review of Advances in Psychiatry. Edited by Grinspoon L. Washington, DC, American Psychiatric Press, 1982, pp 498–510

Ornstein PH: From narcissism to ego psychology to self psychology, in Freud's on Narcissism: An Introduction. Edited by Sandler J, Spector ES, Fonagy P. New Haven, CT, Yale University Press, 1991a, pp 175–194

Ornstein PH: Conflict and compromise—a self psychological perspective, in Conflict and Compromise: Therapeutic Implications. Edited by Dowling S. Madison, CT, International Universities Press, 1991b, pp 133–171

Ornstein PH: Chronic rage from underground: reflections on its structure and treatment, in Progress in Self Psychology, Vol 9. Edited by Goldberg A. Hillsdale, NJ, Analytic Press, 1993, pp 143–157

Ornstein PH, Kay J: Development of psychoanalytic self psychology: a historical-conceptual overview, in Review of Psychiatry, Vol 9. Edited by Tasman A, Goldfinger SM, Kaufmann CA. Washington, DC, American Psychiatric Press, 1990, pp 303–322

Ornstein PH, Ornstein A: Assertiveness, anger, rage and destructive aggression: a perspective from the treatment process, in Rage, Power and Aggression. Edited by Glick R, Roose S. New Haven, CT, Yale University Press, 1993, pp 102–117

Ornstein PH, Ornstein A: Some distinguishing features of Heinz Kohut's self psychology. Psychoanalysis Dialogues 5:385–391, 1995

Chapter 8

An Object Relations Theory Approach to Psychoanalysis With Narcissistic Patients

Lucy LaFarge, M.D.

From the perspective of object relations theory, the manifest symptomatology of narcissism reflects specific disturbances of the narcissistic individual's internal world of self- and object representations. This representational world, which exists largely outside consciousness, is built up from the earliest phase of life. It incorporates memories and fantasies of experiences with objects, both more or less realistically perceived and fantastically distorted by affects, wishes, and defensive needs. Self- and object representations are the matrix on which ego and superego are constructed. In addition, the unconscious world of representations is continuously projected onto external reality, organizing both perceptions and interactions with contemporary objects. Thus, disturbances in the object world result in ego and superego pathology and in pathological interactions with objects. Pathological narcissism reflects a disturbance of a deep layer of representations, the construction of an early, highly distorted, rigid constellation of representations that distorts the further evolution of psychic structure and object relations. The analysis of the narcissistic patient entails the analysis of these pathological constellations as they emerge in transference and countertransference and, ultimately, the analysis of the disturbed affects and object relations that led to their construction.

In this chapter, the author traces the development of object relations theories of narcissism from their origin in Freud's work, with particular attention to their clinical implications. Then, the author describes in some detail, with clinical examples, the nature of the analytical process that unfolds with narcissistic patients and the way that a contemporary object relations theorist might approach these patients and might consider issues such as the selection of patients for analysis, the interpretation of pathological narcissistic structures, the problem of regression, and the readiness of patient's for termination of therapy.

Freud's Concepts of Narcissism

Freud (1914/1957) believed that in contrast to most neurotic patients who could form a normal transference, narcissistic patients had withdrawn libido from objects onto their own egos, where libido was either elaborated as omnipotent fantasy or, unbound by fantasy, expressed in the form of hypochondriacal symptoms. In effect, narcissistic individuals loved only themselves. Thus, they could not make a significant libidinal investment in the analyst, they had little motivation to undergo the rigors of analysis, and crucial data about their inner lives could not be made available for the analyst's interpretation.

Freud (1938/1964) described an early developmental phase in which the mother's breast was experienced narcissistically as a part of the self. He also described a narcissistic form of love relations, in which the loved object was believed to represent an aspect of the lover's own self (Freud 1914/1957). However, in his clinical theory, he did not conceptualize these narcissistic object relations as giving rise to transferences.

Object Relations Theorists and Narcissistic Pathology

Since Freud's time, object relations theorists have seen the narcissistic individual's self-absorption, inaccessibility, and indifference to the analyst not as evidence of an absence of transference, as Freud thought. Instead, they have viewed these qualities as evidence of the activation in the transference of a primitive object relation, one in which self- and object representations are not fully distinct or separate but thought to contain elements of each other. These object relations may be either libidinal or aggressive in content, may serve defensive functions, and are potentially analyzable. Different schools of thought within object relations theory have varied as to their nature and the developmental phase at which they originate.

Klein and the Kleinians

Klein linked narcissistic object relations to the paranoid-schizoid position, an organization of the object world emerging in the first few months of life. At this early developmental phase, splitting and the extensive use of projective mechanisms protected the nascent ego and the good object from annihilation by inborn destructive forces, experienced as a persecutory attack by a hated object (Klein 1946/1975, 1952/1975). At this level of organization, part objects made up internal representations. Body parts were not unified into whole figures, and good and bad aspects of objects were believed to be very different and were defensively kept apart. The sensorial nature of early fantasy led the child to experience internal representations of objects as a part of his or her own body (Isaacs 1952). The use of projective identification, a central defensive operation of this phase, led the child to experience parts of himself or herself as residing within the object.

In Klein's schema, this organization of part-object representations was succeeded within the first year of life by the depressive position, a higher-level organization in which good and bad aspects of self and object were brought together to form whole objects. The primary anxiety shifted away from persecution to the danger of the self's own potential for hatred and destruction of the good object. However, the shift from part objects to whole objects was never final. A predominance of aggression at the earliest phase could impede the integration of good and bad aspects of representations, and loss or heightening of aggression throughout the life cycle could lead to the reemergence of paranoid anxieties and part-object relations.

Within this frame of reference, the narcissistic individual's self-absorption and self-love may be understood as a love for an ideal self believed to contain parts of a beloved object. This self-love represents a defensive flight from internal and external object relations that are believed to be bad. The analyst working with such a patient would interpret the active defensive nature of the patient's withdrawal from the analyst and attempt to uncover the specific fantasy contents of good and bad objects and the wishes directed toward them. The love of narcissistic patients for an object believed to represent themselves (Freud's narcissistic love relations) reflects their attachment to an internal object onto which they have projected idealized parts of their own selves and over whom they continue to feel control and connectedness (Segal 1983). Their exploitativeness and sense of dominion over a bad object believed to be inferior reflect their projective use of the object as a container for bad parts of the self.

The aloofness, grandiosity, and loss of lasting positive ties to objects seen in the more severe forms of narcissism are particularly closely related to the fantasy configurations mobilized as defenses against envy—hatred of the good object because it possesses and controls what is desirable (Klein 1957/1975). Because envy is directed toward the good object, envy and defenses against it interfere with the splitting of good and bad objects that is central to the paranoid-schizoid position. Rosenfeld (1964/1965) described the rigid constellation of omnipotent narcissistic object relations constructed by the narcissistic personality. This defensive configuration protects the narcissistic personality not only from envy but also from the persecutory anxiety of the paranoid-schizoid phase. In his or her approach to the narcissistic patient, the analyst must systematically interpret the patient's defensive denial of dependency on the analyst, of the analyst's autonomous thought and behavior, of the analyst's capacity to help the patient, and of the patient's envy of this capacity. As the analyst does so, the patient's distant stance will give way to a phase of paranoid object relations dominated by oral rage and envy. Ultimately, an awareness of a loving dependence on the analyst will emerge as well as a shift to the more integrated object world, including guilt and concern for the object, which is characteristic of the depressive position. Rosenfeld emphasized the importance of the analyst's forming an alliance with those aspects of the patient that have remained outside the narcissistic organization. The purely narcissistic patient would be unanalyzable. The successful analysis of the narcissistic patient ultimately rests on the integration of narcissistic aspects of the personality with healthier elements.

More recent Kleinians have built on Rosenfeld's concept of a rigid narcissistic fantasy structure that blocks the full experience of persecutory and depressive anxiety and have described a multiplicity of such structures (Joseph 1989; Meltzer 1968/1973; Sohn 1985/1988; Steiner 1993). In addition, whereas Klein and Rosenfeld (in his early work) emphasized the predominant influence of very early, instinctually driven organizations of fantasy on all later developmental epochs to the virtual exclusion of reconstructions of later influences, the contemporary Kleinians (Steiner 1993) and Rosenfeld (in his later work; 1987) moved toward a more detailed linkage of fantasy with individual experiences with external objects.

Winnicott and Balint

Writing contemporaneously with Klein in her later work and with Rosenfeld, Winnicott (1960/1965) and Balint (1968) took issue with the Kleinians' belief that the experience of the mother as part of the self served a primary defensive function. Both authors postulated an early nonconflictual phase in normal development in which the infant experienced the mother as a natural extension of the self. The narcissistic patient had experienced an environmental failure at this early phase and as a result had failed to internalize the mother as a secure part of psychic structure. This belief led to important divergences from classic analytical and Kleinian technique. Both authors saw the analysis of the narcissistic patient as biphasic. The interpretation of pathological structures, of defense and wish, led to a critical moment when the patient would resume as best as possible his or her interrupted line of development, this time with the analyst acting as a new "early object." At this moment, the specific content of the analyst's interpretation was less important than his or her recognition of the patient's situation. Balint, drawing on Ferenczi's work (1933/1955), argued that at these moments, the analyst's elaborated interpretation was detrimental to the patient because it distorted the patient's preverbal wishes by forcing them into the mold of the analyst's language. Winnicott (1975) emphasized the importance of the analytical setting, rather than the analyst's specific interpretations, in the treatment of such patients, particularly at times of regression.

Modell (1984), a current proponent of this view, envisions a sequence of three phases in the analysis of the narcissistic personality. In an initial "cocoon" phase, the patient uses analyst and analytical setting as a holding environment where he or she recapitulates early defensive aloofness and omnipotence; during this phase, the analyst must maintain an essentially noninterpretive accepting stance. In midphase, this defensive structure breaks down, and rage at early environmental failure emerges. In the final phase, which resembles classic transference neurosis, conflict is fully internalized and may be interpreted.

Kernberg

Kernberg's (1975) ego psychology–object relations model of pathological narcissism (described earlier in this volume in

Kernberg, Chapter 2), now the dominant theory in the United States, integrates Rosenfeld's concept of a pathological organization of narcissistic object relations with Jacobson's (1964) melding of ego psychology and object relations and Mahler's (Mahler et al. 1975) developmental theory. The central task of the treatment of the severe narcissistic personality, according to Kernberg, is the analysis of the pathological grandiose self as it emerges in the transference. He advocates that the analyst's stance should be neutral and interpretive throughout the course of the analysis. The narcissistic individual's seeming aloofness screens his or her wish to diminish the analyst, to defend the self against paranoid suspicions of the analyst, or to avoid a dependency that might lead to envy and frustration. Kernberg emphasizes the analyst's use of many channels in understanding the primitive transferences elaborated by these patients. In addition to the patient's verbal associations, his or her actions and the analyst's countertransference provide key data. After a lengthy, often discouraging period during which the analyst must repeatedly interpret the defensive functions of a relatively static transference configuration reflecting an underlying pathological grandiose self, this organization will, if the analysis is successful, give way first to an organization dominated by splitting and oral rage and finally to an organization of integrated whole objects in which more realistic oedipal material is expressed.

Although Kernberg's theoretical model emphasizes general characteristics of pathological narcissism, his clinical approach focuses on the uniqueness of the pathological grandiose self constructed by each patient and the uniqueness of the fantasies and experiences warded off by it. As the analysis progresses and the patient's manifest attitude toward the analyst is interpreted, specific unconscious fantasies underlying both the pathological grandiose self and the self's rejected contents begin to emerge. It is the analyst's detailed interpretation of these specific fantasies that leads to further unfolding of the analysis and ultimately to a lasting analytical result.

The Analytical Process With Narcissistic Patients

Selection of Patients for Psychoanalysis

Although psychoanalysis may afford the best possibility of lasting character change for narcissistic patients, selection criteria for those patients who will benefit from analysis remain quite imprecise. The Kleinians have characteristically analyzed a wide spectrum of patients without variations in technique. Kernberg (1984) considers analysis the treatment of choice for those narcissistic patients who do not function at an overt borderline level. At this level of organization, the narcissistic patient has established a cohesive, stable grandiose self, which permits stable—albeit distorted—object relations, impulse control, and tolerance of some painful affects without severe regression. However, a successful narcissistic patient whose rigid pathological grandiose self is confirmed in external reality may have little motivation for analysis or, if he or she does enter treatment, may be completely inaccessible to the analyst's interventions. In practice, it is a middle group of narcissistic individuals whose defenses do not constitute a closed system; who experience disappointment, pain, and the futility of their adaptation; and who seek and benefit from analysis.

The narcissistic patients who do best in analysis demonstrate higher-level, relatively complex, and realistic object relations alongside omnipotent narcissistic ones. These patients also have some capacity to experience guilt, concern, and depression, reflections of a degree of superego integration. Extensive paranoid reactions, which reflect the projection of unintegrated superego precursors, are a poor prognostic sign. Similarly, narcissistic patients with extensive antisocial features, such as delinquent behavior and widespread lying, have a poor prognosis, although recent explorations of the treatment of patients for whom lying and manipulation are central aspects of the transference convey some optimism about the analyzability of such conditions (Kernberg 1992; LaFarge 1995).

Another poor prognostic sign emphasized by Kernberg is the narcissistic patient's ready regression to primary process thinking. Such patients' cognition is infiltrated by grandiosity, and they tend to expect a magical result not only from the analyst's interventions but also from their own intuition. They are also prone to more severe regression, in which their magical thoughts acquire delusional conviction and their capacity to distinguish between transference fantasy and reality is lost. In general, fantasies and realistic expectations of analysis should be explored in some depth. Often the narcissistic patient agrees to enter analysis too readily, expecting to be made more perfect and taking the offer of analysis as a conquest, a confirmation of his or her special appeal to the analyst. Ultimately, both the diagnosis of pathological narcissism and a decision as to the patient's analyzability may be reached only after a trial period of analysis during which the unfolding of characteristic transferences and the patient's response to the interpretation of narcissistic defenses may be observed.

Opening Phase

In the opening phase of analysis, the patient for whom a pathological narcissistic structure is a dominant mode of defense tends to establish a stable transference configuration in which he or she remains relatively inaccessible to the analyst and the analyst's interpretations. This constellation may be evident from the beginning in a patient who seems uninterested in analysis and the analyst and with whom the analyst in turn feels bored and deadened. More often, the static narcissistic configuration becomes apparent as the analysis fails to deepen, despite the manifestly "analytical" efforts of patient and analyst. It is the analyst's task to identify the specific fantasy structure underlying the patient's rigid narcissistic object relations and to interpret both the many defensive functions that the structure serves and the highly condensed primitive object relations that emerge as defensive functions are interpreted. This task is generally lengthy and involves repeated interpretation of subtle transference manifestations that are hidden in a seemingly bland analytical relationship.

Case 1

Mr. A, a charming, articulate man, easily engaged the analyst's interest in his difficulties both with his cold and rejecting girlfriend and at work, where he had failed to advance despite his obvious talents. In the first few months of analysis, he spoke evocatively of transference fantasies, linking these to frequent interesting dreams. The analyst attempted to clarify the transference themes that emerged and what seemed to be defensive shifts between them. Mr. A would respond to these interpretations by producing memories and fantasies that exemplified whatever the analyst described, but he would never use them to try to understand the meaning of what he said. None of his elaborate transference fantasies appeared to be intensely felt, and none of them ever deepened. Mr. A would often react sharply to real transactions with the analyst—exclaiming angrily or forgetting to pay a bill when she canceled a session—but he never incorporated these reactions in the elaborate "transference fantasies" that dominated his associations, and he would brusquely reject any inquiries about them.

After several months, the analyst's interest in Mr. A began to fade. He had induced in her the same coolness and boredom that he had complained of in his girlfriend and his boss. The analyst came to realize that Mr. A wished to dazzle her and to use her interpretations as a confirmation of his successful self-analysis, while denying that she had any real importance to him. When she interpreted this to Mr. A, he at first criticized her interpretation, accusing her of being unanalytical and talking about their real relationship rather than the transference. As the analyst drew Mr. A's attention again and again to his wish to describe rather than to explore and to his dismissal of the analyst and her interpretations, Mr. A began to question his wish to create a superficial analytical performance, and he became anxious and depressed. If he could not please the analyst this way, he felt like a broken machine. The analyst was seen as a cold and mechanical mother. Neither had anything of value to give to the other.

Mr. A used the analysis to confirm a grandiose fantasy in which he possessed all the tools necessary for self-understanding without any active effort. The analyst was cast as a satellite, a shadow who would confirm his grandiosity. This fantasy structure, which dominated the opening phase of the analysis, returned again and again as material deepened in the succeeding years of the analysis. Repeated analysis of the same defensive constellation revealed that it was a highly condensed fantasy structure. The dazzling performer was at times a son, admired by each parent in turn; a father admired by a child; and an early phallic mother. Similarly, the object relations, warded off by the defensive constellation, incorporated material at many developmental levels, including fantasies of murderous competition as well as oral rage and deprivation.

Case 2

Ms. B defensively used confusion and vagueness in order to keep distant and maintain control over the analyst. In early sessions, Ms. B was often silent. She said that she felt empty and had trouble expressing her thoughts. Her descriptions of events with friends and at school, where she was having trouble studying, were so sparse and vague that the analyst had trouble following them and found herself listening with heightened attention, trying to piece together what Ms. B was saying. The analyst asked questions to clarify both the content of Ms. B's associations and the meaning of her vagueness and silence, but Ms. B's rambling replies only left the analyst more perplexed.

One day Ms. B reported that she had had a frightening dream about Nazis. She began to associate to the dream, speaking of sensory experiences that it had contained: the feel of the grass beneath her bare feet, the texture of the Nazis' uniforms. The analyst was confused by Ms. B's report. Only after Ms. B left did the analyst realize that Ms. B had never told her the dream. When she returned for the next session, the analyst pointed this out. Ms. B replied that her own experience of the dream had been of sensory fragments, some visual, some auditory, and some tactile. She

contrasted this dream with a more coherent dream a few
weeks before, which was also about Nazis. In the second
confused dream, she felt unreal and in fragments, but she
felt more in control than she did in the first dream; her confusion made the Nazi drama unreal and kept her from being
drawn into it. With the analyst as well, Ms. B said, she felt
more secure when she was confused and confusing. The
analyst would not get to know her too fast, and she would
not be "swallowed up" by the analysis.

Ms. B's withdrawal and confusing communication cast the
analyst in the role of a hungry pursuer, seeking after an elusive depriving patient. Analyst and patient enacted a fantasy in which,
via projective identification, the analyst was thought to contain
Ms. B's needs, and Ms. B herself was an idealized figure who
needed nothing. Continuing analysis of Ms. B's defensive confusion over many months led to the uncovering of this fantasy, then
to Ms. B's own oral rage, reflected in fantasies of dismembering
and cooking people who had disappointed her.

Ms. B's conscious self-experience as muddled and defective
screened a central unconscious fantasy of herself as powerful and
pursued, in total control of both her objects and her need for
them. This grandiose fantasy in turn warded off experiences of
frustration, anger, and envy. Oral determinants of this configuration were important, but Ms. B's sense of defect, her grandiosity,
and the needs that she rejected incorporated fantasies at other developmental levels as well. For example, Ms. B experienced herself in succession as sexually ambiguous and defective, then as the
cold rejecting object of the analyst's desire, and finally as driven
by her own sexual desire for the analyst. The repeated analysis of
this pattern led slowly to a shift in Ms. B's self-experience from
one of emptiness to an awareness of her wish to triumph over human needs to a gradual integration of her own desires.

Midphase

In midphase, the balance of the analysis gradually shifts, and the
pathological narcissistic structure that previously dominated the

analysis and appeared static and monolithic appears infrequently for brief periods as new and frightening material threatens to emerge. The analysis is now dominated by the aggressive fantasies that were warded off by an idealized omnipotent self-structure. Most often these emerge first as paranoid fantasies, then as the patient's own violent wishes toward hated objects, and finally as part of the patient's more complex experience of anger at whole objects toward whom he or she feels guilt and concern. This movement from distance to paranoid fantasy, rage, and guilt is repeated again and again in midphase as the predominant experience of paranoid fantasy and part objects gradually shifts to a predominant experience of more realistic whole objects toward whom the patient feels concern.

Case 3

In the first year of analysis, Mr. C saw himself as a master strategist who controlled the analyst's reactions to him, alternately exciting her with tales of his exploits and putting her in her place with crude jokes. He denied any real connection to the analyst, insisting that she might be replaced by a self-help book or a tape recorder that would register his associations. When she pressed him on his manipulativeness and his attempts to close her out of the sessions, he expressed fears that she might control him and that she had planned the analysis and was stimulating him to express thoughts that she had chosen, but he quickly dismissed these thoughts.

In the second year of analysis, Mr. C began to report angry fantasies. One group of these fantasies involved insects that inhabited the country where he had lived as a child. At first, these fantasies appeared only in dreams, and Mr. C did not connect them with his current life or the analysis; then he began to think of them in his waking life and to connect them with his experience of the analyst. After the analyst's long summer vacation, Mr. C reported a dream of a woman infested with bugs. Bugs crawled out of her mouth, and a clump of bugs fell out of her vagina. Mr. C felt terror and loathing when he looked at her. He had no associations to the dream.

A short break a few months later led to a second bug dream, this time of a giant preying mantis whose colorful shell resembled a suit the analyst often wore. Mr. C now spoke of his fear of the analyst. She seemed terrifying and controlling. She might take away essential parts of him. He felt as if she were invading him from her seat behind him, crawling inside his anus. Listening to her interpretations felt like "taking it up the ass." In successive months, Mr. C spoke of his wish to be close to the analyst, to feel comfortable and secure; but any absence or perceived rebuff led him to feel invaded. He began to speak of memories of setting bugs on fire and fantasies of submitting women to torture. He got up from the couch and paced the office, speaking of his wish to invade the analyst's space, take charge of it, and control her. He began to acknowledge his rage at the analyst as he imagined her spending weekends with her family, his rage at his mother when his sister was born, and his feeling that he had no impact on his parents. He felt that he had ruined the first part of the analysis with his crude manipulations and was afraid that he had depleted the analyst so badly that she would no longer try to understand him.

The Problem of Regression

Because pathological narcissistic structures have arisen largely as a defense against paranoid object relations, paranoid transferences are almost inevitable in the analysis of narcissistic patients. Throughout the analysis, paranoid transferences may emerge in response to the patient's disappointment or felt loss of the analyst. The intrusion of external reality into the analysis—in the form of a chance encounter with the analyst or a change in the concrete arrangements of the treatment—is another trigger of paranoid responses, both because such events are open to multiple readings and because these patients have often constructed a fragile idealization of the analyst that cannot incorporate many of the analyst's actual needs or qualities. In midphase, as the grandiose self becomes less powerful, specific aggressive wishes frequently emerge first in projected form as paranoid transferences.

Paranoid regression is most threatening to the analysis when the transference is dominated by the patient's fantasy of an idealized bad object, as described by Rosenfeld (1971). Kernberg (1984) identified the syndrome of malignant narcissism (see Kernberg, Chapter 2, this volume). In this configuration, the patient attempts to triumph over the analyst by destroying the analysis and himself or herself. The patient may lie to destroy communication in the analytical situation or demonstrate destructive power by self-mutilation or suicide (see Maltsberger, Chapter 14, this volume). Kernberg emphasizes the importance of analyzing brief microepisodes of paranoid regression that the patient may attempt to seal over. Untouched, these regressive experiences may crystallize into an unanalyzable delusional structure that will lead to the end of the analysis.

Bion (1967/1984) delineated a more circumscribed syndrome of cognitive regression that may lead to an impasse in the analysis of narcissistic patients. In the patients whom Bion describes, the characteristics of curiosity, arrogance, and stupidity reflect identifications with an infant who wishes to communicate with the mother and with a mother who rejects the infant's communications. The patient enacts an identification with the internalized powerful, bad, and truth-rejecting mother and casts the analyst in the role of the curious infant by attacking the analyst's attempts to understand the patient and to communicate that understanding. Alternately, the patient projects onto the analyst the role of the mother and feels that the analyst wishes to destroy the patient's perceptions and sanity.

Case 4

> Ms. D met with several analysts before making a final selection. In initial face-to-face sessions, she expressed her enthusiasm about the female analyst she had chosen, but her praise had a slightly condescending quality as she emphasized the analyst's cute small office and unpretentious dress as reasons for her choice. In her first session on the couch, her manner shifted abruptly. She lay stiff and silent for sev-

eral minutes. The analyst asked about her silence. "I don't know how you will get out of it," Ms. D replied. After a few more minutes of silence, she added that she felt as if the analyst was trying to get inside her. For several sessions, the analyst asked Ms. D about the reasons for her silence and anger. Ms. D spoke of her fear that the analyst would use the information she provided in order to hurt her. All Ms. D could do was keep silent or lie. Occasionally, she would speak of being impressed that the analyst kept trying and would recall her hopes for the analysis, which now seemed very far in the past. Then she would renew her attacks. The analyst pointed out that whenever Ms. D said anything positive about the analysis, she would quickly contradict herself and begin an attack on the analysis or on the analyst. It seemed like she did not wish to be hopeful about it or even to remember her recent hopes. Gradually, Ms. D's associations shifted to a feeling of humiliation that the analyst was sitting up while she was lying down and that she had to turn to the analyst for help. She began to associate somewhat more freely, speaking of an envied sister and of situations when she had felt dependent on someone who had seemed uninterested in her.

Ms. D had regressed abruptly as she lay down, shifting from an identification with a more positively colored grandiose self to a grandiose self dominated by sadistic wishes. As she expressed her anger, and as the analyst interpreted her wish to destroy the positive aspects of the analysis, she shifted back to a more positive narcissistic structure, and the analysis could proceed. However, this potential for malignant regression remained active, and Ms. D ultimately broke off her analysis in a paranoid regression, believing that the analyst wished to destroy the success that she had achieved in her work.

Late Phase

Throughout the opening phase and midphase, the narcissistic patient's transference to the analyst is most often rigid and stereotyped, colored by extreme affects. In the opening phase, when a pathological narcissistic structure is dominant, the analyst is alternately idealized as the representative of the patient's own protected grandiosity and devalued as the representative of rejected parts of the patient's self. As this grandiose structure breaks down, highly distorted, aggressive transference fantasies emerge. Often the patient projects sadistic wishes onto the analyst and develops a paranoid transference. At other moments, the patient is aware of his or her own anger and sees the analyst as the rightfully hated target of it. These negative transferences alternate with moments of idealization, when the analyst is justly admired.

As the predominantly aggressive transferences of midphase are analyzed, a new transference gradually emerges. Narcissistic patients begin to be aware of sadness, concern, and a feeling of human connectedness in their feelings toward the analyst, who is now seen as a more complex and realistic figure. Patients now see the analyst as a fallible person who has tried to help them as best he or she could. Often patients feel guilt for their own attempts to defeat the analyst by spoiling the analysis. They regret that for so many years they were unable to take in what the analyst gave them or to enjoy the closeness that was offered. This shift toward integration is reflected in the quality of the patients' associations and the structure of individual sessions. Patients are more reflective, and the work has a more collaborative quality as roles are less rigidly defined by projective identification. Fantasies are less bizarre and extreme. More realistic, detailed memories emerge, and the patients' childhood figures take on a more complex, lifelike aspect. Although these patients have often experienced considerable trauma, they no longer see themselves simply as victims of powerful, bad objects. Instead, their disappointments and injuries appear complicated, and their objects seem less powerful and knowing. The felt malevolence of early objects is seen in part as the result of the patients' own projected anger. At this time, genetic interpretations can be made without oversimplifying the patients' material, and patients often make these linkages themselves. The shift toward a more integrated transference occurs repeatedly as threads of negative transference are analyzed and worked through until the more complex, modulated, and sad but loving relationship becomes the dominant one.

The shift toward a more complex, realistic experience of objects is reflected in a shift in the patient's experience of oedipal conflict. Early in the analysis, oedipal material often appears in highly distorted form. One parent may be excluded entirely from the patient's associations, in affirmation of the patient's fantasy that he or she enjoys an unbroken attachment to the other. If both parents appear, envy may be defensively warded off by a fantasy that the two have no meaningful connection to each other. The interpretation of the patient's denial of the link between the parents often leads to the exposure of terrifying fantasies of the primal scene. The patient's resentment of the parents' relationship is expressed in the fantasy that their union is dominated by hatred. The coital parents may be seen as a single terrifying body, willfully stirring the patient's rage as they share the pleasures of sexuality. Under conditions of extreme aggression, this combined figure is perceived as entirely malevolent, mechanical, and stripped of human qualities. As the patient's rage surfaces and is analyzed at midphase, this combined figure of the parents breaks apart into two parents; each is more loved than hated, and each is perceived more realistically. Envy and competition no longer trigger catastrophic rage and regression. At this point, more realistic, oedipal transferences emerge, and the analysis loses its fantastical cast and is on the more familiar territory of the transference neurosis.

As the analysis has progressed, the analyst's countertransference has also shifted. Early in the analysis, the patient's grandiosity often leads to a shared idealization of the analytical pair. At the same time, his or her aloofness and lack of real responsiveness to the analyst often evoke boredom and anger in the analyst. The patient's rage and paranoid reactions at midphase evoke painful counterreactions in the analyst. As the patient's transference to the analyst deepens and becomes more complex, the analyst's countertransference response deepens as well. The analyst feels sadness and sympathy for the pain the patient has suffered and admiration for the patient's determination to analyze and to change.

Case 5

Early in her analysis, Ms. E appeared cool and withdrawn. Often silent, she listened with seeming interest to her (female) analyst's interpretations, then continued with her own thoughts as if the analyst had never spoken. Outside the analysis, she had few friends. She professed horror of the dating scene, seeing women who were sexually active as sluts and men as cruel and exploitative. She described her parents' marriage as friendly but asexual, seeing the mother as a powerful, exciting figure and the father as an inferior satellite who did the mother's bidding.

The analyst's interpretation of Ms. E's aloofness led to the uncovering of an important fantasy of a secret stronghold. Ms. E represented this fantasy concretely in a screen memory of barricading herself in her room as a child and, in a series of dreams, withdrawing into a house or cave to withstand a series of catastrophes: a nuclear holocaust, World War II, or the Vietnam War. The analysis of the meaning of these dangers and the linking of external disaster to Ms. E's own projected rage were central themes of a long midphase.

In the sixth year of analysis, when Ms. E had become considerably more responsive in the sessions and had established several deeper friendships, she reported a dream: She was in hiding in a house like Anne Frank's. The war was over! It was time for Ms. E to come out and reclaim her property. She had to sign a document attesting to her victimization. As she held the document in her hand, Ms. E was aware of both her pride and her pleasure in testifying to her victimization and of her wish to remain in her snug hiding place forever. Associating to her dream, Ms. E spoke of the triumph over the analyst that she felt by remaining a victim. She would have won the analysis! The analyst would never have reached her or helped her!

In the sessions that followed, Ms. E tried to imagine what it would mean to succeed in another way: to go out in the world and make a life for herself. She recognized her own growing power of self-analysis and felt guilty that her new capacity might represent a threat to her analyst, as if she was taking away something that belonged to the analyst. She thought of the analyst's marriage and her parents' marriage. Recalling a movie in which the hero recognizes his father's virtue only at the father's deathbed, she thought with real sadness of her long-standing contempt for her own father. It had not always been so, she said. As a young child, she had admired the father and coveted his company. Only after a business failure in the patient's school years had she begun to see the father as the disappointing devalued figure whom she had described in the analysis. The father now appeared in a host of memories, a more complex figure whom Ms. E had loved and whose union with the mother she had envied.

Termination Phase

In the successful analysis of the narcissistic patient, the analysis in the transference of a pathological narcissistic structure has led first to the emergence of an organization of the object world dominated by splitting and primitive aggression and then to the integration of split representations of self and object into complex realistic representations of whole objects. These changes in the organization of the object world are reflected in shifts in object relations, ego, and superego functions. The attainment of object constancy, which has previously been blocked by the pathological structure, can now be securely achieved. As the narcissistic patient's impoverished object world deepens and becomes more complex, the emptiness and alienation characteristic of pathological narcissism become less prominent, and the patient feels sustained at times of stress and loneliness by the presence of beloved internal objects. Relations with external objects also change, becoming less rigid, stereotyped, and exploitative. The shallow affect associated with narcissistic object relations and the primitive rage associated with splitting are succeeded by the more complex and modulated affects associated with integrated representations. The integration of representations within the superego leads to a tempering of harsh persecutory representations, a heightened tolerance of guilt and internal conflict, and a lessened tendency to paranoid projection of superego elements.

Termination becomes possible when the narcissistic patient has achieved a higher-level, integrated organization of self- and object representations and can maintain this level of organization in a relatively stable manner under conditions of stress and loss. One indication of this achievement is the patient's ability to tolerate separations from the analyst with sadness rather than paranoid regression. Another is the patient's growing capacity for self-analysis. As Steiner (1993) observes, the narcissistic patient at first tolerates the integration of good and bad aspects of self and object only by using the analyst as a container. The patient projects bad elements of his or her inner world onto the analyst, who, by tolerating and interpreting them, helps the patient to accept them as part of himself or herself. Only in a late phase of analysis does the patient relinquish this use of the analyst and recognize and integrate painful aspects of his or her own psychic reality without reliance on projection and on the analyst's presence.

At termination, narcissistic patients must mourn the use of the analyst as a part of themselves as well as the loss of the analyst as a separate person with whom, over the years, they have developed a complex and rich relationship. A prolonged termination phase is often necessary to accomplish this dual task, and the final work of mourning remains for patients' self-analysis after termination. Both defensive revivals of narcissistic structures and transient paranoid regressions are frequent during the termination phase. Patients' relatively autonomous capacity to understand and resolve these reactions consolidates the work of mourning and the sense of mastery with which they leave analysis. Paranoid regression remains a danger after termination, and severe and prolonged regression is an indication for a return for further analytical work. In the end, it is the patients' continuing capacity to tolerate awareness of painful aspects of psychic reality, to analyze their reactions to them, and to right themselves when regression threatens that guarantees their stability after they have left the analyst's care.

References

Balint M: The Basic Fault. London, Tavistock, 1968

Bion WR: On arrogance (1967), in Second Thoughts. London, Maresfield, 1984, pp 43–64

Ferenczi S: Confusion of tongues between adult and child (1933), in The Selected Papers of Sandor Ferenczi, Vol 3. Translated by Mosbacher E. Edited by Balint M. New York, Basic Books, 1955, pp 156–167

Freud S: On narcissism: an introduction (1914), in The Standard Edition of the Complete Psychological Works of Sigmund Freud, Vol 14. Translated and edited by Strachey J. London, Hogarth Press, 1957, pp 67–102

Freud S: An outline of psychoanalysis (1938), in The Standard Edition of the Complete Psychological Works of Sigmund Freud, Vol 23. Translated and edited by Strachey J. London, Hogarth Press, 1964, pp 141–207

Isaacs S: The nature and function of phantasy, in Developments in Psycho-Analysis. [by Klein M, Heimann P, Isaacs S, Riviere J]. Edited by Riviere J. London, Hogarth Press, 1952, pp 67–121

Jacobson E: The Self and the Object World. New York, International Universities Press, 1964

Joseph B: Psychic Equilibrium and Psychic Change. London, Routledge, 1989

Kernberg O: Borderline Conditions and Pathological Narcissism. New York, Jason Aronson, 1975

Kernberg O: Severe Personality Disorders. New Haven, CT, Yale University Press, 1984

Kernberg O: Psychopathic, paranoid and depressive transferences. Int J Psychoanal 73:13–28, 1992

Klein M: Notes on some schizoid mechanisms (1946), in Envy and Gratitude and Other Works, 1946–1963, Vol 3. London, Hogarth Press, 1975, pp 1–24

Klein M: Some theoretical conclusions regarding the emotional life of the infant (1952), in Envy and Gratitude and Other Works, 1946–1963, Vol 3. London, Hogarth Press, 1975, pp 61–93

Klein M: Envy and gratitude (1957), in Envy and Gratitude and Other Works, 1946–1963, Vol 3. London, Hogarth Press, 1975, pp 176–235

LaFarge L: Transferences of deception. J Am Psychoanal Assoc 43: 765–792, 1995

Mahler M, Pine F, Bergman A: The Psychological Birth of the Human Infant. New York, Basic Books, 1975

Meltzer D: Terror, persecution and dread (1968), in Sexual States of Mind. Perthshire, England, Clunie Press, 1973, pp 99–106

Modell A: Psychoanalysis in a New Context. New York, International Universities Press, 1984

Rosenfeld H: On the psychopathology of narcissism: a clinical approach (1964), in Psychotic States: A Psychoanalytical Approach. London, Hogarth Press, 1965, pp 169–179

Rosenfeld H: A clinical approach to the psychoanalytic theory of the life and death instincts: an investigation into the aggressive aspects of narcissism. Int J Psychoanal 52:169–178, 1971

Rosenfeld H: Impasse and Interpretation. London, Tavistock, 1987

Segal H: Some clinical implications of Melanie Klein's work: emergence from narcissism. Int J Psychoanal 64:269–276, 1983

Sohn L: Narcissistic organization, projective identification, and the formation of the identificate (1985), in Melanie Klein Today: Developments in Theory and Practice, Vol 1. Edited by Spillius E. London, Routledge, 1988, pp 271–292

Steiner J: Psychic Retreats. London, Routledge, 1993

Winnicott D: Ego distortion in terms of true and false self (1960), in The Maturational Processes and the Facilitating Environment. London, Hogarth Press, 1965, pp 140–152

Winnicott D: Through Paediatrics to Psychoanalysis. London, Hogarth Press, 1975

Chapter 9

Treatment of Narcissistic Disorders in the Intensive Psychiatric Milieu

Ralph H. Beaumont, M.D.

In 1914, Freud described a group of people who "in their later choice of a love object had taken as a model, not their mother, but their own selves. They are plainly seeking themselves as a love object, and are establishing a type of object choice which must be termed 'narcissistic.' In this observation we have the strongest of the reasons which have led us to adopt the hypothesis of narcissism" (Freud 1914/1957, p. 88). In the same essay, Freud described the characteristics of narcissistic object choice and distinguished it from anaclitic object choice in the following specific way:

> A person may love—(1) According to the narcissistic type: (a) what he himself is (i.e., himself), (b) what he himself was, (c) what he himself would like to be, (d) someone who was once part of himself. (2) According to the anaclitic (attachment) type: (a) the woman who feeds him, (b) the man who protects him, and the succession of substitutes who take their place. (p. 90)

Later in the essay, Freud adds another distinction. For those making narcissistic object choices, he noted, "Nor does their need lie in the direction of loving, but of being loved" (p. 89). The distinction is between those whose need to be loved is in the context of reciprocity for their own loving attachments and those who need to be loved to enhance their investment in themselves.

These distinctions remain paradigmatic today, even with the current theoretical pluralism, in the therapeutic efforts with severely ill patients in the intensive psychiatric milieu (IPM). This is so despite a great many theoretical developments (e.g., Sandler et al. 1991) and accumulations of observational data that have occurred since these distinctions were drawn. In particular, the concept of narcissistic object choice, which Freud saw as the "strongest of the reasons" to adopt the hypothesis of narcissism, contains a central paradox that has shaped the paradigm of narcissism. It has defined the terms of subsequent theoretical and nosological developments, and its dilemmas apparently accompany the daily pragmatic therapeutic involvements in the IPM. The paradox of narcissistic object choice is that it involves simultaneously in one psychic movement the choice of another and of oneself.

Narcissistic Disorders and Treatment Responsiveness

The conceptual strain of this paradox first appeared in Freud's own application of the hypothesis of narcissism to the therapeutic process. Freud considered the vicissitudes of anaclitic instinctual object choices to be etiological for the transference neuroses, which, by virtue of their tendency in the psychoanalytical situation to lead to anaclitic transferential investments in the analyst, were susceptible to analytical influence. Narcissistic object choices, on the other hand, led to narcissistic neuroses, which, because of the relative absence of transferential investment in the analyst, were not responsive to psychoanalytical treatment. Nosologically, Freud focused on paranoia, schizophrenia, and affective disorders as narcissistic conditions without always strictly coupling descriptive presentations to his underlying dynamic nosology.

His clinical considerations concerning potential responsiveness to treatment have led to a great deal of controversy and creative ferment. Many investigators (Federn 1952; Kernberg 1975, 1984; Klein 1935/1975, 1946/1975; Kohut 1971, 1979, 1984; Rosenfeld 1965, 1987; Sullivan 1940, 1962) have challenged the view that narcissistic conditions do not produce therapeutically useful transference and that they are not responsive to psychoanalytical treatment. In this sense, Freud's original distinction between narcissistic and anaclitic object choices has been more paradigmatic than his clinical application of the distinction to questions of responsiveness to treatment. It is as if two distinct conceptually countertransferential positions have emerged in response to the original paradox of narcissistic object choice. Those who share Freud's position of therapeutic conservatism (e.g., Fenichel 1945; Glover 1958; Greenson 1967; Gutterman 1968; Knight 1953/1954; Waldhorn 1960) emphasize the narcissism in narcissistic object choice and remind us of the distinction between narcissistic and anaclitic object choice. Those who see more therapeutic potential for narcissistic conditions (Fairbairn 1952; Klein 1932/1975, 1935/1975, 1946/1975; Kohut 1977, 1984; Sullivan 1940; Winnicott 1951/1958, 1965) emphasize the object relations inherent in narcissistic object choice and tend to collapse the distinction between narcissistic and anaclitic object choice.

Many theoretical developments can be understood in light of these divergent conceptual stances. Kleinian theorists (Klein 1932/1975, 1935/1975, 1946/1975) have found therapeutic potential in collapsing narcissistic object choice into primitive aggression–laden anaclitic object choices within the paranoid-schizoid position, where they are subject to the defensive vicissitudes of splitting and projective identification. Object relations theorists (Mitchell 1988; Sullivan 1940) have tended to eliminate the distinction altogether, emphasizing instead less clearly motivated but highly invariant affect-laden internalized object relations. Interpersonal theorists have used the strategy of eliminating the distinction by literalizing questions about motivations guiding intrapsychic object choices with their emphasis on concrete social contexts. Freudian ego psychologists have used a mixture of approaches.

Many clinicians (e.g., Hartmann 1964; Kris 1975; Stone 1961) have worked with models that include consideration of both narcissistic and anaclitic object choices, with varying but often modest views of the therapeutic potential for conditions related to the former. Some (e.g., Brenner 1982) have eliminated consideration of narcissism altogether. Others (e.g., Arlow and Brenner 1964), following Abraham (1919/1979), have held to Freud's clinical dichotomy while also moving toward collapsing the distinction by relegating narcissistic phenomena to a subordinate defensive role. Narcissistic defenses, with effective interpretation, are seen then as yielding to vicissitudes of instinctualized anaclitic object choices. Self psychologists (e.g., Kohut 1977, 1984), in contrast, have collapsed the distinction by placing the phenomenon of infantile anaclitic object choices in a subordinate defensive role as breakdown products of thwarted strivings for narcissistic fulfillment. At times, self psychologists have emphasized in their considerations of narcissism the self and its nature, representation, differentiation, structure, cohesiveness or lack thereof, continuous and discontinuous properties, and related issues, thereby avoiding the paradoxical clinical complexities of the object choices inherent in narcissistic conditions. Some developmental theorists have subtly diminished the distinction between anaclitic and narcissistic object choices by shifting the emphasis to the difference between need gratification in the presence of and the absence of the gradual developmental accretion of internal object representations. Theories that emphasize trauma in pathogenesis (e.g., Herman 1992; Rothstein 1986; van der Kolk 1984) sometimes collapse the distinction by viewing narcissistic phenomena as traumatic transformations of anaclitic object choices.

These many elaborations, though never resolving the paradigmatic paradox, have yielded a rich harvest of clinical concepts, such as a deeper understanding of early object relations as manifested in both adults and infants; greater insight into narcissistic and pre-oedipal contributions to oedipal developmental vicissitudes; much information about primitive defensive processes; new notions about vicissitudes of narcissistic object relations, including narcissistic transferential phenomena; new perspectives about the relations of the intrapsychic and the interpersonal, including interpersonal defenses and the notion of the "two person psychology" (Modell 1984); new views of trauma and its relation to ego functioning; and concepts about the development and dynamic status of psychic representation. Many of these explanatory constructs have had particular relevance to clinical work in the IPM.

The nosology of narcissism has also been an area of striking innovation. The narcissistic neuroses originally described by Freud have given way to a varied array of descriptive categories, which have often reflected underlying theoretical elaborations of the problem of narcissistic object choice. Among these have been schizoid personality, borderline personality, psychotic personality, pseudoneurotic schizophrenia, the as-if personality, states of identity diffusion, and narcissistic personality. The last disorder has been associated with a variety of phenomenological pictures, ranging from persons with subtle neurotic disturbances of character to profoundly withdrawn individuals with antisocial personality structures and from those manifesting self-absorption, arrogance, and smugness to depressive masochistic persons with vulnerable self-esteem and preoccupied Walter Mitty–like dreamers. Some approaches emphasize the narcissistic pole of the paradox by focusing on the radical withdrawal from and devaluation of object ties. Others emphasize the object tie in narcissistic disorders and give us accounts of disturbed empathy, entitlement, exploitation, subordination, disqualification, collusion, folie à deux, and the like. The borderline concept, drawing heavily on developmental thinking, has employed a strategy of cautious therapeutic ambition by narrowing the distinction between narcissistic and anaclitic investments and locating a sometimes treatable but difficult middle ground.

Intensive Psychiatric Milieu

In one way, the IPM is familiar to most mental health care providers. Patients with severe illnesses are seen for large blocks of time for the purpose of providing treatment in psychiatric hospitals, general hospital psychiatric units, residential treatment programs, halfway houses, day treatment programs, substance abuse rehabilitation programs, psychiatric vocational rehabilitation programs, and so forth. How to define these settings is less certain. It is difficult to define the unique characteristics of techniques as thoroughly studied as psychotherapy and psychoanalysis, let alone the distinctive features of the intensive group settings in which psychiatric treatment, rather than something else, is provided to severely ill people. Indeed, images of bedlam, snake pits, cuckoo's nests, total institutions, and authoritarian oppression of disenfranchised groups often readily prevail.

One approach to definition is by contrast, that is, in terms of what an IPM is not. Treatment in an IPM, for example, is not individual or group psychotherapy. These psychotherapies are treatment modalities defined by boundaries of intermittently scheduled sessions, a high priority on verbal communication, and certain limitations on the responsibility assumed by the caregivers. Although the latter may be metaphorically extensive, it is exercised largely from a distance, with the literal details left almost entirely to the patient. In contrast, in the IPM, the patient is present for extensive continuous periods. Boundaries are necessarily defined in many ways other than through scheduled sessions and the therapist-patient role asymmetry of psychotherapy. Communication is more global, with greater acceptance of the idea that actions and symptoms may often speak louder than words. The responsibility assumed by caregivers for the well-being—and not infrequently the safety—of patients is inevitably more literal and immediate.

The IPM is also not housing, custodial care, or maintenance care. Patients with severe psychiatric illnesses often must deal with social alienation and poverty and need food and shelter. They also frequently require some level of treatment in order to maintain a status quo in terms of pathology and to avoid deterioration. The settings made available for these purposes differ from the IPM, because the latter is characterized by the provision of active and intensive treatment that is expected to result in significant change in severe psychiatric pathology.

The last example of definition by contrast is perhaps both more and—at other telling clinical moments—less obvious. The IPM is not a prison. The latter is characterized by a highly authoritarian social structure. Those present have been judged to be guilty of crimes, and their presence is imposed. The purpose of their incarceration may be seen variously as punishment or segregation from society, but the individual's health and well-being are not the priority. In the IPM, the asymmetries in social structure, however much apparently authoritarian or egalitarian, are subordinated to the purpose of providing treatment, which is understood as the patient's right. The patient's presence is defined by illness, not guilt. Attendance is voluntary, with the exception of dangerousness caused by illness, which is subject to the concurrence of both medical experts and legal authorities.

These examples of definition by contrast are, on one level, simple and obvious but are, in other ways, sometimes laden with ambiguities of profoundly significant emotional moments (especially for the participants in treatment of narcissistic disorders) as well as with transferential and countertransferential importance. The author hopes that the pragmatic relevance of these ambiguities of definition will become apparent in the next section on treatment.

Another kind of definition, sometimes of interest to anthropologists when they describe social and cultural institutions, is definition by creation myth. Although sometimes lacking the advantages of historical veridicality, narratives of this kind—such as dreams, fairy tales, and unconscious fantasies—can be quite revealing not only about origins but also about contemporary dynamics. Foucault (1965) emphasized the legendlike quality of accounts given of the origins of psychiatric hospitals. Among the available accounts are those describing Philippe Pinel, the French Enlightenment physician who is known as a founder of the moral treatment, the nineteenth-century movement emphasizing humane treatment of the mentally ill in hospitals. Zilboorg (1941), the psychoanalyst historian, described Pinel as follows:

> Pinel saw Napoleon come and go and served assiduously under the restored bourbons. He bore the decorations and honors of all these conflicting regimes, yet remained true to himself—a consistent and devout hospital worker to whom the care of the mentally ill was a task beyond and above the historical agitation which he witnessed and which actually knocked at his door, daily and sharply. (p. 319)

Pinel is particularly noted for having unchained the mentally ill during the revolution in Paris. The following is Zilboorg's 1941 account:

> Revolutionary Paris knew no more of psychiatry than did the Paris of Marie Antoinette but certainly it should have appreciated the dramatic act of restoring corporal liberty to those who were eaten to the bone by iron chains. Yet Pinel was informed that he could not carry out his plan without the permission of the Bureau Central and the authorization of the Commune.
>
> Pinel waited a few days and then decided to plead personally before the Commune itself. The spirit of Marat pervaded that august body. Everyone was suspicious. Everyone was afraid that a lurking enemy was ready to kill him and everyone was ready to return in kind. The president of the Commune was Couthon, a cripple who was paralyzed and unable to walk but a man with a passionate soul, imbued with the spirit of strife and aflame with the idea of defending the Revolution against any danger. He turned on Dr. Pinel: "Woe to you if you deceive me and if you hide enemies of the people among your insane!" Pinel quietly explained that what he was presenting to the Commune was the truth. "We shall see," threatened Couthon. The following day, Couthon, before whom everyone trem-

bled, had himself carried directly into the Bicetre. He wanted personally to question the insane. He received in answer for the most part only curses and vulgar apostrophes. Couthon turned to Pinel, "Well, citizen, are you mad yourself that you want to unchain these animals?" Pinel's reply was simple: "Citizen, it is my conviction that these mentally ill are intractable only because they are deprived of fresh air and of their liberty." Couthon retorted, "You may do what you please, but I am afraid that you are the victim of your own presumptions." (p. 322)

In this somewhat mythic narrative, an ironic counterpoint is drawn between the credible engagement of the dynamics of liberation and oppression by Pinel and the more questionable approach of the revolution. Why does an almost parodic contrast have a place in a narrative of the origins of the IPM? The answer is that the dynamics inherent in the liberation provided by Pinel's moral treatment are predominately those of narcissistic object choice in patients with severe psychiatric illness. The paradoxical and ironic contrast is that between narcissistic and anaclitic object choice, with Pinel as the idealized narcissistically gratifying object who rises above the anaclitically disastrous parents, Marie Antoinette and Couthon. Perhaps it is no coincidence that one of Freud's first published elaborations of the dynamics of narcissistic object choice appears in his analysis of the Schreber memoir (Freud 1911/1957), an account of a man with paranoid illness who was treated in a nineteenth-century psychiatric hospital.

Treatment of Narcissistic Disorders in the Intensive Psychiatric Milieu

The paradigmatic yet paradoxical notion of narcissistic object choice has left central questions unresolved in the contemporary discussion of the treatment of narcissistic disorders. For example, to what extent is it necessary that treatment bring about a shift from narcissistic investments and object choices to more anaclitic and, as some would say, mature object relations? Kohut (1971, 1977, 1979, 1984) proposed a second alternative. As he developed his views on narcissistic disorders, he questioned what he saw as his own "maturity morality" (Kohut 1979) and suggested ways in which treatment might involve a shift in the patient to healthier transformations of narcissism and narcissistic object choice. A third frequently endorsed position (e.g., Greenblatt 1972), which finds some support in Freud's doubts about psychoanalytical influence in narcissistic conditions, questions the extent to which intrapsychic change is a feasible treatment goal in patients with narcissistic disorders. According to this view, symptomatic change and environmental adjustment should be sought rather than a shift toward greater intrapsychic adaptation.

Nonspecific and Specific Interventions

How, then, do investments in these and other positions (and, more often perhaps, oscillations among variations in them) manifest themselves in the clinical work in the IPM with these patients? A common approach to interventions in the IPM is to divide them into nonspecific and specific categories. *Nonspecific interventions,* historically derived from the model of Pinel and other originators of the nineteenth-century moral treatment, involve provision for the patients' physical and psychological safety. Patients who come into the IPM are, in this perspective, in some way out of control. Extremes of behavior, thought, affect, and physiological function have occurred. A consensus has been reached that their usual human surround cannot respond adequately to the patients' witting or unwitting sufferings. An environment significantly different from that in which the uncontrollable pathological manifestations occurred is put into place around the patient. The means by which this is accomplished are varied, but the characteristics of the interventions are nonspecific and similar in quality. Some typical examples are presented in Table 9–1.

Table 9–1.   Examples of nonspecific interventions in the intensive psychiatric milieu

Hospitalization

Medical treatment of physiological dysfunction consequent to psychopathology

Provision of food and shelter

Prevention of self-harm through seclusion, restraint, staff observation, etc.

Segregation from the pathogenic environment through the use of a locked setting, privileges, legal commitment, supervised visits, etc.

Consistent, reliable, predictable, and benevolent attention to psychological needs by clinical staff

One aspect of these interventions is an element of concreteness that is far less available in the necessarily more metaphorical realms of psychic representation of the psychotherapeutic situation. Inextricably associated with the IPM are literal means of one kind or another of demonstrating an investment in the psychological and physical well-being of the patient. Such an association could not be better designed to invite, evoke, and provide for the external social elaboration and expression of whatever vicissitudes of narcissistic object relations are dynamically active in the patients' psyches. It is in just such transference- and countertransference-charged social contexts that the ambiguities suggested by my dialectical definition of the IPM often become relevant with great emotional immediacy. Thus, we hear patients exclaim, "This is not a hospital. This is nothing but a hotel!" Or, "What gives you the right to set limits? Do you not understand that this is psychotherapy?" Or, "How can you lock me up in this prison? I have committed no crime." Caregivers, correspondingly, may also respond to the interpersonal ambiguities of the IPM with the authoritarian stance of a prison warden; with psychotherapeutic zeal that neglects other important aspects of the treatment setting; or, like a hotel manager, with concern about profit and the filling of beds but without an overriding interest in providing effective treatment.

Many analytical therapists from widely differing perspectives—including Greenacre (1954), Winnicott (1965), Bion (1970), Stanton and Schwartz (1954), Stone (1961), Kernberg (1984), Gunderson (1978), and Modell (1984)—have emphasized some version of nonspecific measures. Among the more familiar formulations are Winnicott's holding environment and Bion's notion of containment. The following is an example of Winnicott (1956/1958) applying his approach to the IPM in his well-known paper "The Antisocial Tendency":

> Briefly, the treatment of the antisocial tendency is not psycho-analysis. It is the provision of child care which can be rediscovered by the child, and into which the child can experiment again with the id impulses, and which can be tested. It is the stability of the new environmental provision which gives the therapeutics. Id impulses must be experienced, if they are to make sense, in a framework of ego relatedness, and when the patient is a deprived child ego relatedness must derive support from the therapist's side of the relationship. According to the theory put forward in this paper it is the environment that must give new opportunity for ego relatedness since the child has perceived that it was an environmental failure in ego support that originally led to the antisocial tendency. (p. 315)

In a telling addendum, he suggests something about the unique utility of the concrete provisions of the IPM in these patients.

> If the child is in analysis, the analyst must either allow the weight of the transference to develop outside the analysis, or else must expect the antisocial tendency to develop full strength in the analytic situation, and must be prepared to bear the brunt. (p. 315)

In the IPM, *specific interventions* pick up where the results of the consistency and benevolence of nonspecific interventions leave off. These interventions consist of technical procedures used to 1) identify appropriate diagnostic categories and specific pathogenic factors and 2) ameliorate the illnesses identified, both in their symptomatic manifestations and in their underlying etiologies. Various experts find that patients have not only disorders described in the diagnostic manual but also (to mention a few etiological possibilities) biochemical imbalances, disturbed patterns of behavioral reinforcement, cognitive deficits, psychological trauma, unconscious reminisces, interpersonal conflicts, endocrine dysfunctions, intrapsychic conflicts, developmental arrests, demoralization, low self-esteem, superego lacunae, brain lesions, perversions and inhibitions of desire, excessive and primitive hatred, fragmented senses of self, blocked grief, family secrets, interpersonal collusions, folie à deux, attachments to pain and defeat, and electrophysiological and structural brain disturbances. In response to the conditions identified, a wide array of techniques exemplifying the ingenuity of twentieth-century psychiatry are applied. Some familiar examples are listed in Table 9–2.

Effects of Interventions on Narcissistic Pathology

To the extent that nonspecific and specific interventions are effective, as they often are, manifestations of narcissistic pathology diminish. The holding environment of the IPM may enable and reinforce benign and healthy narcissistic object choices and diminish intrapsychic investments in pathogenic narcissistic object relations. The mechanism of therapeutic action of holding interventions may be understood as literal, metaphoric, or some mixture of the two. Literalists, whose explanations often have the endorsement of patients, families, courts, and other interested nonprofessional participants and observers, often view the patient who has responded positively as having been given what was needed and as having benefited from the caring ministrations and concern of the professionals involved. Narcissistic sustenance has been provided by the designated experts with salutary results. More metaphorical explanations suggest that shifts toward less primitive defenses are mediated by convincing transferential demonstrations of the feasibility of object relations

Table 9–2. Examples of specific interventions in the intensive psychiatric milieu

Psychosurgery altering brain structure

Electroconvulsive therapy altering electrophysiological brain function

Psychopharmacological agents altering brain chemistry

Treatment of associated medical conditions altering secondary effects on brain function

Behavior therapy altering behavioral reinforcement hierarchies

Psychodynamic psychotherapy altering intrapsychic dynamics

Therapeutic milieu participation altering interpersonal dynamics

Psychoeducational and topically focused groups altering pathological denial and lack of information

Therapeutic groups altering interpersonal and intrapsychic dynamics

Family psychoeducational counseling altering lack of family support and information

Family therapy altering pathological family dynamics

Recreational and occupational therapy altering pathological patterns of using leisure time

Vocational therapy altering deficits in vocational skills and functioning

Self-help groups altering pathological denial, isolation, and lack of information

Therapeutic school attendance altering educational deficits and patterns of functioning

Provision of a structured privilege system altering deficits in interpersonal autonomy and responsibility

Supportive staff talks altering deficits in reality testing, feelings of demoralization, patterns of interpersonal withdrawal, etc.

Cognitive therapy altering abnormal patterns of cognitive processing

that are less primitive and more satisfactory. Whatever more abstract explanations of intrapsychic shifts are offered, however, many theorists from differing orientations (Brenner 1982; Kohut 1977, 1984; Schwaber 1988; Winnicott 1965) agree that some element of literal gratification of the patient's needs plays a significant role. For holding interventions, in one form or another, the literalist epistemology of therapeutic action tends to prevail. Not coincidentally, this view of the IPM as an idealized source of narcissistic supplies is most unambiguously suggested by the same groups and individuals in the community at large that support the existence of the IPM.

Various specific interventions may effect shifts in the dynamic balance of forces in a narcissistic equilibrium through different mechanisms of action (see Table 9–2). Here, in contrast to holding interventions, epistemological priority tends to be given to the expert caregivers who design, provide, and explain their interventions. A positive result of treatment in a psychodynamically structured therapeutic milieu setting may, for example, be seen as the result of specific interpersonal interactions that diminish the predominance of pathogenic narcissistic object choices and increase more adaptive and therapeutically accessible anaclitic object relations. Explanations of this kind are often applied to efforts with borderline and depressed patients. Winnicott (1956/1958) had a similar explanation in mind when he described the IPM treatment of antisocial adolescents:

> In a favorable case, where there is not too much madness or unconscious compulsion or paranoid organization, etc., the favorable conditions may in the course of time enable the child to find and love a person, instead of confining the search through laying claims on substitute objects that had lost their symbolic value.
>
> In the next stage, the child needs to be able to experience despair in a relationship, instead of hope alone. Beyond this is the real possibility of a life for the child. When the wardens and staff of a hostel carry a child through all the "processes" they have done a therapy that is surely comparable to analytic work. (p. 314)

Other approaches to specific interventions, which have already been mentioned, may point to shifts toward healthier vicissitudes of narcissistic object relations or to symptomatic relief that is independent of accompanying narcissistic dynamics. The former is often applied to patients with descriptively narcissistic personalities, patients with trauma, hypochondriacal patients, and the more accessible schizoid patients. The more symptomatic approach is often taken toward patients with major psychotic disorders, antisocial personalities, many forms of perversion, and severe schizoid conditions.

Even these general associations, however, are most tentative. Taken at face value, they would be confronted not only by challenges involving the observable data of therapeutic results but also by conflicting theories of pathogenesis, and inevitably they would be shown to suffer from the application of transparent procrustean presumptions. For another instance of this difficulty, consider Winnicott's comments on antisocial adolescents presented above. Even given the recent relative ascendancy of many of his views on the therapeutic process, would we not find many experienced and effective clinicians who would question his suggestion that the ability to "experience despair in a relationship, instead of hope alone" is a desirable goal? Indeed, could it not be argued that the application of Winnicott's perspective might countertransferentially drive a patient toward hopelessness and despair?

Other difficulties in the understanding of the treatment of narcissistic disorders, beyond those of the shaky nosological and pathogenetic formulations, also involve the nonspecific and specific interventions mentioned earlier in this chapter. The unfolding events in the treatment of patients with narcissistic disorders in the IPM simply do not follow a course as smooth and predictable as we might wish. This unpredictable course may result when insufficient, conceptually flawed, or operationally ineffective nonspecific and specific measures are applied. It may also occur when otherwise potentially effective interventions are complicated by the influence of transference and countertransference. Some patients with illusions of absolute self-sufficiency (Modell 1984), far from sharing our view of the benevolence or efficacy of our safety-providing interventions, find entirely different explanations of their gains. They may spontaneously go on to understand our efforts, however well intended from our point of view, as intrusive, restrictive, damaging, enslaving, imprisoning, smothering, depriving, strangling, and in any number of ways not unlike earlier environmental insults, imagined or real.

The patient's conception of his or her illness and its cure is often quite different from the caregiver's view of these matters, however much validated the latter may be by professional colleagues. In psychiatric hospital treatment, we are familiar with the manic or schizophrenic patient who thanks the physician for the curative effects of lithium or neuroleptic medication and leaves the hospital as a satisfied customer, only to return shortly thereafter, having stopped the medication, considering himself or herself already cured. Another frequent example is that of the seriously ill adolescent who comes into the hospital embroiled in painful pathogenic conflict with his or her parents. Nonspecific and specific interventions, such as individual psychotherapy, family therapy, milieu group therapy, and medication, often lead to a significant amelioration of symptoms and a reduction in the conflict within the family. The diminished conflict within the family is followed by the development of parallel transferential conflict between the now-united family and the hospital caregivers. The patient feels tortured, deprived, or otherwise maltreated by the hospital caregivers, and the parents join with their recently alienated child in a collusive alliance to devalue the efforts of the treaters.

Sometimes the cure is found to depend more on the caregivers' continued presence than on the application of specific procedures. The caregivers' or the treatment program's presence may ultimately become more interesting to the patient than the symptoms. New symptoms may be produced, as Joseph Breuer uneasily witnessed with Bertha Pappenheim (Anna O) more than 100 years ago (Freud 1925/1959), for the purpose of maintaining or expanding the involvement with the caregivers.

Case Vignette

As an instance of the transferential complexities that can follow the application of nonspecific and specific interventions in the IPM, consider the treatment of Mr. D:

Mr. D, a single man in his late 30s with a long-standing neurological condition, was hospitalized after a suicide attempt by overdose. This occurred shortly after he received a medical opinion that a worsening of his neurological symptoms did not result from identifiable somatic causes. He felt certain that the worsening had been caused by a recent physical injury sustained in an automobile accident. The original deficit had followed an intracranial hemorrhage during his late teens and had left him with motor deficits but no compromise in higher cognitive functioning. He had invested enormous effort in overcoming—or perhaps more accurately, triumphing over—the physical limitations imposed by the deficit. He had also embarked on a successful legal career, as well as an affair with a married female partner in the firm. After his stroke, he had adopted a new name, borrowed from a film actor known for his ferociously defiant and morally righteous roles.

During Mr. D's hospital stay, he adopted a stance of embattled litigiousness toward the driver of the other vehicle. Somehow he convinced the hospital to defer payment of his bill until after his lawsuit was settled. He began pharmacological treatment for depression, started intensive psychotherapy, received physical therapy, and moved to another treatment milieu in a day and residential treatment program affiliated with the hospital. There he responded with outrage, threats of violence and lawsuits, suicidal impulses, and worsened physical symptoms when his therapist, the staff, and other patients attempted to engage his interest in the meaning of his symptoms and his not infrequent provocative behavior. Limit setting, especially when it was accompanied by psychological explanations of its purpose, also brought angry threatening responses. He fired two therapists.

After a few months of apparently unproductive struggles of this kind in the milieu, Mr. D met with a consulting psychoanalyst. He explained to the consultant his moral indignation at what he experienced as vicious and unsubstantiated insinuations and allegations about his motives and character from all sides. The consultant commented on the passionate quality of Mr. D's moral feelings, and the patient readily concurred. Mr. D felt that the consultant had listened to him more than others had done but offered little other comment about the consultation. The consultant observed to the staff that the patient seemed to have a kind of nineteenth-century moralistic version of psychic reality as part of his perspective. In keeping with this, from the consultant's point of view, much of the interpretive attention to intrapsychic and interpersonal conflicts would quite naturally come across as moral invective. The consultant recommended a shift in approach. The staff and therapist were discouraged from offering their interpretations of the meanings of what the patient presented. Instead, the task was to confirm, when it was the case, that they understood the patient's point of view about whatever experiences he discussed in the milieu. Otherwise, the treaters were to provide the ordinary noninterpretive structured aspects of the setting, including certain expectations for participation and respect for certain limits.

Only a few within the milieu staff were able to follow the recommendations, and the patient soon focused his attention on them. Initially ignoring or devaluing the rest, he gradually developed a grudging and somewhat sardonic appreciation of his tormenting interpreters. Within a short time, his symptoms, psychological and somatic, improved dramatically. He found a new therapist who specialized in a kind of therapy that emphasized the importance of concrete somatic matters and included a kind of advanced electronic technology as part of the approach. Mr. D also reimmersed himself in physical rehabilitative efforts with the vigor that had prevailed following his stroke years before. He was able to leave the intensive setting, glowingly gratified and grateful, well before the litigation was settled.

Comments

For Mr. D, addressing the transferential and countertransferential narcissistic disturbance that unfolded during his IPM treatment proved to be crucial to its effectiveness. The holding environment of the setting was not sufficient; nor were the varied specific interventions, including the many interpretations provided by the caregivers. The fact that many of the interpretations were constructed on the basis of carefully gathered data organized into formulations consistent with widely endorsed theories did not matter. The therapeutic action was dependent on the consultant's shared comprehension with Mr. D of the transference-countertransference impasse that had developed and the subsequent application of the mutualized understanding of the situation that had been discovered. The prevailing epistemology was like neither community consensus (which supports holding interventions) nor the professional validation of the caregivers' theories of pathogenesis and care (which support specific interventions). A more individualized, essentially ideographic, epistemology was necessary to derive a mutualized understanding of the treatment situation that could be effective in resolving the transference-countertransference impasse. Only through such a resolution could the beneficial effects of previous nonspecific and specific interventions be liberated.

Complex transference-laden treatment situations that are susceptible to a variety of apparently feasible but incompatible interpretations and interventions complicate treatment endeavors in the IPM. What is the response when, for example, a borderline patient, after cutting herself, complains with angry indignation about her treatment? In one such instance, a patient insisted that she had been driven to harm herself by the hopelessness and despair she felt in response to the therapist-administrator's failure to understand the difficulty of her struggle for self-control while seeking a better living situation. Was this incident the result of a countertransferentially driven interpretation that had implicitly pressured her to be less self-centered and had undervalued her precarious narcissistic balance? If so (and this is what the treaters thought), we might search with her for the ways in which the treatment interventions may have had such a detrimental effect from her point of view. Or, was the incident the transferential confirmation of an interpretation of her defensive withdrawal from mature object relations into a position of rageful pathological entitlement and infantile omnipotence? With this hypothesis, investigators may be inclined to attempt to discover regressive defensiveness that the patient may be aware of as well. If we consider the patient to be acting on the basis of an immovable egosyntonic narcissistic investment in omnipotent control, our effort might be to set limits, to explore the meaning of the limits to the patient, and to seek a mutually verifiable understanding of the patient's experience of them. Any number of formulations and interventions are possible. Without mutual inquiry into the patient's psychic reality and mutual corroboration of what is found, however, no plausible conclusions can be drawn, and the effectiveness of treatment often may be significantly compromised.

Conclusion

The examples offered in this chapter point to the ubiquitous and often decisive presence of the phenomena of transference and countertransference in the IPM. These phenomena are particularly enhanced in the area of the transferential derivatives of narcissistic object choices in these settings for several reasons. The IPM, after all, derives its justification—its own narcissistic sustenance, as it were—from the historical and contemporary premise that it provides environments that can, with greater effectiveness than the patients' usual social surround, enhance the well-being and, from an intrapsychic perspective, the narcissistic status of patients. The intention is carried out, as noted, in a literal manner, accompanied by the participation of those whose expertise is validated by their colleagues and society. Caregivers in the IPM are uniquely positioned, then, not only as observers of but also as participants in the creation of transferential phenomena derived from patients' narcissistic object choices. Because the resolution of these multidetermined transferential phenomena is so often crucial to therapeutic results, the therapeutic action of nonspecific and specific interventions in the IPM must necessarily be supplemented by inquiry. However apparently ill-suited to exploration of intrapsychic conflictual tensions and transferential derivatives some patients may appear to be, the availability of treaters ready to search their patients and their own perspectives for mutually verifiable accounts of patients' experiences in the IPM may be decisive.

Work from a variety of directions in psychoanalysis, including contributions from Gill (1982), Hoffman (1983), Gardner (1983), Schwaber (1983, 1986), and Jacobs (1991), has converged on similar perspectives as to the place of transference in the therapeutic process. Within these perspectives, the patient's transference is no longer seen solely as an idiosyncratic distortion of the reality of the therapist that can be objectively discerned and interpreted only by the therapist. Instead, it is understood as a joint creation that can be authentically comprehended and therapeutically resolved only through mutual inquiry and validation. This perspective applies equally to the psychoanalytical situation and to the transferential derivatives of the narcissistic object choices of patients in the IPM, which are so often prompted by the nonspecific and specific therapeutic measures that define these settings. The mutualized resolution of these transferences may become an essential mode of therapeutic action for patients who would otherwise remain inaccessible to potentially effective treatment. With the help of inquiry, the nonspecific and specific therapeutic interventions of the IPM can at times be found to create resolvable illusions that are both necessary to the future of patients and inherent in the continuing life of these therapeutic milieus.

References

Abraham K: A particular form of neurotic resistance against the psycho-analytic method (1919), in Selected Papers of Karl Abraham. Translated by Bryan D, Strachey A. New York, Brunner/Mazel, 1979, pp 303–311

Arlow J, Brenner C: Psychoanalytic Concepts and the Structural Theory. New York, International Universities Press, 1964

Bion W: Attention and Interpretation. London, Tavistock, 1970

Brenner C: The Mind in Conflict. New York, International Universities Press, 1982

Fairbairn W: Psychoanalytic Studies of the Personality. London, Routledge & Kegan Paul, 1952

Federn P: Ego Psychology and the Psychosis. New York, Basic Books, 1952

Fenichel O: The Psychoanalytic Theory of Neurosis. New York, WW Norton, 1945

Foucault M: Madness and Civilization: A History of Insanity in the Age of Reason. New York, Vintage Books, 1965

Freud S: Psychoanalytic notes on an autobiographical account of a case of paranoia (dementia paranoides) (1911), in The Standard Edition of the Complete Psychological Works of Sigmund Freud, Vol 12. Translated and edited by Strachey J. London, Hogarth Press, 1957, pp 1–84

Freud S: On narcissism: an introduction (1914), in The Standard Edition of the Complete Psychological Works of Sigmund Freud, Vol 14. Translated and edited by Strachey J. London, Hogarth Press, 1957, pp 67–102

Freud S: An autobiographical study (1925), in The Standard Edition of the Complete Psychological Works of Sigmund Freud, Vol 20. Translated and edited by Strachey J. London, Hogarth Press, 1959, pp 1–74

Gardner MR: Self Inquiry. New York, Little, Brown, 1983

Gill M: Analysis of Transference, Vol 1: Theory and Technique. New York, International Universities Press, 1982

Glover E: Ego distortion. Int J Psychoanal 39:260–264, 1958

Greenacre P: The role of transference: practical considerations in relation to psychoanalytic therapy. J Am Psychoanal Assoc 2:671–684, 1954

Greenblatt M: Foreword, in Schizophrenia: Pharmaco-therapy and Psychotherapy. Edited by Grinspoon L, Ewalt J, Shader R. Baltimore, MD, Williams & Wilkins, 1972, pp vii–xiii

Greenson R: The Technique and Practice of Psychoanalysis, Vol 1. New York, International Universities Press, 1967

Gunderson J: Defining the therapeutic processes in psychiatric milieus. Psychiatry 41:327–355, 1978

Gutterman S: Indications and contraindications for psychoanalytic treatment. Int J Psychoanal 49:354–355, 1968

Hartmann H: Essays in Ego Psychology. New York, International Universities Press, 1964

Herman J: Trauma and Recovery. New York, Basic Books, 1992

Hoffman IZ: The patient as interpreter of the analyst's experience. Contemporary Psychoanalysis 19:389–422, 1983

Jacobs TJ: The Use of the Self: Countertransference and Communication in the Analytic Situation. Madison, CT, International Universities Press, 1991

Kernberg O: Borderline Conditions and Pathological Narcissism. New York, Jason Aronson, 1975

Kernberg O: Severe Personality Disorders: Psychotherapeutic Strategies. New Haven, CT, Yale University Press, 1984

Klein M: The Psycho-Analysis of Children (1932). New York, Delta, 1975

Klein M: A contribution to the psychogenesis of manic depressive states (1935), in Love, Guilt, and Reparation and Other Works 1921–1945, Vol 1. New York, Delta, 1975, pp 262–289

Klein M: Notes on some schizoid mechanisms (1946), in Envy and Gratitude and Other Works, 1946–1963, Vol 3. New York, Delta, 1975, pp 1–24

Knight R: Management and psychotherapy of the borderline schizophrenic patient (1953), in Psychoanalytic Psychiatry and Psychology. Edited by Knight R, Fredman C. New York, International Universities Press, 1954, pp 110–122

Kohut H: The Analysis of the Self. New York, International Universities Press, 1971

Kohut H: The Restoration of the Self. New York, International Universities Press, 1977

Kohut H: The two analyses of Mr. Z. Int J Psychoanal 60:3–27, 1979

Kohut H: How Does Analysis Cure? Edited by Goldberg A, Stepansky PE. Chicago, IL, University of Chicago Press, 1984

Kris E: The Selected Papers of Ernest Kris. New Haven, CT, Yale University Press, 1975

Mitchell S: Relational Concepts in Psychoanalysis: An Integration. Cambridge, MA, Harvard University Press, 1988

Modell A: Psychoanalysis in a New Context. New York, International Universities Press, 1984

Rosenfeld H: Psychotic States: A Psychoanalytic Approach. London, Maresfield Reprints, 1965

Rosenfeld H: Impasse and Interpretation. New York, Routledge, 1987

Rothstein C: The Reconstruction of Trauma: Its Significance in Clinical Work. Madison, CT, International Universities Press, 1986

Sandler J, Person E, Fonagy P (eds): Freud's "On Narcissism: An Introduction." New Haven, CT, Yale University Press, 1991

Schwaber EA: Psychoanalytic listening and psychic reality. International Review of Psychoanalysis 10:379–392, 1983

Schwaber EA: Reconstruction and perceptual experience: some further thoughts on psychoanalytic listening. Journal of the American Psychoanalytic Association 34:911–932, 1986

Schwaber E: On the mode of therapeutic action: a clinical montage, in How Does Treatment Help? On the Modes of Therapeutic Action of Psychoanalytic Psychotherapy. Edited by Rothstein A. Madison, CT, International Universities Press, 1988, pp 81–93

Stanton A, Schwartz M: The Mental Hospital. New York, Basic Books, 1954

Stone L: The Psychoanalytic Situation. New York, International Universities Press, 1961

Sullivan H: Conceptions of Modern Psychiatry. New York, WW Norton, 1940

Sullivan H: Schizophrenia as a Human Process. New York, WW Norton, 1962

van der Kolk B: Post Traumatic Stress Disorder: Psychological and Biological Sequelae. Washington, DC, American Psychiatric Press, 1984

Waldhorn H: Assessment of analyzability: technical and theoretical observations. Psychoanal Q 29:478–506, 1960

Winnicott DW: Transitional objects and transitional phenomena (1951), in Through Paediatrics to Psychoanalysis: Collected Papers. New York, Basic Books, 1958, pp 229–242

Winnicott DW: The antisocial tendency (1956), in Through Paediatrics to Psychoanalysis: Collected Papers. New York, Basic Books, 1958, pp 306–315

Winnicott DW: The Maturational Processes and the Facilitating Environment. New York, International Universities Press, 1965

Zilboorg G: A History of Medical Psychology. New York, WW Norton, 1941

Chapter 10

Narcissistic Patients in Group Psychotherapy

Containing Affects in the Early Group

Bennett E. Roth, Ph.D.

I n this chapter, the author addresses a question that persists in the literature and in clinical practice: Can group therapy effectively treat narcissistic conflicts and narcissistic personality disorders? The answer must include attention to the struggle of narcissistic patients to maintain their personal identity in the group—that is, their sense of self—while still being a group member. It must also consider the impact of these psychic struggles on the other members of the group and the group therapist.

Narcissistic patients are discussed in this chapter from the vantage point of identity impairment. The group is seen as an avenue to correct certain usual defenses therapeutically and to help understand the nature of habitual transference patterns. Entry into group therapy is seen as the most important test of a new patient and is discussed from the vantage point of the affect that is aroused in the patient and in the group.

Implied in the question of efficacy of group therapy for narcissistic patients is the idea that another form of treatment can effectively treat severe narcissistic problems. When group psychotherapy is being considered, the answer to this question must depend on the group, the group therapist, and the patient combination in a particular group. Surely well-conducted group therapy can help a group member start to make distinctions between self and other, reduce the tendency to project onto others (often mistakenly confused with the term *identification* by group members), and work on the absence of empathic communication and the presence of exhibitionistic anxiety. Group therapy can offer many corrective experiences in dealing with narcissistic hurts and identifying vulnerability. All these can safely happen in a well-functioning analytical group therapy situation. Is that enough? Can deeper psychic change take place?

When the possibility of deeper psychic change is being contemplated, of particular concern is whether the therapy group can contain the dynamics of these difficult patients, particularly during the long period of negative alliance that is often a hallmark of their treatment. Often there is also concern as to whether group therapy will reproduce the original situation that led to the dysfunctional behavior (Roth 1980).

Although there have been many advances in the theory and clinical technique of dealing with the narcissistic patient in psychoanalysis, these techniques have not found their way into the group therapy literature. One source of this problem is that the multiperson setup of the therapy group does not easily translate to the layered individual transferences that emerge in the dyadic situation. In particular, the group patient does not have the full attention of the analyst. This alone reduces the narcissistic gratification inherent in having someone listen to the flow of associations. Group therapy requires some separation from the primary therapist, listening to others speak, and capacity to form relationships with others in the group (Roth 1990).

The Identity-Impaired Patient

The problematic issues of analytic group therapy may best be summarily described as issues that effect the identity of the impaired patient. For the purposes of describing a common problem, the term *identity-impaired* will be used to describe some dynamic similarities among patients who appear diagnostically different. In this instance, identity-impaired will also stand in contrast to *identity-secure*. Identity-impaired personality organization is described as a dynamic organization existing over time and in varying degrees within persons whose development of primary identity systems, ego self, and sense of self engenders a constant need for maintenance and repair. In other words, their identity is narcissistically vulnerable.

Generally, such persons have avoided major crises in adolescence but continue to seek archaic and grandiose external objects on which to depend and attack or from whom to flee. Selfobject differentiation remains episodically unstable, and boundaries between self and objects of need can frequently become diffuse and unstable. Fearful wishes exist for self-obliteration and dissolution of self via drugs or merging (Khantzian 1993) along with frequently experienced periods of psychic depletion, psychic emptiness, and psychic death.

These paradoxical fears of a need for a grandiose object occur with the sudden withdrawal of or with excessive closeness to either regulatory events or objects. Extreme anxiety and dependency may be experienced by these identity-impaired people without their having the ability to distinguish the origin of the threat as being internal or external. In addition, extreme variations in self-esteem may occur with slight narcissistic injury or seemingly without external cause, leading to variations in self-perception and perception of others without awareness of these fluctuations. Or, from a different perspective, some identity-impaired people seemingly live within brittle, unwavering narrow bands of perception, thinking, and feeling that seem

impervious to experience other than that afforded by psychoac-
tive drugs (Khantzian 1993).

Because of a number of developmental faults, often seemingly
dysfunctional families, and problems with both separateness and
identity, these narcissistic patients usually are a high risk for either
individual or group therapy. Specifically, they may appear to be
unable to maintain rudimentary self-observation functions (introspection, observing ego functions) necessary for a commitment to therapeutic work (Roth 1990). Because of this, it is
frequently necessary for the group therapist to both anticipate
and understand the events that will precipitate a narrowing of
adaptive capacities and that lead to problems of acting out and remaining in the therapy group.

These behavioral problems in the group are particularly difficult for the other members of the group and the therapist. In a
group in which provocative feelings emerge early and frequently,
there often may be attempts to scapegoat these patients. For many
reasons, it is difficult for a group or group members to sustain a
prolonged period of anger and negative transference toward the
therapist, which is essential in the treatment of these problems.

Entry Into the Group

The process of entry into a psychotherapy group often determines the success or failure of group therapy for that patient. For
the new member, the capacity to become a working member of
any group rests on the amount of perceived and felt danger experienced in the real and expected transferences within the group.
In a psychotherapy group, these transferences are experienced in
three distinct forms: 1) to the group, 2) to the group therapist, and
3) to individual members of the group. Broadly speaking, for the
identity-impaired person, although he or she may express a wish
to join the group, any form of psychosocial self-definition will
generate defensive reactions: avoidance, self-isolation, and disen-

gagement from the working alliances. Sometimes this isolation will include drug-taking as a defense.

The new member also has an effect on the existing group hierarchical relations. For the ongoing group, the new member shifts alliances between the group members, arouses curiosity and its defenses, and tests again the trust between the group and the therapist. For the group therapist, the entrance of a new patient is an opportunity to test the trust that exists in the group and the extent to which the group is secure enough to allow a new member to increase its range of behavior.

Affect Management

The management of affect is central to remaining in a therapy group. Affects are part of the phenomena of everyday mental life and are part of the symptomatology of every psychopathological condition. Like anxiety, affects or feelings serve a signal function permitting knowledge about the external world and affecting the perception of both internal and external events. Although it would be expected that affects would have a central place in group psychoanalytical theory and practice, this is not the case. Some difficulty remains in defining them and their role in group dynamics, despite the early awareness of group theorists that affects in groups were contagious (LeBon 1920) and that the leader of the group often determined the range and content of affect (Redl 1942/1980). In the more recent literature, only Stone's (1990) paper clearly has the word "affect" in its title, but a recent review of that paper indicated that it lacks a focus on affects as they occur in the group situation.

The Narcissistic Patient in the Group

Narcissistic patients' entry into an accepting group can evoke deeply felt regressive dependency. Also prominent in the narcissistic dynamics of analytical psychotherapy groups is the appearance of strong negative affects or negative affects in disguised or defensive form (Kernberg 1975). These occur because the group therapy situation, with its forms of regression (Scheidlinger 1980), elicits the kind of early narcissistic transferences that are at the core of these patients' relationships. In addition to being a natural setting for projection and projective identification, the group therapy situation sets up competition for the therapist's attention and becomes an arena in which forms of psychic attachment are lived out. As their (defensive) fantasies of omnipotence are interfered with by being in a multiperson group, patients often cannot control strongly felt emotions that regressively recall the fears associated with this loss of that object relationship. This is particularly so in the treatment of the identity-impaired patient who lacks the capacity to relieve strongly experienced affects without taking action. In particular, negative affects (i.e., affects that are associated with the negative transference and with real trauma or affects surrounding loss) often destabilize these patients' sense of self or identity. At the same time, the articulation of strong affects can reverberate around a group, evoking strong feelings in some group participants and generating destabilizing regressive reactions in other group members.

Furthermore, chronic disturbances in both mood and relationships with others may be rooted in developmental deficits that are revived and recalled in the regressive group situation. In all these situations, catharsis is neither enough nor desirable. In other terms, the expression of affect is too simple a goal in analytical work. Therefore, it becomes part of the therapeutic process for the therapy group and the therapist to be able to allow the expression of these affects and to create an environment to contain and understand the patients' expressed negative and positive transferences. Among the affects that often need to be incorporated are screaming, querulousness, boredom, smugness, arrogance, bitterness, shame, sarcasm, aloneness, jealousy, disillusionment, and ingratitude. When reading this list of emotions and imagining a group filled with such affect, even in fantasy, it is clear that the group therapist's capacity to remain neutral is frequently challenged.

At the same time, as these affects pose problems, analytical group psychotherapy offers a unique setting in which to examine affects and their defenses. With the analytical prohibition against action, affective elements of group interpersonal interaction are heightened. Isolation and repression as defenses are often loosened in the presence of both other people and other multiple affects. In addition, the frequent challenges to intellectualization that take place in a psychotherapy group add to an affective expectancy or readiness. Displacement or splitting of affect from immediate objects of transference to events outside of the group is a common defensive maneuver, and projection and projective identification precipitated by strong affects and anxiety occur rapidly. This is particularly so when the inevitable narcissistic disappointment with the group or the group leader occurs. Frequently, the author has observed that the disappointment that occurs in the group will initially be split away from the group to maintain the idealizing defenses. Or, on the other side, negative and destructive impulses will be directed at the self or some person in the group or harbored against the therapist.

The following case vignettes are from American Group Psychotherapy Association (AGPA) training groups. Exemplified in these recent group experiences is the loosening of affect that occurs as narcissistic defenses become clear.

Case Vignette: Group 1

In general, there is always a somewhat uneven emergence of affect in a psychotherapy group. The following example does not account for this phenomenon; it distills the affect in the situation and presents it in a somewhat cohesive manner. This is particularly true of the first events that took place over four group sessions in 2 days.

> Dana is a young, attractive, well-dressed woman. Susan is a slightly older woman. Early in the first group session, they have this exchange:

Dana (sitting somewhat to the right of the therapist; she is tense and speaks to Susan):   I have been looking at you. Of all the people in the group, you're the only one I would not want to go to lunch with.

Susan: Really, you don't even know me. I haven't said anything.

Dana: I don't need to know anything about you. It's my feeling. It's the way you sit there. It's the way you look, I mean, the expression on your face. But here it is, we are in group, and rather than walk out of here, I want to say it.

Susan: Well, I am sure that you feel better.

Third woman (to Susan):   I would go to lunch with you.

Group therapist (puzzled):   I wonder what that was about.

After lunch:

Susan (starts the afternoon session):   Well, I was wondering whether I was going to have lunch alone. I usually do eat alone, but two people came over to me and said let's have lunch, and I felt better.

Dana: I wouldn't have lunch with you.

Somewhat later:

Dana (to therapist):   You know, I asked a lot of people about you and which group I should take. They said you were arrogant, very arrogant, but smart and a good group therapist and that you could handle me.

Group therapist: And you came to this group anyhow? (group laughs, Dana barely smiles)

Second session (next day):

Susan: I feel I never belonged anywhere. My mother was Irish and my father was Jewish. We lived in a suburb of C. When we would go to the city to be with my father's family, they were warm, and there was always food, and I felt accepted. And then we would go to my mother's family in the suburbs, and it was cold. They never served enough food, and I never felt accepted. I feel for my daughter now because I'm divorced and she's an adolescent, and I feel just like she feels—like I don't know where I belong. That's how I felt when Dana said she wasn't going to lunch, you know.

Group therapist: When she served cold tongue. (Susan nods)

Later:

Dana: I always seem to annoy people. (no connection made to Susan) I'm like my father. He was always angry and confronting people. That was his style. But he wasn't like that with me. My mother wasn't there. She was there physically but not emotionally. I remember my father being there. He was kind and good to me. I remember sitting on his lap and feeling this giant man would protect me. I remember they were always fighting, and he always had admirers around him, people telling him how wonderful he was, but there were always other people who were hurt by him. (crying) Later I felt that he wouldn't accept me. He was always critical of me. It made me tough. People were telling me how critical and nasty he was. I needed him. I need people—like with my kids now, I don't want to do to them what he did to me.

Dana's event was at the very end of the second long group session. The therapist consciously looked at his watch to determine how much time was left in the group before making an announcement about resumption.

Dana (as the therapist is looking at his watch): I know I'm taking up too much group time.

Group therapist: Boy, that was really at the periphery of your vision. How did you see that?

Dana: I'm paranoid. I watch everything and everyone. If you grew up the way I did, you would watch everything and everyone.

Group therapist: What a combination: crying and sad and alert.

Dana: It makes me a good group therapist.

Third session:

Susan: The whole time I am in the group, I felt protected
by Dr. B. He didn't say anything after Dana attacked
me, but I looked at him and he looked at me and I
knew he understood. (to Dana, with anger and contempt) You don't even know me. I'm a nice person,
and you're a bitch. You come into a group and attack
me. This is the first time I've ever been in a group and
you attack.

Group therapist (to Susan):   I guess I knew how angry you
were, and I waited for you to deal with it.

Dana (shrugging):   People say I put holes in them. My
husband says that.

Fourth session:

Dana: I need people close to me, and I don't let them get
close. (crying) Sometimes I feel alone. I get angry
when I am alone and feel ignored. Like my father—
I get angry. But I want them close, as close as my skin.

Group therapist: I remember the scene from *The Singing
Detective* when he's scratching himself and saying,
"I got you under my skin. I got you in the heart of
me."

Lois: "So deep in my heart you are really a part of me."

Lois and group therapist: "I got you under my skin."

Comment

This event can be understood from the perspective of transference, affect regulation, self-esteem, or countertransference. The
group dynamics are about inclusion and exclusion; competition
and rivalry; the exchange and communication of affect through
words, fantasy, and projections; and the establishment of an affective group culture.

It seems that Dana is struggling with certain defenses regarding anger and closeness. In her first exchange, she picks a silent
maternal equivalent in an attempt to establish the shooting range

for her negative affect. Over time, some memory of mother, food, and exclusion was found that pointed to some repressed memories and association-repressed affect. She wants to have people close enough to touch, to shore up her sense of maternal identity, but she is irritating and irritated by not being able to control her own affect. People get under her skin, and a psychosomatic history is likely as a discharge for feelings of self-anger. Perhaps anger, querulousness, and vulnerability are incompatible mood and self-states. She repressively feels small (vulnerable) with the therapist—she has a fantasy of sitting on the therapist's lap, and she wants the sad-eyed woman to go away. Oral issues are hinted at regarding lunch and boundaries of what is felt inside and outside the group. Projections of arrogance of the leader are covered rapidly by her own smug remarks to the therapist and Susan.

Susan expresses affect silently, looking for magical approval without content. The therapist reversed Susan's affect stance by saying that she wanted to protect the therapist and Dana from her anger. Susan identifies with her own adolescent daughter in her confusion of "Whom do I belong with?" and "Who am I?" "You don't know me" is a defensive cover for "You don't know what feeling I have inside me and who I am." This comes along with the complaint of "No one understands me." Dana and Susan represent two sides of the same narcissistic problem: dealing with feelings that destabilize a sense of self or identity. Dana deals with her narcissistic feelings of being small projectively, and Susan deals introjectively with feelings of being rejected, silent, and different.

Case Vignette: Group 2

A woman, Barbara, to the right of the group therapist is crying.

Barbara: I'm really surprised at what I'm feeling (sob) and
remembering. It's terrible. How I felt responsible for
her. I was thinking this as Ann was talking about her
mother and father being physicians. My father left
us—me—us—he just left. And I'm the oldest child,

and I was glad. I thought he was taking me with him, but he wasn't, and I took care of him and then I took care of her. That night I remember. I don't know what started this feeling, but it's awful. I was stuck with her.

John (sitting to the left of the group therapist):   I'm really touched by what you're saying. It really moves me to tears. Dr. B isn't going to like this, I don't know what the rules are here about this, but I want to get up and give you a hug. (There is no response from the therapist. John gets up, walks by the therapist, stops in front of Barbara, and reaches down and takes her hand. She remains seated.) Do you want the hug? (Barbara gets up. The hug is firm from him, reluctant from her. John goes back to his seat, and Barbara sits down.)

Ken: That took balls to do. It felt like to me you were cutting the pretty one out of the group for yourself. (to Barbara) You know I'm attracted to you, and that old man really put a move on you.

Ann: I felt like I was watching a scene of abuse. I always wondered whether I was abused, but how could you let him do that to you?

Gail: Well, I know that my brother, after the accident, came into my room one night, and he said he loved me and, well, I never wanted to admit it.

Ann: I wouldn't go any further than that. How could you trust him after what happened? He let that man abuse her right in front of us. Just boom, like that. He doesn't care about us women at all.

Barbara: I didn't feel abused when he hugged me. I just felt kind of used—like I was there to satisfy him.

Therapist: Like he stopped what you were feeling and you had to take care of him.

John: That's funny, that's what my wife says—that although I'm a psychiatrist, I try to stop her from feeling. Did I do that here?

Barbara: Now I'm angry at you. If that was what you were doing, if you hugged me to stop me from feeling sad and I had to meet your need to be hugged? I'm really angry.

Ken: You know, I'm really turned on to you. You came alive when you got angry, and I want to spend some time with you. I know it's dangerous to say that in a group.

John (to Ken):   That was real strange.

Ken: Jealous?

John: You know the way you look and behave, you look like one of those guys who went to prep school back East. I went to one in Arizona, and you look like the kind of guy who never went home—had no home to go to. We would go home for Christmas, and there was one guy who stayed.

Ken: That is me. Once they sent me to school, that was it. School, camp, then college. My mother wasn't interested, and my father, well—my therapist said he was held together by his vest, and you (to John)?

John: We left Kansas City when I was 16. I went to school, and I never saw my father again. At 17, I went into the army (crying) and killed a lot of men. I was a trained killer: a marksman, a sniper. I stopped counting how many I killed and became a professional killer. (pointing at Ken) I'd get them in my sights and squeeze.

Group therapist: You know, when you walked across the room to hug Barbara, you made a wonderful target.

John: I thought that, too. I still have a lot of guilt. My father was a dirt farmer. Not much choice: be a poor dirt farmer or an M.D. I don't understand why I'm crying now.

Comment

The above case is an oedipal screen event of two men, John and Ken, competing for a crying woman. One wants to silence her affect, whereas the other cannot tolerate her crying and sadness because he finds her more sexual when she is angry. Narcissistic patients injure quickly in group therapy when confronted by their own behavior and sometimes by the therapist's unawareness of the contradictory feelings they are expressing. For that reason, the contradiction of angry/sexual is not highlighted.

The group therapist chose to let the initial events unfold, particularly because Barbara never made eye contact with him or in any way asked for the therapist's intervention. The seeming competition for a sad and crying woman in the group unmasked bitterness, murderous rage, guilt, and abandonment by both male and female patients. The response to Barbara's crying is perceived differently by each member of the group because of the emotional, narcissistic, perceptual regressive set they bring to it—that is, abuse, sexual excitement, guilt, a wish to attack, and the wish to humiliate the therapist to make him weak. For Barbara, she becomes aware that she is caught in a four-way event: John's and Ken's varying approaches to her in the presence of the group and the remembered feeling of her father's loss. For Ken and John, the men in the group, more than competition seems to be aroused, and the issues become complex with envy, absent fathers, and narcissistic rage. This combination is crucial to their sense of self and their need to reaffirm their masculinity. Most interestingly, when the group therapist, as a teaching example, retells the story of the man crossing the room, the therapist is most frequently verbally criticized by the audience for being passive.

Remarks by the group therapist are generally described as interpretative, confronting, or clarifying. Correct and well-timed interpretations in a group setup often evoke emotion from the intended member or reverberate to adjacent members of the group. For certain patients who do not have "a language of emotional or inner life," therapist interventions may include affect naming ("You were angry then"), affect correspondence ("That sounds like the kind of anger you were describing when . . . "), or correcting affect blindness ("You didn't notice that X was sad "). The group therapist interventions are never intended to afford closure. They are intended to keep the group event open without resolution, to afford an opportunity for continued processing of a multilayered event, and to keep the event within the group. It is for that reason that what the group therapist says is often misperceived in the group. In this way, the alliance in the group must always be present.

Technical Problems

Although the general rules for therapist behavior apply in group therapy, there are some unique technical problems (Pines 1990) that arise because of the presence of destructive impulses that often accompany the wish for an omnipotent object, the absence of self-reflection (Roth 1990), and the failure to distinguish self from other. Because of these psychic problems, the so-called narcissistic groups develop into working groups slowly—that is, the members of the group come to a trusting alliance very slowly, reveal themselves slowly, and develop transference other than narcissistic forms even more slowly. The group therapist must be exceedingly tolerant of the slow pace of such groups. Also, when the patient is in both group and individual psychotherapy, the group therapist must be attentive to what is revealed from the "private" sessions and not humiliate patients in the group. This is particularly important with the so-called inferior narcissistic patient, as contrasted with the grandiose or exhibitionistic patient. The former is prone to set up the group to receive humiliation and to attempt to set up a sadomasochistic transference relationship with either the group or the group therapist.

Various tests of the boundaries and rules are common to patients who cannot tolerate social definition—that is, in whom closeness arouses early defenses—and who cannot withstand the potential closeness in the group. Although the group member will make these defensive actions, they must be tactfully and therapeutically handled to avoid scapegoating and injury to the group (e.g., time, payment).

Therapists in this kind of group therapy may be reluctant to wait for the group to develop and may find the early stages of group development difficult (i.e., avoiding the basic rule of surface before depth and not waiting for a strong alliance to develop). Some will be prone to make (deep) interpretations too quickly under the pressure of an acting out by a group member or to join in group avoidance of recognizing such behavior. This is likely to occur when the therapist's own defenses are activated in the group.

Narcissistic patients put unusual stress on group therapists' needs for a good group and for narcissistic gratification from the group. Talking too much, boredom, anger, inattention, lateness, and projective counteridentification are common countertransference reactions during problematic group dynamics. Often, the group therapist's need for appreciation and for doing good work is thwarted by these patients.

Narcissistic patients frequently leave the group suddenly, with and without notice, and thereby disrupt group balance, individual ties, and self-esteem balance within the group. The therapist is frequently blamed for this group loss when he or she cannot understand the sudden departure.

Patients may assume a defensive characterological identity in the group and hide behind that identity, such as the therapist's assistant, silent film star, group historian, or group interrogator (Roth 1990). Under the force of group projection of their need for a grandiose leader, enactment, or group deficit, the group therapist may also assume a role in the group that represents an aspect of his or her character. Or, in the case of group deficits, the therapist may assume a missing but necessary aspect in the group functioning. When this is done, the group therapist is better served by telling the group what he or she is doing. Therapists may become aware of this role through understanding the underlying causes for their distorting information while in supervision.

References

Kernberg OF: Borderline Conditions and Pathological Narcissism. Northvale, NJ, Jason Aronson, 1975

Khantzian E: The ego, the self and opiate addiction: theoretical and treatment conditions, in Psychodynamics and Drug Dependence. Edited by Blaine J, Demetrios C. Northvale, NJ, Jason Aronson, 1993, pp 101–117

LeBon G: The Crowd: A Study of the Popular Mind. New York, Unwin, 1920

Pines M: Group analytic therapy and the borderline patient, in The Difficult Patient in Group Psychotherapy—International. Edited by Roth B, Stone W, Kibel H. Madison, CT, International Universities Press, 1990, pp 31–44

Redl F: Group emotion and leadership (1942), in Psychoanalytic Group Dynamics. Edited by Scheidlinger S. Madison, CT, International Universities Press, 1980, pp 15–68

Roth B: Understanding the development of a homogeneous identify impaired group through countertransference. Int J Group Psychother 30:405–426, 1980

Roth B: The group that would not relate to itself, in The Difficult Patient in Group Psychotherapy. Edited by Roth B, Stone W, Kibel H. Madison, CT, International Universities Press, 1990, pp 127–156

Scheidlinger S: The concept of regression in group psychotherapy, in Psychoanalytic Group Dynamics. Edited by Scheidlinger S. Madison, CT, International Universities Press, 1980, pp 233–254

Stone W: On affects in group psychotherapy, in The Difficult Patient in Group Psychotherapy. Edited by Roth B, Stone W, Kibel H. Madison, CT, International Universities Press, 1990, pp 191–214

Chapter 11

Schema-Focused Therapy for Narcissistic Patients

Jeffrey Young, Ph.D.

Catherine Flanagan, Ph.D.

R ecent developments in the field of cognitive therapy have led to new treatment paradigms for severe character disorders, including narcissistic personality disorder (NPD). As cognitive therapists began to move from treating Axis I disorders such as depression to addressing more chronic, characterological issues, several limitations of Beck's (Beck et al. 1979) early model of cognitive therapy became apparent. Influenced by the constructivist movement (Mahoney 1993), Young (1994) developed an integrative model called *schema-focused therapy,* designed to overcome many of the limitations of Beck's original work. The schema-focused approach combines cognitive, behavioral, experiential, and transference-based techniques, utilizing the concept of a schema as the unifying element. Compared with conventional cognitive therapy, the schema-focused model involves greater use of the therapeutic relationship as a vehicle for change, more emphasis on affective experience, and more extensive discussion of early life experiences.

General Model of Schema-Focused Therapy

According to the theory proposed, 18 Early Maladaptive Schemas (EMS) are at the core of personality disorders (see Appendix). An early maladaptive schema is defined as an extremely broad, pervasive theme regarding oneself and one's relationships with others that was developed during childhood, was elaborated throughout one's lifetime, and is dysfunctional to a significant degree. These 18 schemas are primarily unconscious but can be brought into awareness through various strategies.

Three schematic processes are hypothesized: Maintenance, Avoidance, and Compensation. These processes (which overlap with the psychoanalytical concepts of resistance and defense mechanisms) determine, in part, how easily individual patients can bring their schemas into awareness and change them.

A developmental model is proposed to explain the childhood origins of EMS. Five schema domains are proposed: Disconnection and Rejection, Impaired Autonomy and Performance, Impaired Limits, Other-Directedness, and Overvigilance and Inhibition. Each domain represents a core need required for healthy psychological maturation of the child. Each of the 18 schemas interferes with one or more of these core needs.

Most recently, McGinn and Young (1996) proposed an additional construct in conceptualizing characterological patients: a schema mode, which is defined as a facet of the self involving a natural grouping of schemas and schema processes that has not been fully integrated with other facets. Patients flip from one mode to another, primarily in response to environmental circumstances or life events. For example, borderline patients flip among four modes: the Angry Child, the Abandoned Child, the Punitive Parent, and the Detached Protector. Patients show different cognitions, behaviors, and emotions in each mode; therefore, the therapist must utilize different treatment strategies in response to each mode.

Treatment is divided into two phases: assessment and change. The assessment phase focuses on the identification and activation of the particular schemas that are most relevant for each patient. This process incorporates several assessment methods:

1. Using pattern identification, which involves a life review, linking the presenting problems with childhood and adolescent origins
2. Educating patients about schemas with the "Client's Guide" (Bricker and Young 1993/1994) and *Reinventing Your Life* (Young and Klosko 1994)
3. Reviewing the Schema Questionnaire, a self-report instrument for measuring schemas (Young and Brown 1990/1994)
4. Activating schemas through imagery, dialogues, and inner-child exercises
5. Observing patterns in the therapy relationship

The change phase applies systematic change techniques to modify the schemas most relevant to the individual patient. Four types of intervention are integrated during the change phase:

1. *Cognitive interventions to help patients examine EMS empirically and rationally.* These interventions include testing the validity of schemas through examining past evidence, thus allowing the patient to reframe the past; creating dialogues between schemas and the "healthy self"; and developing flashcards that the patient can carry around to rehearse healthier thinking.
2. *Experiential techniques to bring emotions in synchronization with cognitive changes.* These emotive techniques are drawn largely from gestalt therapy and include imagery, role-playing, inner-child work, and ventilation of affect. These techniques are utilized in relation to significant others from childhood and adult life.
3. *The therapy relationship, especially for issues of emotional deprivation, abuse, and abandonment.* For some patients, the therapist undertakes a limited kind of reparenting to provide a corrective emotional experience. The therapist also confronts schemas in the context of the therapy relationship, similar to what analysts refer to as analyzing the transference.

4. *Behavioral pattern-breaking to change self-defeating behavior patterns.* The therapist assigns graded tasks to help patients change schema-driven behaviors, especially interpersonal patterns, outside of therapy sessions. In some cases, the therapist also works to alter schemas in the context of couples work or with parents.

Schema-Focused Conceptualization of Narcissism

Early Maladaptive Schemas in Narcissism

Our cumulative clinical observations and experience over several years led the authors to propose that the central or core operating schemas in NPD are those of Entitlement, Emotional Deprivation, and Defectiveness.

Entitlement.   The Entitlement schema is in the realm of impaired Limits and translates into behaviors such as insisting that one should be able to do or have whatever one wants, regardless of what others consider reasonable or the cost to others. Entitlement can develop in two ways. Many children develop Entitlement because their parents set too few limits; the parents do not demand that their children respect the rights and feelings of others. Alternatively, some children develop Entitlement as an overcompensation for feelings of defectiveness or deprivation (as elaborated below). It is as if they are making sure that they are never devalued or cheated again by demanding that they have everything their own way.

Entitled people are exploitive and control the behavior of others by keeping it in line with their own desires. The cognitive processes that fuel these self-centered behaviors include ongoing thoughts about how special they are, fantasies about major acquisitions and achievements, expectations that they should be treated with special attention and consideration and should not have to obey the rules that apply to everybody else, and beliefs that they deserve the best.

Emotional Deprivation. Both the Emotional Deprivation schema and the Defectiveness schema are in the domain of Disconnection and Rejection. These schemas interfere with the individual's ability to experience intimacy, love, and acceptance. Emotional Deprivation usually results from a lack of nurturance, empathy, or protection from parents. The underlying feelings are loneliness and emptiness and a sense that something is missing. Patients with Emotional Deprivation often hold exaggerated beliefs that they are not being cared for and understood, that they are not receiving sufficient attention, that others will not be there for them emotionally, and that people are unable or unwilling to meet their needs for emotional support. They often simultaneously yearn for close connection yet feel uncomfortable and back away if they begin to receive it.

Defectiveness. Defectiveness involves a feeling of shame and humiliation because the patient believes that he or she is flawed or inferior and therefore unlovable to significant others. This schema usually results from severe criticism or rejection by parents in childhood. In other cases, Defectiveness may arise from being rejected or excluded by peers. For example, some narcissistic individuals grew up poorer, less attractive, less athletic, or less popular than the group they wanted to be part of.

Patients with Defectiveness do not allow others to get too close for fear of being exposed and humiliated, or they engage in compensatory efforts to make themselves desirable (e.g., meticulous grooming, flattery of others, high achievement). When this schema is triggered by perceived rejection or criticism, the patient often becomes defensive or counterattacks. The ongoing cognitive activity consists of a constant monitoring of one's performance, a comparison of oneself with others, or a morbid preoccupation with or envy of what others have. These patients often believe that the exposure of any flaws will result in humiliation and ultimately in rejection.

Several secondary schemas and schema processes have also been observed that sometimes appear in the narcissistic profile. These include Approval-Seeking, Unrelenting Standards, Subjugation, Mistrust, and Schema Avoidance.

Approval-Seeking. Narcissistic individuals frequently place strong emphasis on Approval-Seeking. This tendency manifests itself through an exaggerated focus on social status, high achievement, physical appearance, and wealth. Many patients with Approval-Seeking are expert in sensing how to gain recognition from the people around them. The origins of Approval-Seeking are twofold. Patients with this schema often have parents who overemphasize "social appearances" at the expense of inner happiness or intimacy. For many narcissistic individuals, Approval-Seeking also can be viewed as an effort to compensate for the Defectiveness schema. By gaining recognition and approval, narcissistic individuals can pump themselves up and thus escape the painful feelings of inadequacy underneath. Approval-Seeking also helps to reinforce the sense of "specialness" that is part of the Entitlement schema. Approval-Seeking is ultimately self-defeating, however, because the patient's sense of self-esteem becomes dependent on the reactions of others, and a secure sense of self cannot be developed.

Unrelenting Standards. Many narcissistic individuals strive to maintain high, perfectionist standards of performance. The origin for these Unrelenting Standards is usually parents who set high expectations for themselves and others. Often, these parents are demanding and critical and convey the sense that anything short of perfection is failure. It is also hypothesized that narcissistic individuals frequently develop Unrelenting Standards as another form of compensation for Defectiveness. By striving for perfection, the patient hopes to ward off internal and external criticism. Most patients with Unrelenting Standards also set high standards for those people they perceive as reflecting on them, such as family members and employees. Furthermore, by surrounding themselves with other perfect, high-status, special people, the narcissistic individual strives to compensate for underlying feelings of defectiveness.

Subjugation. Subjugation is the excessive surrendering of control over one's behavior, emotional expression, and decisions to others, particularly those in authority, because one fears retaliation or abandonment. Subjugation almost always involves the chronic suppression of anger in relation to those perceived to be in control. The origin of Subjugation is usually one or more parents who demand that the child meet the parents' needs instead of the child's. Some narcissistic individuals grew up feeling like objects who performed for the gratification of their parents. They felt like they were treated as extensions of their parents, without regard for their own unique needs, feelings, or preferences. Many narcissistic persons are sensitive to being controlled. This is especially true of what Masterson (1981) calls the "closet narcissist." Their entitlement may, to a certain extent, be a compensation for a sense that, unless they control their environment, others will control them. Narcissistic individuals frequently engage in resentful compliance for fear of rejection.

Mistrust.   The Mistrust schema refers to the expectation that others will hurt, humiliate, cheat, lie, manipulate, or take advantage of the patient. It often involves the sense that one always ends up being cheated relative to others or "getting the short end of the stick." Many narcissistic individuals felt used by their parents to gratify their own needs for social acceptance and status; these patients did not receive an adequate supply of unconditional love and acceptance. As a result, many narcissistic individuals expect to be manipulated or used by others; they feel little security regarding ongoing loyalties. Perceived deception or betrayal can lead to outbursts of rage or vengeful retaliation.

Schema Avoidance.   Most narcissistic individuals engage in a variety of behaviors designed to avoid the painful feelings associated with Emotional Deprivation and Defectiveness. These behaviors generally take the form of stimulation seeking or self-soothing, such as drug or alcohol abuse, and serve to distract narcissistic individuals from their core schemas. By pushing many of these high-risk activities to the limit, narcissistic people may also be attempting to prove that they are special and that the rules that apply to everybody else do not apply to them.

Hypothesized Origins of Narcissism

After reviewing the backgrounds of narcissistic persons in their practices over many years, the authors observed a few common threads in childhood origins. The vast majority of narcissistic patients had one doting parent who instilled a message of "specialness" to the child while depriving the child of true affection and nurturance and a second parent who was ineffectual, disengaged, highly successful, critical, or rejecting.

The origin for the sense of entitlement generally involves a doting parent—usually the mother—who treats the child as special based on either real or exaggerated talents and assets (e.g., gifted, bright, good-looking). The child is given special privileges and treatment, and few limits are set. The child is idealized and expected to do wonderful things. The doting mother channels her unfulfilled needs (e.g., for status, recognition, achievement) onto the child. As a result, her attention and lavish praise are not experienced as genuine, unselfish, or unconditional. Normal physical affection, such as touching, holding, kissing, and hugging, is often absent; there is little genuine empathy for the child's needs and feelings. In a few cases, the child was used as a substitute husband by the mother, and the relationship had an undercurrent of inappropriate sexual longings on the part of the parent.

The father is frequently isolated or detached from the family: the mother and child become a unit from which the father is excluded. The mother may devalue her husband, and the father is often critical, rejecting, punitive, or controlling toward the child. A number of fathers were successful and had attained high status in their profession or career. This often led to an excessive emphasis on work and achievement, combined with a feeling that the family was special. Because the father was so often uninvolved or critical, attention and validation from the father occasionally took on exaggerated importance to the child. The child felt pressure to perform to obtain this approval; criticism or rejection by a high-status father was crippling.

In summary, one typical origin for narcissism involves a child who is overvalued by the mother, is undervalued by the father, and experiences minimal unselfish love from either or both. The differences in parental styles and messages could be further exacerbated by the parents' disapproval of each other or their efforts to compensate for the other's behavior. For example, a mother who sees her husband as depriving might try to compensate by channeling exaggerated amounts of attention in the child's direction. A father who feels that his wife is overindulging his child might try to establish balance by being more rigid, detached, or withholding than he otherwise might be. Ultimately, the child is caught in an unreal world. In order to survive, the child combines as best he or she can the messages and value systems of the two parents: the specialness conveyed directly by the mother and both parents' emphasis on achievement, perfection, and social appearances.

The explanation proposed here overlaps with aspects of theories by Kernberg (1967, 1970), Kohut (1966, 1971), and Millon (1969) described elsewhere in this volume. Emotional deprivation, disappointment, and overevaluation are central components. The combination of one doting but emotionally depriving parent who delivers a message of specialness along with unrealistic expectations and a second nondoting parent who is absent, critical, entitled, cold, disengaging, or rejecting sets the stage for NPD.

Schema Modes in Narcissism

Several of the EMS that were frequently observed in narcissistic patients—Entitlement, Emotional Deprivation, Defectiveness, Approval-Seeking, Unrelenting Standards, Subjugation, and Mistrust—naturally seem to group into three clusters called *schema modes:* the Self-Aggrandizer, the Vulnerable Child, and the Detached Self-Soother. These modes are facets of the self that are more or less cut off from each other. The narcissistic individual shifts from one of the three modes into another in response to events or changes in the environment.

The Self-Aggrandizer. This is the "default" mode for the narcissistic personality; "successful" narcissistic individuals spend most of their time in this mode. The focus of this mode is on gaining approval, recognition, and attention while maintaining control over their environment and having their needs gratified. The Self-Aggrandizer comprises the schemas of Entitlement, Approval-Seeking, Unrelenting Standards, and Mistrust. Narcissistic persons in this mode act superior, status-oriented, entitled, and critical of others. They show little empathy and can be exploitive and manipulative. In the Self-Aggrandizer mode, patients are usually highly competitive and envious, mistrust the sincerity of others, and may engage in fantasies of brilliance and success.

The Vulnerable Child. The Vulnerable Child mode can be triggered in several ways: when narcissistic individuals are cut off from sources of approval and validation, such as when they are alone for extended periods; when they receive negative feedback or criticism; when they fail; or when they achieve less success or gain less attention than others do. In the Vulnerable Child mode, the narcissistic person acutely experiences the loss of special status and is left feeling devalued, alone, and ordinary. This mode comprises the schemas of Defectiveness, Emotional Deprivation, and Subjugation.

The sense of being just average is experienced emotionally by narcissistic individuals as emptiness and loneliness. They feel unloved, humiliated, ignored, and exposed. If this mode persists, they can become demoralized, self-critical, and depressed. In this mode, narcissistic individuals revert to the sense of Emotional Deprivation and Defectiveness they experienced as children when the parents withdrew their approval or when they were left alone. To escape this painful experience, these narcissistic persons will try as hard as possible to regain approval and validation and thus revert to the Self-Aggrandizer or, failing that, to the third mode, the Detached Self-Soother.

The Detached Self-Soother. When narcissistic individuals can no longer tolerate the Vulnerable Child mode and are unable to regain the feeling of being special, or when they are alone, they generally enter into the Detached Self-Soother mode. This mode is a form of schema avoidance—that is, its purpose is to distract from, or numb themselves to, the pain of the Emotional Deprivation and Defectiveness schemas. Detached Self-Soothing can take many forms, such as drug and alcohol abuse, compulsive sexual activity, stimulation seeking (e.g., high-stakes gambling or investing), overeating, fantasies of grandiosity, and "workaholism." Narcissistic individuals will do almost anything to avoid experiencing the Vulnerable Child mode.

Subtypes of Entitlement

Three forms of Entitlement can be distinguished. The first type is NPD, which is referred to as *compensated entitlement* or *fragile entitlement*. In compensated entitlement, the child strives to be special to compensate for underlying feelings of emotional deprivation, defectiveness, and shame. Many patients have Entitlement schemas without meeting the DSM-IV (American Psychiatric Association 1994) criteria for NPD. The second type is *pure entitlement*, which does not involve underlying feelings of deprivation or defectiveness but usually stems from a background of material indulgence ("spoiled") and unlimited privilege. Unlike patients with NPD, patients with pure entitlement are not easily upset by defeats, criticisms, or rejections. They lack the brittleness, envy, and fragility of patients with NPD. Both types have in common, however, the expectation that they should be able to have everything they want on their own terms. The third type is *dependent entitlement*, which involves one's feeling entitled to be taken care of by others. The parents of individuals with dependent entitlement gave them few responsibilities and did everything for them, thus fostering feelings of incompetence and dependence. These patients are unable to make their own decisions and to carry out normal life responsibilities on their own. They expect others to take care of them, and they expect to give little in return. The underlying fear is of being unable to survive autonomously in the world.

Schema-Focused Treatment of Narcissism

Assessment and Diagnosis

One method of assessing NPD is through the nature of the presenting problem as described by the patient. Frequently, narcissistic patients come into therapy because their behavior is causing
problems for a significant person in either their personal or their
professional life (as a result of the Self-Aggrandizer mode), not because they are having acute internal pain. The impetus for therapy can be an intimate partner who believes that the relationship
is in trouble or a boss who has delivered an ultimatum concerning
"attitude." Therapy may also be sought when a relationship has
failed or a job has been lost, and the narcissistic individual is feeling low and mistreated by life. In either case, the narcissistic individual rarely "owns" the problem—someone (wife, boss) or
something (life, luck) is blamed. Finally, some narcissistic persons
present with substance abuse or compulsive behavior (the Detached Self-Soother mode).

A second form of assessment involves observing the patient's
behavior in relationship to the therapist. Narcissistic individuals'
behavior, especially in early sessions, speaks for itself. They talk
about themselves—their achievements, their special talents, their
grandiose plans for the future. They frequently "interview" the
therapist about his or her credentials and experience; the message
is that these patients will not demean themselves to work with
anyone who is not also highly successful, competent, and sophisticated enough to recognize and understand them and their
uniqueness. They have little real interest in the therapist as a person. Special requests and demands are presented, and if they are
not met, patients tend not to return.

A third form of assessment involves observing narcissistic patients' responses to questions about their childhood. They are often very reluctant to talk about the past; it can be remembered in
glowing terms, or else people throughout their life are blamed
unconditionally and written off. Narcissistic patients rarely show

vulnerable emotions or acknowledge pain regarding the past.

A fourth part of the standard assessment procedure involves asking patients to do imagery exercises. The therapist asks them to close their eyes and picture themselves as children. Most narcissistic persons are very resistant to doing this kind of imagery work; they often write it off as "hokey" and become angry and impatient at the suggestion. Patients who agree to try imagery either cannot generate images, produce only images that are vague or without emotional meaning, or, in the most promising cases, have memories of being lonely and devalued.

The assessment of narcissism can be further corroborated by the use of the Schema Questionnaire (Young and Brown 1990/ 1994). This 205-item self-report questionnaire provides a profile of the patient's EMS (to the extent the patient is aware of core feelings). Narcissistic individuals usually score high on Entitlement and Unrelenting Standards (because they believe they are special and admire perfection in themselves and others). Because most narcissistic patients enter therapy in the Self-Aggrandizer mode, they are almost completely unaware of schemas associated with the Vulnerable Child; consequently, they usually score low on all the underlying schemas, especially Emotional Deprivation and Defectiveness.

Focus of Treatment

The primary focus of schema-focused treatment for narcissism is on the patient's close relationships, especially the therapy relationship and romantic relationships. The purpose is to access and nurture the Vulnerable Child (and the accompanying schemas of Emotional Deprivation and Defectiveness) while challenging the Self-Aggrandizer (and the allied schemas of Approval-Seeking, Entitlement, and Unrelenting Standards). By confronting Entitlement and Approval-Seeking, the therapist begins to help the patient to relinquish the default mode of the Self-Aggrandizer. This process becomes easier as the patient—through the Vulnerable Child mode—learns to take in genuine nurturance and caring from the therapist and others without having to be perfect or special. The therapist simultaneously helps the patient tolerate the pain of the Vulnerable Child, so that he or she can acknowledge the validity of his or her emotional needs without flipping into one of the other modes. With the healing of the Defectiveness and Emotional Deprivation schemas, the Self-Aggrandizer becomes increasingly unnecessary as a compensatory strategy. A secondary focus is to discourage the patient from engaging in the Detached Self-Soother mode (and the accompanying avoidance behaviors, compulsions, and addictions) by substituting fulfilling, reciprocal intimate relationships, based on unconditional love, to alleviate the loneliness of the Vulnerable Child.

Within the therapy relationship, the major task is to create an alliance in which the patient can be helped to give and receive nurturance and empathy. This remains a consistent and central focus throughout therapy. Initially, the patient is often unable to recognize that he or she even has difficulty in accepting or giving genuine caring. Another main task is to encourage the narcissistic patient to remain in the Vulnerable Child mode rather than the Self-Aggrandizer or Detached Self-Soother mode, with feelings such as sadness, loneliness, defectiveness, shame, fear of abandonment, and loss. The patient is discouraged from engaging in behaviors in the session that are part of the Self-Aggrandizer mode, including approval-seeking, criticalness, superiority, or bragging. Some narcissistic patients profess an ability to love or empathize that actually turns out to be a form of approval-seeking. Therefore, a third task of therapy is to gently confront this approval-seeking behavior without devaluing the patient ("I care about you—not your performance or how you look"). Likewise, the therapist has to confront the entitlement, again without devaluing the patient. The message is one of mutual caring and reciprocity, a two-way flow.

It is imperative for therapists to remain consistent in their messages and behavior rather than giving in to the patient's demands or criticisms, although the patient may view the therapist's explanation and behavior as selfish, controlling, devaluing, or depriving criticisms. This is the only way in which the patient will ultimately learn what it is to feel really cared for, as well as to recognize his or her own distortion of the therapist's message. The notion of reciprocity—that all relationships, including therapy, are two-way streets—is emphasized throughout the treatment.

Obstacles to Treatment

Completing a successful course of therapy with narcissistic patients is more difficult than with patients with most other diagnoses. Narcissistic patients are much more likely than other patients to drop out of therapy prematurely, especially in the early sessions. There are several possible reasons for this premature termination: 1) they do not accept the goal of therapy (empathy, caring) and think it sounds silly, 2) they think that the therapist is incompetent or not good enough for them, or 3) they do not want their sense of entitlement and specialness to be frustrated. Even if narcissistic patients "buy" the theory, they may have great difficulty in trusting that the therapist's motives are truly as unselfish as they seem and not just a good sales ploy to keep them spending their money. This shift from seeing the therapist as just a paid functionary doing a job to viewing him or her as a genuinely caring person can be a major one.

With many narcissistic patients, the therapist cannot do anything to keep them in treatment short of providing approval and validation of their specialness, which is not advisable and is in fact considered counterproductive. However, therapists occasionally can enhance the leverage they have with the narcissistic patient. *Leverage* here refers to something the therapist has that the patient wants. The most common source of leverage initially is the threat that unless the patient gets help now, he or she will be further rejected or devalued in love or at work. A second source of leverage in some cases is the patient's unacknowledged desire to be close to the therapist and to receive empathy and nurturance. The therapist can utilize the first source by continually reiterating the dire consequences if the patient does not learn to show more vulnerability and consideration toward others. The second source can be enhanced if the therapist tries to create a more open, personal relationship with the patient instead of maintaining neutrality or emotional distance. When the patient feels that the therapist genuinely cares, he or she will be better able to understand and tolerate the therapist's empathy. Otherwise, the patient may misinterpret or experience empathy for the vulnerable child as the therapist pitying the patient, which may lead the patient to feel exposed and then to terminate therapy.

Specific Strategies

In the remainder of this chapter, the authors focus on specific experiential, cognitive, behavioral, and couples-based strategies for working with the narcissistic patient. All of these techniques serve to further the goals of therapy outlined earlier in this chapter.

Experiential Work

Using experiential techniques, the patient is helped to experience his or her feelings of deprivation, defectiveness, and emptiness and is shown how to experience and differentiate the three schema modes. Each mode takes on a visual representation in imagery and becomes a separate character. These three characters interact and have dialogues with one another. For example, the Self-Aggrandizer might devalue the Vulnerable Child for being weak and pitiful. The patient is helped to create a nurturing adult in imagery to care for the Vulnerable Child. At the same time, the Detached Self-Soother and the Self-Aggrandizer are challenged by the nurturing adult until the patient is able to see that these two modes cannot really substitute for genuine comfort, validation, acceptance, and fulfillment.

Cognitive Work

Through cognitive strategies, patients learn to track their thinking in the three modes by identifying the automatic thought sequences that are triggered in certain problem situations and writing them down on a Daily Record of Dysfunctional Thoughts (Beck et al. 1979). Narcissistic persons are helped to identify and correct the cognitive distortions reflected in their automatic thoughts. For example, one target is to identify the all-or-nothing (black-or-white) thinking of the Self-Aggrandizer. "Unless I am special and the center of attention at all times, then I am worthless and ignored." This distortion leads the narcissistic patient to seek attention and approval and compare himself or herself to others on a continuous basis.

Thought sheets, on which patients record their thoughts and feelings in specific upsetting life situations, can be helpful to facilitate empathy, to take the perspective of the other, and to imagine others' thoughts and feelings. The fantasies of the Self-Aggrandizer can also be explored and then translated into more healthy, attainable goals.

By monitoring their thoughts before initiating the Detached Self-Soothing mode, narcissistic patients can learn to recognize the underlying vulnerability and fear of being alone. Thoughts such as, "I should not be alone—it means I am not popular," are identified and discussed. These patients are helped to spend time alone unstimulated and unsoothed and to get to know and understand the Vulnerable Child. By tracking thoughts in the Vulnerable Child mode, they learn to see that again they are distorting the reality of the situation (e.g., one does not have to be special to be cared for). Cognitive distortions, such as Labeling and Jumping to Conclusions, are identified.

Techniques such as the Vertical Arrow are particularly useful in identifying the underlying beliefs and expectations that drive narcissistic individuals' excessive emphasis on appearance, status, money, approval, and attention. The therapist can help the patient to work systematically through statements such as, "If it were true that you were not handsome (or well-dressed, popular, talented, etc.), what would that mean to you? Why would it upset you?" Patients come to see how their rigid absolutistic rules and beliefs drive their perfectionism and lead to the fear of failure and exposure.

Through these types of techniques, the therapist can introduce some margin for error into performance expectations, both
for themselves and for others. Disadvantages of overemphasizing
status and appearance (e.g., a lack of time for the development of
true friendship and connection) are pointed out. Finally, beliefs
and expectations about others being there to "serve them," or
about others "being out for themselves" or "wanting something
from them," are challenged.

Behavioral Pattern Breaking

Cognitive work is typically combined with behavioral pattern-
breaking assignments. For example, narcissistic patients are asked
to spend time alone, without self-soothing through substances or
other forms of stimulation. The clinician suggests that these patients should carry out experiments—such as saying nothing and
just observing while socializing—in order to risk not seeking attention or approval. During leisure time, they are advised to decrease the amount of time they spend in large crowds and to focus
on developing their intimate relationships. They are taught how
to practice empathy in various situations. If they are having problems in their interpersonal interactions at work, this can be an
ideal laboratory for testing empathic gestures and a change of attitude. They are gradually helped to feel how comforting and nurturing it can be to fit in and be one of the crowd rather than always
attempting to stand out.

Case Vignette

Steve,[1] a 30-year-old gay optometrist, entered therapy with
issues related to the Detached Self-Soother mode. He presented with a sexual compulsion that resulted in frequent,
unprotected anal sex. He was afraid of contracting HIV (human immunodeficiency virus). "It would be a waste of such
a unique guy. I have a great life," he stated, but he was un-

---

[1]The patient was treated by the second author.

able to stop himself. He wanted the therapist to just "fix" him, that that was what she "was meant to be good at." His Self-Aggrandizer mode was reflected in his description of himself as a "cool dude"; he dressed downtown hip and nonchalantly criticized the location, decor, and accessibility of the therapist's uptown office.

Like most narcissistic individuals, Steve saw relationships as a form of conquest—validation of the Self-Aggrandizer. Steve had "come out" 3 years previously but still had not had any lasting relationships. This was not a new pattern. At college, he was extremely popular, was always surrounded by girls, was seen at every party, drove fast cars, had lots of sex, but never involved himself for long with any one person. Steve substituted stimulation for intimacy: "I never let anyone get really close," "I get easily bored," "I like to live on the edge." During the last 3 years, his pattern had been one of meeting friends for supper, going home, and then, at midnight or so, going out to cruise gay bars. He would pick someone up, take him home, have (frequently unsafe) sex, and then kick him out.

The day after the sexual partner left, Steve's Vulnerable Child mode would be triggered. He felt terrible. He could not understand why he had no control over the problem—"I can do anything I want, I'm being successful—why can't I lick this?" He felt lonely, empty, and terrified that he would contract AIDS (acquired immunodeficiency syndrome).

The origin of Steve's narcissism is typical of the pattern described earlier in this chapter: a doting mother who used the child to gratify her own needs, in combination with a critical father. Steve grew up in New Jersey and was the second of three sons. His father owned a successful jewelry business and was at the store a lot. His mother was a housewife and at home all the time. His parents argued constantly. Steve became his mother's companion and protector—she told him how special and wonderful he was and how she could not live without him. Later, the tone of their relationship became more sexual as she openly flirted with him. "I became my mother's girlfriend (i.e., confidant) and her husband." His father resented their closeness and blamed Steve for draining the family's finances and for not spending more time at home.

The Self-Aggrandizer was further reinforced through the parents' emphasis on status and success. When Steve was 11, the family moved to an even bigger house in New Jersey, which to this day Steve feels is more like a movie set than a home. The accumulation of material wealth was always a major emphasis, and Steve's mother was easily seduced by her husband's gifts. At these times, she would completely ignore Steve until the fighting started again.

Steve's mother would use him when she felt alienated from her husband but never offered Steve empathy or physical affection. She would often turn to him for support and counsel, telling him that he was the only one who really understood her. Steve felt betrayed and angry by her inconsistency and manipulation but over time learned "to beat her at her own game." He learned to suppress his Vulnerable Child and bolster the Self-Aggrandizer by demanding more special privileges and material extravagances in exchange for his attention and companionship.

The Self-Aggrandizer and Detached Self-Soother were further reinforced by the absence of responsibilities at home or parental limits. He began using people in the same way he felt used. At age 16, Steve was free to do whatever he wanted and, with a car, started to stay out late and experiment with sex and drugs. He made lots of friends but no close attachments. He manipulated people and pushed his companions to the limit to test their loyalty. If they failed, he dismissed them. The pattern of entitlement and lack of intimacy continued throughout college and optometry school. Steve eventually created a successful business of which he was inordinately proud; he also prided himself on being a slave driver as a boss— "but they all love me."

Steve was helped to reconnect to the Vulnerable Child through experiential and cognitive work. He gradually became more in touch with the emptiness and rejection that he had felt throughout his childhood. He was able to connect these feelings with his urges to seek sex. "Thought records" helped him to monitor his thinking leading up to sexual encounters: "Why am I alone here? I've got to keep the energy going." He began to see how the temporary companionship of an anonymous lover offered an illusory solution. In the short run, it reduced the tension and alleviated his feelings of emptiness, but in the long run, this behavior kept him from establishing a lasting connection that would allow him to feel cared for and appreciated.

Experiential exercises were also valuable in helping Steve validate his needs for nurturing and unconditional acceptance. He did imagery exercises in which he vented anger toward his parents for depriving him emotionally. "A mother should give unconditional love—she never did." "A father should be a buddy—he hated me." Ultimately, he realized that he never felt really loved by either of his parents; neither of them really cared about him and how he felt.

The therapist's initial leverage was Steve's fear of contracting HIV; but later, his increased awareness of his loneliness and pain provided the primary motivation for continuing. She encouraged him to spend time alone in his apartment at night and also to choose partners for dating rather than just sex. Steve realized, in the course of spending time with a number of different men, that he was highly critical and manipulative. He also became more keenly aware of the difficulty he had in handling intimacy or gestures of real caring from other people.

The therapy relationship played a critical role in shifting Steve away from the Self-Aggrandizer toward the Vulnerable Child and Healthy Adult. For example, Steve frequently changed his hairstyle to whatever was in style that month. At these times, he always asked for the therapist's feedback and approval: "Well, what do you think? It's great, isn't it?" The therapist was always honest and on one occasion said she did not like it but reassured him that how he looked in no way affected her respect or caring for him. Steve was visibly shaken by this "criticism" but eventually came to believe that the therapist did not think less of him at times like this. Steve made many similar efforts to assert his Self-Aggrandizer—through dressing in new clothing ensembles, mentioning famous people he spent time with, and offering to get the therapist into trendy restaurants or overbooked theater productions. In each instance, the therapist gently confronted his motivation of gaining approval while reasserting her respect for him "just the way he is."

Steve was often manipulative in sessions. He accomplished this through charm, by acting hurt, or by becoming angry. For example, early in treatment, he repeatedly asked to change appointment times to times already assigned to regular patients. When the therapist refused, Steve criticized her for being selfish and uncaring and became angry because she would not adapt her schedule to suit his preferences: "I'm insulted that you won't accommodate my needs." Gradually, the therapist helped Steve to see that he was feeling hurt that she was not valuing and caring for him but that his demands were unrealistic. He was urged to express genuine feelings of vulnerability instead of becoming angry or manipulative. The therapist explained that all patients are treated equally, regardless of their status or demandingness. Through these types of interventions, Steve learned more appropriate ways of getting his needs met while respecting the feelings and desires of other people.

The final stage of treatment involved behavioral pattern breaking. In this phase, the therapist encouraged Steve to develop a committed relationship based on mutuality and vulnerability rather than approval and entitlement. The breakthrough began when Steve met Walter, a young man from Kentucky who was struggling with his own gay identity. Steve's initial role was the macho guy who would show Walter the ropes; this mentoring role gradually developed into a loving relationship. Walter was very up front. He wanted a monogamous relationship based on mutual respect and caring. Steve initially could not tolerate the straightforwardness and sincerity of what Walter offered and ran away into 2 weeks of late-night drugs and sex. But this time, it felt so empty in comparison to what he had had with Walter that he committed himself to try again. Walter agreed to be firm but patient. Learning how to accept and give love was difficult and painful for Steve, but the joy of waking up in Walter's arms and sharing tender moments far outweighed the quick buzz of anonymous sex or drugs.

By the end of treatment, Steve had learned to value and express his vulnerable feelings, to overcome his insistence on being special, to give up the sexual compulsivity that filled up his emptiness, and to relate to other people on the basis of genuine caring and reciprocity.

Conclusion

Schema-focused therapy offers a promising new model for approaching the problem of narcissism. This approach combines the theoretical depth often associated with psychoanalytical theory with the more active and directive techniques central to cognitive, behavior, and experiential therapies. It is hoped that this method will help therapists treat the complex disorder of narcissism in a more focused and efficient manner.

References

American Psychiatric Association: Diagnostic and Statistical Manual of Mental Disorders, 4th Edition. Washington, DC, American Psychiatric Association, 1994

Beck AT, Rush AJ, Shaw BF, et al: Cognitive Therapy of Depression. New York, Guilford, 1979

Bricker DC, Young JE: A client's guide to schema-focused therapy (1993), in Cognitive Therapy for Personality Disorders: A Schema-Focused Approach, Revised. Edited by Young JE. Sarasota, FL, Professional Resource Press, 1994, pp 79–90

Kernberg OF: Borderline personality organization. J Am Psychoanal Assoc 15:641–685, 1967

Kernberg OF: Factors in the treatment of narcissistic personality disorder. J Am Psychoanal Assoc 18:51–58, 1970

Kohut H: Forms and transformations of narcissism. J Am Psychoanal Assoc 14:243–272, 1966

Kohut H: The Analysis of the Self. New York, International Universities Press, 1971

Mahoney MJ: Theoretical developments in the cognitive psychotherapies. J Consult Clin Psychol 61:187–193, 1993

Masterson JF: The Narcissistic and Borderline Disorders. New York, Brunner/Mazel, 1981, p 8

McGinn LK, Young JE: Schema-focused therapy, in Frontiers of Cognitive Therapy. Edited by Salkovskis PM. New York, Guilford, 1996

Millon T: Modern Psychopathology: A Prosocial Approach to Maladaptive Learning and Functioning. Philadelphia, PA, WB Saunders, 1969

Young JE: Cognitive Therapy for Personality Disorders: A Schema-Focused Approach, Revised. Edited by Young JE. Sarasota, FL, Professional Resource Press, 1994

Young JE, Brown G: Schema questionnaire (1990), in Cognitive Therapy for Personality Disorders: A Schema-Focused Approach, Revised. Edited by Young JE. Sarasota, FL, Professional Resource Press, 1994, pp 63–77

Young JE, Klosko JS: Reinventing Your Life: How to Break Free of Negative Life Patterns and Feel Good Again. New York, Plume, 1994

Appendix
Early Maladaptive Schemas

Disconnection and Rejection

Expectation that one's needs for security, safety, stability, nurturance, empathy, sharing of feelings, acceptance, and respect will not be met in a predictable manner. Typical family origin is detached, explosive, unpredictable, rejecting, punitive, unforgiving, withholding, inhibited, or abusive.

1. **Abandonment/instability:** The perceived *instability* or *unreliability* of those available for support and connection. Involves the sense that significant others will not be able to continue providing emotional support, connection, strength, or practical protection because they are emotionally unstable and unpredictable (e.g., angry outbursts), unreliable, or erratically present; because they will die imminently; or because they will abandon the patient in favor of someone better.
2. **Mistrust/abuse:** The expectation that others will hurt, abuse, humiliate, cheat, lie, manipulate, or take advantage. Usually involves the perception that the harm is intentional or the result of unjustified and extreme negligence. May include the sense that one always ends up being cheated relative to others, or "gets the short end of the stick."
3. **Emotional deprivation:** The expectation that one's desire for a normal degree of emotional support will not be adequately met by others. The three major forms of deprivation are 1) deprivation of nurturance—absence of attention, affection, warmth, or companionship; 2) deprivation of empathy—absence of understanding, listening, self-disclosure, or mutual sharing of feelings from others; and 3) deprivation of protection—absence of strength, direction, or guidance from others.
4. **Defectiveness/shame:** The feeling that one is defective, bad, unwanted, inferior, or invalid in important respects or that one would be unlovable to significant others if exposed. May involve hypersensitivity to criticism, rejection, and blame; self-consciousness, comparisons, and insecurity around others;

or a sense of shame regarding one's perceived flaws. These flaws may be *internal* (e.g., selfishness, angry impulses, unacceptable sexual desires) or *external* (e.g., undesirable physical appearance, social awkwardness).

5. **Social isolation/alienation:** The feeling that one is isolated from the rest of the world, different from other people, or not part of any group or community

Impaired Autonomy and Performance

Expectations about oneself and the environment that interfere with one's perceived ability to separate, survive, function independently, or perform successfully. Typical family origin is enmeshed, child's confidence is undermined, parents are overprotective or fail to reinforce child for performing competently outside the family.

6. **Dependence/incompetence:** The belief that one is unable to handle one's *everyday responsibilities* in a competent manner without considerable help from others (e.g., take care of oneself, solve daily problems, exercise good judgment, tackle new tasks, make good decisions). Often presents as helplessness.

7. **Vulnerability to danger (random events):** The exaggerated fear that "random" catastrophe could strike at any time and that one will be unable to prevent it. Fears focus on one or more of the following:

   ■ Medical (e.g., heart attack, AIDS)
   ■ Emotional (e.g., go crazy)
   ■ Natural/phobic (e.g., elevators, crime, airplanes, earthquakes)

8. **Enmeshment/undeveloped self:** Excessive emotional involvement and closeness with one or more significant others (often parents) at the expense of full individuation or normal social development. Often involves the belief that at least one of the enmeshed individuals cannot survive or be happy without the constant support of the other. May also include feelings of being smothered by or fused with others *or* of insufficient individual identity. Often experienced as feeling empty and floundering, having no direction, or—in extreme cases—questioning one's existence.

9. **Failure:** The belief that one has failed, will inevitably fail, or is fundamentally inadequate relative to one's peers and in areas of *achievement* (e.g., school, career, sports). Often involves beliefs that one is stupid, inept, untalented, ignorant, lower in status, less successful than others, and so forth.

Impaired Limits

Deficiency in internal limits, responsibility to others, or long-term goal orientation. Leads to difficulty respecting the rights of others, making commitments, or setting and meeting personal goals. Typical family origin is characterized by permissiveness, indulgence, or lack of direction rather than appropriate confrontation, discipline, and limits in relation to taking responsibility and setting goals. Child may not have been pushed to tolerate normal levels of discomfort or may not have been given adequate supervision, direction, or guidance.

10. **Entitlement/grandiosity:** Insistence that one should be able to do or have whatever one wants, regardless of what others consider reasonable or the cost to others; *or* the excessive tendency to assert one's power, force one's point of view, or control the behavior of others in line with one's own desires without regard to others' needs for autonomy and self-direction. Often involves excessive demandingness and lack of empathy for others' needs and feelings.

11. **Insufficient self-control/self-discipline:** Pervasive difficulty or refusal to exercise sufficient self-control and frustration tolerance to achieve one's personal goals or to restrain the excessive expression of one's emotions and impulses. In its milder form, patient presents with an exaggerated emphasis on *discomfort avoidance*—avoiding pain, conflict, confrontation, responsibility, or overexertion at the expense of personal fulfillment, commitment, or integrity.

Other-Directedness

An excessive focus on the desires, feelings, and responses of others at the expense of one's own needs in order to gain love and approval, maintain one's sense of connection, or avoid retaliation. Usually involves suppression and lack of awareness regarding one's own anger and natural inclinations. Typical family origin is based on conditional acceptance: children must suppress important aspects of themselves in order to gain love, attention, and approval. In many such families, the parents' emotional needs and desires—or social acceptance and status—are valued more than the unique needs and feelings of each child.

12. **Subjugation:** Excessive surrendering of control over one's behavior, emotional expression, and decisions, because one feels *coerced*—usually to avoid anger, retaliation, or abandonment. Involves the perception that one's own desires, opinions, and feelings are not valid or important to others. Frequently presents as excessive compliance combined with hypersensitivity to feeling trapped. Almost always involves the chronic *suppression of anger* toward those perceived to be in control. Usually leads to a buildup of anger that is manifested in maladaptive symptoms (e.g., passive-aggressive behavior, uncontrolled outbursts of temper, psychosomatic symptoms, withdrawal of affection, "acting out," substance abuse).

13. **Self-sacrifice:** Excessive focus on *voluntarily* meeting the needs of others in daily situations at the expense of one's own gratification. The most common reasons are to prevent causing pain to others, to avoid guilt from feeling selfish, or to maintain the connection with others perceived as needy. Often results from an acute sensitivity to the pain of others. Sometimes leads to a sense that one's own needs are not being adequately met and to resentment of those who are taken care of. (Overlaps with concept of codependency.)

14. **Approval-seeking:** Excessive emphasis on gaining approval, recognition, or attention from other people or fitting in at the expense of developing a secure and true sense of self. One's sense of esteem is dependent primarily on the reactions of others rather than on one's own internalized values, standards, or natural inclinations. Sometimes includes an overemphasis on status, appearance, social acceptance, money, competition, or achievement—being among the best or most popular—as a means of gaining approval. Frequently results in major life decisions that are inauthentic or unsatisfying, hypersensitivity to rejection, or envy of others who are more popular or successful.

Overvigilance and Inhibition

Excessive emphasis on controlling one's spontaneous feelings, impulses, and choices in order to avoid making mistakes *or* on meeting rigid, internalized rules and expectations about performance and ethical behavior—often at the expense of happiness, self-expression, relaxation, close relationships, or health. Typical family origin is grim (and sometimes punitive). Performance, duty, perfectionism, following rules, and avoiding costly mistakes predominate over pleasure, joy, and relaxation. Patients usually have an undercurrent of pessimism and worry that things could fall apart if they fail to be vigilant and careful at all times.

15. **Negativity/Vulnerability to error (controllable events):** The exaggerated expectation—in a wide range of work, financial, or interpersonal situations that are typically viewed as "controllable"—that things will go seriously wrong or that aspects of one's life that seem to be going well will fall apart at any time *or* a pervasive, lifelong focus on the negative aspects of life (e.g., pain, death, loss, disappointment, conflict, guilt, resentment, unsolved problems, potential mistakes, betrayal, things that could go wrong) while minimizing or neglecting the positive or optimistic aspects. Usually involves an inordinate fear of making mistakes that might lead to financial collapse, loss, humiliation, being trapped in a bad situation, or loss of control. Because potential negative outcomes are exaggerated, these patients are frequently characterized by chronic worry, vigilance, pessimism, complaining, or indecision.

16. **Overcontrol:** The excessive inhibition of spontaneous action, feeling, or communication, usually to avoid making mistakes, disapproval by others, catastrophe and chaos, or losing control of one's impulses. The most common areas of excessive control involve 1) inhibition of anger and aggression, 2) compulsive order and planning, 3) inhibition of positive impulses (e.g., joy, affection, sexual excitement, play), 4) excessive adherence to routines or rituals, 5) difficulty expressing vulnerability or communicating freely about one's feelings, needs, and so on, or 6) excessive emphasis on rationality while disregarding emotional needs. Often, the overcontrol is extended to others in the patient's environment.

17. **Unrelenting standards:** The underlying belief that one must strive to meet very high *internalized standards* of behavior and performance, usually to avoid criticism. Typically results in feelings of pressure or difficulty slowing down and in hypercriticalness toward oneself and others. Must involve significant impairment in pleasure, relaxation, health, self-esteem, sense of accomplishment, or satisfying relationships. Unrelenting standards typically present as

   ■ Perfectionism, inordinate attention to detail, and an underestimate of how good one's own performance is relative to the norm
   ■ Rigid rules and "shoulds" in many areas of life, including unrealistically high moral, ethical, cultural, or religious precepts
   ■ Preoccupation with time and efficiency, so that more can be accomplished

18. **Punitiveness:** The tendency to be angry, intolerant, harshly critical, punitive, and impatient with those people (including oneself) who do not meet one's expectations or standards. Usually includes difficulty forgiving mistakes or tolerating limitations in oneself or others because of a reluctance to consider extenuating circumstances, allow for human imperfection, empathize with feelings, be flexible, or see alternative points of view.

Source.   Copyright 1994, Jeffrey Young, Ph.D. Reprinted with permission of the Cognitive Therapy Center of New York, 3 East 80th Street, Penthouse, New York, NY 10021.

Chapter 12

Manifestations of Narcissistic Disorders in Couples Therapy

Identification and Treatment

Marion F. Solomon, Ph.D.

A good marriage is one in which one or the other partner rises to the challenge of providing the self object functions that can fill the other's temporarily impaired self needs at a particular moment.

Heinz Kohut
(1984, p. 220)

"**A** good marriage is one in which only one partner is crazy at any given time," quipped Heinz Kohut at the first University of California–Los Angeles conference on "Narcissism: The Psychology of the Self" in 1979. Kohut did not work with couples, nor did he focus on the marital relationship, but he believed marriage to be an extremely important topic for self psychology. When partners exhibit early damage to the self and pathological, narcissistic defenses protect a fragile core, mutative change requires specific strategies for treatment of the relationship and each of the mates. When individual treatment alone may disrupt the marital or family relationship, conjoint therapy coinciding with analysis may be of great benefit. The therapeutic goals of conjoint therapy with narcissistic patients include 1) helping the partners understand each other's archaic, dependent core needs; 2) finding ways to reduce the injuries partners inflict on each other in their collusive attempt to protect vulnerable selves from injury; and 3) healing damaged structures of the self through a reparative relationship.

In this chapter, conjoint marital therapy as a mode of treatment for narcissistic disorders is discussed. The model suggested focuses on a modification of the couples system, sometimes in addition to and sometimes in lieu of individual treatment. Treatment choice often depends on the degree of individual pathology as well as the resources of the couple. A combination of conjoint treatment and individual treatment with separate therapists works best whenever feasible.

Background

The introduction of an object relations theory perspective (Fairbairn 1954; Slipp 1984; Winnicott 1965) in couples therapy (Dicks 1967) paved the way for the attention to narcissistic disturbances and provided a conceptual frame for describing and understanding narcissistic issues in couples. The first author to identify narcissistic disturbances in couples was Lansky (1981), who discussed the underlying shame and humiliation of those who are narcissistically vulnerable.

Lansky described how narcissistically vulnerable partners use each other to temporarily avoid dealing with the emergence of a serious problem. He showed how partners form collusive bonds to defend against fragmentation when feelings of shame arise. Instead of helping each other grow and mature, each may use the other to reinforce a distorted view of reality. The collusive contract is maintained because each partner needs to keep destructive forces at bay. Instead of changing and adapting, the relationship relies on defensive strategies. In such relationships, communication is viewed not as a way to improve a problematic situation but as a danger that might expose underlying fears of falling apart and being humiliated (Lansky 1993). Both partners may think of their relationship as a disaster. They may not be able to explain even to themselves why they remain attached to someone who is so despicable. Yet through years, even decades, of unremitting misery, these attacking relationships endure. Lansky suggests that couples can break disruptive patterns when each partner reclaims his or her own cutoff, disowned parts.

Schwartzman (1984) connected the contributions of self psychology to the treatment of five couples. She noted the different transferences between the narcissistic person who lacks differentiation between self and other and the neurotic patient who is capable of viewing others as distinct and separate. Schwartzman suggested that the therapist may need to temporarily perform needed functions for one or both partners in order to provide the essential self-cohesion needed to enable the couples therapy to proceed effectively.

Scharff and Scharff (1987, 1991) elaborated on the ways that each partner, carrying an internalized exciting or frustrating object, utilizes marital and family relationships to contain intolerable affect and anxiety. Couples therapy, they proposed, requires a secure treatment environment with a focus on understanding beyond language; the ability to tolerate and contain each partner's anxieties; and the ability to make interpretations and carefully note the response, "to look us back in the eye, and to set us straight. . . . They need to be able to do this with [the therapist] if they are to manage to do it with each other" (Scharff and Scharff 1987, p. 63).

Solomon (1989) focused on the range of narcissistic needs, from healthy to pathological, that arise in conjoint therapy and the effect of early, unmet dependency needs on intimate relationships throughout life. In *Narcissism and Intimacy: Love and Marriage in an Age of Confusion,* Solomon (1989) offered strategies for understanding the relations between presented problems and underlying problems and described how various acted-out behaviors have underlying relational and narcissistic issues at the base. When stressful conditions cause a welling up of emotions, patterns of defending the self reemerge. Narcissism is on a continuum from health to pathology. Table 12–1 shows the differences between healthy narcissism, narcissistic disorders, and severe personality disorders, including psychotic or autistic states. It also addresses different types of boundaries, levels of object relations, types of anxieties, ability to give and take emotional support, self-image, awareness of emotions, and types of defenses. In times of stress, the reactions correlate closely with the degree of pathology.

Recognizing the Past in the Present

Couples typically enter marital therapy complaining of severe problems in their relationships. What often emerge are signs of a lack of a cohesive self in one or both partners, along with defenses that partners repeatedly replay in a collusion that protects each of them from the terror so prevalent with narcissistic disorders.

Treatment of narcissistic disorders requires an understanding of the early interactions between parent and child and the representation of interactions that have been generalized and replayed in adult interactions. When couples begin treatment—and if both partners have narcissistic wounds from early emotional, psychological, or physical assaults—a major goal of the therapy is to help each partner move out of the intense self-focus he or she brings to the relationship and into an understanding of his or her needs, fears, and defenses as they are being played out in the relationship.

To understand the dynamics of couples, it may be helpful to

Table 12–1. The narcissistic continuum

	Mature level (self and other are separate entities)	Level of narcissistic vulnerability (primary focus on self)	Archaic level (lives in a separate reality)
Types of boundaries	Solid but intimate relationships may open and become permeable	Unstable boundaries; lack of self-differentiation; merger wish along with fear of losing self	Lack of distinction between self and other or between inner and outer
Ability to give and take emotional support	Flexible and able to reciprocate; has stable representations of self and others	Mind-reading fantasies; projection of own wants and needs onto others; exterior facade of power and success; many friends but no intimates; limited ability to reciprocate	Unaware of needs of others or reciprocity of relationships; dependent and needy
Types of anxieties in emotional situations	Experiences fears and anxiety in stressful situations; may experience jealousy in love triangles	Concerned about identity when not in control; fear of fragmentation and loss of self-cohesion; desire for attention to overcome inner emptiness	Fragments when needs unmet; experiences terror of abandonment, death, nonexistence, destruction, and chaos
Self-image	Feels guilty when things go wrong; capable of reparative actions	Intensely ambitious, power hungry, self-centered with omnipotence and grandiosity; exists to fill needed functions within self	Nothing exists outside of private inner world; surrounded by many dangers

(continued)

Table 12–1. The narcissistic continuum (*continued*)

	Mature level (self and other are separate entities)	Level of narcissistic vulnerability (primary focus on self)	Archaic level (lives in a separate reality)
Awareness of emotions	Able to tolerate negative and positive emotions at the same time; emotions do not interfere with thought processes	Inner world hidden; defenses used to block dangerous emotions; wide variations of affect; sometimes violent; awareness of others' needs and emotions denied	Impaired thought process; fragmented emotions; inner world filled with fear and rage
Types of defenses	Rationalization, intellectualization, sublimation; repression and displacement	Splitting and projective identification; using denigrating, and discarding of people; fear of attack from others	Hallucinations, disavowal, grandiose demands, and fantasies; magical thinking; paranoid ideation; somatization
Focus when problems arise	Focus on positive and negative aspects; reality distorted but not denied; self well defended but cohesive	Sudden surges of emotions; fear of fragmentation; feelings of shame or blame; loss of cohesive thoughts; total focus on meeting self-needs	Complete and mindless self-absorption; feels surrounded by danger and chaos; experiences autistic inner world
Pathological states in times of stress	Neurotic functioning; phobic, obsessive, compulsive, hysterical personality type	Borderline and narcissistic functioning; passive, aggressive, rage reactions; infantile personality type; dissociative states	Psychotic functioning; paranoid, schizophrenic, manic depressive (bipolar), antisocial personality type

Source.   Copyright 1994 by Marion Solomon. *Training Handbook for Couples Therapy,* reprinted by permission of the Lifespan Learning Institute, Los Angeles, CA.

determine where in the developmental sequence the damage took place. The early development of neurotic and more primitive mental disorders, as conceptualized by different theorists, is depicted in Figure 12–1. The top section of Figure 12–1 shows precursors of neurosis. The bottom section includes precursors of more severe narcissistic and borderline disorders.

The early development of narcissistic disorders may affect adult functioning at the level of the earliest object relations. The oedipal complications identified in early psychoanalytical theory and represented on the upper half of the figure imply problems originating at a relatively late developmental point, after age 18 months. Narcissistic pathology originates before the boundaries of self and other have achieved object constancy, before the capacity to be alone has developed sufficiently, and before cognitive processes have developed to the point that the child is able to think about feelings. Defenses designed to protect against intolerable affect are imprinted and replayed throughout life when situations reminiscent of early failures cause reemergence of both old injuries and primitive defenses. The issues that emerge at each stage of development remain as imprinted aspects of the person, bubbling up repeatedly to be reexperienced in continuing connections throughout life.

In work with couples, it is necessary to recognize that symptoms that were formed early in the lives of either or both spouses can appear later in life in a renewed attempt to resolve old issues. In treatment, partners may join together to protect themselves and each other from conflict. In operation, the collusive contract maintains the consistency of each partner's perceptions, protecting them both against overwhelming negative or dangerous emotions.

Underlying many problems that couples identify are issues of power and control, independence and dependence, and closeness and distance. More often than not, couples at first do not even recognize issues other than the crisis that has brought them to treatment. Deeply hidden wounds to self-esteem may make it impossible for the partners to reach agreement about anything.

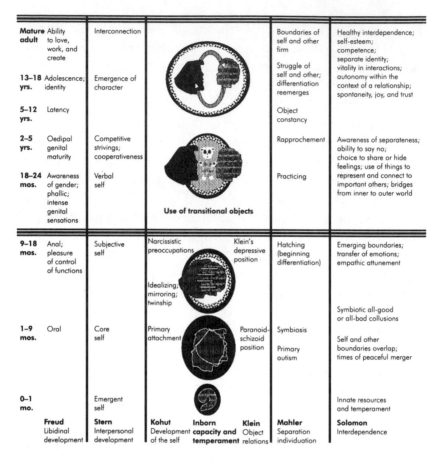

Figure 12–1.   Early development of neurotic and more primitive mental disorders. *Source.*   Reprinted from Solomon M: *Lean on Me: The Power of Positive Dependency in Intimate Relationships.* New York, Simon & Schuster, 1994. Copyright 1994, Marion Solomon. Reprinted by permission of Simon & Schuster, Inc., New York City, and the Lifespan Learning Institute, Los Angeles, CA.

Narcissistic Persons as Partners

Narcissism manifests in a variety of ways in intimate relationships. Characteristics of narcissistic persons' individual functioning have been described elsewhere in this volume. As a couple, they may present in therapy an interaction between a ruthlessly exploiting, dominating individual and an oppressed victim, the proverbial narcissistic partner matched with a masochistic partner (Kernberg 1993). In some instances, the couple makes collusive efforts to maintain an idealized image of the relationship as one of complete mutual satisfaction. In other instances, partners maintain the balance of individual psychopathology by finding and utilizing each other's vulnerable areas, projecting their own hated parts, sometimes locating the fragile boundaries in the other that makes them unconsciously willing receivers of unwanted projections, and ultimately hating what they see of themselves mirrored in their partners. The partners, experiencing the projections as both alien and familiar, feel overwhelmed and may, if forced to stay in this role beyond a tolerable period, feel increasingly weakened and dysfunctional. When a couple enters therapy, what is initially presented as a problem may be a distortion caused by this process of boundary invasion and transmission of split-off affects.

Another manifestation of narcissistic disorder is attachment to a well-known figure in order to bask in reflected glory. Some relationships are created to contain unrecognized fears left over from infancy, dread of abandonment, or the terror created by destructive fantasies. A narcissistic relationship begins with high hopes that this new person will be the one who meets all needs and is perfectly attuned, totally accepting, always available, and never intrusive when not needed. Such an idealized version of a relationship is bound to lead to disappointment when the other emerges with needs and desires of his or her own. The result may be narcissistic rage, devaluation of the relationship, and rapid discarding of the other person.

When difficulties arise, each partner sees the problem coming from the other. When his or her defensive arrangements falter, the vulnerable partner becomes irrational, demanding attention or justice, with a rage that goes beyond the immediate issues. Devaluation and discarding, closing out the painful awareness of another who has failed, is easier than tol-

erating the pain and shame incurred by being in the relationship.

The manifest issues serve as justifications for primitive defensive operations that bring to the forefront fears of abandonment,
disappointment, or not being cared for. Demandingness and entitlement are pervasive features of narcissistic partners in vulnerable marriages because omnipotent expectations can never be
fulfilled. Marriages organized around the containment and expression of massive rage and fear involve the collusive exchange
of projective defenses that ward off debilitating anxiety and fragmentation experiences. The result is a constant preoccupation
with holding oneself together, especially in intimate situations. In
this collusive dance, feelings of emptiness, futility, depression,
and rage abound.

In order to address the complexities of the pathology in such
relationships, vulnerable areas must be contained by the therapist. Healing requires an increased ability to hold and contain
such painful intrusions, thereby changing and making more cohesive the structuring of the self. Kohut (1984) pointed out that a
healing relationship can include a variety of significant others
who serve selfobject functions to support a wounded self. In
successful treatment, the therapist is carried by the momentum
of the analytical process to reactivate in the relationship the
needs of a self that had been thwarted in childhood. A healthy
self includes the ability to identify, seek out, and utilize appropriate selfobjects.

Conjoint sessions therapy with both partners present can be
an important part of the healing process (Solomon 1989, 1994). In
individual therapy, the transference emerges and provides clues
to the early object relations of the patient. In conjoint therapy, the
partners enter treatment with a full-blown transference that can
be observed by the therapist and utilized by rapid movement into
deep levels of the partners' unfilled needs and wounds. Transference develops also between each of the partners and the therapist, thus providing information on unconscious dyadic and
triadic imprinted patterns that are reemerging in the treatment
setting.

Treating the Vulnerable Marriage

All marriages include infantile feelings between the partners. Happy marriages allow freedom for deeply repressed feelings without loss of dignity or security (Nadelson and Paolini 1978). In troubled marriages, the need to express repressed infantile feelings and the awareness that such expression is likely to result in harmful interactions cause regression and defensive reactions. In marriages hampered by narcissistic vulnerabilities and defenses, disagreements serve as opportunities to vent repressed infantile rage and vengefulness in the form of blame.

Therapists generally enter the picture at the point at which discharge of overwhelming emotions takes the form of mutual blaming or acting out. A conjoint session with the two people is a small group. While the therapist responds to each of the individuals, he or she must make interpretations about how the mates use the interactive system and how the system causes each to react in special ways. The therapist must function as decoder of messages by empathically responding to the underlying affects and emotions of each partner, reframing the partner's perceptions along the way. As the treatment progresses, it is possible to slowly uncover the underlying wounds and vulnerabilities. By becoming aware through the emergence of dysfunctional patterns in treatment and by learning to recognize the inner reality of the other, each comes to understand how blame or destructive behavior is being used as a protection against humiliation or fear of abandonment. Connecting the triangle of transference in the session, at-home interactions, and early relationships in family of origin, partners begin to understand their current behavior as learned ways of protecting a damaged fragile self. Although the origins of the problem can be traced back to early life experiences, change takes place in a corrective experience in the here and now of the relationship.

Assessing Prognosis for Treatment

Many needs are the same in the adult as in the child: to be loved, understood, accepted, affirmed, and acknowledged as a valuable person. Other needs are those that emerge later in the developmental sequence: to be autonomous, valued, and needed by another person and seen as a contributing member of a group.

Understanding the needs that were not met and how narcissistic defenses were erected to protect the self from further injury contributes to the formulation of a treatment plan. Many people with narcissistic disorders appear to function as highly successful, accomplished, creative, and attractive individuals. They cultivate and collect "interesting" friends and have learned ways to attract and use others for their own purposes. Sometimes a person with severe narcissistic features appears to be the healthier partner when the couple first enters therapy. Observing the process of the couple's interaction and the transference process with the therapist provides the information necessary to determine the degree of narcissistic pathology and therapeutic treatment plan. During the first few sessions, the therapist may begin by learning to read the "real" message in the partner's words and actions. Listening to the couple, the therapist silently considers the following issues:

1. What are the wounds of each of the partners? Where do they originate? How early? How consistently?
2. What defenses have either or both developed to protect a vulnerable self? How primitive are the defenses? To what extent are these defenses impinging on the partner?
3. What are the goals of each? For themselves individually? For the relationship? How do these goals relate to the values and belief systems of each?

An important part of the early assessment process is not only an understanding of the way each has learned to be in the world but also the determination, based on the beliefs and values of the couple, of what they individually and mutually hope to have in the relationship. The partners may be committed to working out their problems in order to remain in the relationship or may question whether the relationship can meet the needs of one or both of them.

After presentation of problems and implied provocations by the couple, the therapist may elicit information about the internal and external resources of the partners, the mutual collusions that protect vulnerabilities of each, and the deeper underlying individual fantasies and fears that each carries into any intimate relationship.

4. If a change is wanted, how does it occur? What are the unmet needs of each? Is the behavior seen as part of a mutual collusion—a reaction to the partners' projections? Is this behavior used as a defense against intolerable affect? Does the couple use the therapeutic setting to contain unacceptable split-off parts? Can the therapist provide the needed functions temporarily and be a model for the partners? Can therapy provide a space to hold toxic emotions until they can be tolerated by the partners?
5. What is the motivation to change? What are the resources of each partner? What is the tendency to blame? How intense are the symptoms of the problem? How syntonic are the symptoms to other aspects of life? How deep is the resistance to change?
6. Other indicators for prognosis: Is there a capacity to provide needed functions reciprocally? Is there a willingness to invest emotionally in the future of this relationship?

It is possible to differentiate the kinds of reactions that are specific to this relationship and those behaviors that might emerge no matter to whom the partners were married. In relationships marred by narcissistic pathology, defenses originate so early that words cannot define the pain and rage that are part of internal experience. The adult relational problems are an unsuccessful attempt to re-create old wounds in hopes of doing it right this time, of making this one a healing experience.

Ongoing Treatment Considerations

Therapists who listen to the process as the couple shares what is troubling them rather than hearing only the content of their complaints can help both mates become aware of how their particular defenses are utilized repeatedly during certain interchanges. By moving away from specific issues that have become charged with blame and resentment, examining instead how certain defenses have become mobilized to protect a vulnerable or injured self, therapists may be able to help partners understand behavior that otherwise seemed inexplicably withdrawing or attacking. When this kind of demonstration occurs in an atmosphere of safety, it need not be experienced as an attack but can serve to teach each partner to more fully understand the other. In effect, conjoint therapy fosters empathy, which allows the couple to feel safe, clear in relation to their individual dynamics, and more successful in handling the marital relationship effectively.

The therapist must allow the couple's communications, verbal and nonverbal, conscious and unconscious, to flow into a holding place within the therapist. This allows the free play of the therapist's stream of associations at different levels of consciousness to be triggered by nondefensive immersion in the material the couple presents. This does not imply that self (therapist) and other (couple) have become fused or confused. The immersion may be likened to a symbiosis in which the fantasy of merger, far from being based on a desperate neediness, is characterized by open boundaries that are voluntary and temporary. By its nature, this form of immersion is never imposed but rather offered, and it requires that the therapist not be defensively rigid about protecting his or her boundaries. The result is an empathic access to the deeper regions of the couple's affective experience, allowing the therapist to receive and process both partners' feelings, defenses, and pathologies.

During the course of treatment, many therapists experience memories of sights, sounds, and even smells that do not seem to correspond to what is occurring in the treatment session. These are drawn from subliminal representations of the therapist's personal experiences with literature, art, poetry, or other elements of the therapist's personal history. On reflection, therapists may recognize the deeper levels of communication that take place at an unconscious level and may use this understanding to give feedback about the dynamic interaction that is taking place between the partners (Solomon 1989).

Case Example: The Window

Bill and Sandra called the therapist to request some quick help before the following week when they were scheduled to leave for a 6-week vacation to Europe. They feared the vacation would be a disaster. When they came in and began talking to each other, their fear became understandable. Neither one could begin a sentence about almost any subject—her parents, their children, the route they took to get a movie—without the other challenging some detail of what was said. For example:

Bill: Sandy got mad at me for not unlocking the car door for her, and she wouldn't talk to me all the way to the movie.

Sandy: That's not true. I just said that you should have helped me in. You got upset, and I didn't say another word.

Bill: That's not all you said. I remember it exactly.

Bill then went on to give a word by word, 5-minute account of a conversation between them as he recalled it.

Sandy: That's what you always do. (crying she turns to me) I can't remember things the way Bill does, so I always come out wrong.

Bill: I'm just trying to be clear about what happened, and you get upset with me. I feel as if you see me like your father, always finding fault with you. I'm not your father.

Sandy: So you think it's all me and my crazy family. It's nothing that you are doing?

> *Bill:*   I'm not saying that. But I'm trying to figure out what
>   we can do, and you get mad at me.
>
> *Sandy:*   Okay. So it's all my fault.

The therapist wondered how they tolerated living in the same house. They argued over nonissues. But when Sandy said, "I feel like there is something wrong with me. You would have been happier with someone else," Bill, suddenly defending the relationship, said, "I'm not so perfect either. I know you put up with a lot." They wanted to be together but had fears of closeness. Bickering kept them distant but lonely. Distance regulation (Lansky 1981) was a core issue between them.

As the therapist listened to this couple, she recalled a memory of childhood: sitting on a windowsill of a large, seemingly empty house, watching the other children outside play in the snow. The memory of wishing to open the window and climb through to join the others, but being afraid to do so, offered some tools to break the impasse. For a moment, all the palpable feelings of loneliness of that day long ago were re-created in the consulting room. It is such experiences that provide inklings of what goes on between partners or between the couple and therapist—the hurts, fears, and desires that they cut off from themselves and from each other. Such countertransference feelings were used as therapeutic guides to focus on the loneliness and isolation that had permeated their relationship.

Moving From Content to Process

Each partner seeking help for marital problems views the issues within the context of his or her own "truth." Each has a different narrative describing the present and past of the relationship (Spence 1982; White and Epstein 1990). Each is disappointed that the other has failed to meet important needs in ways that seem disconcertingly familiar. Most couples enter therapy with each partner initially believing that the goal of treatment is to change the other partner in some way so that he or she will respond more appropriately. Those who utilize archaic defenses usually do not recognize that the partner has similar needs, nor do they respond well to advice about changing their behavior, as it is likely to be perceived as harsh criticism. Sessions with individual partners typically involve the assignment of blame and shame or attempts to align the therapist against the partner. Conjoint sessions can avoid these disruptions and the ensuing therapeutic impasse.

Repeatedly in the therapy process, one partner turns to the other partner or to the therapist for approval and confirmation. If what is needed is not immediately forthcoming, the disappointment manifested in either verbal communication or body language will reveal the presence or absence of intense needs and strong defenses. As defense mechanisms emerge, the therapist must turn the focus to the underlying needs and wounds that provoked these reactions. Although both partners may be terrified of intimacy, one may seem overinvolved while the other withdraws. When both have experienced love as dangerous, one may appear to be a caregiver while the other seems to demand constant replenishment of emotional needs.

Observing how each partner represents the story of the relationship or of a particular interaction and how each deals with issues of power, control, dependence, and autonomy can provide the therapist with an ample impression of the partners' defensive structures. With partners who have a history of emotional failures, any repeated wounds touch deep fault lines and cause a surge of dangerous emotions. The therapist must provide a relational space in which nameless, frightening emotions are translated into clear messages of physical or emotional reactions: anxiety, anger, terror, neediness, eroticism, love, and hate.

Treatment takes place within the relational space—the area of emotional overlap among husband, wife, and therapist. In this way, conjoint therapy sessions become a safe environment in which destructive patterns that have been part of the relationship can be experienced, acknowledged, and detoxified. The examination of a specific emotional issue becomes part of the therapeutic process between the partners. When needs, hurts, and defenses arise in a session, they are viewed not as problems to be solved or overcome but as opportunities for exploration and as clues to deep structures of the psyche.

Rather than focusing on the content of the couple's disagreements, the therapist focuses on the pattern of interactions between the partners and the therapist: identifying who initiates, who follows, and how each reacts to emotions and identifying the behaviors used to express anger, sadness, fear, and shame as well as positive emotions. The therapist continues to convey the goals of the work to the couple: to uncover the origins of the conflicts that cause their emotional pain, to identify the way each defends his or her vulnerable areas, and finally, to develop understanding and empathy for each other's core needs.

Moving From Presenting to Underlying Issues

The presenting problem may be money, work, sex, children, or a myriad of life difficulties. The problems the couple brings in are examined until an area of narcissistic need, injury, or defense arises. Because partners are prone to shame and blame, and because protective defenses can emerge suddenly with the slightest provocation, the therapist must be especially careful to provide a milieu that they can experience as a temporary haven in which to uncover and examine painful affect. At this point, the couple's process becomes the subject. The therapist temporarily shelves whatever is being discussed to transform the therapeutic setting into a container (Bion 1977) for the intense emotions that inevitably emerge. For example, the therapist commented to Bill, "When Sandy describes how hurt she felt Saturday night when she felt you criticized her, I noticed that your body seemed to become more rigid and your hands formed a fist. It must be hard for you not to react when you listen to the painful feelings that Sandy is describing. Are you aware of any feelings right now?" As the therapist says this, she watches for reactions from each of them.

Does the body tense? Does one partner seem to withdraw or nod in agreement? Do they seem connected with our work together?

Psychodynamic treatment of narcissistically vulnerable partners begins in ways that do not inflict injury through premature confrontations, paradoxical assignments, or unrealistic expectations of rapid lasting change. The therapist listens for signs of early injury and vulnerability to narcissistic or borderline defenses such as splitting or projective identification (Solomon 1989). The couple's responses will provide insight into their core issues and the direction of the therapy. Does Bill deny any feelings, or is he in touch with his anger? Can he relate his feelings of being criticized or shamed in the therapy session? Can he connect the present with the past? Can therapy help him to hold and examine the underlying emotions rather than defend against them? The answers emerge in the therapeutic encounter and provide information on how to proceed in the conjoint sessions.

Translating Narcissistic Defenses

Observing how partners interact when negative emotions are provoked provides needed knowledge of how past relationships are being transferred onto the present ones, both in the relationship of the partners to each other and in the relationship to the therapist. It is not the past per se that must be analyzed and understood, but the unfinished past that the person is attempting to resolve in the present. As is true in individual psychotherapy, although problematic interactional patterns originate in the past, they are part of the current relationship. Although the past is fixed, its infiltration into the present is a dynamic process and therefore open to change.

Sessions are used to examine and clarify how partners unconsciously conceal their attempts to defend a vulnerable self through angry attacks or distancing devices. When Sandy reported in therapy how distant and preoccupied Bill was on a weekend trip together, he angrily cut her off, saying loudly, "So it's all my fault—you did nothing?"

Sandy: Why are you getting so angry? What are you doing? I don't know you any more. Don't scream at me.

Therapist: Now we have a chance to look together at what happens between you that makes you both so incompatible.

Bill: I've been trying to control myself because I was afraid to make you angry. But you don't leave me alone. I sit and watch television and you walk in to tell me I've got to stop and get ready for dinner. I've always got to do something. It's always for you, for your friends.

Sandy (crying):   Why didn't you tell me? Why did you have to get so angry at me?

Bill: There you go crying again. I can't stand it.

Therapist: There is a lot of emotion here that has been buried. You are afraid of your own intense feelings, Bill, and you hate to see Sandy upset. It may have felt easier to leave than to open up the deep well of unresolved emotions. Sandy, you may have known how upset Bill can get. So you try to avoid deep or intense discussions. It is very painful to think you are doing the right things and then hear that it is all wrong.

The therapist must take an active stance as these issues arise. With verbalizations such as, "I see how these feelings must arise at home. Now we have a chance to look carefully and see what provokes the feelings," the therapist and the couple can pull the cognitive process back into highly charged emotional material and begin to connect the past with the present.

As therapy progresses, the partners gradually learn to think and feel at the same time. The therapist assists by constantly reinterpreting the content of interactions to reflect the underlying needs and emotions. When emotions can be held through another's willingness to acknowledge them, they need not trigger overwhelming terror, pain, and emotional chaos (Solomon 1989). The therapist provides a contextual container to hold the relationship while modeling the slow, precise examination of the emotions that arise in the course of the session (Scharff and Scharff 1987, 1991).

Moving From Therapeutic Decoding to Direct Communication Between Partners

In order to provide a safe haven for therapeutic work with the couple, it is crucial to maintain contact in the conjoint sessions with each partner, remaining equally empathic with both. Any sign of favoring one over the other will be experienced as a betrayal. At the beginning of treatment, it is also important to set up a communication pattern wherein transactions go through the therapist; in this way, partners are far less likely to thrust destructive attacks on each other. The therapist is therefore actively reducing the tendency of the couple to collide in pathological ways while providing a model for empathic attunement (Lansky 1981). As the partners listen to each other, revealing themselves to the therapist, and as the therapist connects present problems with past traumas—in terms free of psychological interpretations or labels that could be experienced as humiliating—the partners' ability to understand and respect each other's core needs increases. As the therapist consistently mirrors empathic attunement, partners learn a new mode of responding that goes beneath surface behaviors.

Later in the therapy, the therapist is less active as the mates begin to integrate this new method of attuning to each other's needs, fears, and ways of protecting themselves in stressful situations. As life brings new stressors, there are many opportunities to try what they are learning: share and contain each other's feelings temporarily, tolerate the emergence of their own painful emotions for longer periods, and attune to each other's internal experiences to resolve together ways they will handle stressors.

The work continues by helping each partner develop "emotional literacy." Each partner learns to reclaim dissociated affect, to identify fleeting emotions as they occur rather than splitting them off from conscious awareness, and to contain frightening internal experiences rather than to defend against them or act them out. In large measure, this awareness of affect comes about through the therapist's repeated efforts to safely call attention to emotions as they occur.

Throughout the treatment process, the ongoing focus is on teaching couples to listen and understand in a different way—a "listening literacy." Listening literacy allows partners to develop a tolerance to the feelings that have caused overwhelming shame or anxiety. Vulnerability decreases, and there is less need to protect against overwhelming reactions. Underlying wounds and immediate hurts that would otherwise catalyze overwhelming affects are received and connected to past relationships, and fears of volcanic emotional overflow are dissipated.

Life themes that had seemed incomprehensible and off limits now begin to emerge. Partners gain a new respect for behaviors they had previously disparaged. Lansky noted that each partner learns to understand himself or herself empathically as one who has unwillingly been dealing with past trauma. This is recognized and clarified repeatedly as a result of an understandable and intelligible process rather than as a sign of a defective, incomprehensible, and contemptible product (Lansky 1981).

The couple in treatment repeatedly reactivates transferences that come from early childhood traumas. The therapist, in a nonjudgmental way, examines the current interaction, its genetic reconstructions, and the defenses mobilized to protect a vulnerable self. By slowly, carefully uncovering the ways in which the partner's needs, fears, and protective defenses are utilized to safeguard a fragile self, each partner can be emotionally held and permitted to express vulnerabilities without shameful criticism.

When partners fail to understand or respond appropriately, the therapist is available to provide the emotional holding, understanding, and interpretation of the painful feelings underlying enactments of rage or withdrawal. The result of such treatment often is an increase of tolerance for a partner's misunderstanding along with an increased understanding of the partner's responses that had previously seemed unreasonable, irrational, or mean-spirited. Using the therapist both as interpreter and model for understanding each other, partners are helped to grow individually and together.

Reinforcing the Transformation

As the need to mobilize defenses against old wounds decreases, the opportunity emerges for true change in each of the partners. Narcissistic demandingness may be replaced by normal assertiveness. Timidity and withdrawal as a way to protect against embarrassingly childlike grandiose fantasies may be replaced by a willingness to expose high aspirations and devotion to ideals, as well as by a joyful acceptance of a healthy grandiosity. Chaos and instability between partners diminish as the couple expands their ability to contain explosive reactions. There are opportunities to examine with the therapist a range of emotions, such as shame, guilt, fear, and disgust, that are covered by surface outbursts.

At-home arguments are reframed as opportunities for the couple to try thinking for themselves about feelings as they emerge. Sessions following at-home arguments are another chance to examine which aspects of the couple's individual psyches are still very vulnerable and reactive to narcissistic injury. Thus, the problems themselves become part of the treatment plan, always with the goal of tolerating emotions—to hold them rather than act them out or defend against them and to think as well as feel.

Kohut noted in his last book that an ill-disposed critic accused him of showing his true colors, that is, believing in the curative effect of the "corrective emotional experience" (1984, p. 78). Kohut explained that the concept of a "corrective emotional experience" was tainted by its use as a form of brief analysis in which the therapist play-acted being the opposite of what the patient experienced with parents in childhood.

Perhaps there is a need for a new term, such as a *reparative interpersonal experience*. This is what occurs in successful therapy; in a healing religious experience; and in an ongoing, loving intimate relationship, such as marriage. Providing a sustaining echo of empathic resonance to someone who has lacked it in earlier relationships is a reparative experience that unlocks the gates and releases the interrupted maturational push thwarted in childhood, enabling the developmental process to begin to reassert itself.

Wounds heal slowly. They take a long time to develop and a long time to repair. Nevertheless, the change takes place in the sense of excitement, vitality, and use of inner resources when crises force people to reexamine old patterns and discover new paths to follow. Where there is giving as well as getting, the cycle of narcissistic injury and entitlement fantasies can be broken.

Ultimately, the goal of marital therapy is not only to promote a greater degree of empathy in the relationship but also to rebuild slowly the damaged or enfeebled structures of the self. Each partner comes to trust the marital relationship and the therapist as a safe environment in which intense affect may be experienced in relative safety. Each learns to tolerate painful affect that emerges in the course of interpersonal experience, and both develop capacities that enable them to serve temporarily as a selfobject for the other in times of stress. Each is able to grow through the healing relationship. The therapist provides the container in which the reparative work can take place.

References

Bion WR: Seven Servants. New York, Jason Aronson, 1977
Dicks H: Marital Tensions. London, Routledge & Kegan Paul, 1967
Fairbairn WRD: An Object Relations Theory of the Personality. New York, Basic Books, 1954

Kernberg OF: Narcissism and love relations. Paper presented at the annual meeting of the American Psychoanalytic Association, New York, December 1993

Kohut H: How Does Analysis Cure? Edited by Goldberg A, Stepansky P. Chicago, IL, University of Chicago Press, 1984

Lansky M: Treatment of the narcissistically vulnerable marriage, in Family Therapy and Major Psychopathology. Edited by Lansky M. New York, Grune & Stratton, 1981, pp 163–183

Lansky M: Family genesis of aggression. Psychiatric Annals 23:9, 1993

Nadelson CC, Paolini TJ: Marital therapy from a psychoanalytic perspective, in Marriage and Marital Therapy: Psychoanalytic, Behavioral and Systems Perspectives. Edited by Paolini TJ, McCrady BS. New York, Brunner/Mazel, 1978, pp 89–165

Scharff D, Scharff J: Object Relations Family Therapy. Northvale, NJ, Jason Aronson, 1987

Scharff D, Scharff J: Object Relations Couple Therapy. Northvale, NJ, Jason Aronson, 1991

Schwartzman MS: Narcissistic transferences: implications for the treatment of couples. Dynamic Psychotherapy 2:5–14, 1984

Slipp S: Object Relations: A Dynamic Bridge Between Individual and Family Treatment. New York, Jason Aronson, 1984

Solomon M: Narcissism and Intimacy: Love and Marriage in an Age of Confusion. New York, WW Norton, 1989

Solomon M: Lean on Me: The Power of Positive Dependency in Intimate Relationships. New York, Simon & Schuster, 1994

Spence DP: Narrative Truth and Historical Truth: Meaning and Interpretation in Psychoanalysis. London, WW Norton, 1982

White M, Epstein D: Narrative Means to Therapeutic Ends. New York, WW Norton, 1990

Winnicott DW: The Maturational Process and the Facilitating Environment: Studies in the Theory of Emotional Development. New York, International Universities Press, 1965

Section III

Special Clinical Considerations

Introduction

Elsa F. Ronningstam, Ph.D.

Recently, there has been an increased clinical and empirical interest in the role of normal affect regulation in human development and the influence of dysfunctional affect regulation in psychopathological states. Clinical observations of narcissistic patients have identified an impairment in the capacity to identify, understand, and tolerate feelings; a profound idealization and preference of a state of "affect absence or abstinence"; and an impairment in self-preservative functions. These observations call for the initiation of exchange with other areas of investigation, that is, affect research and suicidology. The two chapters in this section represent important and groundbreaking efforts to conceptualize and explain the origin and manifestations of pathological narcissism in the context of dysfunctional affect and self-regulation. Henry Krystal, M.D., in Chapter 13, describes how normal self-regulatory and self-esteem functioning are influenced by affect regression caused by infant or massive adult psychic trauma. The relation between alexithymia and psychosomatic illness to narcissistic pathology is outlined as well. Suicidal behavior is identified by John T. Maltsberger, M.D., in Chapter 14, in terms of severely disordered self-regulation. He identifies, based on Klein's theory, two types of underlying dynamics in suicidal behavior that specifically apply to narcissistic patients.

Chapter 13

Affect Regulation and Narcissism

Trauma, Alexithymia, and Psychosomatic Illness in Narcissistic Patients

Henry Krystal, M.D.

T he role of the development and regulation of affects in the formation of normal and pathological narcissism has only marginally been commented on in the clinical literature. The same can be said about the role of trauma in the generation of narcissistic disorders. Kernberg (1975) suggests that self-esteem and affects, as part of the self-regulatory functions, are closely related. Referring to Jacobson's work, he noted that self-esteem or self-regard is

> not simply a reflection of "instinctual cathexis": It always reflects a combination of affective and cognitive components, with the predominance of diffuse affective components at more primitive levels of regulation of self-esteem, and a predominance of cognitive differentiation with "toned down" affective implications at more advanced levels of regulation of self-esteem. (p. 317)

Both McDougall (1985) and Kernberg (1975, 1976) recognized the general influence of early trauma in the development of narcissistic personality disorder. More specifically, J. H. Krystal et al. (1994) noted that narcissistic disturbances in posttraumatic states are related to survival guilt as well as to shame caused by helplessness to resist the aggressor and for having submitted. Both shame and guilt contribute to a regression in affects that takes place as part of the trauma process and constitutes a major threat to the ability to restore self-regulation in general and self-esteem and self-respect in particular.

Although the effect of noncommunication in narcissistic patients has been commented on in the literature (Modell 1975), studies of alexithymia have rarely connected this state of pathology to narcissistic personality disorder. No major efforts have so far been directed to explore and analyze the relation between these different areas of inquiry (i.e., affect regulation, trauma, alexithymia, and narcissism).

The purpose of this chapter is to discuss how normal affect regulation and self-esteem regulation can be influenced by the occurrence of infantile psychic trauma or massive psychic trauma later in life. The impact of affect regression on the development of narcissistic disorders is discussed, as well as alexithymia with psychosomatic disorders and specific treatment strategies for narcissistic alexithymic patients. Before addressing these main topics, the composition and development of affects are outlined.

Four Components of Affects

Affective experience can be studied in terms of its attributes and described in terms of four components or aspects.

The *cognitive component* involves the affect's own meaning. Thus, both fear and anxiety have the meaning that something bad is about to happen. Fear is the perception of impending but avoidable danger. In addition to the intrinsic meaning, the cognitive aspect of an emotion has an underlying story. In fear, the danger is external and veridical. In anxiety, it is internal with very little conscious explanation available (for a detailed review of this and subsequent attributions to affect, see H. Krystal 1988a).

The *expressive aspect* of emotions originally was thought of as connected to the autonomic nervous system. This theory followed Freud's idea that if the expression of drives "to the outside" is blocked by inhibition, these aspects of emotions become channels for discharging the drives to the body's interior. Although this conception represents a profound sentience of the connection between the emotions and psychosomatic illness, the direct discharge idea is not supportable by modern biology, physics, or neurology. In fact, the idea that emotions can be eliminated by "expressing" them verbally or through action cannot be accepted in a direct, simplistic way (H. Krystal 1977).

The *hedonic aspect* of emotions needs further clarification. Although most emotions are consistently pleasurable or distressful, it is still necessary to make further distinctions—that is, to separate the idea of pleasure from gratification and to differentiate pain from suffering. In addition, it is possible that an experience can be consciously painful while it is unconsciously gratifying. Anxiety, for example, can be experienced as pleasurable when there is a secret or fantasized sense of security. Moreover, the mechanism of experiencing pain with an unconscious gratification accounts for a major therapeutic problem: the addiction to pain, which, in my observations, is one of the hardest addictions to give up, more difficult than any substance or smoking. The hedonic aspect of emotions is also related to the nature of consciousness of mental events. In the adult, consciousness varies along several spectra (Pribram 1971), and it can at times be difficult to identify the precise state of consciousness in a patient at a given moment. The work with victims of early trauma has shown that these patients go into dissociative states or trances frequently and that hedonic aspects of emotions in each state have to be explored and understood (H. Krystal 1981).

The *activating aspect* of emotions not only involves the familiar psychomotor retardation of depression and the excitement in mania but also controls all the functions of the organism. Especially notable is the regulation of the immune system. As a result, whereas the expressive aspect of emotions is the connection to the psychosomatic diseases, the activating aspect of emotions represents the link with psychobiology. Finally, it also feeds back to the cognitive aspect of emotions—for example, severely depressed patients have only 20% less frequent disturbances in cognition than do schizophrenic patients, albeit of a different kind.

Individuals who have these four aspects of emotions in a mature form (i.e., differentiated and recognizable) and are capable of adequate reflective self-awareness or self-observation may, when experiencing an emotion, recognize: "I am experiencing a feeling." This is the recognition of a subjective experience. Recognizing the occurrence of a feeling makes it possible to monitor to what extent the feeling—particularly its intensity—is derived from and proportional to the current situation and to what extent past memories distort or intensify the present emotional reaction.

Genetic View of Emotions

Observations have been accumulating that support the idea of a gradual and orderly development of the human capacity to experience emotions. Hadley (1992) collected evidence from developmental neuroanatomy and neurophysiology and correlated this with clinical observations, and an excellent review about the genetic aspects of emotions can be found in Brown's (1993) work. Some authors (Demos 1982; Izard 1971, 1977; Tompkins 1962, 1963, 1968) have proposed that a certain number of basic affects are available shortly after birth. The studies, based on direct observations of infants and children (Emde 1983; Emde et al. 1976; Greenspan 1981; Pine 1979; Solyom 1987; Solyom et al. 1983), have provided important scientific evidence. My own clinical work on concentration camp survivors, other posttraumatic patients, and psychosomatic patients, as well as those with heroin addiction undergoing withdrawal (H. Krystal 1993, 1994; H. Krystal and Raskin 1963), resulted in an exploration of the genetic view of affects—that is, the development of affects evolving from three affect-precursor states (Figure 13–1).

Global reaction patterns are observed in the newborn: the state of well-being and contentment; the state of distress; and a third, rarely noted, reaction pattern called "freezing," that is, becoming totally immobilized. This last pattern is universal in young animals, but in the human infant it usually disappears at about age 2 months (Papousek and Papousek 1975), which is a reason that it is often overlooked. However, freezing as an affect precursor needs to be highlighted because it returns in trauma and accounts for a variety of dissociative symptoms. In traumatized children, it returns in trances, and later in adults, it returns in psychotherapy.

These affect precursors fulfill their potentials within specific developmental lines: affect differentiation, verbalization, and desomatization (H. Krystal 1975, 1988a). Through these developmental lines—and combined with the attachment to primary caregivers who encourage, help, and "reward" this process—normal development takes place. Starting with differentiation in vocalization, the epigenetic development of emotions proceeds from the state of well-being to differentiation of all the affects that are generally pleasurable (or as Rado [1969] called them, "welfare affects"), such as love, security, contentment, joy, and pride. Out of the distress state evolve painful feelings (Rado's "emergency affects"), such as anger, guilt, jealousy, shame, anxiety, and fear.

Pain is in a unique position because it cannot become a separate experience (Figure 13–1) from the earlier distress affect precursor pattern. Most of the tracts are not yet mature, and there is not yet a functional "body image" or representation. In affect regression, it is common that pain returns and becomes a part of affects or, on a conscious level, takes the place of affect awareness. Another common type of regression is the loss of sense of time. Anyone who has severe physical and emotional pain loses the sense of time and expects that the suffering will go on "forever."

Along with the process of affect maturation, the "good enough caregiver" demonstrates to the child the uses of emotions: they can serve as signals to the self, and once recognized and put into words, they can produce desired results speedily.

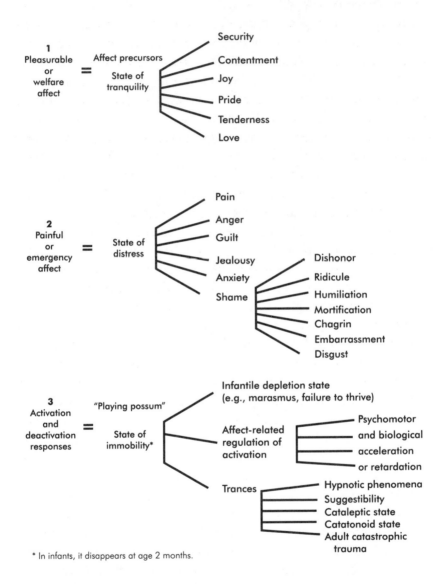

* In infants, it disappears at age 2 months.

Figure 13–1. Affect differentiation.
Source. Reprinted from Krystal H: *Integration and Self-Healing.*
Hillsdale, NJ, Analytic Press, 1988, p. 44. Used with permission.

Along with the identification with patterns of the caregiver, the child is shown ways to regulate emotions and to keep them within a bearable range for their greatest utility as signals. This determines the optimal utility of emotions, called "affect tolerance," which has to do with the reactions to having an emotion and the capacity to handle and contain this emotion (H. Krystal 1975, 1978a, 1978b, 1988a).

Affect Regulation and Defenses Against Affects

Under normal optimal circumstances, the process of affect regulation is characterized by the individual's comfort with his or her emotions and by the ability to use the emotions as signals for self-regulation. To the extent that emotions are verbalized and desomatized, they are most suitable to function as signals for information processing and as subliminal "switches" in the mental operations. Normal affect regulation permits the individual to experience a feeling and to discern both its connection to the current situation and its relation to memories of past experiences, particularly past narcissistic injuries and rages. The process of sorting out the feelings in this fashion permits the individual to decide which of the repertoire of possible responses are in his or her best long-term and short-term interest and to act accordingly. This capacity leads to a lifelong realistic development of self-reliance, normal narcissistic self-regulation, and a healthy self-esteem.

Certain experiences cause habitual tendencies to develop intense emotional reactions that can threaten to overwhelm the individual. Under these circumstances, some people are able to develop defenses against emotions, such as denial of contents, reversal, displacement, or turning feelings toward the self. These defenses must be distinguished from affect regression.

Regression in affect functioning is usually caused by the occurrence of a psychic trauma. It is important to note that trauma may occur at birth or anytime thereafter and therefore can greatly vary in cause, course, and aftereffect. Affect regression is characterized by a regression in the affective manifestations caused by affect dedifferentiation, deverbalization, and resomatization (H. Krystal 1971, 1974, 1978a; H. Krystal and Raskin 1970). This development is in sharp contrast to the normal developmental lines of affects mentioned earlier (H. Krystal 1975, 1988a). In milder forms of affect regression, the affects appear diffuse, undifferentiated, and primitive; in its more severe forms, emotions manifest themselves virtually exclusively in their somatic component.

At the most severe level of regression, emotions appear only as physical reactions and are not useful for information processing—that is, they become a nuisance or a source of distress under these circumstances. Two developmental trends can be discerned. Some people become stoical and suppress or ignore all their emotional reactions as irrelevant or as physical distractions, like a circumstantial itch. They live entirely on the basis of their reasoning, and their judgment is dedicated to the proposition that they alone know what matters. Such behavior lends itself to narcissistic superiority, indifference, and the covering up of their own weakness by the domination and exploitation of everyone around them. These people become narcissistic psychosomatic patients. The opposite types are people who become intolerant of the useless physical components of their emotions, which they experience as unbearable and painful, and which they forever try to block or cover up in any way possible. These individuals tend to develop the world's spectrum of addictions. Affect regression is a crucial precondition for the development of psychosomatic illness; that is, there can be no psychosomatic disease with alexithymia without affect regression, although affect dysregulation is another major cause of psychosomatic illness (Taylor 1987).

Trauma

Fear is the signal of impending danger. However, it is assumed that the danger is avoidable or manageable. When an individual is confronted with danger that is determined to be unavoidable or inescapable, and no help can possibly be forthcoming, he or she surrenders to it. This view is in harmony with Freud's (1926/1959) statement that "the essence and meaning" of the cause of psychic trauma is "[t]he subject's estimation of his own strength . . . and . . . his admission of helplessness . . . in the 'Erlebte Situation,' i.e., the subjective helplessness in the face of what he experiences as unavoidable, inescapable danger, and his surrender to it" (p. 166).

Once an individual surrenders to his or her subjectively determined inevitable fate, the affect changes from fear to a catatonoid reaction (H. Krystal 1978a; M. M. Stern 1951a, 1951b), and this is the onset of the traumatic state. The individual gives up most or all of his or her initiatives and obeys orders. This state is similar to a hypnotic state but is immensely more powerful in that the more the subject obeys orders, the deeper he or she goes under, until he or she reaches a cataleptic or "robot" state. It is possible to remain in this state for long periods.

If the traumatic state continues, a progressive numbing of pain and painful affects begins and broadens to involve other affects and the sense of being a worthwhile individual. At the same time, a parallel process is reaching malignant proportions: the progressive blocking of all mental activities (cognition, perception, recall, scanning, information processing, judgment, planning, and problem solving). Finally, just a vestige of these functions and the capacity for self-observation are retained. In this state, most normal narcissistic functions—self-preservation, self-regard, self-defense, self-respect, and self-concern (see Stone, Chapter 1, this volume)—collapse, and the person experiences a massive and dangerous depreciation in self-esteem and capacity to maintain narcissistic functioning. In the aftereffects of such trauma, different pathological narcissistic compensatory processes are initiated, which can promote denial of failures, isolation or a splitting off of intolerable affects or somatic symptoms, maintenance of omnipotent or grandiose fantasies, and experiences of superiority or belief in invulnerability. Often intricate and complex developments with the incorporation of pain into a grandiose self-structure take place, and pain instead of pleasure becomes part of a pathological form of self-esteem regulation (Cooper 1989).

Two types of trauma can be distinguished: the infantile psychic trauma and the adult trauma. The infantile psychic trauma can occur during the process of promoting affect tolerance, which is probably one of the most important, difficult, and challenging aspects of parenting. The purpose is to allow the child to tolerate increasing emotional tension. The good-enough caregiver monitors the baby, steps in and relieves distress if the child exceeds his or her ability to retain and regain composure, and, if possible, comforts the child. If that is not achievable, the parent takes advantage of the distractibility of the child. If the parent is unable or chooses not to do so, then the infant's excitement mounts until the child reaches a point of virtual inconsolability. This can be identified as the point of onset of the infantile trauma.

Reactions that arise in the infant probably are similar to those in adults during the adult psychic trauma. The major difference is that the young child has a built-in device so that instead of terminating in psychogenic death, he or she will go to sleep. However, it is important to differentiate this sleep from the sleep of a contented, cajoled child who goes to sleep in a cloud of magical narcissistic security, possibly with feelings of having virtually merged with the mother. The infant who goes to sleep in utter misery is at risk, and if these episodes happen repeatedly, the child may start showing a failure to thrive or marasmus and may die of intercurrent infection as Spitz (1946) observed.

The aftereffects of infantile psychic trauma frequently do not terminate abruptly but continue into psychosomatic disturbances in infancy. These include sleeping and feeding disturbances; colic; intervals of eczema; asthma; and failure of affective attunement, which can develop into affective maladjustment (Harmon et al. 1982).

The survivors of infantile trauma were usually completely brainwashed about the perfection of their childhood, but as adults they would present themselves as psychosomatic or addictive patients, usually with no memory or family history. In addition, they had a combination of alexithymia, anhedonia, aprosodia, and so-called doomsday orientation, a profound, unshakable conviction and certainty of the return of the infantile psychic trauma. Posttraumatic patients believe that "lightning always strikes twice," especially when they are spectacularly successful or try to usurp the functions reserved for the idolatrous primary object. Other consequences occur. For example, residuals of infantile trauma are preverbal. The affects are undifferentiated and arrested in their development, and these early memories do not automatically become verbal (D. N. Stern 1985). These patients later show alexithymia, anhedonia, and a predisposition to psychosomatic diseases or addiction. The abused or traumatized children experience a desertion and betrayal by the parents who are "supposed" to be omnipotent and perfect. However, the traumatized persons turn the aggression against the self, and as patients they present themselves with problems of shame and guilt.

The trauma causes impaired self-respect and self-esteem because the confrontation with an unavoidable trauma, the surrendering to it, and the survival of the event leave the individual with the memory of a failure of his or her feeling of narcissistic omnipotence and the power of magical thinking. The ability to restore the state of denial of death, in which everybody must function, is impaired. Helplessness and the inability to defend the self or loved objects leave a lasting residue of shame and sometimes survivor guilt. Under these circumstances, all the defenses and reactions apply, but chronic anxiety remains, as well as a depressive lifestyle, even during periods of compensatory overachievements.

The consequences of severe psychic trauma include a greatly increased insecurity as represented both by a chronic state of hypervigilance and by a fixation on past trauma. This development modifies the individual's sense of time (commonly resulting in expectation of foreshortening of his or her life) and limits the individual's ability to assert himself or herself. In some cases (e.g., posttraumatic stress disorder), memories and visual representations of the traumatic experiences may actually invade present precepts with flashbacks from the past. (For further discussion of the aftereffects of massive psychic trauma, see Wilson and Rafael [1993], specifically Chapter 71 [H. Krystal 1993].)

Alexithymia

In general, alexithymia involves a diminution of the usefulness of affects for information processing. More specifically, H. Krystal (1979) defines alexithymia as consisting of disturbances in three areas:

1. *Affective functions.* The alexithymic person is impaired in his or her ability to name and localize emotions (H. Krystal 1968, 1971, 1978a, 1978b; Sifneos 1967) and to recognize and use emotions as signals to himself or herself. The affects are experienced as vague and confusing and remain undifferentiated and unverbalized. Nemiah and Sifneos (1970a, 1970b) described alexithymia in psychosomatic patients and pointed out (confirmed by the use of a questionnaire) that these individuals, when questioned about their emotional responses, tended to answer with a description of what they would do in the stressful situation rather than being able to tell how they felt. Niederland (1961, 1968a, 1968b, 1981) repeatedly described these phenomena in Holocaust survivors.

2. *Cognitive functions.* Persons with alexithymia are unable to verbalize and describe emotions and sensations, have a sterility and monotony of ideas, and have impoverished imaginatory processes. Operative thinking (Marty and de M'Uzan 1963; Marty et al. 1963) dominates at the expense of symbolic and imaginative processes. The associations of alexithymic persons are activated by stimulus rather than being determined by drive (Nemiah and Sifneos 1970a, 1970b).

3. *Self- and object representations.* Alexithymic patients have self- and object representations characterized by detachment and indifference in relation to both external objects and live internal object representation. Patients have an impaired capacity for self-care (H. Krystal 1978b), experience a sort of numbness to avoid pain, and tend to become loners (McDougall 1974).

Among the aftereffects of this development is evidence that although the original trauma left the individual with impaired self-respect, the functional numbness and insensitivity of alexithymia can provide a kind of spurious secondary gain of narcissistic grandiosity caused by the inability to use feelings for information processing. The alexithymic individual is not able to differentiate between present and past origins of the feelings or to use feelings as a base for deciding suitable responses or actions. In the absence of these capacities, the individual is destined to swing from infantile grandiose self-views to feelings of helplessness and shame. In alexithymic patients, who are usually not aware of these defects, it is noticeable how they regulate themselves by reasoning combined with a compensatory attitude of superiority and contempt toward those who experience emotions. The impaired self-care often found in alexithymic patients is another consequence of affect regression.

Alexithymic, anhedonic, aprosodic patients usually have multiple mental and physiological disturbances (e.g., quadruple-increased norepinephrine secretion and disturbances of endogenous opioid regulation). These lasting physiological changes influence and modify these patients' cognition, memory, and even states of consciousness (J. H. Krystal et al. 1994; van der Kolk 1993).

Alexithymic patients have other outstanding characteristics as well. One is the inability to express wish-fulfilling fantasies. This is caused by a history of infantile trauma that interrupts the normal development of the transitional process (H. Krystal 1988b) and has far-reaching implications for the later capacity for "solacing" (Horton and Sharp 1981). Works on attachment (Ainsworth et al. 1978; Bowlby 1977; Main 1977; Parkes and Stevenson-Hinde 1982) have highlighted the importance of empathic caregiving for the development of visible and hidden attachment behavior (Hofer 1981, 1982, 1983) and of transitional objects (Gadini 1970, 1975, 1987). This process starts up concretely but becomes increasingly imaginative, musical, and poetic (Deri 1984). It contributes to self-respect in childhood (Ablon et al. 1993; Copolilo 1967), which serves as a lasting reserve for future development of new self-representations corresponding to the transformation and integration of the wholesome narcissism in adolescence (Benson 1980; Benson and Pryor 1973; Sugarman and Jaffe 1989). These conditions form the base for the capacity for wish-fulfilling fantasies. Another characteristic of alexithymic patients is their inability to associate, which initially can appear as a "super-realistic" cognitive approach, making psychoanalytical treatment less appropriate.

The degree and severity of alexithymia can vary from person to person or within the same person. Several well-tested instruments have been designed to measure alexithymia. A few sources can be helpful and reliable (Emde et al. 1976; J. H. Krystal 1988; Ten Houten et al. 1985a, 1985b, 1985c, 1985d; Von Rad 1983; Von Rad and Lolas 1982; Von Rad et al. 1977) as can a test that will likely become the standard, the Toronto Alexithymia Scale (Bagby et al. 1990; Taylor 1984b, 1985).

Alexithymia and Psychosomatic Illness

Because of the predominant affect regression in the state of alexithymia, situations and experiences that would otherwise produce useful affect signals for information processing and decision making tend to cause an organ response of chronic hyperactivity. This hyperactivity goes on silently until the organ (generally a viscus) is damaged, and the lesion is produced. The outcome is a physical illness of combinatorial etiology, because both hereditary and environmental factors may contribute to the development of such illness.

Psychosomatic illness can be considered as one of the most solid and dependable "protections" against the recognition of narcissistic defects and inadequacies in object relations (i.e., the consequences of severe narcissistic injuries). McDougall (1982–1983, 1985, 1989) suggested that although the patient may present with only one illness, this picture may be already a defensive containment of a "psychosomatosis," which is the physical equivalent to psychosis.

As mentioned earlier in this chapter, there can be no psychosomatic disease with alexithymia without affect regression. Accordingly, if a patient has both alexithymia (which includes aprosodia) and anhedonia, there is a high degree of certainty that the syndrome is posttraumatic. If there is absolutely no history of trauma, then the likelihood is very high that a history of infantile psychic trauma is buried in the individual's and family's past.

Treatment

Analytical approaches to the treatment of patients with alexithymia and psychosomatic diseases combined with narcissistic disorders cannot be made with the principles of treatment developed for the neuroses. Instead, psychotherapy has to focus on demonstrating and explaining the nature of the patient's emotional, affective, and cognitive disturbances (H. Krystal 1982, 1982–1983; H. Krystal and Raskin 1970; McDougall 1972, 1974, 1984), with consideration of their multifactorial causality (Pollock 1977). If psychoanalysis or any type of anxiety-provoking therapy will be used, the patient's impaired affect tolerance must be considered. The most important principle in the treatment of the alexithymic psychosomatic patient is that reconstruction of damaged structures has to precede the reconstruction of any traumatic memories. Part of the mind where trauma persists is characterized by primal repression, which refers to an absence of psychic structure. Direct emergence of primal repression is therefore risky but may be reached and worked with in the presence of a noninternalized, valuing, nurturing relationship called "primary relatedness" (Kinston and Cohen 1986), which is the interactional context for enhanced growth. In other words, the therapeutic work should concentrate for a long time on reconstruction of structures before the usual psychoanalytical idea of reconstruction can begin. Some of the important and necessary areas of focus and therapeutic tasks in the treatment of patients with this combination of pathology follow.

Work on Affect Tolerance

When affect tolerance is being addressed, the patients' thoughts of emotions and reactions to having emotions are discussed. The ideas of affects as magical punishment, signs of weakness or effeminacy, or other similar fantasies have to be explored. In this work, the intent is to catch up on the regressions, deficiencies, and arrests that these patients have experienced in the genetic development of affect.

Work on Affect Differentiation

Working on affect differentiation involves naming of affects, "interpreting" the story behind the affects, and using elucidation, confrontation, and interpretation to highlight the differences between the adoptive mature responses and the occasions when the patient shows an infantile affective response. Such occasions also highlight the infantile or abnormal narcissistic patterns, and the analyst, in the atmosphere of the current idealizing and mirroring transferences, can show empathy to the exposed infantile disturbances.

Return of the Infantile Psychic Trauma

Narcissistic patients with alexithymia and psychosomatic illness strongly believe that the infantile psychic trauma will return in one or another form. Self-caring, self-soothing, and self-regulation are inhibited in these patients (Edgecumbe 1983; Khantzian and Mack 1983; H. Krystal 1978b, 1979, 1982–1983, 1988a; Zinberg 1975). The author has often observed the connection between these inhibitions and transference residuals from infancy that are a result of psychic trauma. In treatment, these inhibitions and reconnections must be thoroughly explored and evaluated.

Identification With the Other Side

One of the deepest and most profoundly repressed "secrets" is the "identification with the other side" (of the victim-oppressor dyad) (H. Krystal 1988a), which usually is revealed at some point in the continuing work with the deformations of the patient's narcissistic self-acceptance. In conjunction with this is the additional secret of a primitive unconscious form of love toward the perpetrator or victim, respectively, which the individual forms despite profound overwhelming subjugation and sadistic assault. Such phenomena can be seen in horses that become attached for life to the person who "broke them." Many sadomasochistic marriages also rest on this foundation (Meloy 1992).

Activation of Denial and Defenses

It is well known through many sources, especially the work of Dorpat (1985), that when patients are confronted with an anxiety situation (what he calls the "painful object"), instant denial is activated. This in turn initiates a variety of defenses, including the kind designated against keeping the memory and the affect object together. Consequently, in the situation that Freud defined as "traumatic," it can be assumed that "the incompatibility forces itself upon the ego and at which the latter decides on the repudiation of the incompatible idea" (Breuer and Freud 1893–1895/1955, p. 123). There is ample evidence that defensive distortions of perception, cognition, and recall are called up frequently by painful affective signals (H. Krystal and A. D. Krystal 1993; Westerlundh and Smith 1983). A basic principle must be stressed in this context: two types of affect are operative in the organism, one that can be registered consciously and another, the subliminal signal affect, that operates in information and perception processing like automatic switches within computers (Bucci 1985; H. Krystal 1988a).

As has been pointed out (H. Krystal 1985), defenses against trauma involve all of the individual's mental and emotional functions. Posttraumatically, the responses to affective signals become enormously exaggerated (Giora 1981, 1991; Reiser 1990).

Work on Shame, Guilt, and Narcissistic Dysregulations

At some point, when the patient has revealed the psychic trauma and related emotional, behavioral, and cognitive strategies, it is important to discuss the patient's feelings of shame and guilt. These feelings tend to attach him or her to the trauma and its perpetrators and to impair the patient's capacity to maintain adequate self-esteem and self-care.

Development of Transference

In treatment with psychosomatic alexithymic patients, transference does not for the most part develop in a neurotic sense (Marty and de M'Uzan 1963). The patients are cool, polite, and quite willing to continue attending analytical sessions, waiting patiently for "the doctor to cure them." In the meantime, they are presenting the same material, and this leads to countertransference of boredom. The occurrence of aggressive and sexual fantasies in the analyst is an important clue to the nature of the patient's "missing affects" (Taylor 1984a, 1984b).

These patients rarely report dreams. When they do, the dreams tend to be one-sentence productions to which they cannot associate. If pressed, they may be able to "squeeze out" some additional detail to the manifest contents of the dream. It is clear that these patients cannot utilize psychoanalytical psychotherapy. Sifneos (1972–1973) pointed out that an accurate interpretation actually may produce a life-threatening exacerbation to a psychosomatic patient.

If psychosomatic alexithymic patients remain in treatment until they have been able to understand and feel what the therapist is talking about, it is necessary to bring to their attention that they have severe inhibitions in self-care, self-soothing, transi-tional processes, and self-regulation; that they treat themselves as robots; and that they have no empathy for anyone. By this time, it would be possible to interpret that their transference—which is basically that they want the therapist to take over the operation of all their vital and affective functions, starting with those that are malfunctional—is a version of an idolatrous transference. The pa-tients have lived their lives submitting themselves to substitutes for the primal object, which they experience exactly as any relig-ious group does.

Treatment of Anhedonia

There is really no exact knowledge about how to treat anhedonia. The author has tried a technique that functions with recovering depressive patients: the patient should resume the activities he or she previously enjoyed. However, anhedonia is difficult to re-lieve, because it introduces the additional area of nonverbal pre-symbolic affects and traumatic residues. It also involves a complex anatomical and neurophysiological control system, which in-volves the orbital-frontal cortex (Schore 1994).

Conclusion

In this chapter, the interaction between the functions of emotions in general and the issue of self-esteem regulation in the context of trauma and affect regression in particular has been briefly reviewed. On reflection, it appears natural that the self-representation and the psychosocial responses to significant oth-ers would be markedly influenced by the status and availability of emotions in a form most effective in judging life and individual worth. The history of psychoanalysis has been a factor in the de-velopment of insights in certain order, according to the kinds of patients worked with. It was possible to work with "good neurotics" without spending a great deal of time and effort on examining the relationship of their emotions to psychosomatic diseases and self-esteem regulation. However, the ever-expanding scope of psychoanalysis has inspired work with patients with whom it was imperative to pay attention to these issues. In this chapter, observations from posttraumatic, alexithymic psychosomatic patients were integrated with views of narcissistic disorders in an effort to understand more about their interrelation.

References

Ablon SA, Brown D, Khantzian EJ, et al (eds): Human Feelings: Explorations in Affect Development and Meaning. Hillsdale, NJ, Analytic Press, 1993

Ainsworth MDS, Blehar MC, Walters E, et al: Patterns of Attachment: A Psychological Study of the Strange Situation. Fogel, NJ, Lawrence Erlbaum, 1978

Bagby RM, Taylor GJ, Parker TDA, et al: Cross-validation of the factor structure of the Toronto Alexithymia Scale. J Psychosom Res 34:47–51, 1990

Benson RM: Narcissistic guardians: developmental aspects of transitional objects, imaginary companions, and career fantasies. Adolesc Psychiatry 8:253–264, 1980

Benson RM, Pryor DB: When friends fall out: developmental interference with the function of some imaginary companions. J Am Psychoanal Assoc 210:457–473, 1973

Bowlby J: The making and breaking of affectional bonds, I: aetiology and psychopathology in the light of attachment theory. Br J Psychiatry 130:201–210, 1977

Breuer J, Freud S: Studies on hysteria (1893–1895), II: case histories, in The Standard Edition of the Complete Psychological Works of Sigmund Freud, Vol 2. Translated and edited by Strachey J. London, Hogarth Press, 1955, pp 19–181

Brown D: Affective development, psychopathology, and adaptation, in Human Feelings: Explorations in Affect Development and Meaning. Edited by Ablon SA, Brown D, Khantzian EJ, et al. Hillsdale, NJ, Analytic Press, 1993, pp 5–66

Bucci W: Dual coding: a cognitive model for psychoanalytic research. J Am Psychoanal Assoc 33:571–608, 1985

Cooper A: Narcissism and masochism: the narcissistic-masochistic character. Psychiatr Clin North Am 12(3):541–552, 1989

Copolilo HP: Maturational aspects of the transitional phenomenon. Int J Psychoanal 48:237–246, 1967

Demos EV: Facial expressions of infants and toddlers: a descriptive analysis, in Emotion and Early Interaction. Edited by Field T. Fogel, NJ, Lawrence Erlbaum, 1982, pp 127–160

Deri SK: Symbolization and Creativity. New York, International Universities Press, 1984

Dorpat TL: Denial and Defense in the Therapeutic Situation. Northvale, NJ, Jason Aronson, 1985

Edgecumbe E: On learning to talk to oneself. Bulletin of the British Psychoanalytic Society 5:1–13, 1983

Emde RN: The prerepresentational emotional self and its affective care. Psychoanal Study Child 38:165–192, 1983

Emde RN, Gaensbauer TJ, Hamron BJ: Emotional Expressions in Infancy. New York, International Universities Press, 1976

Freud S: Inhibition, symptoms, and anxiety (1926), in The Standard Edition of the Complete Psychological Works of Sigmund Freud, Vol 20. Translated and edited by Strachey J. London, Hogarth Press, 1959, pp 77–175

Gadini R: Transitional objects and the process of individuation. Journal of the American Academy of Child Psychiatry 4:347–364, 1970

Gadini R: The concept of the transitional object. Journal of the American Academy of Child Psychiatry 14:731–736, 1975

Gadini R: Early care and the roots of internalization. International Review of Psychoanalysis 14:321–333, 1987

Giora Z: Dream styles and the psychology of dreaming. Psychoanalysis and Contemporary Thought 4:291–381, 1981

Giora Z: The Unconscious and Its Narratives. Budapest, Hungary, Turin Publishing House, 1991

Greenspan SI: Psychopathology and Adaptation in Infancy and Early Childhood. New York, International Universities Press, 1981

Hadley JL: The Instincts Revisited. Psychoanalytic Inquiry 12:396–418, 1992

Harmon RJ, Wagonfeld S, Emde RN: Anaclitic depression: a follow up from infancy to puberty. Psychoanal Study Child 37:67–94, 1982

Hofer MA: Toward a developmental basis for disease predisposition: the effect of early maternal separation on the brain, behavior and cardiovascular system, in Brain, Behavior and Bodily Disease. Edited by Werner H, Holdes MA, Stunkard AJ. New York, Raven, 1981

Hofer MA: Some thoughts on "the transduction of experience" from a developmental perspective. Psychosom Med 44:19–28, 1982

Hofer MA: On the relationship between attachment and separation processes in infancy, in Emotion: Theory, Research and Experience: Emotions in Early Development, Vol II. Edited by Pluchik R. New York, Academic Press, 1983

Horton PL, Sharp SL: Solace: The Missing Dimension in Psychiatry. Chicago, IL, University of Chicago Press, 1981

Izard CE: The Face of Emotions. New York, Basic Books, 1971

Izard CE: Human Emotions. New York, Plenum, 1977

Kernberg OF: Borderline Conditions and Pathological Narcissism. New York, Jason Aronson, 1975

Kernberg OF: Object Relations and Clinical Psychoanalysis. New York, Jason Aronson, 1976

Khantzian E, Mack JE: Self-preservation and the case of the self. Psychoanal Study Child 38:209–232, 1983

Kinston W, Cohen J: Primal repression: Clinical and theoretical aspects of the mind: the realm of psychic states. Int J Psychoanal 67:537–555, 1986

Krystal H: Study of juvenile survivors of concentration camps. Reported to the "Children of Disaster" workshop. American Psychoanalytic Association, NY, 1968

Krystal H: Trauma: consideration of its intensity and chronicity, in Psychic Traumatization. Edited by Krystal H, Niederland WG. Boston, MA, Little, Brown, 1971, pp 11–28

Krystal H: The genetic development of affects and affect repression. Annual of Psychoanalysis 2:98–126, 1974

Krystal H: Affect tolerance. Annual of Psychoanalysis 3:179–210, 1975

Krystal H: Aspects of affect theory. Bull Menninger Clin 41:1–26, 1977

Krystal H: Trauma and effect. Psychoanal Study Child 33:81–118, 1978a

Krystal H: Self-representation and the capacity of self care. Annual of Psychoanalysis 6:209–247, 1978b

Krystal H: Alexithymia and psychotherapy. Am J Psychother 33:17–28, 1979

Krystal H: The hedonic element in affectivity. Annual of Psychoanalysis 9:93–114, 1981

Krystal H: Psychotherapy with alexithymic patients, in Psychosomatic Medicine: Theoretical, Clinical and Transcultural Aspects. Edited by Krakowski AJ, Kimball CP. New York, Plenum, 1982, pp 737–744

Krystal H: Alexithymia and the effectiveness of psychoanalytic treatment. International Journal of Psychoanalytic Psychotherapy 9:353–388, 1982–1983

Krystal H: Trauma and stimulus barrier. Psychoanalytic Inquiry 5:131–161, 1985

Krystal H: Integration and Self-Healing. Hillsdale, NJ, Analytic Press, 1988a

Krystal H: On some roots of creativity, in The Hemispheric Specialization. Edited by Hoppe KD. Philadelphia, PA, WB Saunders, 1988b, pp 475–491

Krystal H: Beyond DSM-III-R: Therapeutic considerations in post traumatic stress disorders, in International Handbook of Traumatic Stress Syndromes. Edited by Wilson JP, Rafael B. New York, Plenum, 1993, pp 841–853

Krystal H: Psychic trauma and psychoanalytic approaches to somatization and addiction. Paper presented at the 5th Annual Day in Psychoanalysis, the Toronto Psychoanalytic Society, Toronto, Canada, April 1994

Krystal H, Krystal AD: Psychoanalysis and neuroscience in relationship to dreams and creativity, in Creativity and Affect. Edited by Shaw MP, Runko MA. Norwood, NJ, Ablex Publishing, 1993, pp 185–212

Krystal H, Raskin HA: Addiction and Pain. Mimeographed, 1963

Krystal H, Raskin HA: Drug Dependence. Detroit, MI, Wayne State University Press, 1970

Krystal JH: Assessing alexithymia, in Integration and Self Healing. Edited by Krystal H. Hillsdale, NJ, Analytic Press, 1988, pp 286–310

Krystal JH, Bennett A, Bremmer JD, et al: Towards a cognitive neuroscience of dissociation and altered memory function in post traumatic
disorders, in Neurobiological and Clinical Consequences of Stress:
From Normal Adaptation to PTSD. Edited by Friedman MJ, Charney
DS, Deutch AY. New York, River Press, 1994, pp 239–269

Main M: Analysis of peculiar form of reunion behavior seen in some
day-care children: its history and sequelae in children who are home
reared, in Social Development in Childhood: Daycare Programs and
Research. Edited by Webb R. Baltimore, MD, Johns Hopkins University Press, 1977

Marty P, de M'Uzan M: La pensee operatoire. Revue Psychoanalitique
27 (suppl):345–356, 1963

Marty P, de M'Uzan M, David C: L'investigation psychosomatique. Paris,
Presses Universitaires Paris, 1963

McDougall J: The anti-analysand in analysis, in Ten Years of Psychoanalysis in France. New York, International Universities Press, 1972,
pp 213–246

McDougall J: The psychosoma and psychoanalytic process. International Review of Psychoanalysis 1:437–459, 1974

McDougall J: Alexithymia, psychosomatosis, and psychosis. International Journal of Psychoanalytic Psychotherapy 9:379–388, 1982–1983

McDougall J: The "dis-affected" patient: reflections on affect pathology.
Psychoanal Q 53:386–409, 1984

McDougall J: Theaters of the Mind. New York, Basic Books, 1985

McDougall J: Theaters of the Body: A Psychoanalytic Approach to Psychosomatic Illness. New York, WW Norton, 1989

Meloy JR: Violent Attachments. Northvale, NJ, Jason Aronson, 1992

Modell A: A narcissistic defense against affects and the illusion of self-
sufficiency. Int J Psychoanal 56:275–282, 1975

Nemiah JC, Sifneos PE: Affect and fantasy in patients with psychosomatic disorders, in Modern Trends in Psychosomatic Medicine—2.
Edited by Hill OW. London, Butterworth, 1970a, pp 26–34

Nemiah JC, Sifneos PE: The psychological management and treatment
of patients with peptic ulcer. Adv Psychosom Med 6:169–173, 1970b

Niederland WG: The problem of the survivor. Journal of the Hillside
Hospital 10:233–247, 1961

Niederland WG: Clinical observations of the "survivor syndrome." Int J
Psychoanal 49:313–315, 1968a

Niederland WG: An interpretation of psychological stresses and defenses in concentration camp life and the late after-effects, in Massive Psychic Trauma. Edited by Krystal H. New York, International Universities Press, 1968b, pp 60–70

Niederland WG: Survivor syndrome: further observations and dimensions. J Am Psychoanal Assoc 29:413–426, 1981

Papousek H, Papousek M: Cognitive aspects of preverbal social interaction between human infants and adults, in Parent Interaction (Ciba Symposium). New York, Associated Publishers, 1975

Parkes CM, Stevenson-Hinde J (eds): The Place of Attachment in Human Behavior. New York, Basic Books, 1982

Pine F: On the expansion of the affect array. Bull Menninger Clin 43:79–95, 1979

Pollock GH: The psychosomatic specificity concept: its evaluation and reevaluation. Annual of Psychoanalysis 5:141–168, 1977

Pribram KH: Languages of the Brain. Englewood Cliffs, NJ, Prentice-Hall, 1971

Rado S: The emotions, in Adaptational Psychodynamics: Motivation and Control. Edited by Klein H. New York, Science House, 1969, pp 21–30

Reiser MF: Memory in Mind and Brain. New York, Basic Books, 1990

Schore AN: Affect Regulation and the Origin of the Self: The Neurobiology of Emotional Development. Hillsdale, NJ, Lawrence Erlbaum, 1994

Sifneos P: Clinical observation on some patients suffering from a variety of psychosomatic diseases. Acta Medica Psychosomatica: Proceedings of the Seventh European Conference on Psychosomatic Research. Rome, September 11–16, 1967, pp 452–458

Sifneos P: Is dynamic psychotherapy contraindicated for a large number of patients with psychosomatic disease? Psychother Psychosom 21:133–136, 1972–1973

Solyom AE: New research on affect regulation development: universal and theoretical considerations. Psychoanalytic Inquiry 7:331–347, 1987

Solyom AE, Homes TM, Hoffman P: Infant clinical assessment procedure: its implications for diagnosis and treatment in the second and third years. Infant Mental Health Journal 4:104–115, 1983

Spitz RA: Anaclitic depression. Psychoanal Study Child 2:313–342, 1946

Stern DN: The Interpersonal World of the Infant. New York, Basic Books, 1985

Stern MM: Pavor nocturnus. Int J Psychoanal 32:302–309, 1951a

Stern MM: Anxiety, trauma, and shock. Psychoanal Q 20:179–203, 1951b

Sugarman A, Jaffe LS: A developmental line of transitional phenomena, in The Facilitating Environment: Clinical Implications of Winnicott's Theories. Edited by From G, Smith BL. New York, International Universities Press, 1989, pp 88–129

Taylor GJ: The boring patient. Can J Psychiatry 29:217–222, 1984a

Taylor GJ: Alexithymia: concept, measurement, and implications for treatment. Am J Psychiatry 141:725–732, 1984b

Taylor GJ: Verbal measures of alexithymia: what do they measure? Psychother Psychosom 43:32–37, 1985

Taylor GJ: Psychosomatic Medicine and Contemporary Psychoanalysis. Madison, CT, International Universities Press, 1987

Ten Houten WD, Hoppe KD, Bogen JE, et al: Alexithymia and the split brain, I: lexical-level content analysis. Psychother Psychosom 43:202–208, 1985a

Ten Houten WD, Hoppe KD, Bogen JE, et al: Alexithymia and the split brain, II: sential-level content analysis. Psychother Psychosom 44:1–5, 1985b

Ten Houten WD, Hoppe KD, Bogen JE, et al: Alexithymia and the split brain, III: global-level content analysis. Psychother Psychosom 44:89–94, 1985c

Ten Houten WD, Hoppe KD, Bogen JE, et al: Alexithymia and the split brain, IV: Gotschalk-Gleser content analysis. Psychother Psychosom 44:113–121, 1985d

Tompkins SS: Affect, Imagery, Consciousness: The Positive Affects, Vol 1. New York, Springer, 1962

Tompkins SS: Affect, Imagery, Consciousness: The Positive Affects, Vol 2. New York, Springer, 1963

Tompkins SS: Affects: primary motives of man. Humanitas 3:321–345, 1968

van der Kolk BA: Biological considerations about emotions, trauma, memory and the brain, in Human Feelings: Explorations in Affect Development and Meaning. Edited by Ablon SA, Brown D, Khantzian EJ, et al. Hillsdale, NJ, Analytic Press, 1993, pp 221–258

Von Rad M: Alexithymie: Emipirische Untersuchungen Zur Diagnostik und Therapie Psychosomatisch Kranker. Berlin, Springer-Verlag, 1983

Von Rad M, Lolas F: Empirical evidence of alexithymia. Psychother Psychosom 38:91–102, 1982

Von Rad M, Lalucat L, Lolas F: Differences in verbal behavior in psychosomatic and psychoneurotic patients. Psychother Psychosom 28:83–97, 1977

Westerlundh B, Smith G: Perceptgenesis and the psychodynamics of perception. Psychoanalysis and Contemporary Thought 6:597–640, 1983

Wilson JP, Rafael B (eds): International Handbook of Traumatic Stress Syndromes. New York, Plenum, 1993

Zinberg NE: Addiction and ego function. Psychoanal Study Child 30:567–588, 1975

Chapter 14

Pathological Narcissism and Self-Regulatory Processes in Suicidal States

John T. Maltsberger, M.D.

I t is doubtful that patients with narcissistic personality disorder (NPD) of the DSM-IV (American Psychiatric Association 1994) type are ever lost to suicide (except under the rarest circumstances) unless they also have depression or a substance abuse disorder. There is much to suggest that the same statement holds true for patients who fall into the other personality disorder groups. Unfortunately, DSM-IV criteria for a major depressive episode require 2 weeks of morbidity before that diagnosis can be made. The instability of patients in the personality disorder groups renders them subject to sudden exacerbations of depressive mood that can precipitate a suicide before the 2-week waiting period to qualify for a major depressive episode diagnosis has passed.

Suicide in Narcissistic Patients

If patients with uncomplicated NPD (as defined by the DSM-IV rubric) are not at great risk to commit suicide, it is nevertheless true that they are very likely to fall into crises in the narcissistic functional sense that can result in suicide, and they are very likely to develop major depressive episodes. Perry (1990), in an overview of suicide in personality disorder patients, commented that the NPD patients' difficulty in maintaining reasonable self-esteem, coupled with their painful emotional reactions to failure, criticism, and humiliation, might make them vulnerable to suicide. To some extent, there is empirical evidence that this is true for those who have NPD.

Stone (1989) reported that in a group of borderline personality disorder patients those who also met the diagnostic criteria for NPD or had other prominent narcissistic features were at higher risk for suicide than ordinary borderline patients. Furthermore, in a study of narcissistic, antisocial, and noncomorbid borderline patients (McGlashan and Heinssen 1989), a slight (but nonsignificant) elevation in suicide rate was found in the narcissistic borderline group compared with the "pure" borderline personality group. Thirty-three characteristics for pathological narcissism were investigated (Gunderson et al. 1990), and among these were nonmanipulative suicidal behavior and ideation as reactions to criticism and defeat. This characteristic did not prove to be specifically prevalent or significantly discriminating for NPD patients in relation to other near-neighbor personality disorders or to psychiatric patients in general (Ronningstam and Gunderson 1989).

Between NPDs and antisocial personality disorders, Kernberg (1984, 1992) located a transitional group of patients who had "malignant narcissism" (see Kernberg, Chapter 2, this volume). They experienced pleasure and self-inflation when behaving aggressively, and some took pleasure in cruel perversions. These patients, profoundly aloof in their relationships to others, were especially prone to mutilate and, in some instances, to kill themselves, taking a cold satisfaction and asserting their control over life and death to the horror and despair of relatives and psychiatric staff (Kernberg 1984). Elsewhere, Kernberg (1992) defined the syndrome of malignant narcissism as the "combination of narcissistic personality disorder, antisocial behavior, ego-syntonic aggression or sadism directed against others or expressed in a particular type of triumphant self-mutilation or attempts at suicide, and a strong paranoid orientation" (p. 67). Suicides in such patients often conform to the metamorphic type, which is discussed below. Their magical grandiosity can express itself in the belief that through bodily self-destruction, an indestructible aspect of the self survives to live on in a better way; they conceive themselves to be masters over death (Kernberg 1992).

Kernberg chose to emphasize the importance of sadism and hate in these patients, a state of affairs that makes establishing and maintaining attachments to others problematical at best and often impossible. Their incapacity to master excessive aggressive and angry excitement is directly related to the instability of their self-organization. This difficulty forms the main theme of this chapter.

Definitions

The word *self*, like the word *narcissism*, invites great confusion. Because any discussion of pathological narcissism in suicidal states must address both narcissistic and self phenomena, some definitions are offered.

The functional definition of narcissism proposed by R. D. Stolorow (1975) is a helpful one, well suited for the purposes of the present discussion. "Mental activity is narcissistic," he wrote, "to the degree that its function is to maintain the structural cohesiveness, temporal stability and positive affective coloring of the self-representation" (p. 179).

Following Hartmann (1950), R. D. Stolorow defined the self as "the whole person of an individual, including his body and body parts as well as psychic organization and its parts" (p. 179). This definition is similar to those found in ordinary dictionaries. The self-representation is defined as "the unconscious, preconscious and conscious endopsychic representations of the bodily and mental self in the system ego" (pp. 179–180). It follows that an object representation is a corresponding, congruent set of representations of another person in the ego of the subject.

Disarticulation of Self-Representations in Suicidal States

Many, or even most, suicide-vulnerable patients have unstable self-representations which, under certain circumstances (such as in severe depression or angry excitement), are likely to divide in pieces. At such moments, the patient's body representation, disarticulated from the rest of the self-representation, may become associated with the representations of internal "bad" objects. This places the patient's body at risk for suicidal attack. Sullivan (1953) referred to "not-me" experiences in infancy, associated with intense anxiety and dread that relate to dissociative, psychotic, and dream experiences in adulthood.

Some patients repudiate their bodies and treat them as "not-me" entities. The body may be experienced as the wellspring of unendurable suffering. If patients thrust their bodies far enough in the "not-me" direction, they may objectify them. When the patients' bodies are objectified, some assume an essentially paranoid attitude toward their own flesh. Through suicide, they can attempt to rid themselves of it as a persecutory enemy (Maltsberger 1993b). This is decompensation or failure in narcissistic functioning at its most profound level: the structural cohesiveness and temporal stability of the self-representation are lost. Furthermore, the positive affective coloring of the broken-off representational fragment of the patient's body is abandoned.

Fragmentation of the self-representation can be formulated in traditional psychoanalytical terms as a form of ego regression, in which the capacity for self-object differentiation is lost. Jacobson (1964) discussed the tendency to confuse self and objects in depressed states; she formulated the problem in terms of confusion between self- and object representations. Modell (1963) identified the incapacity to differentiate self and object as nuclear in the failure of the capacity to "reality test" and discussed patients whose transferences reflected imperfect capacity for self-object discrimination. This theme was later expanded by McGlashan (1983).

Numerous writers have understood the potential for self and object confusion as the consequence of regression to (or partial arrest at) a developmental stage later than Freud's primary narcissistic (or autoerotic) stage (Freud 1914/1957) but earlier than the stage of object love. Mahler (1972) is preeminent among them; she refers to the "subphase of rapprochement" as critical in the child's transition between early symbiosis and the autonomy of later self- and object differentiation.

Hendrick (1936) noticed unusual aggressivity in certain primitive character types that interfered with the ego's executant functions. My observation of suicide-prone patients places most of them in this group. Hendrick suggested that the persistence of primitive aggressive fantasies reflected the failure of the identification process that would dissipate them had an undisturbed development occurred.

The unusual aggressive endowment of these patients appears to relate to their incapacity to keep stable self- and object representations clearly apart from each other. Their aggressivity, and the accompanying representational fragility, may arise in part from a constitutional or neurochemical limitation in the capacity to internalize and identify with "good" objects and to achieve stable self-object differentiation (Modell 1963). On the other hand, empirical reports point to the importance of traumatization throughout childhood and adolescence (not only in Mahler's early subphase) in the development of borderline personality disorder and multiple personality disorder, two diagnostic groups with high incidences of self-mutilative and suicidal behavior (Links 1990; Wagner and Linehan 1994). Many within these two groups also satisfy the diagnostic criteria for NPD, especially when the syndrome of Kernberg's malignant narcissism is present. The aggressivity of their fantasies and their sadomasochistic dispositions arises in the context of significant psychological and often brutal physical and sexual developmental misfortune.

Kohut (1971) blurred the distinction between the self and the self-representation, but he suggested that some suicides are to be understood not as attacks of the superego on the ego, but instead as attempts of the suffering ego to do away with the self in order to wipe out the offending, disappointing reality of failure. "In other words," he wrote, "the self-destructive impulses are to be understood here not as analogous to the suicidal impulses of the depressed patient but as the expression of narcissistic rage" (p. 181).

The distinction he draws between depressive suicides and those that arise from narcissistic rage directed against the self reflects, in my opinion, his terminological confusion. Plainly, the "suffering ego" to which Kohut refers cannot be separated from the "self" if one understands ego to be a psychic system within the self, as self is defined by Hartmann and the dictionary. If one reads Kohut to denote by "ego" the broader mental "self," the implication is that the broader "self" turns against some other part of the "self" and attacks it in order to escape mental suffering. This confused language nevertheless expresses an observable clinical fact: in suicide, one part of the patient's self turns against another part (the patient's body and what is associated with it) and destroys it.

Normal and Disturbed Self-Regulation

In the course of normal development, internalization of the child's relationship to the parents results in the building up of essential ego and superego structures and permits increasingly autonomous narcissistic function as maturation proceeds. Suicide-prone patients have a number of ego and superego deficiencies that from time to time make narcissistic autonomy and satisfactory self-esteem regulation impossible and that permit affective flooding of such painful intensity that their lives are threatened. They have great difficulty in mastering anxiety and are prey to feelings of panic that they cannot master (Weissman et al. 1989). They cannot sustain reasonable self-regard, and they often feel unreal.

Gradual identification with comfort-giving adults permits the ego to build up an anxiety-mastering structure. The child's ability to cope with separation and other experiences of external danger slowly increases as identification takes place; eventually, experiences of overwhelming anxiety are tamed and the capacity to experience and make use of signal anxiety appears (Tolpin 1971). Object permanence becomes possible with ego maturation, and so does the capacity for reality testing. The mental ability to keep self-aspects sorted out and separate from aspects of others is essential for psychic survival, and, as we shall see, sometimes it is essential for physical survival. Self-object confusion may well prove to be a sine qua non for suicide (Adler 1989; Adler and Buie 1979; Fraiberg 1969).

Normal narcissistic functioning in adulthood requires a reasonably stable superego system in which self-criticism is realistic but kindly, and the ego-ideal, firmly established, is comparatively realistic and does not require grandiose or omnipotent performance. In the course of undisturbed development, introjection and identification operate to transform the child's relationships with his parents into pre-oedipal superego anlage and into the post-oedipal superego proper (Sandler 1960). Traumatized children, however, have difficulty in establishing a satisfactory superego system. The dissociative experiences in childhood and adolescence that accompany physical and sexual abuse are likely to interfere with normal structuralization. To the extent that introjections of unempathic, neglectful, or brutal parental experiences are taken into the developing superego, unusually aggressive and punitive self-attitudes are likely to result with the advance of maturation. The self-kindliness of the normal superego will be lacking (Schafer 1960).

Clinical experience with suicidal patients suggests that the hostile introjects deriving from traumatic or otherwise painful parental experiences commonly fail to become well integrated with the superego system, although these are likely to maintain, under most circumstances, a loose affiliation with it. When more affiliated with the superego than not, their influence is experienced as a brutal, occasionally insane conscience. This is the state of affairs in many psychotic depressions.

In psychotic and many other grave depressions, it is not the patient who raves: the patient's conscience raves at the patient. Conscience dominates the inner stage, scolding and devaluating, while the rest of the self suffers the conscience's censure in more or less mute submission. The essence of the patient's experience is that one part of the self attacks the rest. "I am a worthless scum," or "I am radioactive," the patient (conscience having the floor) may insist, with intense conviction. The self-devaluations may rise to delusional proportions; although utterly at variance with reality, some patients insist that their negative self-valuations are entirely correct. Sometimes the delusional tendency is not confined to convictions of debased self-value but expands into claims such as "I am a monster," "devil," or "murderer."

As subjectively experienced, many superego operations have the color of an object relationship. To the extent that the introjections that give rise to the superego remain "undigested" or "unmetabolized" (remain charged with aggressive and sexual energy and have not been assimilated through secondary identification), the conscience may be experienced as an internal watcher, or, worse, as a martinet or even a concentration camp guard (Fairbairn 1943; Freud 1915/1962, 1923/1962; Meissner 1971).

Although troublesome aggressively charged introjects are usually more or less affiliated with the superego and give rise to experiences that seem to come from within the self, the affiliation is not always secure. There is a tendency for these structures to assume transient qualities of an inner object representation when they are subjectively less experienced as part of the self.

To the extent that an ill-integrated, aggressively overcharged introject remains affiliated with the superego, the patient's subjective experience is that of uneasy conscience or other inner censure (the experience of conscience is one of shame or guilt; there are other experiences of self-censure). The aggressive vector belonging to the introject adds itself to that of the superego. The censure seems to come from within the self, and the patient is likely to assent to it as just.

When the affiliation of the hostile introject to the superego is sufficiently loosened, the patient may experience censure from within, but the censure does not seem to come from a part of the self. It is as though something or someone foreign has invaded the self and has set itself up within the mind as a hostile alien. From this configuration arises experiences of demonic possession or possession-like states:

> A 30-year-old patient, Ms. A, with an intractable major depression and a significant level of malignant narcissism with powerful suicidal impulses, reported the following dream, reflecting the action of a hostile introject ill-integrated into the superego as an inner persecutor. "There was a hairy man in bed with me; he looked like a gorilla He punched me and hit me and swore at me all night, insulting me, and would not let me lie in any position that was comfortable."

"Bad" Internal Objects

Although it is customary for writers to distance themselves from Klein's implausible theories of infantile mental development (Klein 1958), we are indebted to her for directing attention to ill-integrated, aggressively colored introjects, which she chose to call "bad objects." Indeed, she related bad internal objects to the problem of suicide and proposed two suicide scenarios.

In the first, the patient attempts to preserve the "good" internal objects and that part of the ego that is identified with them by destroying the other part of the ego, which is identified with the bad objects and the id. In the second, she suggests that the good inner objects are identified with real objects in the external world. Suicide in this context represents an attempt to rid the world, felt to be good, of the bad ego, which is identified with the bad object and the patient's id (Klein 1935).

These Kleinian formulations can be translated into contemporary and more precise language. In the first, the self-representation is split, and the bad introject, expressing itself as an object representation on the inner stage, has become fused with a repudiated fragment of the self-representation. This fragment typically includes the patient's body representation, although Klein does not state this. The aggressive and sexual impulses, which trouble many suicidal patients, center in the physical self, which is experienced as the seat of the id. Mental self-aspects appear to be less securely bound to the body representation than are the representations of the self-as-feeling (Maltsberger 1993b; Rothstein 1988; Sandler 1990; Sandler and Rosenblatt 1962). In this case, one can usually identify the fantasy that the mental aspects of the self will survive suicide. In the second, the self-representation is also split, but the fantasy is that the portions of the self destined to survive suicide become fused with object representations.

Metamorphic Suicide

At the root of most suicides of Klein's first type is a fantasy of metamorphosis: the aim of suicide is to effect some transformation of person in the service of escaping an insupportable present into a better future beyond death. To shed one's body, as a pupa breaks out of its chitinous shell or cocoon after maturing into an adult, is the core fantasy (Maltsberger and Buie 1984).

In their fantasies of postmortem survival, these patients repudiate parts of themselves (those parts destined to die) but do not repudiate other parts, which are expected to live on. Metamorphic suicides reflect the mental or thinking self acting on the body self as object; the body self is to die, the mental self is not.

Metamorphic suicide can occur in patients whose grandiosity, cruelty, and object detachment rise to malignant proportions. In such persons, the integration of the body self into the overall self-representation is very loose. Fragmentation of the self-representation is highly characteristic in these patients, and the principal fissure line along which cleavage is likely to occur lies between the mental and physical representational selves. When borderline patients injure themselves, they commonly feel depersonalized and claim their bodies are unreal or even alien (Maltsberger 1993b).

> Ms. A, the patient whose rest was prevented by the dream of a gorilla-man, blamed her female body for her failure to excel as an Olympic swimmer. In a chronic narcissistic rage, she often brooded on suicide by hanging. She imagined hanging herself to death off the end of a crane, whereupon someone would come with a knife to fillet out the core of herself (head, neck, and some of the thoracic parts) so it could be hoisted away for transplant into a waiting perfect male body.

In the suicides of profound depression, an ambivalently loved lost object is taken into and "identified" with the ego. The ego then becomes the object of attack by the superego (Freud 1915/1962). Some of these suicides can be reformulated in the same way if we take it that the patient's self-representation splits and that its physical portion is fused with the "bad" object representation. The superego's attack is then directed against the body as a bad alien object.

In some cases, the bad object is representationally fused with the split-off representation of the body self, whereupon it presents itself on the inner stage as an enemy to be killed off and cast away. Adolescent suicide attempts frequently follow this scenario. Shocked and troubled by the body changes that accompany puberty and by the impulses that accompany them, adolescents may objectify their bodies. No longer experienced as part of oneself, but rather as a "not-me" persecutor, the body may become the object of a suicidal attack (M. Laufer and M. E. Laufer 1984; M. E. Laufer 1991).

Sometimes patients assign responsibility for mental suffering (depression, sometimes hallucinations or delusions) to the physical self. In some of these cases, the body representation is experienced as the seat of influencing machinery and may be attacked as an inner persecutor (Maltsberger and Buie 1984; Tausk 1919/1948). Although the patient in the following case example did not have NPD, her experience nevertheless sheds a good deal of light on the phenomenon of self-fragmentation in suicide.

> Ms. B, a 28-year-old chronically suicidal patient, killed herself, leaving behind an explanatory note. It said she could no longer bear the persecutions of a robot that had taken up residence in her head, controlling her thoughts, telling her what to say in therapy. She explained that her suicide was intended to free herself of it.

This dynamic pattern is not restricted to psychotic patients but also appears in others who have been sexually abused as children. In the course of sexual traumatization, children commonly dissociate themselves from the physical ordeal to which they are subjected. These early dissociative experiences probably interfere with the development of a self-representation with good mind and body integration. Abuse victims are prone to representational splitting in adulthood; this makes them suicide vulnerable (Orbach 1994).

> Mrs. C, a 43-year-old professional woman with an NPD, began psychotherapy in a dangerous suicidal state. She had been sexually brutalized by her father in childhood. When she recalled scenes of incest, she wanted to tear out her hair and strike herself. When it was pointed out to her that she thought to hurt herself, not her father, at the moments of reliving her memories, the patient said, "What's the difference? What does a child of three know about anything? My body? It was not my body that was doing the hurting, my body that was giving me pain. It was his. I learned to hate it early. That's where the hurting and the fear and the humiliation was. I was trapped by him and my body was his cage." (Maltsberger 1993b, p. 158)

Execution Suicide

The second suicidal scenario suggested by Klein resembles a later formulation of Freud's (1923/1962). The superego withdraws itself from the ego in some cases, he wrote, abandoning it to die. If the subject projects his good objects into the external world, then a suicidal attack may be understood as an effort to rid the good outer world, with which the patient affiliates the mental self, from the badness that can be left behind by killing the patient's body (Klein 1935).

Formulating this in representational terms, we may say that the self-representation is split and that the observing, executive aspect of the self puts the body representation—once again experienced as a representation of a bad object—to death.

Superego projection, or projection of aggressive superego fragments, is a familiar transference phenomenon. In suicidal cases, the therapist may be experienced as desiring the patient's death, concurring that suicide is the best choice.

> Mrs. D, a 35-year-old married professional woman with several young children, had an intractable depression and profound narcissistic disturbance. She not only considered herself to be worthless—a failure as wife, mother, and worker—but also believed she could never get better. She developed a secret delusional transference in which she was convinced that both her present and her previous therapists were secretly sure she was worthless and wanted her to go ahead with suicide. This delusional belief was described in a diary discovered after she took her life. She had watched her therapist closely for weeks for evidences that he disliked her and wanted her out of his life. The language of the diary showed that the therapist was highly idealized; the negative judgment of herself she projected into him she sadly accepted as correct.

Patients may succeed in entangling therapists in trans-ference-countertransference binds so that the therapist, perceived as a potential executioner, may be provoked or persuaded to become an accomplice in suicide (Asch 1980; Hendin 1994;

D. S. Stolorow and R. D. Stolorow 1989). In such an instance, the re-projected hostile introject is experienced more as an external and less as an internal object, concurring that the self is bad and must die.

In execution suicide, the action of the "bad objects," or hostile introjects, appears to be ubiquitous. On the one hand, their influence is evident in the negative self-judgment these patients form: their superegos are "hostile." Through projection, others are experienced as concurring in negative judgment. Subjectively, the patient does not experience either conscience or the repudiating outer object as bad or destructive. The negative judgments on the self are accepted as realistic and correct. The bad self is then objectified and put to death by the executant self, and, of course, the body self is the victim, split off and identified as bad.

The patient may be saved from suicide in such an instance if the self-representation is able to free itself from the grips of the hostile superego and to project it, and its affiliated hostile introjects, into the therapist. A paranoid state may then appear, enabling the patient to fight against a persecution by running away.

In summary, some suicides may be understood as the self attempting to rid itself of something bad (the body self experienced as the seat of unacceptable impulses and identified as a loathsome bad object) in the service of metamorphosis. In other suicides, the self attempts to destroy the body as the locus of intolerable suffering (the body self as a persecuting bad object). Finally, the executive mental self may identify with the deadly judgment of the superego, supported by concurring negative judgment—real or fantasized—of an external object. (In representational terms, the split-off representation of the executive mental self allies itself with the deadly superego, reinforced by concurring negative judgment that seems to come from an external object.) An attack is then carried out against the patient's body representation, which is experienced as a bad inner object.

Self-Disintegration in Suicidal Patients' Dreams

In conclusion, representational instability in suicidal states is sometimes reflected in patients' manifest dream content. Kohut

(1977) described a special variety of dream "attempting, with the aid of verbalizable dream-imagery, to bind the tensions of traumatic states (the dread of overstimulation, or of the disintegration of the self)" (pp. 108–109). He named such dreams "self-state" dreams and said they were similar to the dreams of children, to the dreams of traumatic neuroses, and to "hallucinatory" dreams occurring with toxic states or high fever (pp. 108–109). Although there has been some controversy surrounding the meaning of such dreams (Slap and Trunnell 1987), the general phenomenon of self-state dreams is familiar in psychoanalytical work.

In short, the manifest self-state dreams of suicidal patients sometimes depict the breakup of the self. Patients may dream that body parts are literally disarticulated from the body, that the body is being shaken to pieces, or that obvious body symbols (a house, for example) are being broken to pieces (Maltsberger 1993a). Dreams of this kind are a further phenomenon demonstrating the specific disintegration of the self-representation in the course of the ego regression that accompanies suicide.

Clinicians who remain sensitive to the phenomena of representational breakup will be better equipped to assess the level of suicide risk. These phenomena invite further research. The future empirical study of the development of traumatized children, with special attention to the implications of early dissociative experiences for adult vulnerability to suicide, should go far to deepen our understanding and to place it on a firm scientific basis.

References

Adler G: Uses and limitations of Kohut's self psychology in the treatment of borderline patients. J Am Psychoanal Assoc 37:761–785, 1989

Adler G, Buie DH: Aloneness and borderline psychopathology: the possible relevance of child development issues. Int J Psychoanal 60:83–96, 1979

American Psychiatric Association: Diagnostic and Statistical Manual of Mental Disorders, 4th Edition. Washington, DC, American Psychiatric Association, 1994

Asch SS: Suicide and the hidden executioner. Int J Psychoanal 7:51–60, 1980

Fairbairn WRD: The repression and the return of bad objects (with special reference to the "war neuroses"). Br J Med Psychol 19:327–341, 1943

Fraiberg S: Libidinal object constancy and mental representation. Psychoanal Study Child 24:9–47, 1969

Freud S: On narcissism (1914), in The Standard Edition of the Complete Psychological Works of Sigmund Freud, Vol 14. Translated and edited by Strachey J. London, Hogarth Press, 1957, pp 67–102

Freud S: Mourning and melancholia (1915), in The Standard Edition of The Complete Psychological Works of Sigmund Freud, Vol 14. Translated and edited by Strachey J. London, Hogarth Press, 1962, pp 239–260

Freud S: The ego and the id (1923), in The Standard Edition of the Complete Psychological Works of Sigmund Freud, Vol 19. Translated and edited by Strachey J. London, Hogarth Press, 1962, pp 3–66

Gunderson J, Ronningstam E, Bodkin A: The diagnostic interview for narcissistic patients. Arch Gen Psychiatry 47:676–680, 1990

Hartmann H: Comments on the psychoanalytic theory of the ego. Psychoanal Study Child 5:76–96, 1950

Hendin H: Seduced by death: doctors, patients, and the Dutch cure. Issues in Law and Medicine 10:123–168, 1994

Hendrick I: Ego development and certain character problems. Psychoanal Q 5:320–346, 1936

Jacobson E: The Self and the Object World. New York, International Universities Press, 1964

Kernberg O: Severe Personality Disorders. New Haven, CT, Yale University Press, 1984

Kernberg O: Aggression in Personality Disorders and Perversions. New Haven, CT, Yale University Press, 1992

Klein M: A contribution to the psychogenesis of manic-depressive states. Int J Psychoanal 16:145–174, 1935

Klein M: On the development of mental functioning. Int J Psychoanal 39:84–90, 1958

Kohut H: The Analysis of the Self. New York, International Universities Press, 1971

Kohut H: The Restoration of the Self. New York, International Universities Press, 1977

Laufer M, Laufer ME: Adolescence and Developmental Breakdown: A Psychoanalytic View. New Haven, CT, Yale University Press, 1984

Laufer ME: Body image, sexuality and the psychotic core. Int J Psychoanal 72:63–71, 1991

Links PS: Family Environment and Borderline Personality Disorder. Washington, DC, American Psychiatric Press, 1990

Mahler MS: On the first three subphases of the separation-individuation process. Int J Psychoanal 53:333–338, 1972

Maltsberger JT: Dreams and suicide. Suicide and Life-Threatening Behavior 23:55–62, 1993a

Maltsberger JT: Confusions of the body, the self, and others in suicidal states, in Suicidology: Essays in Honor of Edwin S. Shneidman. Edited by Leenaars A. Northvale, NJ, Jason Aronson, 1993b, pp 148–171

Maltsberger JT, Buie DH: The devices of suicide: revenge, riddance, and rebirth. International Review of Psychoanalysis 7:61–72, 1984

McGlashan TH: The "we-self" in borderline patients: manifestations of the symbiotic self-object in psychotherapy. Psychiatry 46:351–361, 1983

McGlashan TH, Heinssen RK: Narcissistic, antisocial and noncomorbid subgroups of borderline disorder. Psychiatr Clin North Am 12:653–670, 1989

Meissner WW: Notes on identification 2: clarification of related concepts. Psychoanal Q 40:277–302, 1971

Modell AH: Primitive object relationships and the predisposition to schizophrenia. Int J Psychoanal 44:232–292, 1963

Orbach I: Dissociation, physical pain, and suicide: a hypothesis. Suicide and Life-Threatening Behavior 24:68–79, 1994

Perry JC: Personality disorders, suicide and self-destructive behavior, in Suicide: Understanding and Responding. Edited by Jacobs D, Brown H. Madison, CT, International Universities Press, 1990, pp 157–169

Ronningstam E, Gunderson J: Descriptive studies of narcissistic personality disorder. Psychiatr Clin North Am 12:585–602, 1989

Rothstein A: The representational world as a substructure of the ego. J Am Psychoanal Assoc 36 (suppl):191–208, 1988

Sandler J: On the concept of the superego. Psychoanal Study Child 15:128–162, 1960

Sandler J: On internal object relations. J Am Psychoanal Assoc 38: 859–880, 1990

Sandler J, Rosenblatt B: The concept of the representational world. Psychoanal Study Child 17:128–145, 1962

Schafer R: The loving and beloved superego in Freud's structural theory. Psychoanal Study Child 15:163–188, 1960

Slap JW, Trunnell EE: Reflections on the self state dream. Psychoanal Q 61:251–262, 1987

Stolorow DS, Stolorow RD: My brother's keeper: intensive treatment of a case of delusional merger. Int J Psychoanal 70:315–326, 1989

Stolorow RD: Toward a functional definition of narcissism. Int J Psychoanal 56:179–185, 1975

Stone M: Long-term follow-up of narcissistic borderline patients. Psychiatr Clin North Am 12:603–620, 1989

Sullivan HS: The Interpersonal Theory of Psychiatry. Edited by Perry HS, Gowel ML. New York, WW Norton, 1953

Tausk V: On the origin of the "influencing machine" (1919), in Schizophrenia: The Psychoanalytic Reader. Edited by Fliess R. New York, International Universities Press, 1948, pp 31–64

Tolpin M: On the beginnings of a cohesive self: an application of the concept of transmuting internalization to the study of the transitional object and signal anxiety. Psychoanal Study Child 26:316–354, 1971

Wagner AW, Linehan MM: Relationship between childhood sexual abuse and topography of parasuicide among women with borderline personality disorder. Journal of Personality Disorders 8:1–9, 1994

Weissman MM, Klerman GL, Markowitz JS, et al: Suicidal ideation and suicide attempts in panic disorder and attacks. N Engl J Med 321:1209–1214, 1989

Section IV

Research

Introduction

Elsa F. Ronningstam, Ph.D.

Until the inclusion of narcissistic personality disorder
(NPD) in DSM-III in 1980 (American Psychiatric Association 1980),
most knowledge about pathological narcissism was generated
through clinical case observations, usually in psychoanalytical or
long-term psychotherapeutic settings. The DSM criteria sets for
personality disorders have instigated an extensive systematic research tradition in which NPD gradually has been included. The
conceptualization of NPD in terms of observable and verifiable
criteria stimulated studies of narcissistic patients through structured and semistructured interviews and made it possible to investigate the validity and differential diagnostic aspects of NPD
and pathological narcissism. Results from these research efforts
were influential when, for the first time, the DSM-IV (American
Psychiatric Association 1994) Axis II task force could base their decisions about the NPD criteria set on extensive empirical psychometric research on diagnostic efficiency and comorbidity of NPD
(Gunderson et al. 1991). In Chapter 15, Leslie C. Morey, Ph.D., and
Janice K. Jones, B.S., present extensive investigations of the discriminating validity of NPD and the internal characteristics of
each NPD criterion. Based on these results, a number of new criteria are proposed that could diminish the diagnostic overlap and
improve discriminant validity of the NPD category.

A second tradition consists of a series of studies on discriminating criteria, descriptive validity, and long-term stability of
NPD using the Diagnostic Interview for Narcissism (Gunderson

et al. 1990). This research, based on a theoretically eclectic psycho-analytical and psychodynamic conceptualization of NPD (including both object relations theoretical and self psychological aspects), operationalizes a broader set of characteristics for NPD, including those in DSM-III-R (American Psychiatric Association 1987) and DSM-IV. The results described in Chapter 16 by Elsa F. Ronningstam, Ph.D., have been influential in the decisions regarding the delineation of the DSM-IV Axis II criteria set for NPD and have challenged the understanding of NPD as a long-term trait pathology. In this chapter, the interface between pathological narcissism and major Axis I disorders is also discussed.

A third research tradition, emanating from extensive investigation of psychopathy in forensic populations, has focused on the interface between psychopathy and narcissism using the psychopathy checklist as an instrument for measurement. This research, influenced by Kernberg's conceptualizations of the manifestations of NPD and malignant narcissism, has been particularly useful in highlighting and answering questions about the differential diagnosis between NPD and antisocial personality disorder. A series of research studies on the association between narcissism and psychopathy are reviewed by Stephen D. Hart, Ph.D., and Robert D. Hare, Ph.D. (Chapter 17), who suggest that there is a partial diagnostic overlap and that narcissism is associated with one facet of psychopathy.

Other noteworthy empirical efforts are a series of longitudinal studies of narcissistic (Plakun 1990) and narcissistic borderline patients (McGlashan and Heinssen 1989; Stone 1989) presented in other volumes. These studies have contributed to a valuable understanding of the influence of pathological narcissism on long-term adaptation. A tradition that originates from psychological research studies of the narcissistic personality using the Narcissistic Personality Inventory (Raskin and Hall 1979; Raskin and Terry 1988) has generated extensive knowledge on aspects of narcissism in nonclinical populations and delineated the construct of narcissism in relation to other phenomena such as creativity, empathy, and self-esteem.

The first effort to empirically study pathological narcissism and NPD in nonadult samples is presented in Chapter 18 by Paulina F. Kernberg, M.D., and her colleagues Fady Hajal, M.D., and Lina Normandin, Ph.D. Despite disputes regarding the presence of personality disorder during developmental ages, the results convincingly point out the possibility of identifying NPD and narcissistic characteristics in adolescents by using a version of the Diagnostic Interview for Narcissism adapted for record review of adolescents.

References

American Psychiatric Association: Diagnostic and Statistical Manual of Mental Disorders, 3rd Edition. Washington, DC, American Psychiatric Association, 1980

American Psychiatric Association: Diagnostic and Statistical Manual of Mental Disorders, 3rd Edition, Revised. Washington, DC, American Psychiatric Association, 1987

American Psychiatric Association: Diagnostic and Statistical Manual of Mental Disorders, 4th Edition. Washington, DC, American Psychiatric Association, 1994

Gunderson J, Ronningstam E, Bodkin A: The Diagnostic Interview for Narcissistic Patients. Arch Gen Psychiatry 47:676–680, 1990

Gunderson J, Ronningstam E, Smith L: Narcissistic personality disorder: a review of data on DSM-III-R descriptions. Journal of Personality Disorders 5:167–177, 1991

McGlashan T, Heinssen R: Narcissistic, antisocial and noncomorbid subgroups of borderline personality disorder. Psychiatr Clin North Am 12:653–670, 1989

Plakun E (ed): New Perspectives on Narcissism. Washington, DC, American Psychiatric Press, 1990

Raskin RN, Hall CS: The narcissistic personality inventory. Psychol Rep 45:590, 1979

Raskin RN, Terry H: A principal-component analysis of the narcissistic personality inventory and further evidence of its construct validity. J Pers Soc Psychol 54:890–902, 1988

Stone M: Long-term follow-up of narcissistic borderline patients. Psychiatr Clin North Am 12:621–642, 1989

Chapter 15

Empirical Studies of the Construct Validity of Narcissistic Personality Disorder

Leslie C. Morey, Ph.D.

Janice K. Jones, B.S.

The diagnosis of narcissistic personality disorder (NPD) has been the focus of some controversy since the introduction of specific diagnostic criteria for the disorder in DSM-III (American Psychiatric Association 1980). One important area of theoretical controversy has involved the nosological status of the concept: does it represent a distinct diagnostic entity, or does it refer to a range of personality pathology that is common to or overlapping with other personality disorder concepts? This question is one that has been apparent in the historical evolution of accounts of narcissism, and addressing it has become critical with the advent of empirical studies over the past few decades. A construct validation framework (Morey 1991a) may begin to answer this question. To demonstrate such construct validity, several investigations are necessary. Does NPD reflect a coherent pattern of interrelated features? Can these features be successfully discriminated from those of other disorders? Finally, does a diagnosis of NPD have meaningful links to etiology and treatment?

In this chapter, the authors review the results of a few studies that have come out of their research group that may serve as a beginning point to address some of these questions. Although the focus is on their own research, other well-designed studies have tended to arrive at similar conclusions. Note that these studies have specifically addressed the concept of NPD as it has been defined in the various editions of DSM (American Psychiatric Association 1980, 1987, 1994). As reviewed elsewhere in this volume, various other descriptions of narcissism have been offered over the years, and the construct validity of each of these accounts merits investigation. However, it is the DSM concept that has been the focus of this research.

A comparison of NPD diagnoses under DSM-III and DSM-III-R (Morey 1988a) found a substantial increase in frequency of patients with a DSM-III-R diagnosis of NPD. In a sample of 291 inpatients, 6.2% received a diagnosis of NPD when DSM-III was used, whereas 22.0% were given a diagnosis of NPD by DSM-III-R criteria—a 350% increase. This finding suggests that the change from a monothetic criterion system to a polythetic diagnosis increases the number of people who are given a diagnosis of the disorder. As is discussed in more detail below, Morey (1988a) also found that the coefficient alpha of the DSM-III-R NPD criteria was considerably greater than the one obtained for the DSM-III narcissistic criteria (Morey 1985), suggesting that the revisions improved the internal consistency of the criteria. However, the NPD criteria exhibited problematic discriminativeness from other personality disorders, particularly histrionic personality disorder.

Internal Characteristics of Diagnostic Criteria for Narcissistic Personality Disorder

In recent years, increasing attention has been given to examining the criteria sets presented in DSM according to the type of psychometric criteria that have been applied to psychological tests (Blashfield and Livesley 1991; Morey 1991a; Nelson-Gray 1991).

One such psychometric criterion, that of internal consistency, seems particularly applicable, because it provides an estimate of the association between different diagnostic symptoms that supposedly reflects a common syndrome. Analytically, this involves determining the correlation between these different symptoms. It is precisely this association or intercorrelation that results in the identification of a constellation of features as a syndrome. As such, internal consistency analyses are of importance because they search for a correlational structure that should be inherent in natural classes. In summary, internal consistency is an important issue in the evaluation of definitions of personality disorder, because this concept addresses components of both the reliability and the validity of these definitions.

There are many ways to measure the internal consistency of a collection of diagnostic features. One useful metric is coefficient alpha (Cronbach 1951). Alpha represents an estimate of the average correlation between different halves of a feature list; thus, values close to +1.00 imply very high correlations between the different diagnostic features. It should be noted that it would not necessarily be desirable to have criteria with a coefficient alpha of +1.00, because this would mean that all criteria would correlate perfectly, and the presumably different criteria would therefore be redundant (Loevinger 1954). Nonetheless, it is reasonable to propose that in a collection of diagnostic features, those features that are diagnostic of the same syndrome should be intercorrelated, assuming that the sample is fairly heterogeneous and contains a reasonable number of subjects manifesting the syndrome.

Other means of examining internal consistency focus on the relationship of an individual criterion to the other criteria that constitute the diagnosis. Metrics that have been used for this purpose include the sensitivity, specificity, positive and negative predictive powers, and part-whole correlation coefficients. When used in this manner, sensitivity refers to the likelihood of having the criterion symptom given that one has the diagnosis, and specificity is the probability that a person does not display the symptom given that he or she does not have the diagnosis. Sensitivity and specificity estimates are expected to be constant across different types of samples. In contrast, positive and negative predictive power estimates will vary as a function of the composition of the sample. Positive predictive power reflects the likelihood of having the diagnosis given that the criterion in question is manifest, whereas negative predictive power is the probability of not having the diagnosis given that the particular criterion is absent. Finally, various part-whole correlations (such as the phi coefficient or point-biserial correlations) reflect the association between an individual criterion and the whole set of criteria that constitute the diagnosis.

The internal consistency of the set of diagnostic criteria for NPD has been examined in a number of studies (Pfohl et al. 1986; Widiger and Sanderson 1987), including studies from our group (Morey 1985, 1988a, 1988b). These estimates have varied somewhat across studies (coefficient alphas of 0.68 for DSM-III criteria in Widiger and Sanderson 1987, 0.69 for DSM-III-R criteria in Morey 1988a, but only 0.39 for DSM-III criteria in Morey 1985), but the values for the NPD criteria yield coefficient alphas that seem to be typical of most other Axis II disorders.

However, the study by Morey (1988a) also pointed out a problem with the internal characteristics of the NPD criteria. These criteria were found to be the most redundant, in an empirical sense, of all of the DSM-III-R personality disorder definitions. Redundancy in that study was defined by the ability to predict the presence or absence of a given personality disorder diagnosis if the presence or absence of the other personality disorders was already known. This result suggests that some of the intercorrelation between the NPD diagnostic criteria may be artifactual. For example, the same basic characteristic may be described in two different criteria, such as "grandiosity" and "entitlement," perhaps both reflecting greater than average self-esteem.

There also appears to be some variability at the level of the individual criteria with respect to internal consistency. Table 15–1 reports part-whole (phi) correlations of the individual DSM-III criteria with the overall diagnosis from Morey (1985), whereas Table 15–2 presents various measures of association derived from the data presented by Morey (1988a, 1988b). These numbers re-

Table 15–1. Part-whole correlations for DSM-III criteria for narcissistic personality disorder

Criterion	Part-whole correlation	
	Narcissistic	Borderline
Grandiose self-importance	.64	−.17
Narcissistic fantasies	.66	−.26
Exhibitionistic	.73	.31
Indifference or rage at critics	.70	.12
Entitlement	.78	.00
Interpersonal exploitativeness	.79	.24
Overidealized/devalued relationship	.58	.33
Lack of empathy	.59	.27

Source.   Adapted from Morey 1985.

veal several interesting findings. For example, "entitlement" is present in nearly every patient with a diagnosis of NPD, although in isolation it is a fairly poor predictor of NPD because of its limited specificity. The best predictors of the NPD diagnosis appear to be "grandiosity" and "preoccupation with success fantasies," both of which yield positive predictive values of 68%. The criteria involving "reacts to criticism" and "feelings of envy" tend not to be very highly associated with the other criteria; not coincidentally, the former criterion was dropped from DSM-IV, and the latter was substantially revised.

With respect to the coverage of the criteria for NPD, it should be pointed out that a variety of diagnostic features from other personality disorders are typically found to be associated with NPD. Table 15–3 presents a list of symptoms that, when the data from Morey (1988a, 1988b) are used, yield a positive predictive power greater than 45%. In other words, when any of the symptoms listed in Table 15–3 are present, there is at least a 45% chance that

Table 15–2. Internal consistency measures for DSM-III-R narcissistic personality disorder criteria

					Sensitivity				
Items	A1	A2	A3	A4	A5	A6	A7	A8	A9
PAR	.88	.25	.28	.62	.30	.66	.23	.30	.30
SCZ	.59	.22	.25	.50	.22	.50	.09	.41	.13
STY	.74	.07	.48	.59	.48	.63	.19	.27	.11
ANT	.61	.83	.50	.44	.39	.89	.33	.72	.28
BOR	.76	.26	.23	.50	.33	.65	.25	.31	.23
HST	.71	.44	.46	.52	.49	.86	.59	.49	.22
AVD	.80	.14	.22	.60	.30	.48	.28	.27	.28
DEP	.69	.17	.12	.55	.29	.49	.29	.21	.29
OBC	.74	.04	.26	.39	.22	.48	.17	.26	.39
PAG	.72	.47	.47	.56	.39	.83	.31	.58	.28
NAR	.84	.48	.66	.67	.78	.98	.55	.62	.37

					Specificity				
Items	A1	A2	A3	A4	A5	A6	A7	A8	A9
PAR	.49	.80	.81	.67	.76	.47	.81	.73	.88
SCZ	.41	.79	.79	.63	.74	.43	.79	.74	.84
STY	.43	.78	.81	.63	.77	.45	.80	.72	.84
ANT	.41	.83	.81	.61	.76	.46	.81	.75	.85
BOR	.50	.81	.79	.66	.78	.49	.83	.74	.88
HST	.45	.86	.86	.64	.81	.52	.91	.78	.86
AVD	.48	.76	.79	.68	.76	.41	.83	.78	.89
DEP	.44	.78	.76	.65	.76	.42	.83	.70	.88
OBC	.43	.78	.79	.60	.74	.43	.80	.72	.86
PAG	.43	.83	.82	.63	.77	.48	.82	.77	.86
NAR	.49	.87	.91	.68	.89	.56	.90	.82	.90

(continued)

Table 15–2. Internal consistency measures for DSM-III-R
narcissistic personality disorder criteria *(continued)*

Items									

Items	A1	A2	A3	A4	A5	A6	A7	A8	A9
PAR	.33	.26	.29	.35	.26	.26	.26	.23	.41
SCZ	.11	.11	.13	.14	.10	.10	.05	.16	.09
STY	.12	.03	.21	.14	.18	.10	.09	.10	.07
ANT	.06	.25	.15	.07	.10	.10	.10	.16	.11
BOR	.43	.41	.36	.43	.43	.39	.41	.37	.48
HST	.26	.46	.47	.29	.42	.33	.64	.38	.30
AVD	.35	.18	.27	.41	.32	.23	.38	.26	.48
DEP	.26	.18	.13	.31	.26	.20	.33	.17	.41
OBC	.10	.02	.10	.08	.07	.07	.07	.07	.20
PAG	.15	.28	.27	.17	.19	.18	.19	.26	.22
NAR	.32	.51	.68	.37	.68	.38	.60	.49	.52

Positive predictive power (header spanning A1–A9 above)

Negative predictive power

Items	A1	A2	A3	A4	A5	A6	A7	A8	A9
PAR	.93	.79	.80	.86	.79	.83	.79	.79	.82
SCZ	.89	.89	.89	.91	.88	.87	.88	.91	.89
STY	.94	.89	.94	.94	.93	.92	.91	.91	.90
ANT	.94	.99	.96	.94	.95	.98	.95	.98	.95
BOR	.81	.69	.68	.73	.70	.73	.69	.68	.69
HST	.85	.85	.85	.83	.85	.93	.89	.85	.80
AVD	.84	.70	.73	.82	.75	.68	.75	.72	.77
DEP	.83	.76	.75	.83	.79	.74	.80	.76	.81
OBC	.95	.90	.93	.92	.92	.91	.92	.92	.94
PAG	.92	.92	.92	.91	.90	.95	.89	.93	.89
NAR	.92	.86	.90	.88	.93	.99	.88	.89	.84

(continued)

Table 15–2. Internal consistency measures for DSM-III-R
narcissistic personality disorder criteria *(continued)*

	Phi coefficient								
Items	A1	A2	A3	A4	A5	A6	A7	A8	A9
PAR	.31	.05	.09	.25	.05	.10	.05	.02	.20
SCZ	.00	.01	.03	.08	.03	.04	.09	.10	.03
STY	.10	.11	.21	.13	.17	.04	.01	.01	.04
ANT	.01	.39	.18	.03	.08	.17	.09	.05	.13
BOR	.25	.08	.02	.16	.12	.13	.09	.05	.13
HST	.14	.30	.32	.14	.29	.31	.51	.25	.09
AVD	.21	.11	.00	.25	.07	.10	.12	.02	.20
DEP	.11	.05	.12	.17	.05	.07	.12	.08	.20
OBC	.09	.12	.03	.00	.02	.05	.02	.01	.12
PAG	.10	.24	.24	.12	.12	.21	.10	.26	.12
NAR	.28	.36	.57	.30	.64	.45	.46	.41	.32
	Point biserial correlation								
Items	A1	A2	A3	A4	A5	A6	A7	A8	A9
PAR	.43	.07	.12	.35	.17	.10	.08	.10	.24
SCZ	.00	.00	.03	.10	−.07	.00	−.13	.18	.00
STY	.19	−.09	.17	.22	.03	.16	−.01	.09	.05
ANT	.06	.51	.31	.01	.36	.18	.15	.39	.00
BOR	.33	.14	.07	.27	.23	.14	.11	.11	.22
HST	.21	.30	.40	.22	.41	.36	.52	.26	.17
AVD	.30	−.13	−.01	.27	−.01	.08	.06	.00	.19
DEP	.21	−.09	−.10	.21	−.01	.06	.18	−.03	.19
OBC	.12	.01	.11	.10	.00	.09	.01	.10	.15
PAG	.14	.34	.31	.14	.35	.18	.20	.37	.18
NAR	.40	.51	.62	.44	.65	.62	.54	.51	.38

Note. $N = 291$. Items (total frequency in sample): A1 = reacts to criticism
(171); A2 = exploitative (61); A3 = grandiose (62); A4 = uniqueness (115);
A5 = preoccupied with fantasies (74); A6 = entitlement (163); A7 = requires
attention and admiration (58); A8 = lack of empathy (81); A9 = feelings of
envy (46). Personality disorders: PAR = paranoid; SCZ = schizoid; STY =
schizotypal; ANT = antisocial; BOR = borderline; HST = histrionic; AVD =
avoidant; DEP = dependent; OBC = obsessive-compulsive; PAG = passive-
aggressive; NAR = narcissistic. *Source.* Adapted from Morey 1988a, 1988b.

Table 15–3. Other Axis II diagnostic criteria that demonstrate substantial predictive power for narcissistic personality disorder (NPD)

Criterion (parent diagnosis)	Positive predictive power for NPD (%)
Fights as a child (antisocial)	60.3
Defaults on financial obligations (antisocial)	48.6
Has no regard for truth (antisocial)	46.2
Is center of attention (histrionic)	59.6
Has shifting and shallow emotions (histrionic)	50.0
Believes doing a much better job (passive-aggressive)	46.0
Criticizes or scorns others (passive-aggressive)	48.4

Source.   Adapted from Morey 1988b.

the patient's condition will meet criteria for NPD. Three of these criteria are antisocial criteria, and two each were DSM-III-R criteria for histrionic and passive-aggressive personality disorders. These criteria further solidify the picture of the individual with NPD as an unempathic and affectively labile patient. Because the association of these criteria with NPD is in many instances greater than the association with their parent diagnoses, the addition of these criteria to the NPD diagnostic list would increase its internal consistency.

   In summary, the diagnostic criteria for NPD appear to have reasonable internal consistency, although some evidence indicates that this consistency has been achieved by using criteria that are somewhat redundant.

Clinical Diagnosis of Narcissistic Personality Disorder

Another means of attempting to examine the construct validity of the NPD diagnosis is to analyze how the diagnosis is actually used

by clinicians. A study by Morey and Ochoa (1989) found that adherence to DSM-III criteria for NPD was modest at best. In that
study, a kappa coefficient of 0.31 was obtained when clinical diagnosis was compared with a diagnosis algorithmically derived
from DSM criteria. One of the major discrepancies involved the
frequency with which the diagnoses were assigned, with clinicians assigning the NPD diagnosis at a rate double that expected
from a strict application of the diagnostic criteria. This result suggests that clinicians believe that certain types of narcissistic patients are not adequately covered by DSM criteria.

A closer examination of these results provides some further
insight into the diagnostic process applied by the clinicians in the
Morey and Ochoa (1989) study. Table 15–4 lists the largest correlates—both positive and negative—of the "overdiagnosis" of
NPD—that is, when the diagnosis was applied and the patient's
symptoms did not meet DSM criteria. These diagnostic features
seem to be of three types. First, some NPD diagnostic features
seem to be considered pathognomonic by clinicians when pres-

Table 15–4. Correlates of "overdiagnosis" of narcissistic personality
disorder (NPD)

Criterion (parent diagnosis)	Correlation with NPD overdiagnosis
Grandiosity (narcissistic)	.40
Narcissistic fantasies (narcissistic)	.35
Vain and demanding (histrionic)	.28
Egocentric, self-indulgent (histrionic)	.25
Entitlement (narcissistic)	.24
Requires attention and admiration (narcissistic)	.21
Manipulative suicidal threats (histrionic)	−.20
Recurrent suicidal threats/gestures (borderline)	−.18
Pessimistic (self-defeating)	−.16
Self-damaging acts (borderline)	−.16

Source.   Adapted from Morey and Ochoa 1989.

ent; these include "grandiosity," "preoccupation with success fantasies," "entitlement," and "requires constant attention." Apparently, these features are considered such compelling evidence of narcissism that when any of these is present, the diagnosis is given, even in the absence of other supporting evidence. Second, some diagnostic features associated with NPD overdiagnosis involve histrionic criteria: "vain and demanding" and "egocentric and self-indulgent." The presence of these features on the list suggests that clinicians view NPD as having a somewhat greater association to histrionic personality disorder than to other personality disorders. Third, a set of diagnostic features associated with the overdiagnosis of NPD includes negative correlates. The negative sign suggests that clinicians use these features as de facto exclusion criteria; when these features are present, clinicians are less likely to assign an unwarranted diagnosis. Interestingly, three of these four criteria involve self-destructive behaviors. This result implies that clinicians are skeptical about the likelihood of overt self-destructiveness in patients who are truly narcissistic.

Discriminant Validity:
Narcissistic Personality Disorder
and Diagnostic Overlap

One of the most critical issues concerning the construct validity of NPD involves its distinctiveness from other disorders. At the diagnostic level, some studies have found considerable overlap between NPD and other personality disorders. Using DSM-III-R definitions, Morey (1988a) discovered that overlap with other Cluster B personality disorders was substantial, particularly with histrionic personality disorder (53.1% of NPD patients also received this diagnosis) and borderline personality disorder (46.9%); there was less overlap with antisocial personality disorder (15.6%). However, this overlap was not restricted to Cluster B disorders; substantial overlap was also obtained with paranoid

(35.9%), avoidant (35.9%), and passive-aggressive (28.1%) personality disorders. In fact, it appears that NPD is one of the worst offenders on Axis II with respect to diagnostic overlap, and DSM-IV revisions of the criteria for the disorder were directed primarily at alleviating this problem.

A detailed examination of the individual criteria may give some indication as to the source of this overlap problem. In general, features with adequate discriminant validity should be more associated with their parent syndrome than with features representing a different syndrome (Morey 1985), but for many of the NPD criteria, this is not always the case. As described earlier, Table 15–2 presents a variety of associational metrics relating NPD criteria to other personality disorder diagnoses. This table shows that each of the NPD criteria bears substantial relationships to other disorders, and some are particularly problematic. "Reacting to criticism with rage" is more predictive of borderline personality than it is of NPD. "Interpersonal exploitativeness" demonstrates positive predictive powers above 0.40 for both borderline and histrionic personality. "Belief in uniqueness" is more predictive of avoidant and borderline personalities than NPD, whereas "requires attention and admiration" is more predictive of histrionic personality.

Distinguishing Narcissistic Personality Disorder From Other Cluster B Disorders

As noted above, DSM-III-R criteria for NPD yielded a patient group with particular overlap problems with other Cluster B personality disorders. In the following sections, the authors discuss some ways, both empirically and conceptually, that these disorders might be distinguished from NPD.

Distinguishing Narcissistic From Borderline Personality

Borderline personality and pathological narcissism have long been assumed to have certain conceptual similarities (Kernberg

1975), and, as such, findings demonstrating diagnostic overlap are not unexpected. Nonetheless, with comorbidity rates approaching 50%, it becomes critical to identify the fundamental differences between these two diagnostic constructs. DSM-IV suggests that the relative stability of self-image is useful in distinguishing the two disorders, but most theoretical accounts suggest that the inflated self-esteem of the narcissistic personality is actually quite fragile and vulnerable to insult, and the anger that often ensues may seem quite borderline in nature. DSM-IV does mention two diagnostic features that are quite distinct in the two disorders. First, as noted by Morey and Ochoa (1989), the narcissistic person is rarely overtly self-destructive. Self-damaging acts and serious suicidal gestures are rare in this group (Morey 1988b). Second, the narcissistic person is free of the dependency features shown by the borderline person, including the preoccupation with abandonment noted in DSM-IV. A third set of features that appears to distinguish the two disorders involves the passive-aggressive features that were listed in DSM-III-R. In particular, "believing one is doing better than one is," "protesting the demands of others," "critical of authority," and "resenting the suggestions of others" are all much more associated with NPD than with borderline personality disorder (Morey 1988b).

Data have been gathered using the Personality Assessment Inventory (PAI; Morey 1991b) that serve to point out important differences between these diagnostic groups. The PAI is a multiscale inventory designed to assess constructs of significance in a wide variety of clinical settings. The test has 22 nonoverlapping full scales that may be divided into four broad areas: 4 validity scales designed to measure the operation and influence of self-report response styles, 11 clinical scales that measure diagnostic constructs of contemporary relevance, 5 treatment consideration scales that provide information critical in treatment planning, and 2 interpersonal scales designed to identify the respondent's characteristic style of relating to others. The PAI validity scales were developed to provide an assessment of the potential influence of distorting response tendencies on PAI test performance. They include inconsistency, infrequency, positive impression, and negative impression response sets. The clinical scales of the PAI were assembled to provide information about critical diagnostic features of 11 important clinical constructs: somatic complaints, anxiety, anxiety-related disorders, depression, mania, paranoia, schizophrenia, borderline features, antisocial features, alcohol problems, and drug problems. The treatment consideration scales of the PAI were assembled to provide indicators of potential complications in treatment that would not necessarily be apparent from diagnostic information. These five scales are tapping aggression, suicidal ideation, stress, social nonsupport, and treatment rejection. Finally, the interpersonal scales of the PAI were designed to provide an assessment of the interpersonal style of subjects along two dimensions: 1) a warmly affiliative versus a cold rejecting axis and 2) a dominating and controlling versus a meekly submissive style.

PAI scale and subscale raw scores were transformed to T scores (which have a mean of 50 and a standard deviation of 10) in order to provide interpretation relative to a standardization sample of 1,000 community-dwelling adults. This sample was carefully selected to match 1995 U.S. census projections on the basis of gender, race, and age; the educational level of the standardization sample was selected to be representative given the required fourth-grade reading level. Figure 15–1 presents a comparison of the mean profiles of a group of 33 patients with an NPD diagnosis with those of a group of 78 patients with borderline personality disorder. Several differences are apparent in these profiles. First, as expected, the borderline group had higher scores on the borderline features (BOR) scale. However, many other differences are evident. The NPD group had significantly lower levels of suicidal ideation as well as less anxious and depressive symptomatology. The NPD group had somewhat higher scores on the mania (MAN) scale, and this reflects the grandiosity typical of this group. Finally, the NPD group was above average with respect to interpersonal dominance, whereas the borderline group was below average. This result is consistent with the greater dependency in the borderline patient and the heightened need for interpersonal control in the narcissistic patient.

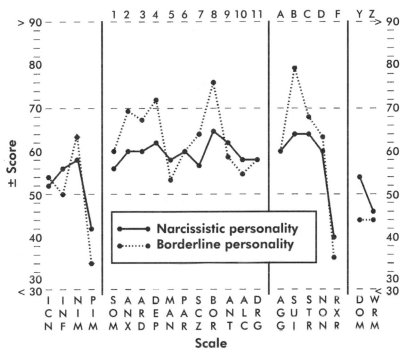

Figure 15–1. Profiles of narcissistic personality ($N = 33$) and borderline personality ($N = 78$) on the Personality Assessment Inventory. ICN = inconsistency; INF = infrequency; NIM = negative impression; PIM = positive impression; SOM = somatic complaints; ANX = anxiety; ARD = anxiety-related disorders; DEP = depression; MAN = mania; PAR = paranoia; SCZ = schizophrenia; BOR = borderline features; ANT = antisocial features; ALC = alcohol problems; DRG = drug problems; AGG = aggression; SUI = suicidal ideation; STR = stress; NON = social nonsupport; RXR = treatment rejection; DOM = dominating style; WRM = warmly affiliative. *Source.* Morey 1991b.

Distinguishing Narcissistic From Histrionic Personality

According to the data from Morey (1988a), the diagnostic overlap with histrionic personality disorder (53.1%) represents the greatest comorbidity for NPD and indeed reflects one of the highest overlap values for all of Axis II. Additionally, a number of dimensional factorial studies often identified these two disorders as related (Morey and Le Vine 1988). Part of the commonality between the two disorders is that they both include traits that, in lesser extremes, are desirable in the general population (such as positive self-esteem for NPD and social facility for histrionic personality disorder). In contrast, very few of the other Axis II disorders involve traits that are desirable in any degree. In general, these desirable traits are rather uncommon in clinical patients, and both disorders may share the characteristic that it is more difficult to distinguish them from "normality" than from most other clinical syndromes.

DSM-IV suggests that a relative lack of emotional display, excessive pride in achievements, and a disregard for others may be useful in distinguishing narcissism from histrionic personality. However, some of these points need some qualification. For example, data from Morey (1988c) indicate that both disorders appear to cause substantial deficits in patients' capacity for empathy. With respect to emotional display, narcissistic patients appear to be considerably more likely to display anger and hostility, both overtly and in a passive-aggressive manner, than do histrionic patients. In fact, the periodic expression of hostility appears to be one of the most reliable symptomatic differentiators for the two disorders.

Distinguishing Narcissistic From Antisocial Personality

In terms of diagnostic overlap, the proportion of NPD patients whose symptoms also meet criteria for antisocial personality is relatively small (15.6%), and, on the surface, it would appear that the issue of overlap is less critical. However, given the relatively low prevalence of antisocial personality disorder (6.2% of patients with personality disorders in that study), the overlap results indicate a fivefold increase in risk for antisocial personality when a diagnosis of NPD is present (Morey 1988a).

A study of the clustering of associations between specific DSM criteria underscores the empirical relationship between these disorders. Morey (1988c) reported the results of a cluster analysis of all DSM-III-R personality disorder diagnostic criteria and found a cluster structure that generally resembled that implicit in DSM. Interestingly, however, the criteria for NPD were the least likely to cluster together; these criteria tended to fragment across different disorders. Although some NPD criteria spread across various disorders (including paranoid, histrionic, and borderline), most of the narcissistic features combined with the nonaggressive antisocial features to form one large cluster. This cluster was named psychopathic, because the inclusion of the exploitative narcissistic personality features and the removal of the overtly aggressive antisocial aspects create a syndrome reminiscent of the older concept of psychopathy (e.g., Cleckley 1941; Hare 1985). A small cluster of antisocial features involving aggression (history of fighting during childhood, aggressiveness, impulsivity) was less associated with these psychopathic features. Interestingly, the distinction drawn by the clustering algorithm also resembles a conceptual distinction drawn by Millon (1986) between the "active-independent" and "active-discordant" personality orientation. These results imply that a sizable core of the NPD criteria relates to a personological element of psychopathy that was not well represented in DSM-III or DSM-III-R. Given the conceptual importance of narcissism in understanding the psychopathic personality, this is certainly a valuable inclusion. However, it still leaves unanswered the question of the discriminant validity of NPD as a distinct diagnostic entity.

A close examination of results from the individual criteria suggests certain key areas of distinction between the two disorders. For example, "reacts to criticism with rage" (a criterion eliminated in DSM-IV) turns out to be virtually unassociated with antisocial personality disorder. In fact, nearly all criteria dealing with affective reactivity (such as the paranoid feature "easily slighted") appear to be much more characteristic of NPD than of antisocial personality disorder. This result is supported by differences in the PAI profiles of the two diagnostic groups; a comparison of the mean PAI profiles from the aforementioned group of 33 patients with an NPD diagnosis and a group of 75 patients with an antisocial personality disorder diagnosis is shown in Figure 15–2. In this

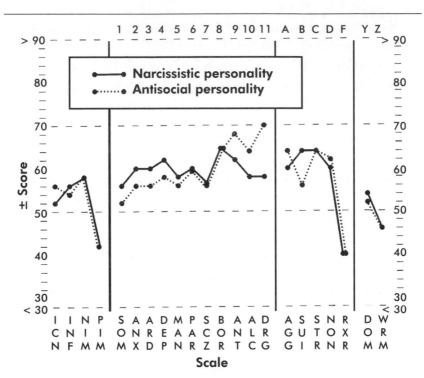

Figure 15–2.   Profiles of narcissistic personality ($N = 33$) and antisocial personality ($N = 75$) on the Personality Assessment Inventory. ICN = inconsistency; INF = infrequency; NIM = negative impression; PIM = positive impression; SOM = somatic complaints; ANX = anxiety; ARD = anxiety-related disorders; DEP = depression; MAN = mania; PAR = paranoia; SCZ = schizophrenia; BOR = borderline features; ANT = antisocial features; ALC = alcohol problems; DRG = drug problems; AGG = aggression; SUI = suicidal ideation; STR = stress; NON = social nonsupport; RXR = treatment rejection; DOM = dominating style; WRM = warmly affiliative. *Source.*   Morey 1991b.

figure, it is apparent that the affective manifestations (e.g., anxiety and depression) are more pronounced in the NPD group than in the antisocial patients. In contrast, the antisocial patients display more behavioral acting out, particularly in the area of alcohol and drug abuse. These results support the generally greater interpersonal and affective responsiveness of the NPD patient compared with the more "delinquent" type of antisocial patient identified by DSM criteria.

Conclusion

Although diagnostic criteria for NPD have now been represented in three different editions of DSM, the theoretical status of the construct remains somewhat unclear. Determining whether narcissism represents a nosological entity or a range of personality pathology that is common to other personality disorders is quite difficult. Our data provide a number of findings that suggest, at least with NPD as defined in DSM, that the latter interpretation may be more accurate. First, the internal consistency of the diagnostic criteria for NPD is not particularly impressive, despite the fact that several of the criteria are empirically redundant. Second, NPD is one of the worst offenders on Axis II in terms of diagnostic overlap. Third, the criteria for NPD are not particularly empirically coherent; some are more highly related to other personality disorder constructs (particularly antisocial, borderline, and histrionic) than to the parent NPD construct. Fourth, clinicians tend to deviate considerably from DSM criteria in assigning the diagnosis.

However, there is also some support for considering NPD as a disorder in its own right. For example, the profile for NPD on a standardized psychological test (the PAI) can be distinguished in important ways from the profiles for other personality disorders that are typically found to overlap considerably with NPD. Data also suggest that the NPD criteria may tap an important feature of the construct of "psychopathy" that is not adequately addressed by DSM criteria for antisocial personality, thus improving the coverage of Axis II. Finally, certain key features can be identified that separate NPD from other Cluster B disorders: the absence of self-destructiveness separates NPD from borderline personality; the expression of interpersonal hostility separates it from histrionic personality; and affective reactivity separates it from antisocial personality. However, none of these potentially important discriminating features is included in the DSM-IV definition of the disorder. This may partially account for the typically problematic discriminant validity of the DSM operationalization of Axis II construct; there is a focus on convergent validity in the formulation of diagnostic criteria at the expense of discriminant validity.

One way to improve the discriminant validity of the NPD diagnosis would be to return to the monothetic approach to diagnostic criteria used in DSM-III. The exclusive reliance on polythetic criteria in DSM-III-R may have been one reason that diagnostic overlap actually worsened in the transition from DSM-III to DSM-III-R (Morey 1988a). A selection of such criteria with careful regard to discriminant validity would greatly sharpen the NPD diagnosis, although it would also lower the apparent prevalence of the disorder. Drawing from the various results presented in this chapter, such criteria might look as follows. All four of the following must be present:

1. **Inflated self-esteem with marked affective reactions (such as rage or depression) to assaults on this self-esteem.** The inflated self-esteem reflects a core trait of NPD and in itself reflects a distinguishing characteristic from borderline personality disorder. The vulnerability of this self-esteem has been reported in numerous theoretical accounts of the disorder, and the empirical data described here support the notion that this is a distinguishing characteristic of the disorder. The affective reactivity that follows narcissistic injury distinguishes NPD from the relatively unresponsive antisocial type and the more affectively stable hypomanic individual.

2. **Marked need for interpersonal control.** The PAI results presented earlier in this chapter are consistent with numerous other studies of the narcissistic personality (DeJong et al. 1989; Morey 1985; Wiggins and Pincus 1989) in identifying dominance as a characteristic interpersonal pattern. Although NPD shares this feature with antisocial personality

disorder, this characteristic can distinguish the narcissistic person from borderline and histrionic persons, who are more concerned with attachment issues than with control issues.

3. **Noteworthy expressions (either active or passive) of interpersonal hostility.** Although hostility is not typically regarded as a core feature of NPD, and the level of hostility is not as extreme as might be noted in other disorders, the data presented here suggest that its presence (particularly passive-aggressive features) can distinguish NPD from histrionic personality disorder as well as from the Cluster C personality disorders. Clinically, it seems that the mode of expression of hostility in the narcissistic person varies as a function of the status of the target: those in an "inferior" position to narcissistic individuals (e.g., employees, service personnel) are overtly belittled, whereas those in a position superior to them (e.g., their employer or even their clinician) are the targets of passive hostility.

4. **Lack of overtly self-destructive tendencies.** This exclusion criterion discriminates NPD from borderline personality disorder, both empirically (Morey 1988a) and in the minds of clinicians (Morey and Ochoa 1989). This criterion may also serve to distinguish the depression in these patients following narcissistic injury from depression that arises independent of characterological issues.

The advantage of using a conjoint (monothetic) application of these criteria is that each individual criterion need not be highly predictive of the disorder to be useful. For example, "lack of overtly self-destructive tendencies" plays little role in distinguishing NPD from normality, but it serves the valuable function of distinguishing it from borderline personality disorder, with which NPD has much in common. The monothetic-discriminant approach would treat the individual diagnostic criteria as necessary parts of a total configuration rather than as a collection of features that are all independently and presumably equally reflective of the disorder.

Reducing the diagnostic overlap with other disorders is only the first step in improving the discriminant validity of NPD. As mentioned earlier in this chapter, establishing meaningful links to etiology and treatment is a critical aspect of demonstrating the construct validity of NPD. Although empirical work in this regard has begun and is indeed reflected in this volume, there remains a great need for differential studies. How is the etiology of NPD different from that of other Cluster B personality disorders? What are the mechanisms of treatment that would lead to improvement in NPD but not in, for example, borderline personality disorder? If these critical differences cannot be identified and supported empirically, the discriminant validity of the construct of NPD must be called into question. Nonetheless, a vital first step in this research must involve sharpening the diagnostic picture, and a few suggestions that might assist this process have been presented.

References

American Psychiatric Association: Diagnostic and Statistical Manual of Mental Disorders, 3rd Edition. Washington, DC, American Psychiatric Association, 1980

American Psychiatric Association: Diagnostic and Statistical Manual of Mental Disorders, 3rd Edition, Revised. Washington, DC, American Psychiatric Association, 1987

American Psychiatric Association: Diagnostic and Statistical Manual of Mental Disorders, 4th Edition. Washington, DC, American Psychiatric Association, 1994

Blashfield RK, Livesley WJ: Metaphorical analysis of psychiatric classification as a psychological test. J Abnorm Psychol 100:262–270, 1991

Cleckley H: The Mask of Sanity. St. Louis, MO, CV Mosby, 1941

Cronbach LJ: Coefficient alpha and the internal structure of tests. Psychometrika 16:297–334, 1951

DeJong CAJ, van den Brink W, Jansen JAM, et al: Interpersonal aspects of DSM-III Axis II: theoretical hypotheses and empirical findings. Journal of Personality Disorders 3:135–146, 1989

Hare RD: Comparison of procedures for the assessment of psychopathy. J Consult Clin Psychol 53:7–16, 1985

Kernberg OF: Borderline Conditions and Pathological Narcissism. New York, Jason Aronson, 1975

Loevinger J: The attenuation paradox in test theory. Psychol Bull 51:493–504, 1954

Millon T: A theoretical derivation of pathological personalities, in Contemporary Directions in Psychopathology. Edited by Millon T, Klerman G. New York, Guilford, 1986, pp 639–670

Morey LC: A psychometric analysis of five DSM-III categories. Personality and Individual Differences 6:323–329, 1985

Morey LC: Personality disorders under DSM-III and DSM-III-R: an examination of convergence, coverage, and internal consistency. Am J Psychiatry 145:573–577, 1988a

Morey LC: A psychometric analysis of the DSM-III-R personality disorder criteria. Journal of Personality Disorders 2:109–124, 1988b

Morey LC: The categorical representation of personality disorder: a cluster analysis of DSM-III-R personality features. J Abnorm Psychol 97:314–321, 1988c

Morey LC: The classification of mental disorder as a collection of hypothetical constructs. J Abnorm Psychol 100:289–293, 1991a

Morey LC: The Personality Assessment Inventory Professional Manual. Odessa, FL, Psychological Assessment Resources, 1991b

Morey LC, Le Vine DJ: A multitrait-multimethod examination of MMPI and MCMI personality disorder scales. Journal of Psychopathology and Behavioral Assessment 10:333–344, 1988

Morey LC, Ochoa ES: An investigation of adherence to diagnostic criteria: clinical diagnosis of the DSM-III personality disorders. Journal of Personality Disorders 3:180–192, 1989

Nelson-Gray RO: DSM-IV: empirical guidelines from psychometrics. J Abnorm Psychol 100:308–315, 1991

Pfohl B, Coryell W, Zimmerman M, et al: DSM-III personality disorders: diagnostic overlap and internal consistency of individual DSM-III criteria. Compr Psychiatry 27:21–34, 1986

Widiger T, Sanderson C: The convergent and discriminant validity of the MCMI as a measure of the DSM-III. J Pers Assess 57:228–242, 1987

Wiggins JS, Pincus AL: Conceptions of personality disorders and dimensions of personality. Psychological Assessment 1:305–316, 1989

Chapter 16

Narcissistic Personality Disorder and Pathological Narcissism

Long-Term Stability and Presence in Axis I Disorders

Elsa F. Ronningstam, Ph.D.

In this chapter, the author discusses two aspects of pathological narcissism: its long-term stability and its presence in Axis I disorders. The discussion is based on a literature review and on results from a series of studies that are part of a more extensive

Parts of this chapter have been reprinted by permission from Ronningstam E, Gunderson J: "Narcissistic Personality—a Stable Disorder or a State of Mind." *Psychiatric Times* 2:35–36, 1996. Copyright 1996, Psychiatric Times; and Ronningstam E: "Pathological Narcissism and Narcissistic Personality Disorder in Axis I Disorders." *Harvard Review of Psychiatry* 3:326–340, 1996. Copyright 1996, Mosby-Year Book, Inc.

effort to investigate the validity of narcissistic personality disorder (NPD) and the specific nature of pathological narcissism.

Studies of Long-Term Stability of Pathological Narcissism

NPD has been considered highly resistant to change. Contributing factors are absence of interfering symptomatology; effective denial of problems, failures, and shortcomings; extensive compensatory fantasies and self-aggrandizing beliefs; opportunities for external gratification; sustained treatment resistance; and perpetual behavioral and interactional patterns (Millon 1981). The presence of severe superego pathology, sexual deviations, and overt borderline functioning worsens the prognosis for NPD patients. Tolerance of depression and mourning and capacity for feeling and admitting guilt improve prognosis (Kernberg 1975). Contrary to other severe personality disorders that are expected to remit or "even out" over time, NPD can actually worsen in middle age (Kernberg 1980). Profound narcissistic pathology in elderly people has also been reported (Berezin 1977; Kernberg 1977).

In the first longitudinal study of patients with a primary diagnosis of NPD, Plakun (1989) retrospectively investigated the records of 17 narcissistic and 33 borderline patients. Follow-up measures 14 years after admission showed that NPD patients had more and longer rehospitalizations than the borderline comparison group. They also had longer sustained outpatient treatment or sometimes the reverse, no psychotherapy at all, compared with borderline patients. Narcissistic patients had relatively low—but still slightly higher—suicide attempt rates and had at follow-up a lower level of global and social functioning than did the borderline patients. These results support the idea of a poor prognosis for NPD.

Background

A series of studies was completed with the purpose of identifying characteristics for NPD and investigating the descriptive validity of NPD (Gunderson and Ronningstam 1991; Ronningstam and Gunderson 1988, 1989). To conduct the studies, the Diagnostic Interview for Narcissism (DIN; Gunderson et al. 1990) was developed by operationalizing characteristics for pathological narcissism derived from the literature (Ronningstam 1988) and our clinical experiences. This semistructured interview includes 33 characteristics for pathological narcissism, 10 of which overlap with those in DSM-III-R and DSM-IV (American Psychiatric Association 1987, 1994). The characteristics are grouped into five sections: grandiosity, interpersonal relations, reactiveness, affects and mood states, and social and moral adaptation.

Systematic studies of narcissistic patients were done to establish the interview's psychometric properties and reliability. The interview was used to identify the descriptive and discriminating criteria for NPD in comparison with a broad range of psychiatric patients (Ronningstam and Gunderson 1990). The studies showed that 11 characteristics significantly discriminated NPD from a control group of all others, including both general psychiatric patients and near-neighbor dramatic cluster personality disorders, that is, borderline personality disorder (BPD) and antisocial personality disorder ($P < .01$, df = 80; see Table 16–1). They also showed that NPD was significantly distinguishable from the near-neighbor samples of BPD and antisocial personality disorder, with 91% and 100% correct group classification (Ronningstam and Gunderson 1991, 1995). These results provided strong evidence for the descriptive validity of NPD diagnosis.

Changes in Pathological Narcissism

As a next step in the investigation of the validity of NPD, a prospective follow-up study was done of 20 patients with a clinical

Table 16–1. Comparison of mean scores for narcissistic personality disorder (NPD) patients and a control group of all other patients on 33 statements (ST) in Diagnostic Interview for Narcissism: results from two-tailed t test (df = 80)

Statement	NPD ($n = 24$)	All others ($n = 58$)	t value	P value[a] NPD vs. all others
Section I: grandiosity				
ST 1 Exaggeration[b]	1.13	0.43	4.60	.001
ST 2 Belief in invulnerability	1.04	0.62	2.50	.02
ST 3 Grandiose fantasies[b]	1.75	1.00	3.77	.001
ST 4 Belief in not needing others	0.58	0.53	0.26	.80
ST 5 Uniqueness[b]	1.25	0.50	5.53	.001
ST 6 Superiority	1.46	0.40	7.16	.001
ST 7 Self-centered/ referential	1.75	1.12	3.32	.001
ST 8 Boastful/pretentious	1.50	0.62	4.80	.001
Section II: interpersonal relations				
ST 9 Needs attention/ admiration[b]	1.83	1.33	3.29	.001
ST 10 Idealization	1.67	1.53	1.00	.32
ST 11 Devaluation/contempt	1.67	1.48	1.20	.23
ST 12 Envious[b]	1.29	1.19	0.60	.56
ST 13 Entitlement[b]	1.46	0.95	2.81	.006
ST 14 Arrogant/haughty[b]	0.88	0.29	3.54	.001
ST 15 Exploitiveness[b]	1.00	0.88	0.58	.56
ST 16 Lacks empathy[b]	0.96	1.05	−0.56	.58
ST 17 Uncommitted to anyone	1.00	0.98	0.09	.93
Section III: reactiveness				
ST 18 Hypersensitive	1.58	1.64	−0.37	.71
ST 19 Reactions to criticism/defeat[b]	1.67	1.62	0.31	.75
ST 20 Suicidal/ self-destructive reactions	0.71	0.72	−0.07	.94
ST 21 Aggressive reactions	1.21	1.14	0.33	.74
ST 22 Reaction to others' envy	1.17	0.60	2.74	.007

(continued)

Table 16–1. Comparison of mean scores for narcissistic personality disorder (NPD) patients and a control group of all other patients on 33 statements (ST) in Diagnostic Interview for Narcissism: results from two-tailed t test (df = 80) (*continued*)

| Statement | Mean score | | | P value[a] NPD vs. all others |
	NPD (*n* = 24)	All others (*n* = 58)	*t* value	
Section IV: mood states				
ST 23 Emptiness	1.29	1.59	−1.55	.13
ST 24 Boredom	1.33	1.50	−0.85	.40
ST 25 Meaninglessness	1.17	1.14	0.12	.90
ST 26 Futility	1.21	1.21	0.01	.10
ST 27 Badness (−)[c]	−0.91	−0.95	0.21	.84
Section V: social/moral adaptation				
ST 28 High achievements	1.83	0.90	5.16	.001
ST 29 Superficial values	0.79	0.88	0.48	.64
ST 30 Disregard for values/rules	1.54	1.10	2.21	.03
ST 31 One or a few crimes	0.54	0.19	2.20	.03
ST 32 Antisocial pattern (−)[c]	−0.50	−0.72	1.02	.31
ST 33 Perversions/ promiscuity	0.87	0.88	−0.02	.98

Note. Statements appearing in italic typeface signify the 11 discriminating statements for NPD ($P < .01$).

[a]P level results from two-tail probability t test. With the Bonferroni correction, $P < .002$ is significant.

[b]DSM-III-R and DSM-IV criteria for NPD.

[c]Presence of ST 27 and ST 32 characteristics is scored negatively against the diagnosis of NPD.

diagnosis of NPD (Ronningstam et al. 1995). The DIN was administered to the patients at baseline and 3 years later at follow-up. The patients' baseline scores were compared with their follow-up scores. In addition, an unstructured interview explored the person's interval history of personal, vocational, and treatment events and identified factors that could have contributed to changes in the person's behavior and experiences.

The results showed that the overall level of pathological narcissism had significantly decreased ($t = 5.26, P < .0001, df = 19$), particularly in the areas of interpersonal relations ($t = 3.94, P < .001, df = 19$), grandiosity ($t = 3.64, P < .002, df = 19$), and reactiveness ($t = 3.20, P < .005, df = 19$). Sixty percent of the subjects were significantly improved (i.e., their total scaled score had decreased ≥ 5 points), and 40% remained unchanged on a high level of pathological narcissism. The results also indicated that the unimproved group at baseline had a higher level of pathological narcissism in the area of interpersonal relations, especially in their capacity to become involved in committed long-term relationships. The unstructured interviews revealed that three types of intervening corrective life events contributed to a decrease in the level of pathological narcissism, that is, experiences related to achievements, interpersonal relations, and disillusionments.

The results from this first prospective study of narcissistic patients suggest that what appeared to be an NPD at baseline actually included two types of pathology, one being a context- or state-dependent type of pathology and the other being a more long-term and stable trait pathology. In other words, it seems as if patients with identifiable narcissistic pathology and NPD can have grandiosity with a higher degree of changeability, as well as pathologically narcissistic relations that can remain stable over time. These results raise the question whether people with NPD differ in their capacity to gain from life events or environmental influence—that is, whether people with certain types of narcissistic psychopathology that include more narcissistic interpersonal relations have more difficulties in accommodating to or benefiting from environmental experiences. The results question the construct validity of NPD and suggest that the core construct of pathological narcissism and NPD actually can include different characteristics or forms of psychopathology that at baseline can appear similar (e.g., grandiosity with higher degree of changeability and pathological narcissistic relations that can remain stable over time).

Intervening Life Events Contributing to Change

The most common life event that contributed to change in pathological narcissism was the experience of *corrective achievements*, such as graduations, promotions, recognitions, and acceptance to sought-for schools, programs, or positions. These events contributed to a more realistic and accepted sense of the self with less need for grandiose fantasies and exaggerations of talents. The following case vignette describes such development.

Case 1

Mr. A, an extremely intelligent, shy but arrogant 25-year-old college student, came for psychotherapy because he had been depressed for several years. Although he was an exceptionally competent student, he constantly felt unappreciated. He tended to devote his time in lectures to "giving the teachers and professors a hard time" by criticizing them and asking "impossible" questions in order to prove their incompetence and embarrass them in public. He described himself as extraordinarily superior with feelings of disdain and confusion toward people he experienced as different from himself (i.e., those who had lower standards and different values than his). He also described himself as intellectually unique because of his specific theoretical and philosophical perspective and high academic standards. He had several close friends among his male peers, but he had experienced severe problems in relating to young women, such as difficulties connecting and feeling shy and insecure.

Mr. A came from a very competitive and successful fam-

ily background. His father was a famous lawyer in his early
60s, and Mr. A described a complicated relationship with
mixed feelings toward the father. On the one hand, he
highly admired and idealized his father; on the other, he
despised the father's demands, values, and expectations
and tended to take every opportunity to protest against
him. Although he envied his father and fantasized about becoming as successful, he also felt inferior and believed that
he would never become as successful. He often felt deeply
misunderstood by his father. After successfully graduating
from college, Mr. A decided to work as a pizza deliverer, a
decision that he considered to be unusually risky but in line
with his "unique approach" to life.

At follow-up 3 years later, Mr. A reported a number of
important changes and developments in his life. He had
been in individual psychotherapy for 1½ years and had specifically focused on depression and insecurity. A new job as
a university teacher had, according to Mr. A, contributed to
the most important change in his behavior and attitude
toward himself and others. As a teacher, he had the opportunity to create the specific teaching atmosphere and technique he felt that his former teachers were unable to do.
Through his work, he had learned to interact with people,
been forced to and actually successfully managed to understand people with different ideas and values, and made efforts to develop specific teaching methods to facilitate
learning and intellectual growth for his students. Mr. A
described himself as more tolerant of criticism. His sense of
pride was associated with a far more realistic self-appraisal
and markedly diminished derogative, arrogant behaviors.
His relationship with his father was still conflictual, but a
more sincere desire to identify with the competent successful father had appeared. His relationships with women had
improved, and a 2-year relationship with a girlfriend contributed to a change in Mr. A's self-esteem.

As Mr. A's experiences of realistic academic competence
and professional responsibility increased, his need for exaggerated superior and unique self-experience and grandiose
fantasies diminished, as did his need to antagonize and de-

value others' achievements. Arrogant, passive-aggressive oppositional behavior and animosity were replaced by active, goal-oriented professional striving, and Mr. A's underlying capacity for interpersonal relations could develop in that context. It is notable that at baseline he did not present severe manifestations of narcissistic interpersonal relations (i.e., exploitiveness, lack of commitment, severe deep envy, and inability for empathy).

The experience of *corrective relationships*—when the person was able to establish a long-term, close, and mutual relationship—seemed to diminish pathological narcissism in three cases. Two of the subjects had actually become engaged, and one was in the process of being married. Changes were evident in the diminished need for devaluation, entitlement, and exploitive behavior.

Case 2

Ms. B, an attractive, intelligent, self-assertive, and articulate woman in her 30s, was caught stealing drugs at a drug company where she had been working as a research assistant since her graduation from college. It became evident that during the last 5 years, she had been using increasing amounts of intravenous drugs, and, more recently, she had been using them on a daily basis.

She came from a working-class background with parents who had high expectations. She graduated from college magna cum laude. However, the parents decided not to support her continuing graduate school. She experienced this as a treachery.

Ms. B described herself as superior, especially compared with other drug abusers, because she had been able to keep herself "clean" and use more sophisticated methods to gain access to drugs. Although hard to please, she usually got what she wanted. She dreamt about becoming a famous journalist, and she loved to drive her car recklessly, believing that she would not be caught. After graduation from college, three problem areas gradually emerged and became more apparent despite Ms. B's intense efforts to deny their presence and consequences. A feeling of indecisiveness and lack of certainty made it difficult for her to identify her purpose and track in life. A pattern of relationships developed, especially to boyfriends, characterized by quick intense involvement and abrupt withdrawal when the relationship stabilized and became closer. She especially feared spending sustained time with the same man sharing feelings, intimacy, and personal private matters. A fear of becoming bored and failing at work also became more prominent, despite her high level of competence.

At follow-up, Ms. B described several notable changes in her life. One-half year of detoxification and drug abuse–focused treatment and 2 years of psychotherapy had contributed to a remission of drug dependency and highlighted underlying problems of low self-esteem and inferiority feelings. This realization led to a decision to pursue graduate school to study business. However, the most important and fundamental change, according to Ms. B, was that she had met a man with whom she had established a relationship. For the first time in her life, she experienced being in love, and she was actually in the process of getting married. Contrary to all previous men with whom she briefly had been involved, she felt that her husband-to-be accepted her and was stronger than her without defeating her. She could feel secure and able to stay in the relationship without becoming unbearably bored, restless, or aggressive. This experience had a major impact on improving her self-esteem.

Her self-description was no longer exaggerated and focused on her specialness. Instead, she was more realistic and pointed out changes within several areas. She had thought she did not need other people; now she realized that she did and that she actually enjoyed them. In the past, she felt that she was different from other people and constantly misunderstood; now she realized that she had actually made people unnecessary in her life through her tough, independent, and self-sufficient demeanor. Grandiose fantasies remained but were now related to success within the field she was studying. She still had strong feelings of envy, and she had difficulties empathizing with other people's sadness—it made her feel helpless and disgusted.

Ms. B's low self-esteem, compensatory grandiosity, reck-lessness, and drug dependency developed out of increasing difficulties in the context of close and intimate relation-ships. However, the absence of more severe narcissistic fea-tures in her interpersonal relationships at baseline—that is, deep devaluating, condescending, ruthless, paranoid, and exploitive attitudes and behavior—made it possible to at-tach emotionally, first to treaters and later to a man. The cor-rectional achievements, such as being accepted to graduate school, also contributed to improve her self-esteem.

The third event, *corrective disillusionment,* involved experiences that challenged the person's previous grandiose self-experience and actually resulted in an adjustment toward a more realistic self-concept, more in accord with his or her actual capabilities. This could be the realization of personal, intellectual, or voca-tional limitations; failure to achieve goals in life; or confrontation of losses or lost opportunities in life. However, if these disillu-sions are too severe and experienced without support, worsen-ing narcissistic pathology can develop.

Case 3

Mr. C, a man in his mid-40s, considered himself to be goal oriented and superintelligent with strong puritan values, quick reasoning skills, and an extraordinary leadership ca-pacity. Although happily married with two teenage sons and one younger daughter, he considered himself to be a loner, not interested in wasting time on meaningless social activities. He had a top managing position in a Canadian company where he had worked since graduation from high school. Showing a bragging, self-praising, and self-centered manner and devaluating behavioral styles of others, he admit-ted that he actually envied them for their social belonging.

On reaching his early 40s, two things happened in Mr. C's life. When his company suddenly and unexpectedly underwent a major expansion, he was sent to a challenging business school for graduate education in order to meet the company's new needs for business expertise. At this time, his sons reached adolescence and developed lifestyles, value systems, and spheres of interest that Mr. C found himself disgusted and threatened by. He could not find reasonable and adequate ways to communicate with or to influence his sons. He considered himself a failure as a parent and struggled with intense aggressive impulses, urges to detach from them totally, or desires to punish them in various ways.

Because Mr. C had been a straight-A student in college and the most intellectually appreciated person in his environment, he was at first stunned and consternated when he discovered the high level of intelligence among the students in the graduate program. It was with a combination of humbleness, envy, and admiration that he gradually accepted that most of the other students were extremely capable and that he, despite enormous efforts, could manage to maintain only a B–B+ level.

At follow-up, Mr. C, who was in the process of moving back and reinstating himself into a new position in his company, was remarkably more humble and had less intense aggressive reactions, bragging, and self-inflating behavior. He felt that he had reached the maximum of his capacity both professionally and as a father. Although satisfied with his results in graduate school, he felt dethroned and incompetent in his parental role, as he realized that he could not convince his sons about the importance of his own values and lifestyle. However, his intense anger was replaced with a new and more realistic ambition to become a friend and supporter of his sons.

This man's experience of shortcomings and limitations in both professional and personal spheres was challenging for his self-esteem. Sustained support from his loyal wife and his own personal flexibility and capacity to integrate initially unacceptable aspects of himself made it possible to modify his grandiose self-experience into more realistic concepts. Although grandiosity and reactiveness improved, the narcissistic interpersonal style with devaluation, envy, and some arrogance remained.

Narcissistic Personality Disorder and Pathological Narcissism in Axis I Disorders

The relation between pathological narcissism and major mental illness has recurrently been discussed in the clinical literature, and the presence of both narcissistic traits and a narcissistic character structure in several of the Axis I disorders has been suggested. Whereas the introduction of NPD in DSM-III (American Psychiatric Association 1980) affirmed its status as a separate diagnostic personality disorder category, it also highlighted pathological narcissism as a long-term, persistent, dysfunctional character trait, clearly differentiated from the Axis I disorders. Although some empirical studies have confirmed the descriptive and construct validity of NPD, other studies have failed to do so and instead pointed out considerable diagnostic comorbidity with other Axis II disorders. In addition, state dependency and co-occurrence of pathological narcissism and Axis I disorders have been found.

The fact that pathological narcissism can be considered both a trait with one or several significant features and a diagnostic category with a core constellation of characteristics makes the issue of diagnostic overlap and interaction with Axis I disorders especially consequential. Is the character structure of NPD present in one or several Axis I disorders, or is there a specific predominance of narcissistic traits that co-occur with certain mental illnesses? What follows is a review of the clinical and empirical literature highlighting the presence of pathological narcissism and NPD in each of the major Axis I disorders. A more extensive and methodological discussion of this topic has been published elsewhere (Ronningstam 1996).

Axis I Disorders in Patients With Narcissistic Personality Disorder

Major depression and dysthymia were the most common Axis I disorders found in 42%–50% of patients with NPD (38 inpatients and outpatients and 34 consecutively admitted inpatients). Sub-stance abuse disorder was the second most common (24%–50%), followed by bipolar disorder (5%–11%) (Ronningstam and Gun-derson 1988, 1990; E. Ronningstam, unpublished data, October 1993).

Narcissistic Personality Disorder in Patients With Axis I Disorders

Major depression and dysthymia.   Acute depression as a reaction to severe narcissistic injuries, failures, or losses, often in combination with suicidal ideations, is what brings the normally symptom-free narcissistic patient to psychiatric treatment. Depression, obviously the most common Axis I disorder in narcissistic patients, usually occurs in the context of a failure in the self-regulatory processes that support the pathological grandiose self and is often accompanied by feelings of rage and irritability. A specific type of depression occurs in midlife when the narcissistic individual is confronted with aging and the inevitable limitations in life (Kernberg 1980; Svrakic 1985). Dysthymia or dysphoria—characterized by a chronic state of boredom, emptiness, aloneness, stimulus, hunger, dissatisfaction, and meaninglessness (Kernberg 1990; Millon 1981)—is a reaction to unavoidable gradual disillusionment with the self. Cooper (1988, 1989) described how depression becomes part of the self-regulatory features and the maintenance of self-esteem in the narcissistic-masochistic character. These dynamics of depression, usually combined with feelings of shame and guilt, are important to take into consideration when identifying and understanding the covert forms of NPD (Cooper and Ronningstam 1992).

This interrelationship between NPD and depression or dysthymia is not reflected in the 12 reports on the presence of personality disorders in depression (see Table 16–2). Eight of the twelve studies reported NPD prevalence rates of 0%–5%. Two studies (Alnaes and Torgersen 1989; Marin et al. 1993) found that patients with mixed depressed/dysthymic/cyclothymic disorder had higher rates of NPD (5%–11%). A possible explanation of these low NPD rates can be the lack of measures reflecting depression as a reaction to sudden or gradual loss of the support of the grandiose self in narcissistic patients. Another explanation relates to the lack of NPD criteria that reflect the underlying chronic dysthymia referred to in the clinical literature. The predominant view of narcissistic patients as appearing superior, arrogant, and exploitive fails to incorporate the vulnerable aspects of the narcissistic personality as well as the fragile, impaired self-regulatory functions that contribute to depression.

Substance use disorders.   Wurmser (1974) has specifically highlighted narcissistic disturbances as a precondition for developing addictive behavior. He also suggested that an overwhelming narcissistic crisis—that is, "an actualization of a lifelong massive conflict about omnipotence and grandiosity, meaning and trust" (p. 826) accompanied by feelings of disillusionment, rage, depression, and anxiety—may contribute to the manifestation of addictive illness. The addiction is an attempt to reestablish lost omnipotence and grandiosity or can be used as a defense against intolerable feelings of rage, shame, and depression. Khantzian (1980, 1982, 1985) noted that the use of narcotics diminishes the regressive and disorganizing influence of intensive rage and aggression on the ego. Of specific relevance for narcissistic patients are some postulated effects of cocaine, such as heightened sense of mastery, control, and grandeur (Wurmser 1974); increased sense of self-esteem; and greater tolerance for frustration (Wieder and Kaplan 1969).

All six empirical studies (see Table 16–2) reporting on personality disorders in alcohol and substance abuse disorders indicated relatively high rates of NPD for drug abusers (13%–38%) and lower rates for alcohol abusers (6%–7%). The samples of NPD patients identified in these studies are notable because of their large size ($n = 8$–60). NPD is the most frequently identified personality disorder in the study by Marsh et al. (1988) and the second most frequent (after antisocial personality disorder) in

Table 16–2. Overview of available data on the prevalence of narcissistic personality disorder (NPD) in patients with Axis I disorders

Study	Axis I disorder	Assessment instrument	Sample	Prevalence of NPD		Subthreshold traits	
				n	%	n	%
Depression							
Shea et al. 1987	Major depression	PAF DSM-III	249 outpatients	1	<1	2	0.8
Reich and Noyes 1987	Major depression (acutely ill)	SIDP PDQ MCMI (BR > 84) DSM-III	24 outpatients	0* 0** 2***	0* 0** 8.3***		
Reich and Troughton 1988	Major depression (recovered)	SIDP PDQ MCMI (BR > 84) DSM-III	19 outpatients 17 outpatients	0* 2*** 2**	0* 10.5*** 11.8**		
Joffe and Regan 1988, 1989	Major depression	MCMI (BR > 74) MCMI (BR > 84) DSM-III	42 outpatients Acute Remitted	2**** 1*** 9**** 4***	4.8**** 2.4*** 21.4**** 9.5***		

Study	Disorder	Method	Sample	n	%
Alnaes and Torgersen 1989	Major depression, dysthymia, cyclothymia	MCMI (BR > 74) DSM-III	64 depressed	3	4.7
			27 depressed and dysthymic or cyclothymic	3	11.1
			80 dysthymic or cyclothymic	4	5.0
			101 other mental disorders	11	10.9
Alnaes and Torgersen 1990	Major depression, depression, anxiety	SIDP DSM-III	Outpatients 58 depressed	1	1.7
			39 depressed and anxious	1	2.6
Libb et al. 1990	Major depression	MCMI (BR > 84) DSM-III	Outpatients 73 depressed	1	1.4
			28 depressed		
			Before treatment	0	0
			After treatment	1	3.6
Jackson et al. 1991	Unipolar affective disorder (depression/dysthymia), mixed Axis I	SIDP DSM-III	Inpatients 30 unipolar	1	3.3
			21 mixed	1	4.8

(continued)

Table 16–2. Overview of available data on the prevalence of narcissistic personality disorder (NPD) in patients with Axis I disorders (continued)

Study	Axis I disorder	Assessment instrument	Sample	Prevalence of NPD		Subthreshold traits	
				n	%	n	%
Pfohl et al. 1991	Major depression	SIDP	78 depressed inpatients	0	0		
			35 control subjects	1	2.9		
Zimmerman et al. 1991	Major depression	PDQ SIDP DSM-III	94 depressed inpatients	1**	1.1**		
			114 depressed inpatients	1*	0.9*		
			102 depressed relatives	1*	1.0*		
			116 depressed relatives	0**	0**		
Marin et al. 1993	Episodic depression, dysthymia, dysthymia with major depression	PDE DSM-III-R	Mixed inpatients and outpatients				
			19 episodic depressed	0	0		
			25 dysthymic	0	0		
			24 dysthymic with major depression	2	8.3		
			49 total dysthymic patients	2	4.1		

(continued)

Study	Diagnosis	Instrument/Criteria	Sample	Rate	
Pepper et al. 1995	Major depression (episodic), dysthymia (early onset)	PDE DSM-III-R	Outpatients 97 dysthymic 45 depressed	Patient report 4 0	4.1 0
			73 dysthymic 31 depressed	Informant report 4 4	5.5 12.9
Bipolar disorder					
Pica et al. 1990	Bipolar disorder (recent onset)	SIDP DSM-III	26 inpatients	Patient report 1	3.8
				Patient and informant report 3 3	11.5 15.0
Kutcher et al. 1990	Bipolar disorder (euthymic)	PDE DSM-III-R	20 adolescent inpatients (mean age 17.5 years)		
O'Connell et al. 1991	Bipolar disorder	PDQ-R DSM-III-R	50 outpatients	7	14.0
Turley et al. 1992	Bipolar disorder (recent onset)	MCMI-II (BR > 84) SIDP DSM-III	19 inpatients	9*** 2*	47.4*** 10.5*
Peselow et al. 1995	Bipolar disorder (hypomanic)	SIDP DSM-III	66 outpatients	Patient report 12	18.2
				Informant report 18	27.3

Table 16–2. Overview of available data on the prevalence of narcissistic personality disorder (NPD) in patients with Axis I disorders (*continued*)

Study	Axis I disorder	Assessment instrument	Sample	Prevalence of NPD		Subthreshold traits	
				n	%	*n*	%
Peselow et al. 1995 (*continued*)			47 outpatients	Baseline/patient report			
				8	17.0		
				Baseline/informant report			
				11	23.4		
				Recovery/patient report			
				2	4.3		
				Recovery/informant report			
				8	17.0		
Stormberg et al. 1992	Bipolar disorder (acute mania, euthymia)	DIN NPD (TSS ≥ 9) DSM-III-R diagnosis (≥ 5 of 9 criteria)	18 inpatients	Manic			
				6[†]	33.3[†]		
				10[††]	55.6[††]		

Study	Disorder	Assessment	Sample	Euthymic		NPD/BPD	
Schizophrenia							
Hogg et al. 1990	Schizophrenia (recent onset)	SIDP MCMI (BR > 84) DSM-III	40 inpatients* 37 inpatients***	2† 2†† 2* 13***	11.1† 11.1†† 5.0* 35.1***		
Eating disorders							
Piran et al. 1988	Anorexia (restrictive), anorexia + bulimia	Clinical interviews DIB MMPI DSM-II	Inpatients 30 anorexic 38 anorexic + bulimic	0 0	0 0	0 3	0 7.9
Gartner et al. 1989	Anorexia, anorexia + bulimia, bulimia	PDE DSM-III-R	Inpatients 6 anorexic 21 anorexic + bulimic 8 bulimic	1 2 1	16.7 9.5 12.5		
Yates et al. 1989b	Bulimia	PDQ DSM-III-R	30 bulimic outpatients 30 control subjects (community population)	1 0	3.3 0		

(continued)

Table 16–2. Overview of available data on the prevalence of narcissistic personality disorder (NPD) in patients with Axis I disorders (*continued*)

Study	Axis I disorder	Assessment instrument	Sample	Prevalence of NPD		Subthreshold traits	
				n	%	n	%
Ronningstam 1992	Anorexia	DIN (TSS ≥ 9) DSM-III-R diagnosis (≥ 5 of 9 criteria)	17 outpatients 3 inpatients	2[†]	10.0[†]		
				6[††]	33.3[††]		
		DSM-IV diagnosis (≥ 5 of 9 criteria) PDQ-R		2[§]	10.0[§]		
				6[**]	33.3[**]		
Obsessive-compulsive disorder (OCD)							
Stanley et al. 1990	OCD	SCID-II DSM-III-R	25 outpatients	0	0		
Baer et al. 1990	OCD	SIDP DSM-III	96 outpatients	0	0	SCID-II subthreshold 4	16.0

						NPD criteria	
Mavissakalian et al. 1990	OCD	PDQ DSM-III	51 outpatients	0	0	A. 8 B. 12 C. 9 D. 2 E. 12	15.7 23.5 17.6 3.9 23.5
Sciuto et al. 1991	OCD	SIDP-R DSM-III-R	30 outpatients	1	3.3		
Pfohl et al. 1991	OCD	SIDP DSM-III	37 outpatients	2	5.4		
Anxiety and panic disorders							
Mavissakalian and Hamann 1986	Agoraphobia + panic disorder	PDQ DSM-III	60 outpatients	0	0	A. 5 B. 5 C. 9 D. 3 E. 2	8.3 8.3 15.0 5.0 3.0
Reich and Noyes 1987	Panic disorder (acutely ill)	SIDP PDQ MCMI (BR > 84) DSM-III	83 outpatients	0* 1** 5***	0* 1.2** 6.0***		

(continued)

Table 16–2. Overview of available data on the prevalence of narcissistic personality disorder (NPD) in patients with Axis I disorders *(continued)*

Study	Axis I disorder	Assessment instrument	Sample	Prevalence of NPD		Subthreshold traits	
				n	%	*n*	%
Reich and Troughton 1988	Panic disorder (recovered)	SIDP	57 outpatients	0*	0*		
		PDQ		6**	10.5**		
		MCMI (BR > 84)		8***	14.0***		
		DSM-III	40 control subjects (general population)	0**	0**		
				5***	12.5***		
Mavissakalian et al. 1990	Panic disorder + agoraphobia	PDQ DSM-III	187 outpatients	0	0	NPD criteria A. 16 B. 18 C. 27 D. 5 E. 21	8.6 9.6 14.4 2.7 11.2
Gasperini et al. 1990	Generalized anxiety disorder	SIDP DSM-III	46 outpatients	2	4.3		
			50 control subjects (general population)	5	10.0		

(continued)

Study	Disorder	Criteria	Sample	N	%
Aluaes and Torgersen 1990	Anxiety disorder	SIDP DSM-III	92 outpatients	5	5.4
Sciuto et al. 1991	Panic disorder + agoraphobia	SIDP-R DSM-III-R	48 outpatients	2	4.2
Alcohol and substance use disorders					
Craig 1988	Opiate addiction	MCMI (BR > 84) DSM-III	121 inpatients	22	18.2
Marsh et al. 1988	Opiate addiction	MCMI (BR > 74) DSM-III	159 outpatients	60	37.7
Yates et al. 1989a	Cocaine abuse, alcohol abuse	PDQ DSM-III	Inpatients		
			55 cocaine abusing	19	32.2
			47 alcohol abusing	3	6.4
			69 control subjects (community population)	1	1.4
Yeager et al. 1992	Substance abuse (opiates, cocaine, polydrug)	MCMI (BR > 84) DSM-III	144 inpatients in residential treatment	43	29.9
			1,000 control subjects (general psychiatric outpatients in psychotherapy)	117	11.7

Table 16–2. Overview of available data on the prevalence of narcissistic personality disorder (NPD) in patients with Axis I disorders (*continued*)

Study	Axis I disorder	Assessment instrument	Sample	Prevalence of NPD		Subthreshold traits	
				n	%	n	%
DeJong et al. 1993	Alcohol addiction, polydrug addiction	SIDP DSM-III	Inpatients 178 alcohol addicted	12	6.7		
			86 drug addicted	11	12.8		
Weiss et al. 1993	Cocaine dependence	SCID-II DSM-III-R	50 inpatients	8	16.0		

Note. PAF = Personality Assessment Form developed by the National Institute of Mental Health; SIDP = Structured Interview for DSM-III Personality Disorders; PDQ = Personality Disorders Questionnaire; MCMI = Millon Clinical Multiaxial Inventory; BR = base rate; PDE = Personality Disorder Examination; PDQ-R = Personality Disorders Questionnaire–Revised; MCMI-2 = Millon Clinical Multiaxial Inventory II; DIN = Diagnostic Interview for Narcissism; TSS = Total Scaled Score (0–13) in DIN; DIB = Diagnostic Interview for Borderline Patients; MMPI = Minnesota Multiphasic Personality Inventory; BPD = borderline personality disorder; SCID-II = Structured Clinical Interview for DSM-III Personality Disorders; SIDP-R = Structured Interview for DSM-III-R Personality Disorders.
*Prevalence rate obtained with SIDP; **Prevalence rate obtained with PDQ; ***Prevalence rate obtained with MCMI (BR > 84); ****Prevalence rate obtained with MCMI (BR > 74); †Prevalence rate obtained with DIN; ††Prevalence rate obtained with DSM-III-R criteria; §Prevalence rate obtained with DSM-IV criteria.
Source.   Reprinted from Ronningstam E: "Pathological Narcissism and Narcissistic Personality Disorder in Axis I Disorders." *Harvard Review of Psychiatry* 3:326–340, 1996. Copyright 1996, Mosby-Year Book, Inc. Used with permission.

the study by Craig (1988). Yates et al. (1989a) concluded that co-caine abusers are more likely than non–cocaine abusers to have NPD traits, and they actually consider NPD to be a risk factor for the development of cocaine abuse.

These interactional findings raise several questions about the factors that make some but not all NPD patients become drug abusers. Are there major differences in superego functioning (or components representing dependency or addiction in the underlying character functions, or other underlying personality traits) that make some narcissistic patients more prone to drug abuse, whereas others develop other symptom disorders? The limited measures of NPD leave these questions unanswered, and more research with refined diagnostic instruments is indicated to further explore this comorbidity.

Bipolar disorder.   Several authors have commented on the presence of narcissistic pathology in bipolar patients (Gibson et al. 1959; Milden 1984; Rado 1928). Aleksandrowicz (1980) concluded that "bipolar patients tend to have a vulnerable narcissistic personality sensitive to environmental cues 'field dependent' and relying on a significant person's approval for a narcissistic balance" (p. 318). Depression and mania are suggested to be two ways of directing and expressing rage and shame. Morrison (1989) suggested that a shame-based depression in the narcissistically vulnerable person triggers manic episodes as reactions to shame over a sense of incompleteness.

Characteristics that are similar to pathological narcissism have been observed in acutely manic patients. Freeman (1971) noted that pathological narcissism is "positively expressed" in mania, "either in grandiose delusions, a sense of omnipotence or a heightened eroticism" (p. 484). Akhtar (1989) suggested characteristics that are common in both narcissistic and hypo-manic patients, such as grandiosity, self-absorption, and feelings of inferiority and boredom.

Six empirical studies reported on the presence of NPD in bipolar patients, and two of them included bipolar patients with hypomania or acute mania (see Table 16–2). A higher-than-average prevalence of NPD (4%–47%) was found in these studies, and NPD occurred at a much higher rate when the patients were actively hypomanic or manic (17%–56%) compared with when they were euthymic (4%–15%).

One study investigated the presence of pathological narcissism in bipolar patients—both when euthymic and acutely manic—using DIN (Stormberg et al. 1992). Bipolar disorder was diagnostically separable from NPD, and 11% of euthymic patients with bipolar disorder met DSM-III-R criteria for NPD. Bipolar patients, when manic, scored significantly higher than control subjects but not differently from NPD patients on 6 of the 14 most predominant criteria for pathological narcissism: uniqueness, superiority, self-centered and referential behavior, boastful and pretentious behavior, entitlement, and exploitiveness. Actually, NPD patients differ from acutely manic patients only on the criteria of profound envy and needs for admiring attention.

Although both empirical and theoretical studies point to a relationship between pathological narcissism and bipolar disorder, note that mania and pathological narcissism are conceptually and phenomenologically different. Mania is a state characterized by elevated or expansive mood, often accompanied by grandiose delusions or other psychotic features, whereas pathological narcissism occurs within a stable self-structure and involves the regulatory processes of self-esteem. The experiential, affective, and behavioral manifestations can nevertheless appear quite similar. These significant conceptual and phenomenological differences are not reflected in measures used in the empirical studies. In addition, the lack of criteria and instruments for identifying and measuring covert features of NPD may contribute to an artificial overlap between NPD and bipolar disorder that relies heavily on the overt similarities in behavioral and affective states and ignores major underlying differences. On the other hand, as a consequence of these measurement limitations, the presence of a narcissistic personality structure, such as narcissistic vulnerability, sensitivity, shame, and impaired self-regulatory functions, in bipolar patients cannot be verified.

Schizophrenia. The early psychoanalytical literature recognized the relation between narcissism and psychotic disorders or paraphrenia as a regression to a state of primary narcissism. In addition, the observation that the capacity to develop classical transference in psychoanalysis was absent in patients with a diagnosis of narcissistic neurosis (Freud 1914/1957) further connected these psychopathological states. In contrast to these views, Kernberg (1990) claimed that a diagnosis of NPD is contraindicated in psychotic illness because of the loss of reality testing in psychosis.

Only one investigation (Hogg et al. 1990) reported on personality disorders in patients with schizophrenia (see Table 16–2). Quite divergent results with two different instruments (5% and 35% prevalence for NPD) were obtained. The lack of measures to identify the major conceptual differences between NPD and schizophrenia—that is, the capacity for reality testing—can cause an overvaluation of shared features and provide misleading inferences regarding comorbidity.

Eating disorders. Several authors have found narcissistic disturbances in patients with anorexia nervosa (Hogan 1983a, 1983b, 1983c; Meyer 1965; Wilson 1983). Sours (1974) mentioned "exalted self-esteem from amazing self-control" (p. 568) as a sign of anorexia, and Goodsitt (1985) outlined several narcissistic features—grandiosity, exhibitionism, responsiveness, power, and control—as evidence of the anorexic patient's incapacity to maintain self-esteem. Self-esteem is restored through control of the body self and ingestion. Johnson and Connors (1987) suggested two character disorders in patients with eating disorders, borderline and false self/narcissistic disorders. The latter is characterized by an attempt to "compensate for or hide interoceptive deficits" (p. 114) and is associated with greater ego resources than the former.

Four studies (see Table 16–2) investigated NPD in individuals with eating disorders (i.e., anorexia, bulimia, and mixed anorexia and bulimia). The results were inconsistent. The NPD rates vary from 0% to 33%, with 8% of the patients having both NPD and BPD.

One study (Ronningstam 1992), using DIN, focused specifically on the occurrence of pathological narcissism in anorexic patients (both restricted and bulimic type). The results showed that anorexia in these patients was diagnostically separable from NPD, and in 10% of patients with anorexia, DSM-IV criteria for NPD were also met. However, they scored significantly higher than general psychiatric patients and not differently from narcissistic patients on two of the most discriminating characteristics for pathological narcissism: a sense of superiority and a sense of uniqueness. The current measures of the interface between anorexia and NPD are limited, and the inconsistent results might reflect the lack of measures of underlying covert narcissistic pathology.

Obsessive-compulsive disorder.   Although Axis II obsessive-compulsive personality disorder has been included in the differential diagnosis of NPD (Akhtar 1989; Kernberg 1990), the association between NPD and Axis I obsessive-compulsive disorder has rarely, if ever, been discussed in the clinical literature. This absence of comorbidity is also reflected in the five studies included here (see Table 16–2), which report very low rates of NPD (0%–5%).

Anxiety and panic disorder.   NPD and anxiety disorders have seldom been related in the clinical literature. However, Gabbard (1983) discussed panic and anxiety reactions related to problems with self-esteem regulation in individuals with stage fright. The seven studies reporting on Axis II disorders in anxiety and panic disorders (see Table 16–2) have generally found very low rates (0%–5%).

Discussion

The prevalence of NPD in Axis I disorders usually does not exceed that found in the general clinical population or in patients with personality disorders (i.e., 2%–22%) (Gunderson et al. 1991; Morey 1988). Somewhat higher prevalence rates were found in studies of anorexic patients (10%–20%) and in studies of bipolar patients (4%–15%; 47% with the Millon Clinical Multiaxial Inventory [MCMI]). High NPD rates were reported throughout the studies of patients with drug abuse disorders (13%–32%; 38% with MCMI). Empirical studies often failed to confirm accounts of pathological narcissism suggested in the theoretical and clinical literature, for example, in depression and anorexia.

The possibilities of making generalizations and valid conclusions about the interface between NPD and individual Axis I disorders are limited. Several methodological problems and divergences in the empirical studies contribute to a circumscribed comparability. One problem is variation because of differences in the samples' demographics and cultural backgrounds (Australian, Italian, American, Middle European, and Scandinavian). Another is the small sample sizes of NPD patients (usually $N <$ 5 subjects) that make results and conclusions especially tentative. The third problem is that conceptual and constructional variations among the instruments used for measuring both Axis I and Axis II diagnoses (structured, semistructured, or unstructured interviews; questionnaires; self-reports; and rating scales) prevent reliable consensus regarding the prevalence rates, both between studies using the same instrument and within studies using different instruments.

Despite these limitations, the lack of evidence from the empirical studies supporting the idea of a predominant significant relation between NPD and any specific Axis I disorder is obvious. In no case does the presence of a specific Axis I disorder make the presence of NPD more likely. The opposite is also true: in no case does the presence of NPD automatically implicate a specific Axis I comorbidity. It is, however, reasonable to conclude from the integration of clinical and empirical data that there are complex interactions between pathological narcissism and specific syndromes. These interactions are influenced by other aspects of the nature of narcissistic pathology as well, especially the covert vulnerability and sensitivity, but also by the comorbid patients' deficiencies in self- and affect-regulatory functions. This raises questions about environmental versus biological or genetic factors that influence the origin and development of a particular comorbid disorder.

The relation between NPD and depression or dysthymia suggests a certain vulnerability in narcissistic patients for developing these syndromes (i.e., an acute failure in the individual's narcissistic balance and capacity to maintain processes of pathological self-esteem regulation that support the pathological grandiose self can lead to acute major depression). Specific patterns in the course of NPD can also actually generate these syndromes (i.e., the long-term process that takes place, involving continuous confrontations with and gradual realization of behaviors and circumstances related to the narcissistic pathology).

In relation to substance use disorders, it seems as if the course of NPD in some individuals can involve a receptiveness or vulnerability for certain types of drug abuse. The interactions between the abuse of drugs—especially cocaine and opiates—and pathological narcissism may serve two functions: to gratify the pathological, unrealistic grandiose self-experience and to defend against intolerable feelings of pain, self-disillusion and depreciation, depression, and rage. In other words, the drug abuse or addiction can serve to compensate for dysfunctional self-regulatory processes and for severe defects in the capacity to identify and tolerate affects.

A specific relation can be identified between anorexia and pathological narcissism. Anorexic symptomatology can become part of the process of pathological self-esteem regulation in the comorbid patient. Low body weight, highly controlled food intake, ascetic lifestyle, and social isolation are linked with a sense of superiority and uniqueness, the central aspect of the pathological grandiose self. In other words, the anorexic syndrome becomes a part of the pathological self-esteem regulation, serving to defend against intolerable self-images and underlying rage. As a consequence, a particularly strong resistance to relinquish the anorexic behavior and introduce alternative behaviors and attitudes can be found in these patients (Hsu 1980).

The interaction between NPD and bipolar disorder is somewhat more complex given the dualistic nature of bipolar disorder. The substantially higher rates of NPD in acute manic and hypomanic phase (17%–55%) raise the question as to whether certain narcissistic traits are revealed during these states in which repressive defenses are absent and ego functions are impaired (Lewin 1941; Pao 1971) but obscured during periods of euthymia, during which higher levels of defense and ego functions are present (Stormberg et al. 1992). This suggests the possibility of an underlying NPD structure that could predispose to bipolar disorder. Alternatively, it is also possible that the manifestations of mania resemble the characteristics of pathological narcissism and NPD but that there is no characterological relationship between the disorders.

Future research should focus on developing methods for identifying and measuring the central underlying characteristics for pathological narcissism and related defects in affect and self-esteem regulation. It is obvious that the criteria for defining the diagnostic category of NPD and overt features of pathological narcissism, although having stimulated important empirical research, still are insufficient in providing complete information about the nature of narcissistic disorders.

References

Akhtar S: Narcissistic personality disorder: descriptive features and differential diagnosis. Psychiatr Clin North Am 12(3):505–530, 1989

Aleksandrowicz DR: Psychoanalytic studies of mania, in Mania—An Evolving Concept. Edited by Belmaker R, van Praag HM. Utrecht, The Netherlands, MTP Press, International Medical Publisher, 1980, pp 309–322

Alnaes R, Torgersen S: Personality and personality disorders among patients with major depression in combination with dysthymic or cyclothymic disorder. Acta Psychiatr Scand 79:363–369, 1989

Alnaes R, Torgersen S: DSM-III personality disorders among patients with major depression, anxiety disorders and mixed conditions. J Nerv Ment Dis 178:693–698, 1990

American Psychiatric Association: Diagnostic and Statistical Manual of Mental Disorders, 3rd Edition. Washington, DC, American Psychiatric Association, 1980

American Psychiatric Association: Diagnostic and Statistical Manual of Mental Disorders, 3rd Edition, Revised. Washington, DC, American Psychiatric Association, 1987

American Psychiatric Association: Diagnostic and Statistical Manual of Mental Disorders, 4th Edition. Washington, DC, American Psychiatric Association, 1994

Baer L, Jenike MA, Riccardi II JN, et al: Standardized assessment of personality disorders in obsessive compulsive disorder. Arch Gen Psychiatry 47:826–830, 1990

Berezin M: Normal psychology of the aging process, revisited—II. the fate of narcissism in old age: clinical case reports. J Geriatr Psychiatry Neurol 10:9–26, 1977

Cooper A: The narcissistic-masochistic character, in Masochism: Current Psychoanalytic Perspectives. Edited by Glick RA, Meyers DI. New York, Analytic Press, 1988, pp 117–138

Cooper A: Narcissism and masochism—the narcissistic-masochistic character. Psychiatr Clin North Am 12:541–552, 1989

Cooper AM, Ronningstam E: Narcissistic personality disorder, in American Psychiatric Press Review of Psychiatry, Vol 11. Washington, DC, American Psychiatric Press, 1992, pp 80–97

Craig RJ: A psychometric study of the prevalence of DSM-III personality disorders among treated opiate addicts. Int J Addict 23:115–124, 1988

DeJong CAJ, van der Brink W, Harteveld FM, et al: Personality disorders in drug addicts. Compr Psychiatry 34:87–94, 1993

Freeman T: Observations on mania. Int J Psychoanal 52:479–486, 1971

Freud S: On narcissism (1914), in The Standard Edition of the Complete Psychological Works of Sigmund Freud, Vol 14. Translated and edited by Strachey J. London, Hogarth Press, 1957, pp 67–102

Gabbard GO: Further contributions to the understanding of stage fright: narcissistic issues. J Am Psychoanal Assoc 31:423–431, 1983

Gartner A, Marcus R, Halmi K, et al: DSM-III-R personality disorders in patients with eating disorders. Am J Psychiatry 146:1585–1591, 1989

Gasperini M, Battaglia M, Diaferia G, et al: Personality features related to generalized anxiety disorder. Compr Psychiatry 31:363–368, 1990

Gibson R, Cohen MB, Cohen R: On the dynamics of the manic depressive personality. Am J Psychiatry 115:1101–1107, 1959

Goodsitt A: Self psychology and the treatment of anorexia nervosa, in Handbook of Psychotherapy for Anorexia Nervosa and Bulimia. Edited by Garner DM, Garfinkel PE. New York, Guilford, 1985, pp 55–87

Gunderson JG, Ronningstam E: Is narcissistic personality disorder a valid diagnosis? in Personality Disorders: New Perspectives on Diagnostic Validity. Edited by Oldham JM. Washington, DC, American Psychiatric Press, 1991, pp 105–119

Gunderson J, Ronningstam E, Bodkin A: The diagnostic interview for narcissistic patients. Arch Gen Psychiatry 47:676–680, 1990

Gunderson J, Ronningstam E, Smith L: Narcissistic personality disorder: a review of data on DSM-III-R descriptions. Journal of Personality Disorders 5:167–177, 1991

Hogan C: Psychodynamics, in Fear of Being Fat. Edited by Wilson P. New York, Jason Aronson, 1983a, pp 115–128

Hogan C: Object relations, in Fear of Being Fat. Edited by Wilson P. New York, Jason Aronson, 1983b, pp 129–149

Hogan C: Transference, in Fear of Being Fat. Edited by Wilson P. New York, Jason Aronson, 1983c, pp 153–168

Hogg B, Jackson H, Rudd R, et al: Diagnosing personality disorders in recent-onset schizophrenia. J Nerv Ment Dis 178:194–199, 1990

Hsu LK: Outcome of anorexia nervosa: a review of the literature. Arch Gen Psychiatry 37:1041–1046, 1980

Jackson HJ, Whiteside HL, Bates GW, et al: Diagnosing personality disorders in psychiatric inpatients. Acta Psychiatr Scand 83:206–213, 1991

Joffe R, Regan J: Personality and depression. J Psychiatr Res 22:279–286, 1988

Joffe R, Regan J: Brief report: personality and depression: a further evaluation. J Psychiatr Res 23:299–301, 1989

Johnson C, Connors ME: The Etiology and Treatment of Bulimia Nervosa. New York, Basic Books, 1987

Kernberg OF: Borderline Conditions and Pathological Narcissism. New York, Jason Aronson, 1975

Kernberg OF: Normal psychology of the aging process, revisited—II. discussion. J Geriatr Psychiatry Neurol 10:27–45, 1977

Kernberg OF: Internal World and External Reality. New York, Jason Aronson, 1980

Kernberg OF: Narcissistic personality disorder, in Psychiatry, Vol 1. Edited by Michels R, Cooper AM, Guze SB, et al. New York, JB Lippincott, 1990, pp 1–12

Khantzian EJ: An ego-self theory of substance dependence: a contemporary psychoanalytic perspective, in Theories on Drug Abuse (NIDA Research Monograph 30). Edited by Lettieri DJ, Sayers M, Pearson HW. Rockville, MD, National Institute on Drug Abuse, 1980, pp 29–33

Khantzian EJ: Psychological (structural) vulnerabilities and the specific appeal to narcotics. Ann N Y Acad Sci 398:24–32, 1982

Khantzian EJ: The self-medication hypothesis of addictive disorders: focus on heroin and cocaine dependence. Am J Psychiatry 142:1259–1264, 1985

Kutcher S, Marton P, Korenblum M: Adolescent bipolar illness and personality disorder. J Am Acad Child Adolesc Psychiatry 29:355–358, 1990

Lewin BD: Comments on hypomanic and related states. Psychoanal Rev 28:86–91, 1941

Libb W, Stankovic S, Freeman A, et al: Personality disorders among depressed outpatients as identified by MCMI. J Clin Psychol 46:277–284, 1990

Marin DB, Kocsis JH, Frances AJ, et al: Personality disorders in dysthymia. Journal of Personality Disorders 7:223–231, 1993

Marsh DT, Stile SA, Stoughton NL, et al: Psychopathology of opiate addiction: comparative data from MMPI and MCMI. Am J Drug Alcohol Abuse 14:17–27, 1988

Mavissakalian M, Hamann S: DSM-III personality disorders in agoraphobia. Compr Psychiatry 27:471–479, 1986

Mavissakalian M, Hamann S, Jones B: A comparison of DSM-III personality disorders in panic/agoraphobia and obsessive-compulsive disorder. Compr Psychiatry 31:238–244, 1990

Meyer JE: Anorexia Nervosa. Stuttgart, Germany, Thieme, 1965

Milden R: Affective disorders and narcissistic vulnerability. Am J Psychoanal 44:345–353, 1984

Millon T: Disorders of Personality DSM-III: Axis II. New York, Wiley, 1981

Morey L: Personality disorders in DSM-III and DSM-III-R: an examination of convergence, coverage, and internal consistency. Am J Psychiatry 145:573–577, 1988

Morrison A: Shame: The Underside of Narcissism. Hillsdale, NJ, Analytic Press, 1989

O'Connell R, Mayo J, Sciutto M: PDQ-R personality disorders in bipolar patients. J Affect Disord 23:217–221, 1991

Pao P-N: Elation, hypomania, and mania. J Am Psychoanal Assoc 19:787–798, 1971

Pepper CM, Klieg DN, Anderson RL, et al: DSM-III-R Axis II comorbidity in dysthymia and major depression. Am J Psychiatry 152:239–247, 1995

Peselow ED, Sanfilipo MP, Fieve RR: Relationship between hypomania and personality disorders before and after successful treatment. Am J Psychiatry 152:232–238, 1995

Pfohl B, Black DW, Noyes R, et al: Axis I and Axis II comorbidity findings: implications for validity, in Personality Disorders: New Perspectives on Diagnostic Validity. Edited by Oldham JM. Washington, DC, American Psychiatric Press, 1991, pp 145–161

Pica S, Edwards J, Jackson H, et al: Personality disorders in recent-onset bipolar disorders. Compr Psychiatry 31:499–510, 1990

Piran N, Lerner P, Garfinkel P, et al: Personality disorders in anorexic patients. Int J Eat Disord 7:589–599, 1988

Plakun E: Narcissistic personality disorder: a validity study and comparison to borderline personality disorder. Psychiatr Clin North Am 12(3):603–620, 1989

Rado S: The problem of melancholia. Int J Psychoanal 9:420–438, 1928

Reich J, Noyes R: A comparison of DSM-III personality disorders in acutely ill panic and depressed patients. Journal of Anxiety Disorders 1:123–131, 1987

Reich J, Troughton E: Comparison of DSM-III personality disorders in recovered depressed and panic disorders. J Nerv Ment Dis 176: 300–304, 1988

Ronningstam E: Comparing three systems for diagnosing narcissistic personality disorder. Psychiatry 51:300–311, 1988

Ronningstam E: Pathological narcissism in anorexic subjects. Paper presented at the 145th annual meeting of the American Psychiatric Association, Washington, DC, May 2–7, 1992

Ronningstam E: Pathological narcissism and narcissistic personality disorder in Axis I disorders. Harvard Review of Psychiatry 3:326–340, 1996

Ronningstam E, Gunderson J: Narcissistic traits in psychiatric patients. Compr Psychiatry 29:545–549, 1988

Ronningstam E, Gunderson J: Descriptive studies on narcissistic personality disorder. Psychiatr Clin North Am 12:585–602, 1989

Ronningstam E, Gunderson J: Identifying criteria for narcissistic personality disorder. Am J Psychiatry 147:918–922, 1990

Ronningstam E, Gunderson J: Differentiating borderline personality disorder from narcissistic personality disorder. Journal of Personality Disorders 5:225–232, 1991

Ronningstam E, Gunderson J: Differentiating antisocial personality disorder from narcissistic personality disorder. Paper presented at the 148th annual meeting of the American Psychiatric Association, Miami, FL, May 20–25, 1995

Ronningstam E, Gunderson J, Lyons M: Changes in pathological narcissism. Am J Psychiatry 152:253–257, 1995

Sciuto G, Diaferia G, Battaglia M, et al: DSM-III-R personality disorders in panic and obsessive compulsive disorders: a comparison study. Compr Psychiatry 32:450–457, 1991

Shea T, Glass D, Pilkonis P, et al: Frequency and implications of personality disorders in a sample of depressed outpatients. Journal of Personality Disorders 1:27–42, 1987

Sours JA: The anorexia nervosa syndrome. Int J Psychoanal 55:567–576, 1974

Stanley M, Turner S, Borden J: Schizotypal features in obsessive-compulsive disorder. Compr Psychiatry 31:511–518, 1990

Stormberg D, Ronningstam E, Gunderson J, et al: Pathological narcissism in bipolar patients. Paper presented at the 145th annual meeting of the American Psychiatric Association, Washington, DC, May 2–7, 1992

Svrakic DM: Emotional features of narcissistic personality disorder. Am J Psychiatry 143:720–724, 1985

Turley B, Bates G, Edwards J, et al: MCMI-II personality disorders in recent-onset bipolar disorders. J Clin Psychol 48:320–329, 1992

Weiss RD, Mirin SM, Griffin ML, et al: Personality disorders in cocaine dependence. Compr Psychiatry 34:145–149, 1993

Wieder H, Kaplan EH: Drug use in adolescents: psychodynamic meaning and pharmacogenic effect. Psychoanal Study Child 24:399–431, 1969

Wilson P (ed): Fear of Being Fat. New York, Jason Aronson, 1983

Wurmser L: Psychoanalytic considerations of the etiology of compulsive drug use. J Am Psychoanal Assoc 22:820–843, 1974

Yates W, Fulton AI, Gabel JM, et al: Personality risk factors for cocaine abuse. Am J Public Health 79:891–892, 1989a

Yates W, Sieleni B, Reich J, et al: Comorbidity of bulimia nervosa and personality disorders. J Clin Psychiatry 50:57–59, 1989b

Yeager RJ, DiGuiseppe R, Resweber PJ, et al: Comparison of Millon personality profiles of chronic residential substance abusers and general outpatient population. Psychol Rep 71:71–79, 1992

Zimmerman M, Pfohl B, Coryell W, et al: Major depression and personality disorder. J Affect Disord 22:199–210, 1991

Chapter 17

Association Between Psychopathy and Narcissism

Theoretical Views and Empirical Evidence

Stephen D. Hart, Ph.D.
Robert D. Hare, Ph.D.

Research on both psychopathy and narcissism has expanded rapidly during the past two to three decades. For the most part, the two fields have evolved separately, without much coordina-

The authors wish to thank M. R. (Rick) Levenson, Ph.D., and Elsa F. Ronning-stam, Ph.D., for their helpful comments on an earlier version of this manuscript. All research on the PCL:SV described herein was funded by a grant from the John D. and Catherine T. MacArthur Foundation's Research Network on Mental Health and the Law under the direction of John Monahan, Ph.D., School of Law, University of Virginia.

tion or cross-fertilization. This is unfortunate, because—as others have noted and as is discussed below—there may be potentially important similarities between the two disorders. In this chapter, theory and research on the association between psychopathy and narcissism are summarized. The authors begin by outlining the traditional clinical construct of psychopathy and by clarifying the difference between psychopathy and antisocial personality disorder. Next, the authors briefly discuss some key clinical-theoretical perspectives on the association between psychopathy and narcissism. This is followed by a review of the relevant empirical literature. They conclude by identifying some unanswered questions and by recommending avenues for future research.

The Nature of Psychopathy

Clinical Features

Psychopathy—also known as sociopathy and dissocial or antisocial personality disorder—is a specific form of personality disorder with a distinctive pattern of interpersonal, affective, and behavioral symptoms. Modern clinical descriptions of the psychopathic person have been extremely consistent over time, beginning with Cleckley's classic text, *The Mask of Sanity* (1941), and continuing to the present (e.g., Buss 1966; Craft 1965; Hare 1970; Karpman 1961; McCord and McCord 1964; Millon 1981). These clinical descriptions are representative of the views of researchers and clinicians, according to content analyses (Albert et al. 1959; Fotheringham 1957) and to opinion polls of mental health professionals, forensic personnel, and even the lay public (Davies and Feldman 1981; Gray and Hutchinson 1964; Livesley 1986; Rogers et al. 1992, 1994; Tennent et al. 1990). The descriptions can be summarized as follows: interpersonally, psychopathic persons are grandiose, arrogant, callous, superficial, and manipulative; affectively, they are short-tempered, unable to form strong emotional bonds with others, and lacking in guilt or anxiety; and behaviorally, they are irresponsible, impulsive, and prone to delinquency and criminality.

Diagnostic Issues

Although there is little debate over the key features of psychopathy, in recent years there has been considerable disagreement about how best to diagnose the disorder. There are two major approaches (Hare et al. 1991; Lilienfeld 1994). The first, which can be called the Cleckleyan tradition, argues that an adequate diagnosis must be based on the full range of psychopathic symptomatology. According to this perspective, a focus on behavioral symptoms (e.g., irresponsibility, delinquency) to the exclusion of interpersonal and affective symptoms (e.g., grandiosity, deceitfulness) may lead to the overdiagnosis of psychopathy in criminal populations and to underdiagnosis in noncriminals (Lilienfeld 1994; Widiger and Corbitt 1993). The Cleckleyan tradition was reflected in the first two versions of DSM (American Psychiatric Association 1952, 1968) and currently is reflected in the criteria for dissocial personality disorder in ICD-10 (World Health Organization 1990). It also is reflected in the revised Psychopathy Checklist (PCL-R; Hare 1980, 1991), which forms the basis for much of our research described below.

The second perspective, which can be called the Washington University tradition, is based on a number of influential works published by people who worked or trained at that institution (e.g., Feighner et al. 1972; Robins 1966). One of the fundamental assumptions of this approach is that assessment should focus on publicly observable antisocial behaviors, because clinicians are incapable of reliably assessing interpersonal and affective characteristics (Robins 1978). The Washington University tradition heavily influenced DSM-III, DSM-III-R, and DSM-IV (American Psychiatric Association 1980, 1987, 1994).

Criteria sets based on the two traditions generally show moderate to high levels of diagnostic agreement, even in forensic settings (Hare 1980, 1985; Widiger et al. 1996). However, criteria sets based on the Washington University approach, such as those in

DSM-III, diagnose antisocial personality disorder in the majority (50%–80%) of incarcerated offenders, whereas criteria based on the Cleckleyan tradition, such as the PCL-R, diagnose psychopathy in about 25% of the same offenders (Hare 1983, 1985; Hare et al. 1991). This has led many to criticize severely DSM-III, DSM-III-R, and DSM-IV criteria for confusing psychopathy with criminality (Hare 1985; Hare et al. 1991; Rogers and Dion 1991; Stevens 1994; Wulach 1988). Indeed, DSM-IV acknowledges that the Washington University approach may be inadequate for use in forensic settings. Another problem with criteria based on this approach is that it has poor predictive validity in forensic settings (Hare et al. 1991), unlike Cleckleyan criteria such as the PCL-R (Hare and Hart 1992; Hare et al. 1992, 1993; Hart et al. 1994). For these reasons, the authors prefer the Cleckleyan tradition and focus their discussion on this approach whenever possible.

Assessment Issues

Although highly structured methods that rely on self-reports of behavior and attitudes may be useful for the assessment of many aspects of normal and pathological personality, such methods are inappropriate for the assessment of psychopathy (Hare and Hart 1992; Hare et al. 1989, 1991, 1993; Lilienfeld 1994). Several reasons account for this. For example, deceitfulness (e.g., lying, manipulation) is a key clinical feature of the disorder. There is every reason to expect that psychopathic individuals will attempt to minimize or deny their antisocial behavior. For example, Hare (1985) described in a previous report one psychopathic person who, while incarcerated in a federal prison, managed to obtain copies of a major psychological test and its scoring key. This inmate ran a successful and lucrative consulting business for some time, coaching other prisoners on how to respond to the test, which was administered as part of routine correctional and pre-parole assessments. In light of such gross deceitfulness, it is difficult to put much faith in an individual's response to common interview and self-report questions such as, "As an adult, have you lied a lot?" or "As an adult, have you on several or more occasions committed acts for which, if you had been caught, you could have been arrested?"

There are other reasons for mistrusting the self-reports of psychopathic persons, even apart from the matter of conscious deceitfulness. First, the grandiosity and superficiality of psychopathic individuals give them a strong tendency to present themselves in an unrealistically positive light. This tendency may be "unconscious," that is, habitual or otherwise outside the realm of normal awareness. Second, psychopathic individuals, because of their shallow affect and lack of empathy, may have a poor understanding of how they impress and have an effect on others. They may truly believe that others perceive them to be "nice guys" or "responsible employees," in spite of a history of callous and irresponsible behavior. Third, recent research suggests that psychopathic individuals may have a major disturbance of affective and linguistic processing (Hare et al. 1988). This may impair their comprehension and communication of emotionally toned language. These same problems may also hamper the assessment of narcissism by self-report (Gunderson et al. 1990).

Research supports our mistrust of self-report assessments of psychopathy. Several studies that used popular psychological tests—such as the Minnesota Multiphasic Personality Inventory (Butcher et al. 1989; Hathaway and McKinley 1940), the Millon Clinical Multiaxial Inventory (MCMI; Millon 1983, 1987), and the California Psychological Inventory (Gough 1957, 1987)—found low to moderate correlations between various psychopathy-related scales and clinical diagnoses made using PCL-R and DSM criteria (Hare 1985; Hart et al. 1991, 1994). The results are not simply the result of method variance, because the correlations among self-reports were as low as the correlations between self-reports and clinical diagnoses. Another important finding is that self-reports tend to be biased in their assessment of psychopathy, measuring some symptoms much better than others (e.g., Harpur et al. 1989; Hart et al. 1991).

Ironically, the most appropriate use of self-report measures of psychopathy may be in research on "normal" (i.e., nonpatient) populations. For example, Levenson et al. (1995) developed a self-report inventory that attempted to capture faithfully the Cleckleyan concept of psychopathy using an "antisocial desirability" manipulation that allows the respondent to report psychopathic traits while maintaining the impression of positive self-presentation. That is, psychopathic traits are presented as thought-out, "philosophical" positions. This scale was associated with self-reported antisocial behavior in a population of university students and was correlated with self-report measures of personality constructs that are conceptually related to psychopathy.

The Psychopathy Checklist

For reasons discussed above, our view is that psychopathy should be assessed with expert observer (i.e., clinical) ratings. The ratings should be based on a review of case history materials, such as interviews with family members and employers and examination of criminal and psychiatric records, and supplemented with interviews or behavioral observations whenever possible (Hare 1991; Hart et al. 1992, 1994). The authors have spent considerable effort during the past 15 years developing and validating rating scales of psychopathy in the Cleckleyan tradition based on this approach.

The original Psychopathy Checklist (PCL; Hare 1980) was a 22-item rating scale, later revised and shortened to 20 items (Hare 1985, 1991). The PCL and PCL-R were designed for use in forensic populations. Items are scored on a 3-point scale (0 = item does not apply, 1 = item applies somewhat, 2 = item definitely applies). Because the two scales are highly correlated (see Hare et al. 1990), the authors focus below on the PCL-R. Table 17–1 lists the PCL-R items, which are defined in detail in the test manual. Total scores can range from 0 to 40; scores of 30 or higher are diagnostic of psychopathy. There is a considerable body of evidence supporting the validity of the PCL and PCL-R, including laboratory research suggesting that psychopathic individuals have unusual patterns of cognitive and psychophysiological response to aversive, emotional, and linguistic stimuli (Hare et al. 1988; Harpur and Hare 1990; Newman and Wallace 1993) and forensic research suggesting that psychopathic individuals have criminal careers

Table 17–1. Items in the Hare Psychopathy Checklist—Revised (PCL-R)

Item	Description	Loads on factor
1.	Glibness/superficial charm	1
2.	Grandiose sense of self-worth	1
3.	Need for stimulation/proneness to boredom	2
4.	Pathological lying	1
5.	Conning/manipulative	1
6.	Lack of remorse or guilt	1
7.	Shallow affect	1
8.	Callous/lack of empathy	1
9.	Parasitic lifestyle	2
10.	Poor behavioral controls	2
11.	Promiscuous sexual behavior	—
12.	Early behavioral problems	2
13.	Lack of realistic, long-term goals	2
14.	Impulsivity	2
15.	Irresponsibility	2
16.	Failure to accept responsibility for own actions	1
17.	Many short-term marital relationships	
18.	Juvenile delinquency	2
19.	Revocation of conditional release	2
20.	Criminal versatility	—

Note. — = Item does not load on either factor.
Source. Reprinted from Hare RD: *The Hare Psychopathy Checklist—Revised.* Toronto, Ontario, Multi-Health Systems, 1991. Copyright 1991, Multi-Health Systems Inc., 908 Niagara Falls Boulevard, North Tonawanda, NY 14120-2060 (800-456-3003). Used with permission.

characterized by early-onset delinquency, high-density offending, and instrumental violence (Forth et al. 1990; Hare et al. 1992, 1993; Hart et al. 1994).

The second scale is the screening version of the PCL-R (PCL:SV; Hart et al. 1995). It is a brief, easy-to-administer, 12-item scale (see Table 17–2) based directly on the PCL-R but intended for use in nonforensic populations and as a screening test for psychopathy in forensic populations. The PCL:SV is scored in the same

Table 17–2. Items in the Screening Version of the Psychopathy
　　　　　　Checklist (PCL:SV)

Part 1	Part 2
1. Superficial	7. Impulsive
2. Grandiose	8. Poor behavior controls
3. Deceitful	9. Lacks goals
4. Lacks remorse	10. Irresponsible
5. Lacks empathy	11. Adolescent antisocial behavior
6. Doesn't accept responsibility	12. Adult antisocial behavior

Source. Reprinted from Hart SD, Cox DN, Hare RD: *Manual for the Psychopathy Checklist: Screening Version (PCL:SV).* Toronto, Ontario, Multi-Health Systems, 1995. Copyright, Multi-Health Systems Inc., 908 Niagara Falls
Boulevard, North Tonawanda, NY 14120-2060 (800-456-3003). Used with
permission.

manner as the PCL-R, yielding total scores that can range from
0 to 24. The two scales are highly correlated ($r = .80$; see Hart et al.
1995).

The Association Between
Psychopathy and Narcissism

Theoretical Views

Many writers have commented on the overlap between psychopathy and narcissism at a descriptive or phenotypical level
(Bursten 1973, 1989; MacKay 1986; McGlashan and Heinssen
1989; Wulach 1988). The point is made perhaps most eloquently
by Stone (1993, p. 292): "All commentators on psychopathy . . . al-
lude to the attribute of (pathological) narcissism—whether under
the rubric of egocentricity, self-indulgence, or some similar term.
In effect, all psychopathic persons are at the same time narcissistic
persons." The nature of the association between the two disorders
has been discussed at length by Kernberg (1970, 1989; see also
Chapter 2, this volume) and Meloy (1988). Both work within an

object relations framework; however, Kernberg's primary emphasis is narcissism, whereas Meloy's is psychopathy.

The parallels between psychopathy and Kernberg's conceptualization and description of the manifestations of narcissistic personality are clear; indeed, Kernberg noted that the two disorders "present the same general constellation of traits" and that "the antisocial personality may be considered a subgroup of the narcissistic personality" (1970, p. 5). Even closer conceptually to psychopathy is what Kernberg calls "malignant narcissism," a form of narcissistic personality disorder with severe superego pathology (Kernberg, Chapter 2, this volume).

Despite their similarities, though, Kernberg still differentiates psychopathy and narcissism (including malignant narcissism). One major difference is that psychopathic persons have a total incapacity for loyalty, remorse, and concern for others. Another is that psychopathic individuals are unable to see a moral dimension in others. They do not have a good sense of time and are unable to make realistic plans for the future. Finally, Kernberg noted that the antisocial behavior of narcissistic individuals tends to be of the "passive-parasitic" variety, whereas psychopathic persons are more overtly aggressive.

Meloy (1988) views psychopathy as a "deviant developmental process" (p. 311) with a core feature that is "the coexistence of a benign detachment and aggressively pursued, sadistically toned attempts to bond" (p. 59). He also recognized the close link between psychopathy and narcissism, stating that "the weight of clinical research supports the hypothesis that psychopathic personality organization is one subtype of narcissistic personality disorder, albeit an extreme and dangerous variant" (p. 7). His conclusion is based in part on clinical observations of apparent similarities in the Rorschach protocols of psychopathic and narcissistic patients (Meloy 1988; see also Gacono and Meloy 1994; Gacono et al. 1990). Like Kernberg, though, Meloy differentiated between the two disorders along several lines, noting that psychopathy is characterized by, among other things, prominent aggression, sadism, a "malignant ego ideal," and a tendency toward paranoid ideation (rather than depression) when under stress (pp. 19–20).

Empirical Evidence

Conceptual overlap.   One important line of evidence comes from studies that focus on the internal structure of psychopathic traits. It appears that whenever a reasonably comprehensive set of symptoms is examined, two clusters emerge: one comprising interpersonal and affective symptoms such as grandiosity, superficiality, and remorselessness; and the other comprising behavioral symptoms such as irresponsibility and antisociality. The first cluster is, conceptually, very similar to narcissism, perhaps lending support to clinical views that all psychopathic individuals are narcissistic.

Harpur et al. (1988) factor-analyzed the 22 items of the PCL and attempted to identify a factor structure that was stable across samples, sites, and investigators. They had PCL ratings from six samples, with a total sample size of 1,119. For each sample, they extracted between two and eight factors and then subjected the factors to a variety of orthogonal and oblique rotations. The stability of various solutions both within and across samples was determined using split-half cross-validation and congruence. The results strongly supported an oblique two-factor solution. Factor 1, labeled the "selfish, callous and remorseless use of others," comprised items tapping egocentricity; superficiality; deceitfulness; callousness; and a lack of remorse, empathy, and anxiety. On the other hand, Factor 2, labeled a "chronically unstable and antisocial lifestyle" or "social deviance," comprised items tapping impulsivity, sensation-seeking, irresponsibility, aggressiveness, and criminality. The two factors were correlated at about $r = .50$. Identical factor structures have been reported for the PCL-R (Hare et al. 1990) and the PCL:SV (Hart et al. 1995) (see Tables 17–1 and 17–2). The two factors are differentially correlated with important external variables, such as violence, substance use, and personality variables (Hare 1991; Harpur et al. 1989; Hart et al. 1995).

The two-factor structure found with the PCL and related measures is also found in analyses based on other assessment procedures. Livesley et al. (1989, 1992) developed self-report scales to measure a wide range of personality disorder symptoms described in the clinical literature (i.e., not limited to the domain of traits found in DSM-III-R). They conducted factor analyses of the scales in both patient and nonpatient samples. With respect to the prototypical symptoms of psychopathy, they found a two-factor structure isomorphic to that reported by Hare et al. (1990); they labeled the factors "interpersonal disesteem" and "conduct problems." Livesley and Schroeder (1991) replicated these findings when they reanalyzed only those symptoms contained in DSM-III-R criteria for antisocial personality disorder. One interesting finding was that interpersonal disesteem also emerged as a primary factor underlying traits of narcissistic personality disorder.

Harpur et al. (1990) conducted a factor analysis of DSM-III Cluster 2 (dramatic–erratic–emotional) personality disorder symptoms—including symptoms of antisocial and narcissistic personality disorder—in a large sample of community residents (relatives of psychiatric patients and a control group consisting of relatives of nonpatients). All subjects were assessed with the Structured Interview for DSM-III Personality (SIDP; Stangl et al. 1985), a reliable and well-validated instrument. Several factors emerged, including two that comprised symptoms of antisocial and narcissistic personality disorder and that were isomorphic to the PCL factors.

Rogers and colleagues asked 331 forensic psychiatrists (Rogers et al. 1994) and 250 members of the lay public (Rogers et al. 1992) to rate the prototypicality of a long list of psychopathy-related symptoms. They performed a factor analysis of the ratings and retained four factors for extraction. Although there were some relatively minor differences, in both samples the first two factors were isomorphic to the PCL factors: the first reflected impulsive and irresponsible behavior (i.e., Factor 2 of the PCL), and the second reflected manipulation and lack of guilt (i.e., Factor 1 of the PCL). The remaining two factors reflected violent and nonviolent delinquency, respectively.

Finally, the authors note that the two-factor structure of psychopathic symptoms is apparent in several self-report measures of psychopathy (Hare 1991; Levenson et al. 1995; Rogers and Bagby 1995).

Diagnostic overlap.   Let us turn now from studies of the internal structure of psychopathic traits to studies of the association between measures of psychopathy and narcissism. If, as was suggested in previous sections, narcissism is a basic factor underlying about half of all psychopathic symptoms, the two disorders should have high rates of comorbidity, and their traits should be highly correlated.

Numerous studies have examined the overlap among DSM-III or DSM-III-R personality disorders, including narcissistic and antisocial personality disorders. Rather than discuss them individually, the authors discuss a review by Widiger et al. (1991). Summarizing the findings of four studies ($N = 568$), Widiger et al. (1991) found that, on average, the co-occurrence of antisocial and narcissistic personality disorder was about 16%. That is, of all patients with a diagnosis of either antisocial or narcissistic personality disorder, 16% had both disorders. Although quite high in absolute terms, this co-occurrence rate was lower than that for some other disorders. For example, antisocial personality had co-occurrence rates of 26% with borderline personality disorder and 18% with passive-aggressive personality disorder; and narcissistic personality disorder had a 17% co-occurrence rate with histrionic personality disorder. When the investigators analyzed various dimensional measures (e.g., symptom counts) rather than categorical diagnoses, they found an average correlation between narcissistic and antisocial personality disorder of .33 across nine studies. Once again, antisocial personality disorder was more strongly related to borderline personality disorder and passive-aggressive personality disorder ($r = .37$ and $.35$, respectively) than to narcissistic personality disorder; and narcissistic personality disorder was more strongly related to histrionic personality disorder ($r = .35$) than to antisocial personality disorder.

One problem with the studies summarized by Widiger et al. (1991) concerns the assessment of personality disorder: most of the studies used structured interviews or self-report inventories, which may have been susceptible to the effects of deceitfulness on the part of psychopathic individuals. A second problem is that the studies all used DSM criteria for antisocial personality disorder rather than a measure of psychopathy in the Cleckleyan tradition. A third problem is that participants in most of the studies were civil psychiatric patients, a population with a relatively low base rate of psychopathy relative to forensic populations (e.g., Hart et al. 1994; Widiger and Corbitt 1993). As a result of these problems, the Widiger et al. (1991) analyses may underestimate the association between narcissistic personality disorder and measures of Cleckleyan psychopathy, such as the PCL-R.

Only a few studies have examined the association between narcissism and the PCL-R. Hart and Hare (1989) studied 80 men remanded to a forensic hospital for pretrial psychiatric evaluation. Patients' conditions were assessed with the PCL-R and diagnosed with DSM-III Axis I and II criteria. They were also given prototypicality ratings on each personality disorder using a 10-point scale ($1 = $ low, $10 = $ high). The correlation between PCL-R total scores and ratings of narcissistic personality disorder was moderate ($r = .39$) and second in magnitude only to the correlation with antisocial personality disorder ($r = .71$). Not surprisingly, scores on Factor 1 of the PCL-R correlated more highly with ratings of narcissism ($r = .49$) than with ratings of any other personality disorder; in contrast, scores on Factor 2 of the PCL-R correlated most highly with ratings of antisocial personality disorder ($r = .71$) and much lower with ratings of narcissistic personality disorder ($r = .39$).

Hart et al. (1991) studied the correlation between the PCL-R and measures of personality disorder on the MCMI-II (Millon 1987) in a sample of 119 adult male prisoners. In that study, the correlation between PCL-R total scores and MCMI-II base rate scores on narcissistic personality disorder was .31; the correlations with Factor 1 and 2 scores were $r = .24$ and .28, respectively. As one would expect, the PCL-R correlated more highly with antisocial personality disorder; otherwise, the correlations with narcissistic personality disorder were higher than those with any other disorders except for aggressive-sadistic and paranoid personality disorder.

Hart et al. (1994; see also Hart et al. 1995) examined the correlations between the PCL:SV and various measures of personality disorder. In one sample of 40 adult male prisoners who completed the MCMI-II, base rate scores for narcissistic personality disorder were correlated at $r = .44$ with PCL:SV total scores, .48 with scores on Part 1 (comparable to Factor 1 of the PCL-R), and .30 with scores on Part 2 (comparable to Factor 2 of the PCL-R). Although substantial, these correlations were smaller than those between the PCL-R and several disorders other than antisocial personality, including borderline, schizotypal, passive-aggressive, and aggressive-sadistic personality disorder.

In a second sample of 38 civil psychiatric patients, Hart et al. (1994) examined correlations between the PCL:SV and dimensional ratings of personality disorder based on the Personality Disorder Examination (PDE; Loranger 1988), a structured interview for DSM-III-R Axis II. The PCL:SV and PDE ratings were completely independent, made by different raters on the basis of different interviews. Aside from the expected correlations between the PCL:SV and antisocial personality disorder, the highest correlations were between PCL:SV total scores and narcissistic personality disorder ($r = .58$). Part 1 scores correlated more highly with narcissistic personality disorder than did Part 2 scores ($r = .63$ and .41, respectively). Indeed, narcissistic personality disorder was the single strongest correlate of Part 1 scores.

The authors know of only one study that has examined the association between psychopathy and narcissism as a normal personality dynamic. The PCL-R manual presents correlations with the Narcissistic Personality Inventory (NPI; Raskin and Hall 1979; Raskin and Terry 1988) in a sample of 100 adult male prisoners. The correlations between the NPI total score and the PCL-R total, Factor 1, and Factor 2 scores were $r = .34, .33,$ and .34, respectively. Looking at the NPI subscales, the highest correlations were with authority and exploitativeness ($r = .40$ and .29, respectively, with PCL-R total scores).

Conclusion

The available empirical evidence appears to support the theoretical view that a strong association exists between psychopathy and narcissism. There are some important qualifiers to this conclusion, however. First, the association between the disorders is not sufficiently large in magnitude to suggest that psychopathy is simply a "subgroup" or "subtype" of narcissistic personality disorder. The diagnostic overlap is far from complete, and many psychopathic individuals do not have symptoms that meet the criteria for narcissistic personality disorder. Second, narcissism is associated primarily with one of the two major facets of psychopathic symptomatology. In other words, narcissism is related to only one-half of the construct of psychopathy. Third, both psychopathy and narcissistic personality disorder are as strongly related to other personality disorders as they are to each other. In light of these comments, psychopathy can be viewed as a higher-order construct with two distinct, albeit related, facets, one of which is very similar to the clinical concept of narcissism; this two-facet conceptualization of psychopathy is illustrated in Figure 17–1.

Despite these qualifications, the association between psychopathy and narcissism would seem to be a fruitful avenue for further research. It raises many questions. What is the exact extent and nature of the association between the disorders? Is it simply descriptive, or is there a common diathesis—say, temperamental, genetic, or neurocognitive? Does the association remain consistent across various modes of functioning (e.g., behavioral, cognitive, interpersonal)? What is the difference between the disorders with respect to family history, course, and treatment response?

In our view, future research should begin by conducting a series of studies focused specifically on the psychopathy-narcissism association in various populations. For reasons described earlier in this chapter, the authors recommend that researchers avoid relying solely on self-report inventories. They also recommend avoiding omnibus-structured interviews of personality disorder, which sacrifice depth of assessment for breadth of coverage. Instead, researchers should consider using clinical rating scales such as the PCL-R (in forensic settings) or PCL:SV (in other settings) and the Diagnostic Interview for Narcissism (DIN; Gunderson et al. 1990). Although these scales require considerable time

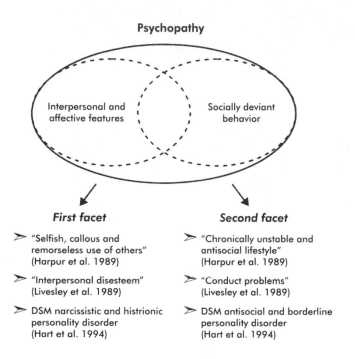

Psychopathy

Interpersonal and affective features

Socially deviant behavior

First facet

➤ "Selfish, callous and remorseless use of others" (Harpur et al. 1989)

➤ "Interpersonal disesteem" (Livesley et al. 1989)

➤ DSM narcissistic and histrionic personality disorder (Hart et al. 1994)

Second facet

➤ "Chronically unstable and antisocial lifestyle" (Harpur et al. 1989)

➤ "Conduct problems" (Livesley et al. 1989)

➤ DSM antisocial and borderline personality disorder (Hart et al. 1994)

Figure 17–1.   A two-facet conceptualization of psychopathy.

and expertise to administer (at least relative to self-reports), they provide detailed and reliable information. They can also provide a variety of dimensional measures in addition to categorical diagnoses.

Regardless of the assessment techniques used, researchers should consider using samples from several different populations. In particular, it will be important to determine whether the association between the disorders is similar across forensic populations, in which the base rate of psychopathy is relatively high but in which little information is available about the base rate of narcissistic personality disorder; in psychiatric populations, in which the base rate of narcissistic personality disorder is relatively high and the base rate of psychopathy generally is quite low; and in the community, wherein both disorders are rare.

References

Albert RS, Brigante TR, Chase M: The psychopathic personality: a content analysis of the concept. J Gen Psychol 60:17–28, 1959

American Psychiatric Association: Diagnostic and Statistical Manual: Mental Disorders. Washington, DC, American Psychiatric Association, 1952

American Psychiatric Association: Diagnostic and Statistical Manual of Mental Disorders, 2nd Edition. Washington, DC, American Psychiatric Association, 1968

American Psychiatric Association: Diagnostic and Statistical Manual of Mental Disorders, 3rd Edition. Washington, DC, American Psychiatric Association, 1980

American Psychiatric Association: Diagnostic and Statistical Manual of Mental Disorders, 3rd Edition, Revised. Washington, DC, American Psychiatric Association, 1987

American Psychiatric Association: Diagnostic and Statistical Manual of Mental Disorders, 4th Edition. Washington, DC, American Psychiatric Association, 1994

Bursten B: The Manipulator. New Haven, CT, Yale University Press, 1973

Bursten B: The relationship between narcissistic and antisocial personalities. Psychiatr Clin North Am 12:571–584, 1989

Buss AH: Psychopathology. New York, Wiley, 1966

Butcher JN, Dahlstrom WG, Graham JR, et al: Minnesota Multiphasic Personality Inventory (MMPI-2): Manual for Administration and Scoring. Minneapolis, MN, University of Minnesota Press, 1989

Cleckley H: The Mask of Sanity. St. Louis, MO, Mosby, 1941

Craft MJ: Ten Studies Into Psychopathic Personality. Bristol, England, John Wright, 1965

Davies W, Feldman P: The diagnosis of psychopathy by forensic specialists. Br J Psychiatry 138:329–331, 1981

Feighner JP, Robins E, Guze SB, et al: Diagnostic criteria for use in psychiatric research. Arch Gen Psychiatry 26:57–63, 1972

Forth AE, Hart SD, Hare RD: Assessment of psychopathy in male young offenders. Psychological Assessment: A Journal of Consulting and Clinical Psychology 2:342–344, 1990

Fotheringham JB: Psychopathic personality: a review. Canadian Psychiatric Association Journal 2:52–74, 1957

Gacono CB, Meloy JR: Rorschach Assessment of Aggressive and Psychopathic Personalities. Hillsdale, NJ, Lawrence Erlbaum, 1994

Gacono C, Meloy JR, Heaven T: A Rorschach investigation of narcissism and hysteria in antisocial personality disorder. J Pers Assess 55: 270–279, 1990

Gough H: Manual for the California Psychological Inventory. Palo Alto, CA, Consulting Psychologists Press, 1957

Gough H: California Psychological Inventory: Administrator's Guide. Palo Alto, CA, Consulting Psychologists Press, 1987

Gray KC, Hutchinson HC: The psychopathic personality: a survey of Canadian psychiatrists' opinions. Canadian Psychiatric Association Journal 9:452–461, 1964

Gunderson J, Ronningstam E, Bodkin A: The diagnostic interview for narcissistic patients. Arch Gen Psychiatry 47:676–680, 1990

Hare RD: Psychopathy: Theory and Research. New York, Wiley, 1970

Hare RD: A research scale for the assessment of psychopathy in criminal populations. Personality and Individual Differences 1:111–119, 1980

Hare RD: Diagnosis of antisocial personality disorder in two prison populations. Am J Psychiatry 140:887–890, 1983

Hare RD: A comparison of procedures for the assessment of psychopathy. J Consult Clin Psychol 53:7–16, 1985

Hare RD: The Hare Psychopathy Checklist—Revised. Toronto, Ontario, Multi-Health Systems, 1991

Hare RD, Hart SD: Psychopathy, mental disorder, and crime, in Mental Disorder and Crime. Edited by Hodgins S. Newbury Park, CA, Sage, 1992, pp 104–115

Hare RD, Williamson SE, Harpur TJ: Psychopathy and language, in Biological Contributions to Crime Causation. Edited by Moffitt TE, Mednick SA. Dordrecht, The Netherlands, Martinus Nijhoff, 1988, pp 68–92

Hare RD, Forth AE, Hart SD: The psychopath as prototype for pathological lying and deception, in Credibility Assessment. Edited by Yuille JC. Dordrecht, The Netherlands, Kluwer, 1989, pp 24–49

Hare RD, Harpur TJ, Hakstian AR, et al: The revised psychopathy checklist: reliability and factor structure. Psychological Assessment: A Journal of Consulting and Clinical Psychology 2:338–341, 1990

Hare RD, Hart SD, Harpur TJ: Psychopathy and the DSM-IV criteria for antisocial personality disorder. J Abnorm Psychol 100:391–398, 1991

Hare RD, Forth AE, Strachan K: Psychopathy and crime across the life-span, in Aggression and Violence Throughout the Life Span. Edited by Peters R, McMahon RJ, Quinsey VL. Newbury Park, CA, Sage, 1992, pp 285–300

Hare RD, Strachan C, Forth AE: Psychopathy and crime: an overview, in Clinical Approaches to the Mentally Disordered Offender. Edited by Hollin CR, Howells K. Chichester, England, Wiley, 1993, pp 165–178

Harpur TJ, Hare RD: Psychopathy and attention, in The Development of Attention: Recent Research and Theory. Edited by Enns J. Amsterdam, North-Holland, 1990, pp 501–516

Harpur TJ, Hakstian AR, Hare RD: Factor structure of the psychopathy checklist. J Consult Clin Psychol 56:741–747, 1988

Harpur TJ, Hare RD, Hakstian AR: A two-factor conceptualization of psychopathy: construct validity and implications for assessment. Psychological Assessment: A Journal of Consulting and Clinical Psychology 1:6–17, 1989

Harpur TJ, Hare RD, Zimmerman M, et al: Dimensions underlying DSM-III personality disorders: Cluster 2. Paper presented at the annual meeting of the American Psychological Association, Boston, MA, 1990

Hart SD, Hare RD: The discriminant validity of the psychopathy checklist in a forensic psychiatric population. Psychological Assessment: A Journal of Consulting and Clinical Psychology 1:211–218, 1989

Hart SD, Forth AE, Hare RD: The MCMI-II and psychopathy. Journal of Personality Disorders 5:318–327, 1991

Hart SD, Hare RD, Harpur TJ: The Psychopathy Checklist: an overview for researchers and clinicians, in Advances in Psychological Assessment, Vol 8. Edited by Rosen J, McReynolds P. New York, Plenum, 1992, pp 103–130

Hart SD, Dutton DG, Newlove T: The prevalence of personality disorder among wife assaulters. Journal of Personality Disorders 7:329–341, 1993

Hart SD, Hare RD, Forth AE: Psychopathy as a risk marker for violence: development and validation of a screening version of the revised psychopathy checklist, in Violence and Mental Disorder: Developments in Risk Assessment. Edited by Monahan J, Steadman HJ. Chicago, IL, University of Chicago Press, 1994, pp 81–98

Hart SD, Cox DN, Hare RD: Manual for the Psychopathy Checklist: Screening Version (PCL:SV). Toronto, Ontario, Multi-Health Systems, 1995

Hathaway SR, McKinley JC: A multiphasic personality schedule (Minnesota), I: construction of the schedule. J Psychol 10:249–254, 1940

Karpman B: The structure of neurosis: with special differentials between neurosis, psychosis, homosexuality, alcoholism, psychopathy, and criminality. Archives of Criminal Psychodynamics 4:599–646, 1961

Kernberg OF: Factors in the treatment of narcissistic personalities. J Am Psychoanal Assoc 18:51–85, 1970

Kernberg OF: The narcissistic personality disorder and the differential diagnosis of antisocial behavior. Psychiatr Clin North Am 12:553–570, 1989

Levenson MR, Kiehl KA, Fitzpatrick CM: Assessing psychopathic attributes in a noninstitutionalized population. J Pers Soc Psychol 68: 151–158, 1995

Lilienfeld SO: Conceptual problems in the assessment of psychopathy. Clinical Psychology Review 14:17–38, 1994

Livesley WJ: Trait and behavioral prototypes of personality disorder. Am J Psychiatry 143:728–732, 1986

Livesley WJ, Schroeder M: Dimensions of personality disorder: the DSM-III-R cluster B diagnoses. J Nerv Ment Dis 179:320–328, 1991

Livesley WJ, Jackson DN, Schroeder M: A study of the factorial structure of personality pathology. Journal of Personality Disorders 3:292–306, 1989

Livesley WJ, Jackson DN, Schroeder M: Factorial structure of traits delineating personality disorders in clinical and general population samples. J Abnorm Psychol 101:432–440, 1992

Loranger AW: Personality Disorder Examination (PDE) Manual. Yonkers, NY, DV Communications, 1988

MacKay JR: Psychopathy and pathological narcissism: a descriptive and psychodynamic formulation on the antisocial personality disorder. Journal of Offender Counseling, Services, and Rehabilitation 11:77–93, 1986

McCord W, McCord J: The Psychopath: An Essay on the Criminal Mind. Princeton, NJ, Van Nostrand, 1964

McGlashan TH, Heinssen RK: Narcissistic, antisocial, and noncomorbid subgroups of borderline disorder—are they distinct entities by long-term clinical profile? Psychiatr Clin North Am 12:653–670, 1989

Meloy JR: The Psychopathic Mind. Northvale, NJ, Jason Aronson, 1988

Millon T: Disorders of Personality: DSM-III Axis II. New York, Wiley, 1981

Millon T: Millon Clinical Multiaxial Inventory Manual, 3rd Edition. Minneapolis, MN, National Computer Systems, 1983

Millon T: Manual for the Millon Clinical Multiaxial Inventory-II, 2nd Edition. Minneapolis, MN, National Computer Systems, 1987

Newman JP, Wallace JF: Psychopathy and cognition, in Psychopathology and Cognition. Edited by Kendall P, Dobson K. New York, Academic Press, 1993, pp 293–349

Raskin R, Hall CS: A narcissistic personality inventory. Psychol Rep 45:590, 1979

Raskin R, Terry H: A principal-components analysis of the narcissistic personality inventory and further evidence of its construct validity. J Pers Soc Psychol 54:890–902, 1988

Robins LN: Deviant Children Grown Up. Baltimore, MD, Williams & Wilkins, 1966

Robins LN: Aetiological implications in studies of childhood histories relating to antisocial personality, in Psychopathic Behavior: Approaches to Research. Edited by Hare RD, Schalling D. Chichester, England, Wiley, 1978, pp 255–271

Rogers R, Bagby M: Dimensions of psychopathy: a factor analytic study of the MMPI Antisocial Personality Disorder scale. International Journal of Offender Therapy and Comparative Criminology 38:297–308, 1995

Rogers R, Dion K: Rethinking the DSM-III-R diagnosis of antisocial personality disorder. Bull Am Acad Psychiatry Law 19:21–31, 1991

Rogers R, Dion K, Lynett E: Diagnostic validity of antisocial personality disorder: a prototypical analysis. Law and Human Behavior 16:677–689, 1992

Rogers R, Duncan J, Lynett E, et al: Prototypical analysis of antisocial personality disorder: DSM-IV and beyond. Law and Human Behavior 18:471–484, 1994

Stangl D, Pfohl B, Zimmerman M, et al: A structured interview for the DSM-III personality disorders: a preliminary report. Arch Gen Psychiatry 42:591–596, 1985

Stevens GF: Prison clinicians' perceptions of antisocial personality disorder as a formal diagnosis. Journal of Offender Rehabilitation 20:159–185, 1994

Stone M: Abnormalities of Personality: Within and Beyond the Realm of Treatment. New York, WW Norton, 1993

Tennent G, Tennent D, Prins H, et al: Psychopathic disorder: a useful clinical concept? Med Sci Law 30:38–44, 1990

Widiger TA, Corbitt E: Antisocial personality disorder: proposals for DSM-IV. Journal of Personality Disorders 7:63–77, 1993

Widiger TA, Frances AJ, Harris M, et al: Comorbidity among Axis II disorders, in Personality Disorders: New Perspectives on Diagnostic Validity. Edited by Oldham JM. Washington, DC, American Psychiatric Press, 1991, pp 163–194

Widiger TA, Cadoret R, Hare RD, et al: DSM-IV antisocial personality disorder field trial. J Abnorm Psychol 105:3–16, 1996

World Health Organization: International Classification of Diseases and Related Health Problems, 10th Edition. Geneva, Switzerland, World Health Organization, 1990

Wulach JS: The criminal personality as DSM-III-R antisocial, narcissistic, borderline, and histrionic personality disorder. International Journal of Offender Therapy and Comparative Criminology 32:185–199, 1988

Chapter 18

Narcissistic Personality Disorder in Adolescent Inpatients

A Retrospective Record Review Study of Descriptive Characteristics

Paulina F. Kernberg, M.D.
Fady Hajal, M.D.
Lina Normandin, Ph.D.

Personality disorders as diagnostic categories for children and adolescents remain controversial. DSM-IV (American Psychiatric Association 1994) follows the principle that "Personality Disorder categories may be applied to children or adolescents in those relatively unusual instances in which the individual's particular maladaptive personality traits appear to be pervasive, persistent, and unlikely to be limited to a particular developmental stage or an episode of an Axis I disorder" (p. 631). Rutter (1981, 1984) pointed out the need to go beyond the idea that child psychopathology consists of only symptoms or disturbed behaviors. Indeed, the concept of personality during development serves as an overarching structure that organizes its genetic constitutional, cognitive, and experiential components. Rutter added that the continuity of personality during development may refer to the continuity of a structural process or mechanism. Moreover, this structural process is more important than the particular forms of expression of personality. In other words, it is not unusual that a person with an avoidant personality disorder has a history of shyness. Kernberg (1988, 1989, 1991) described the existence of persistent (lasting for more than 1 year) maladaptive ways of dealing with oneself and the environment in children. Children seem to have descriptive characteristics similar to those present in adults with personality disorders with additional appropriate developmental features, such as play characteristics, peer relationship characteristics, and particular variations of separation anxiety.

Abrams (1993) described a profile of pathological narcissism as seen through the Thematic Apperception Testing for Children. The test scores in children with narcissistic personality disorder (NPD) profile seemed to have a specific quality: caricatural incompetent people with buffoon stories. Despite achievement, the child feels rejected and empty and perceives adults as ineffectual, unprotecting, and unnurturing figures. People are not seen as distinct individuals with clear identities. Bardenstein (1994) reported on children with NPDs, defined by DSM-III-R (American Psychiatric Association 1987) criteria as seen through the Rorschach Exner system. Hyperalertness, oppositionalism, a high incidence of reflection images, distortion of experience, and a high level of egocentricity are characteristics of these children.

Systematic assessments of borderline personality disorders in adolescents were done by applying the Diagnostic Interview for Borderlines (DIB; Gunderson et al. 1981) to hospitalized adolescents (McManus 1984). It was then natural to consider an attempt to apply the Diagnostic Interview for Narcissism (DIN; Gunderson et al. 1990) for record review of hospitalized adolescents as a preliminary step toward live interviews. Adolescence is a developmental stage in which narcissistic traits are at their height.

However, the adolescent inpatient does not have the grandiosity, the attitude of devaluation, and the disturbed interpersonal relations found in adolescents with NPD.

The relevance of this study relates to the role of coexisting narcissistic traits in worsening the prognosis of patients with borderline personality disorder. Increased suicidal risk (Stone 1989) and a higher likelihood of rehospitalization (Plakun 1990) have been observed in such patients. The use of clinical records for retrospective diagnostic evaluations has several advantages. These records contain multiple observations of each patient done by multiple observers over time. This might add to the convergent validity. Moreover, the descriptions of the patients' everyday interactions written in the clinical records without preconceived notions, when present, might add power to findings. This chapter presents an investigation of the occurrence of NPD in a sample of inpatient adolescents by using conceptual criteria and a specific diagnostic instrument.

Method

A modified version of DIN (Gunderson et al. 1990), the Adolescent Adaptation to Record Review of DIN, was applied to a sample of adolescent inpatients. The purpose was to evaluate the presence of NPD in adolescents by using several sources of information. DIN is a semistructured interview developed specifically for evaluating 33 characteristics of pathological narcissism and the diagnosis of NPD in clinical samples. The structure and content of the interview have been described earlier (see Ronningstam, Chapter 16, this volume). Results from studies using DIN on narcissistic patients (Ronningstam and Gunderson 1989, 1990) showed that these patients scored specifically high on the statements related to grandiosity—that is, a sense of superiority and uniqueness, exaggeration of talents, boastful and pretentious behavior, grandiose fantasies, self-centered and self-referential behavior—making these features the most outstanding for NPD.

The narcissistic sample had a predominance of males (71%) and was recruited from both inpatient (46%) and outpatient (54%) settings.

Instrument

In the Adolescent Adaptation to Record Review of DIN, the basic structure of the original DIN was kept unchanged. The five sections described grandiosity, interpersonal relations, reactiveness, affects and mood states, and social and moral adaptation. The use of probes to collect evidence for evaluating statements and the numerical scoring of the statements was unchanged. Likewise, the concluding evaluation scales regarding certainty of diagnosis of NPD (rated on a scale of 0–7) and level of pathological narcissism (also rated on a scale of 0–7) were kept. However, some major modifications needed to be introduced to adapt the instrument more to the adolescent population and the method of record review.

1. The questions were changed to the third person, such as "Do you think the adolescent is . . . ?," in order to address the chart reviewer rather than the patient directly.
2. A category was added to the ratings, "DK—do not know," for use whenever the feature is mentioned ambiguously or without specific illustrations in the chart.
3. The scoring process of the individual questions was modified. Features were not addressed directly as questions to the patient. Instead, an appraisal of each feature was searched for in the medical record, and a qualitative scoring system was introduced with the categories "definitely, likely, not at all, do not know." This appraisal was also helpful for making an independent judgment about the statement. The sections and total scores remain numerically additive. For example, the section for grandiosity has eight statements. The maximum score for this section is 16, which means high evidence of grandiosity, because these features have been mentioned several times by several sources.

A score of 8 means that the grandiosity is present, but not as strong, and a score of 0–3 means that it is not present.

4. Two areas were added. One asks about the narcissistically disturbed adolescent's sense of entitlement. The second asks about the frequency of antisocial behaviors: "Do you think the adolescent usually lies?" and "Do you think the adolescent misconduct is usually followed by remorse?"

5. Several questions were added to the inquiry about sexual activity patterns: "Do you think the adolescent is not constrained by the sexual inhibitions that people usually have, such as exhibiting or exhibitionistic behavior?", "Do you think the adolescent has a same-sex orientation?", and "Do you think the adolescent does not date?" In addition, a question exploring the connection between sexual patterns and exhibitionism was included: "Do you think that the adolescent is more interested in the image he/she projects than in his/her actual sexual life, which can lack eroticism and fulfillment? If yes, do you think that the fact that it is unusual bothers him/her?" To improve the inquiry about the adolescent sexual behaviors, "superficial fleeting encounters, exhibitionism, and/or lack of eroticism and fulfillment" were added. "Promiscuity or perversions" was excluded, because of its lack of clinical specificity for NPDs in adolescence.

6. The absence of several relevant items in DIN was noted, such as separation anxiety, pseudoinsight, substance abuse, alcohol abuse, and somatization. These are frequently present in individuals with NPDs. The narcissistic adolescent's capacity to have a very close or best friend was also noted. Usually the peer interactions show disturbed clinical patterns, caused by the adolescent's self-centeredness, entitlement, exploitiveness, and lack of empathy (Kernberg 1989). In the section on reactiveness, "separation" as a cause to intense reactions was added, as well as "somatization in reaction to criticisms, defeat, and separation-abandonment." Based on clinical and literature references (Akhtar 1992; Kernberg 1989), the category "aloofness, rage, and somatization" was added to the forms of reaction to frustration.

In addition, there is a clinical observation that the academic grades of narcissistically disturbed adolescents show a checkered pattern from very high grades to very low grades. This is probably due to the difficulties these patients have in working for achievements. Their sense of entitlement contributes to this, as does the fact that they learn to obtain admiration for its own sake rather than for the actual value of acquiring knowledge. Moreover, their grandiosity does not allow them to easily accept that they do not know everything. Hence, they tend to show very high grades for those subjects that come very easily to them and very low grades for those subjects that require an effort on their part.

Cutoff Point for Inclusion

Because data were elicited from a retrospective review of records, strict criteria for inclusion were applied. A cutoff point of 20% was used for inclusion of statements into the statistical analysis. This means that of the individual statements subsumed under each section—that is, grandiosity (8), interpersonal relations (9), reactivity (8), affects and mood states (5), and social and moral adaptation (6)—only statements that were rated in more than 80% of the subjects were entered into the analysis. An exception was made for the statements in affects and mood states. Because features of affects and mood states were reported less consistently in the records, the cutoff point for inclusion was raised to 36.7%. With the cutoff point of 20%, 26 analyzable statements were obtained: all 8 statements from the grandiosity section, 6 from the interpersonal relations section, 7 from the reactivity section, 0 from the affects and mood states section, and 5 from the social and moral adaptation section. Furthermore, because some but not all subjects fulfilled the criteria for inclusion for each section, different numbers of subjects were entered into each analysis.

Following the cutoff point of 20%, 26 statements—corresponding to 72% of the total number of statements constituting the original instrument—were used in the major analysis. Included were all 8 statements from the grandiosity section, 6 from interpersonal relations, 7 from reactivity, 0 from affects and mood states, and 5 from social and moral adaptation. Subject inclusion into the analysis was based on correspondence between the number of statements rated by the reviewers and the number of statements finally included under each section. That means that for a subject to be included into the analysis of the interpersonal relations section, the reviewers must have attributed a score of 0–2 to each of the 6 final statements in this section. This explains why the number of subjects varies for each section: 24 in the grandiosity section, 20 in interpersonal relations, 21 in reactivity, 14 in affects and mood states (based on a cutoff point of 36.7%), and 20 in social and moral adaptation.

The group of 10 statements that figured less regularly than all others—missing in 53%–80% of the records and hence excluded from the analysis—were: S10 "Unrealistically idealizing other people," S12 "Having recurrent and/or deep feelings of envy towards other people," and S16 "Lacking empathy and being unable to both understand and feel for other people's experiences" in the interpersonal relations section; S23 "Reacting with somatization in response to criticism, defeat, disappointment, or separation" in the reactivity section; S26–S30 "Deep sustained feelings of emptiness, boredom, meaninglessness, futility and badness" in the affects and mood states section; and S32 "the adolescent has superficial and changing values and interests" in the social and moral adaptation section.

Subjects

A sample of 30 adolescents served as subjects in this study. The sample was drawn from the population of adolescents, ages 13–19, who had been hospitalized at the New York Hospital, Westchester Division, for an average of 60–90 days. Data were extracted from a randomized sample of medical records (1981–1992). It comprised adolescents of both sexes divided into two groups: 1) adolescents having received a diagnosis of an NPD at admission or discharge and 2) adolescents having received no Axis II diagnosis either at admission or at discharge.

Results

The narcissistic group included 15 adolescents (7 boys and 8 girls). They ranged in age from 14 to 19 years (mean = 16.13, SD = 1.23, median = 16). Their duration of hospitalization ranged from 14 to 221 days (mean = 65.20, SD = 60.97). The no Axis II disorder group included 15 adolescents (7 boys and 8 girls). They ranged in age from 14 to 20 years (mean = 16.66, SD = 1.89, median = 17). Their duration of hospitalization ranged from 13 to 252 days (mean = 78.9, SD = 64.23).

There were no significant differences between the two groups on the basis of the three demographic variables of sex, race, and age. Narcissistic boys seemed to be hospitalized longer than narcissistic girls (M_{boys} = 82.71, SD = 61.57; M_{girls} = 62.69, SD = 62.68), but not to a significant degree (F = 0.58, NS). Caucasian subjects were overrepresented (n = 24) compared with African American (n = 5) and Hispanic (n = 1) subjects. However, there was no difference between this sample and all other hospitalized adolescents with regard to ethnicity.

An investigation of the established clinical diagnosis of NPD in the narcissistic group noted in the records showed that 5 subjects received the diagnosis at admission and retained it at discharge, whereas 10 received it at discharge exclusively. The differences in overall severity of narcissism between these two subgroups were not significant as measured by the total score (F = 0.46, P < .51; $M_{admission}$ = 32.00; $M_{discharge}$ = 34.2).

Evidence of two statements was found in all 30 subjects: S13 "The adolescent reports or behaves entitled, i.e., has unreasonable expectations of favors or other special treatment" (interpersonal); and S18 "The adolescent is hypersensitive" (reactiveness).

Further analyses showed that the statement about entitlement (S13) highly discriminates between narcissistic and no Axis II disorder adolescents (F = 12.25, P < .002; M_{Narc} = 1.33, SD_{Narc} = 0.72, $M_{No\ Axis}$ = 0.40, $SD_{No\ Axis}$ = 0.74). However, no significant difference was reached with hypersensitivity (S18) alone.

More than 72% of the statements were found analyzable at a cutoff point of 20%. The missing statements were equally distributed between the two groups ($\chi^2 = $ NS).

Reliability Estimates

Acceptable interrater reliability was established for the entire instrument by using three charts (two narcissistic and one no Axis II diagnosis). Results showed that the reliability measures of the presence or absence of relevant information to support individual statements appraised by kappa were .72. The intraclass correlation (ICC), measuring the level of agreement of the severity of the statements, ranged from .52 to .74 with a mean of .61. Highest reliability was obtained on statements in the interpersonal section (ICC = .74), followed by reactiveness (ICC = .63) and grandiosity (ICC = .60). The social and moral adaptation and the affects and mood states obtained acceptable agreement (ICC = .53 and .52, respectively).

Group Comparisons

Five dependent variables were analyzed: grandiosity, interpersonal relations, reactiveness, affects and mood states, and social and moral adaptation. As mentioned earlier in this chapter, because none of the statements in the section on affects and mood states were present in more than 63.5% of the records, the cutoff point was lowered from 81% to 63.5% for this section to be included in this analysis. The section scores were entered into the analysis. Results showed that the group of narcissistic adolescents presented more evidence of narcissism on every section compared with no Axis II disorder adolescents (see Table 18–1 and Figure 18–1).

A regression analysis with maximum variance improvement technique was subsequently used to investigate which of these five dependent variables and the duration of hospitalization could best

Table 18–1. Comparisons of mean scores in narcissistic and no Axis II disorder adolescents on the Adolescent Adaptation to Record Review of the Diagnostic Interview for Narcissism (DIN)

Sections in DIN	n	M	SD	df	F	P
Grandiosity						
Narcissistic	10	8.0	4.55	1	4.00	< .05
No Axis II disorder	14	4.3	4.45			
Interpersonal relations						
Narcissistic	10	7.9	2.18	1	13.50	< .001
No Axis II disorder	10	3.7	2.83			
Reactiveness						
Narcissistic	11	8.5	2.30	1	4.93	< .05
No Axis II disorder	10	6.0	2.94			
Affects and mood states[a]						
Narcissistic	7	2.14	1.46	1	5.26	< .05
No Axis II disorder	7	0.71	0.76			
Social and moral adaptation						
Narcissistic	12	5.25	2.05	1	5.83	< .05
No Axis II disorder	8	2.63	2.83			

Note. n = number of patients; M = mean; SD = standard deviation; df = degrees of freedom; F = value for F test; P = probability value.
[a]Affects and mood states based on cutoff for inclusion at 36.7%.

predict the evidence of narcissism. Results showed that the best one-variable model accounting for the highest variance (R^2 = 52.7%) was constituted by the section interpersonal relations (F = 8.91, P < .05). However, the best two-variable model producing the highest variance (R^2 = 87.6%) was grandiosity and reactiveness in combination (F = 24.71, P < .001). It increases still further (90.7%) by adding social and moral adaptation (F = 19.65, P < .01).

Sex Differences

Comparisons of individual statements and demographics suggest some sex differences within the NPD group. Boys with NPD

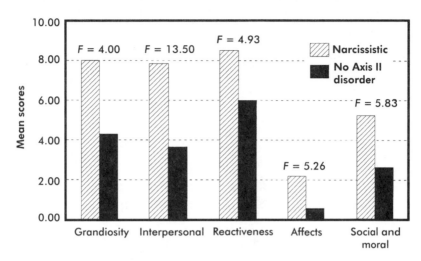

Figure 18–1.   Comparison of narcissistic and no Axis II disorder adolescent groups on five section scores.

tended to have longer hospitalizations than girls. They also regarded themselves as more superior than the girls did ($F = 5.17$, df = 3, $P < .01$). Likewise, boys with NPD were more boastful or pretentious than girls with NPD ($F = 3.07$, df = 3, $P < .05$) and tended to show more disregard for usual and conventional values or rules in society ($F = 4.8$, df = 3, $P < .01$). In turn, narcissistic girls tended to react significantly more than narcissistic boys and all other no Axis II disorder patients with detachment, pseudoindifference, and aloofness in response to criticism, defeats, disappointments, or separation ($F = 4.79$, df = 3, $P < .01$) (see Table 18–2).

Frequency analysis was done after a first review of the medical records to investigate the level of pathological narcissism among the 30 subjects. Obtaining a score of 4–7 on the concluding evaluation scale "level of pathological narcissism" equals a high level; a moderate level of narcissism is represented by a score of 2, 3, or 4; and no evidence of pathological narcissism is scored 1 or 0. Results showed that two no Axis II disorder subjects were estimated by the raters to express a high level of narcissism and five a moderate level of narcissism. In other words, nearly 50% of this

Table 18–2. Summary of significant group differences by diagnostic group and sex

Statement	Summary
S5	The adolescent regards himself/herself as unique compared with other people.
	Narcissistic > No Axis II disorder
S6	The adolescent regards himself/herself as generally superior to other people.
	Boys > Girls
	Narcissistic > No Axis II disorder
S7	The adolescent behaves self-centeredly or self-referentially.
	Narcissistic > No Axis II disorder
S8	The adolescent appears or behaves in a boastful or pretentious way.
	Boys > Girls
S9	The adolescent has a strong need for attention or admiration on the basis of whom the adolescent greatly admires or idealizes.
	Narcissistic > No Axis II disorder
S11	The adolescent devalues other people, including feelings of contempt.
	Narcissistic > No Axis II disorder
S13	The adolescent reports or behaves entitled (i.e., has unreasonable expectations of favors or other special treatment).
	Narcissistic > No Axis II disorder
S14	The adolescent appears or behaves in a condescending, arrogant, or haughty way.
	Narcissistic > No Axis II disorder
S24	The adolescent has reacted with detachment, pseudoindifference, or aloofness in response to criticisms, defeats, disappointments, or separation.
	Narcissistic girls > Others
S33	The adolescent shows a disregard for usual/conventional values or rules of society.
	Boys > Girls

subgroup had moderate to high levels of pathological narcissism. Conversely, all narcissistic subjects were seen as expressing either a moderate ($n = 9$) or a high ($n = 6$) level of narcissism. The global assessment of functioning ranged between 40.0 and 76.0, with a mean tendency of 55.1 ($n = 11$) for narcissistic and 57.3 ($n = 9$) for no Axis II disorder patients. The difference was not statistically significant.

Discussion

This study shows that it is possible to obtain information about personality disorders in the patients' records based on the notes of support staff of nurses and activity therapists. These staff groups are more likely to provide such information than are the psychiatrists, who tend to focus on Axis I diagnoses in their notes. The study also shows that it is possible to identify pathological narcissism and NPD in adolescence by reliably applying the modified version of DIN to chart review.

Unexpectedly, moderate to high levels of pathological narcissism were found in nearly 50% of no Axis II disorder patients. The NPD diagnosis was either overlooked or not included in the list of diagnoses in this group. Several reasons for this are possible: the clinician may not have considered this diagnosis, may have chosen to call it oppositional disorder based on the theoretical background, or may have acted on a reluctance to diagnose Axis II disturbances in adolescence. Moreover, these findings of a moderate to severe level of narcissism in the no Axis II disorder group may be because of the likelihood that adolescent patients more readily resort to narcissistic defensive styles in order to cope with an Axis I psychiatric illness. Omnipotent control, devaluation, self-idealization, splitting, and denial may be used by normal adolescents as well to counteract regressive tendencies. Also, the presence of an Axis I diagnosis hinders the clinician's ability to make an Axis II diagnosis.

In a separate survey of records of 24 consecutively admitted adolescent patients (F. Hajal, "The Inpatient Treatment of Narcissistic Adolescents," unpublished manuscript, May 1991), the admitting Axis I diagnoses included one oppositional disorder. On discharge, the Axis I diagnosis of oppositional disorder had increased to 7. In turn, the admitting Axis II diagnoses had only one NPD, whereas, on discharge, Axis II had risen to 12 NPDs. In comparison, DIN proved to be useful in this regard. DIN enables a systematic analysis of several areas of functioning (grandiosity, interpersonal relations, reactiveness, affects and mood states, social and moral adaptation) and of statements describing individual characteristics. The confluence of these data would suggest strongly the presence of a level of narcissism distributed in a dimensional spectrum of severity, reaching a maximum density among patients meeting the criteria for NPD. Thus, the highest density of patients rated as severe NPD was actually among the group that received the diagnosis. Patients with moderate to severe NPD were in the group with no Axis II diagnoses.

In the separate survey of 24 consecutively admitted adolescents mentioned above, 50% were moderately or slightly improved in an intermediate inpatient treatment, whereas another 50% left the hospital with an undetermined outcome. Discharge plans indicated that 67% of NPD patients proceeded to residential treatment. Another 6% went to day programs, and 15% were discharged to home and had outpatient treatment with medical approval. Finally, another 12% were discharged against medical advice. In Plakun's study (1990), the cohorts of NPD were more likely to be considered as having achieved their goals on discharge. This probably is a result of a collusion with the patient's wish to have achieved goals without having really attained them.

In the present survey of 30 records, a persuasive finding is that in most cases the discharge diagnoses of Axis II disorders were more reliable than the admission diagnoses. Length of observation in the hospital was certainly contributory. Those given an Axis II diagnosis at admission maintained their Axis II diagnoses, but these disorders were not significantly different in severity compared with those diagnoses given to adolescent patients on discharge.

Statements that probed subjective emotional states or psychological processes, such as idealization of others, and most of the statements in the section on affects and mood states were less consistently reported. This is probably related to staff recording priorities and the emotional alienation these patients tend to induce because of their aloofness and haughtiness. Thus, they coerce the staff to circumvent the interaction around feelings with the patients. Another possibility is the staff's lack of familiarity as to their diagnostic importance.

Contrary to the cohort of adult narcissistic patients described by Ronningstam and Gunderson (1990), in this study, interpersonal relation alone was as important or more important than grandiosity. High levels of reactiveness were found due to separation as well as to other sources of frustration common to adults. Moreover, this record review supports the clinical findings of antisocial behaviors in NPD likely linked to their grandiosity and sense of entitlement. Indeed, the likelihood of the existence of NPD in adolescence is increased from 87.6% to 90.7% if social and moral adaptation items are added to grandiosity and reactivity.

The Axis II NPD sample showed an equal sex distribution—that is, there were as many girls as boys in the adolescent sample. This agrees with Plakun's (1990) study but contrasts with the predominance of men reported by Ronningstam and Gunderson (1989, 1990). However, the mode of expression of NPD in girls may be different from that in boys. The girls show more aloofness and detachment vis-à-vis frustration, whereas boys are more boastful and tend to disregard rules more often. These findings provide independent validation to gender differences in narcissistic styles found in a population of medical students (Richman and Flaherty 1990). In this study, men tended to show more interpersonal exploitiveness, entitlement, and lack of empathy, and women tended to have higher scores on reactions to slights. These authors reported significant associations of narcissistic traits with low self-esteem and depression, such as feelings of envy, uniqueness of problems, and upset over slights, that need to be replicated in adolescents. Sexual expressions were characterized by exhibitionism, lack of dating, or dating to show off. Reactiveness played a larger role in adolescents than in adults.

Case Vignette

A Caucasian female patient, age 17 years, was brought to the hospital for refusing to leave home for several months because she had gained much weight and did not want to appear in public looking obese. While in a boarding school in another state, she had felt very different from her peers and, as a result, decided to run away to be with her boyfriend who was in college. When he rejected her, she felt humiliated, dropped out of school, and returned home where she secluded herself. At home, she was abusive toward her parents and experienced periods of ragefulness and violent tantrums. Two weeks before admission, she became mute with her parents. She had erratic eating and sleeping habits (sleep reversal), and she complained of having concentration problems.

She had been verbally precocious, showing high academic potential in school early on. She was an underachiever in her high school years, even though she was bright (IQ 118) and articulate. She had shown a talent in poetry and in acting and was described as a perfectionist. As a child, she seemed extraordinarily fearful and dependent and placed an unusual emphasis on her fantasy life and her wish to be exceptional. She still frequently withdrew into fantasy, expressing grandiose fantasies of perfection and beauty. Described as lacking self-confidence, she often expressed self-deprecating statements. She had difficulties with peers all along, appeared aloof in nursery school, and stated that she always felt very different from other students in the various schools she attended.

In the hospital, she exhibited labile mood and at times cognitive confusion, and her thinking had at times a paranoid flavor. She showed much preoccupation over her parents or staff controlling her life. She would become depressed over perceived imperfections and then would get upset and cry. She had a fixed idea about her body being ugly and deformed. While in the hospital, she had a number of narcissistic features, including grandiosity, marked feelings of rage, feelings of inferiority, and humiliation in response to rejection by or indifference of others.

In the hospital, she remained aloof, distancing herself from peers and staff by way of sarcasm, intellectualization, and splitting. To her therapist she responded largely in an idealized self-manner, telling him and everyone else on the unit what a wonderful person he was. Whenever he confronted her about her manipulative behavior or told her something he expected her to do, she would shift from idealizing to devaluing him and assault him with a barrage of vindictive statements. Generally, these negative reactions would last about a day or two, and then she would revert to her previous idealizing stance.

On psychological testing, her reality testing was variable, but she maintained an adequate sense of reality. She showed a paranoid oppositional stance with defiance of social norms, which gave her a rebellious unconventional appearance. She seemed excessively self-centered and self-preoccupied with a lack of understanding of others. Her attitude of affective detachment and interpersonal remoteness yielded to intense affective reactivity to others, with controlled primitive aggression and sadistic impulses surfacing at periods of interpersonal stress. Her cognitive test scores showed a progressive decline in intellectual functioning. Self-hatred, self-mockery, scorn, contempt (against her body and her femininity) contrasted with narcissistic self-inflation and grandiosity. She showed on testing little capacity for anxiety or guilt, as well as little capacity to trust or depend on other people.

On DIN, as adapted for adolescents and for record review, this patient's scores were the following: grandiosity—4 (on a scale of 0–4); interpersonal relations—3 (on a scale of 0–3); reactiveness—3 (on a scale of 0–3); affects and mood states—2 (on a scale of 0–2); and social and moral adaptation—1 (on a scale of 0–2).

These scores point to a high degree of certainty of NPD (7 on a scale of 0–7) and a very high level of pathological narcissism (7 on a scale of 0–7). Her scoring patterns were derived from raw scores that were transformed into scaled scores in this profile. That is, out of a total of 70 items, this patient had 51 in terms of raw scores, and out of 14 points of scaled scores, this patient had 13.

Vignette Discussion

This clinical vignette illustrates well some of the characteristic features of narcissistic adolescents. Most striking is their conceit and their contemptuous sneering attitude manifested not only toward their peers but also toward the adults around them. As a result, the adolescents present with a characteristic antiadult stance that may appear at times as adolescent rebelliousness, an unconventional affection. In fact, it has a more insidious basis in a sense of grandiosity and omnipotence and in a cynical attitude toward adults and their capacity to care for them and their inflated needs. Pervasive is their need for control. They feel a sense of entitlement that this is how things should be, that their wishes, needs, and desires come first. Their basic mode of interpersonal relatedness is one of control and exploitiveness, with little capacity for empathy and little desire for time connectedness or intimacy. Their relationships with important objects around them fluctuate from zeniths of idealization to nadirs of devaluation and contempt (as well as feeling persecuted by these objects). When frustrated, they are all too ready to fly into rages in which they can be destructive toward others or themselves. Their sense of omnipotence and craving for self-validation lead them to act in ways that can be self-destructive (risk-taking, thrill-seeking behaviors— e.g., engaging in extensive substance abuse). They are at increased risk for suicidal and at times homicidal acting out, especially when in the throes of acute affective hypomanic or depressive states (to which they seem to be prone).

In the hospital, these narcissistic adolescent patients manifest a basic oppositional stance, some remaining unengaged in treatment. As a general rule, they show more investment in their individual psychotherapy, devaluing the rest of their treatment in the hospital. They remain aloof and condescending toward their peers, unless they take on antileader, antisocial roles fomenting trouble and disruption on the unit. Rage reactions are characteristic as they often break into explosive outbursts when confronted or frustrated. Exhibitionistic as well as sexual flirtatious behavior is frequently present in this group of patients. These adolescents are envied by the other patients for their power to manipulate other patients and staff and to get their way around the hospital. Their attitude toward school is very devaluing, even though, as a group, they are generally bright. Despite their above-average intelligence, their academic performance is at best erratic; they are consistent underachievers.

References

Abrams DM: Pathological narcissism in an eight year old boy: an example of Bellak's T.A.T. and C.A.T. diagnostic system. Psychoanalytic Psychology 10(4).573–591, 1993

Akhtar S: Narcissistic personality disorder, in Broken Structures: Severe Personality Disorders and Their Treatment. New York, Jason Aronson, 1992, pp 47–78

American Psychiatric Association: Diagnostic and Statistical Manual of Mental Disorders, 3rd Edition, Revised. Washington, DC, American Psychiatric Association, 1987

American Psychiatric Association: Diagnostic and Statistical Manual of Mental Disorders, 4th Edition. Washington, DC, American Psychiatric Association, 1994, pp 631, 659, 661

Bardenstein K: Rorschach features of narcissistic children. Paper presented at the annual conference of the Society for Personality Assessment, Chicago, IL, March 1994

Gunderson J, Kolb JE, Austin V: The diagnostic interview for borderline patients. Am J Psychiatry 138:896–903, 1981

Gunderson J, Ronningstam E, Bodkin A: The diagnostic interview for narcissistic patients. Arch Gen Psychiatry 47:676–680, 1990

Kernberg P: Children with borderline personality organization, in Handbook of Clinical Assessment of Children and Adolescents, Vol 2. Edited by Kestenbaum CJ, Williams DT. New York, New York University Press, 1988, pp 604–625

Kernberg P: Narcissistic personality disorder in childhood. Psychiatr Clin North Am 12:671–694, 1989

Kernberg P: Personality disorders, in Textbook of Child and Adolescent Psychiatry. Edited by Weiner JM. Washington, DC, American Psychiatric Press, 1991, pp 515–533

McManus M: Assessment of borderline symptomology in hospitalized adolescents. J Am Acad Child Adolesc Psychiatry 23:685–694, 1984

Plakun EM (ed): Empirical overview of narcissistic personality disorder, in New Perspectives on Narcissism. Washington, DC, American Psychiatric Press, 1990, pp 101–149

Richman JA, Flaherty JA: Gender differences in narcissistic styles, in New Perspectives on Narcissism. Edited by Plakun EM. Washington, DC, American Psychiatric Press, 1990, pp 71–100

Ronningstam E, Gunderson J: Descriptive studies on narcissistic personality disorder. Psychiatr Clin North Am 12:585–601, 1989

Ronningstam E, Gunderson J: Identifying criteria for narcissistic personality disorder. Am J Psychiatry 147:918–922, 1990

Rutter M: Stress, coping, and development: some issues and some questions. J Child Psychol Psychiatry 22:323–356, 1981

Rutter M: Continuities and discontinuities in socio-emotional perspectives, in Continuities and Discontinuities in Development. Edited by Emde RN, Harmon RJ. New York, Plenum, 1984, pp 41–68

Stone MH: Long-term follow up of narcissistic/borderline patients. Psychiatr Clin North Am 12:621–641, 1989

Afterword

Elsa F. Ronningstam, Ph.D.

Several important aspects of narcissism and narcissistic personality disorder (NPD) await further exploration. One aspect relates to the role of aggression and vulnerability in the underlying characterological structure of NPD—how it compares with both the overt grandiose, exploitive, and arrogant type of NPD and the covert shy, inhibited, and shame-ridden type, as well as with other personality disorders and states of mental illness. Another aspect refers to the development and functioning of affect and self-regulatory processes in narcissistic patients and the role of trauma and other experiential factors in the formation of a narcissistic character disorder. A third area concerns continuing investigation of malignant narcissism, psychopathy, and antisocial behavior, especially in clinical samples of narcissistic patients. Comparative outcome studies of different treatment modalities and in-depth studies of the psychotherapeutic process with narcissistic patients is a fourth very important area of investigation. In addition to the present NPD category, the inclusion of a criteria set for the covert type of NPD (with hidden grandiose desires and self-experience) in the next edition of the DSM diagnostic system would instigate further and comparative empirical research.

The title of this volume, *Disorders of Narcissism: Diagnostic, Clinical, and Empirical Implications*, reflects the purpose of contributing a comprehensive description of the origins and manifestations of pathological narcissism. It is hoped that the extraction of a few predominant lines in the conceptual and descriptive development of narcissism has served to bring some clarity to and improve the understanding of the complexity of the concept. My foremost hope is that this book can encourage and stimulate further and more integrative efforts to explore and conceptualize the nature of narcissism and NPD. I also hope that future efforts will be directed toward an increased correspondence between clinical observations of the diverse nature of pathological narcissism and the theoretical and diagnostic conceptualizations of NPD.

Index

*Page numbers printed in **boldface** type refer to tables or figures.*